Parental Substance Misuse and Child Welfare

of related interest

The Child's World
Assessing Children in Need
Edited by Jan Horwath
ISBN 1 85302 957 2

A Multidisciplinary Handbook of Child and Adolescent Mental Health for Front-line Professionals
Nisha Dogra, Andrew Parkin, Fiona Gale and Clay Frake
ISBN 1 85302 929 7

Risk Assessment in Social Care and Social Work
Edited by Phyllida Parsloe
ISBN 1 85302 689 1

Effective Ways of Working with Children and their Families
Edited by Malcolm Hill
ISBN 1 85302 619 0
Research Highlights in Social Work 35

Good Practice in Risk Assessment and Risk Management 1 and 2
Edited by Hazel Kemshall and Jacki Pritchard
Good Practice Series 3
Good Practice Series 5
Two volume set ISBN 1 85302 552 6

The Early Years
Assessing and Promoting Resilience in Vulnerable Children 1
Brigid Daniel and Sally Wassell
ISBN 1 84310 013 4

The School Years
Assessing and Promoting Resilience in Vulnerable Children 2
Brigid Daniel and Sally Wassell
ISBN 1 84310 018 5

Adolescence
Assessing and Promoting Resilience in Vulnerable Children 3
Brigid Daniel and Sally Wassell
ISBN 1 84310 019 3
Set ISBN 1 84310 045 2

Childhood Experiences of Domestic Violence
Caroline McGee
ISBN 1 85302 827 4

Parental Substance Misuse and Child Welfare

Brynna Kroll and Andy Taylor

Foreword by Jane Aldgate

Jessica Kingsley Publishers
London and Philadelphia

First published in the United Kingdom in 2003
by Jessica Kingsley Publishers Ltd
116 Pentonville Road
London N1 9JB, England
and
325 Chestnut Street
Philadelphia, PA 19106, USA

www.jkp.com

Library of Congress Cataloging in Publication Data
A CIP catalog record for this book is available from the Library of Congress

British Library Cataloguing in Publication Data
A CIP catalogue record for this book is available from the British Library

ISBN 1 85302 791 X

Printed and Bound in Great Britain by
Athenaeum Press, Gateshead, Tyne and Wear

Contents

ACKNOWLEDGEMENTS   6

FOREWORD BY PROFESSOR JANE ALDGATE   9

Part One: Introduction

1   Parental Substance Misuse and Child Welfare   15

2   Parental Substance Misuse and Child Maltreatment   27

Part Two: Parenting and Substance Misuse in Context

3   The Dynamics of Substance Misuse   57

4   Attachment and Reinforcement: Maintaining the Habit   85

5   The Impact of Substance Misuse on Parenting   99

Part Three: The Effects of Parental Substance Misuse on Child Welfare

6   The World of the Child: Attachment, Vulnerability, Risk and Resilience   137

7   Growing Up with Parental Substance Misuse   163

8   Parental Substance Misuse and Child Development   193

Part Four: Practice and Policy Implications

9   Mind the Gap: Dilemmas for Practice   219

10   Towards an Holistic Approach to Assessment   241

11   From Assessment to Intervention: A Family Perspective   269

12   The Way Forward?   297

APPENDIX 1 DRUGS AND ALCOHOL: CLASSIFICATION AND EFFECTS   307

APPENDIX 2 SCODA GUIDELINES   317

REFERENCES   321

SUBJECT INDEX   341

AUTHOR INDEX   347

Acknowledgements

This book would not have been possible without contributions from family, friends, colleagues, social work students and clients. All the staff and students at the Department of Social Work and Probation Studies, Exeter University, have given us tremendous encouragement throughout the lengthy period it took to complete this book. Particular thanks are due to Gordon Jack, our Head of Department, and to Deirdre Ford and Johanna Woodcock, University of Plymouth. We have learnt a great deal from their invaluable contributions and their help and advice has been much appreciated. In addition, we would like to express our gratitude to all the social welfare professionals who agreed to give up their valuable time to be interviewed for our research. Special thanks are also due to Charlie, for his patience and understanding, and for his contribution to the cover, and to our respective families.

Finally our thanks to Professor Jane Aldgate for her foreword and to our editor, Amy Lankester-Owen.

For Charlie

Foreword

Jane Aldgate

Protecting children from maltreatment is a fundamental aim of child welfare services in the UK. How that maltreatment is defined remains a shifting sand, dictated by many factors and reflecting contemporary knowledge and attitudes of the time. The last twenty years have seen major steps forward in the understanding of child maltreatment and more importantly, of its impact on children throughout their childhood and beyond. The Children Act 1989 took an important step forward in moving the child maltreatment agenda from one which was preoccupied with uncovering abuse of different kinds: physical, sexual, emotional and neglect, to one which asked practitioners to shift their focus towards identifying the impact of that maltreatment on children. Such a move was assisted by the principles underpinning the Children Act 1989, which recognised the diversity of influences that help shape children's development, including children themselves.

Our understanding of significant harm and its prevention revived several key theoretical perspectives: children are individuals with unique potential; children thrive when they grow up in the context of nourishing food, warmth, physical nurture and enduring loving relationships with significant adults. Children's lives embrace many domains beyond that of their relationships with their parents or immediate carers. This includes school, peers, siblings and a positive community. The unique environment that makes up the experience of each individual child provides a constellation of factors which are often delicately balanced against one another. It would be unreasonable to expect any child to have a perfect childhood, even if we were capable of defining what that might be. What we do know is that positive factors can compensate for negative influences. Seeing a child's life within what is now termed 'an ecological framework' has shifted thinking from an approach which tended to diagnose the negatives and ignore the positives to one which sees the life of each child in the round and at the centre of any diagnostic process.

As thinking has shifted to putting the child at the centre of any assessment of significant harm, there has been a parallel move to understand the dynamics of parenting. This change poses tensions for policy makers and practitioners. On the other hand, the Children Act 1989 asks practitioners to recognise the significance for children of growing up in their families and to work with parents to enhance their parental responsibility, a message reinforced by the current interdepartmental government framework for the assessment of children in need and their families. This framework emphasises that practitioners need to help parents build on their strengths, in other words, to offer services that help and support families wherever possible, keeping in mind at all times the parenting orders, which are outwith the Children Act 1989 and which overtly sanction parents who cannot control their children's actions outside the home. In 2002 we have had the first case of a parent being sent to prison for persistently failing to send her child to school. This ambiguity in policy directives is confusing at the best of times but it is the real world in which child care practitioners live and work.

Our organisation of practice has not helped to resolve these issues. Many social services departments have completely separated the organisation and delivery of their services for children and adults. This is particularly so in the area of adult mental health, where the system may respond well to the impact of illness upon adults without being able to support those patients in their parenting capacity easily at the same time. With the advent of a more interdisciplinary approach to services for families, which at the time of writing is beginning to take shape within the reform of the National Health Service and social services, it is hoped that such problems and omissions will be resolved to the benefit of both children and their parents.

Ten years ago, books on child protection hardly ever placed substance misuse on the agenda. Like domestic violence, substance misuse was seen hovering in the background in child protection cases, but its significance as an issue in its own right was often overlooked in the preoccupation with the diagnosis of abuse. It began to gain recognition as a significant issue for policy makers following the publication of a series of research studies on child protection commissioned by the Department of Health. From then, there was a growing number of publications which began to look at both the prevalence and the nature of evidence which connects childhood experiences with adult capacities, while avoiding the trap of a deterministic approach by locating their arguments within an ecological model of adult development. Such an approach recognises the value of research-informed, focused intervention which can make a difference to the lives of individual parents and their children.

Reading this book, one cannot see substance abusing parents as anything other than real people who have significant problems that require a positive response from practitioners. The book stresses that parents need to feel their stories are heard and acted upon. At the same time, the authors recognise that this positive response does not preclude recognition of the seriousness of substance misuse. What the book revives is the fundamental tenet that childcare social workers have known for many generations. It is only in the minority of cases that children are removed from their families. In the majority of cases, with a clear understanding of the problems of substance misuse, a meticulous assessment of parental capacities and weaknesses, and knowledge of a range of effective interventions, child welfare practitioners may use their authority positively to work with both children and families to protect children from significant harm.

Jane Aldgate,
Professor of Social Care,
The Open University.

Part One
Introduction

1

Parental Substance Misuse and Child Welfare

Boy, 7, hands in mother's heroin to his teacher

(*The Times* 31 October 1998)

For those of us who have been long concerned with the effects of parental substance misuse on children, this *Times* headline did not, perhaps, come as a surprise. The little boy in question explained his behaviour as a response to his concern about his mother's drug use and told his teacher he wanted her to stop using heroin. It was one of several similar cases in the period of a week which came and went with little impact, apart from a comment from Keith Hellawell, the 'drugs tsar', who dismissed them as 'isolated incidents' (*The Times* 31 October 1998).

Of course, we do not know with any degree of certainty how many children are affected by parental substance misuse since, as we shall see, it is characterised by denial and secrecy. What we do know is that such incidents are not as isolated as some might hope and that, for many children living with parental substance misuse, life can be difficult, dangerous and frightening. This book focuses on what we consider to be important issues about parental substance misuse and parenting, child development and child welfare raised by incidents like the one described above. Our aim is not to judge, label or ascribe blame but to explore the debates that relate to various aspects of our main themes and throughout we have attempted to maintain a balanced view. This means that we do not shy away from identifying the negative aspects of parental substance misuse, particularly for children. However, we also acknowledge the realities, stresses and tensions that contribute to the way in which people develop and sustain a relationship with either drugs or alcohol. Our central purpose is to enable professionals from a wide range of disciplines to think about a range of important questions. Is it possible to misuse drugs and/or alcohol and be a good parent? What are the factors that either make this possible or militate against it? What is it like to be a child in a family where parents misuse substances? What are the needs of such children and how can they be met? Have children actually become invisible in this context, as Robinson and Rhoden (1998) propose and as some accounts of children suggest (Barnard and Barlow forthcoming; Laybourn, Brown and Hill 1996)? If the hypothesis that many children are invisible is correct (and clearly it is open to exploration and debate) what are the reasons for this? If, as a parent, your principal attachment is to a substance, how does this affect your capacity to form attachments to your children (Kroll and Taylor 2000)? Are current interventions with parents who misuse substances effective in assessing risks to children or are children falling into gaps in service provision – the spaces between professional territories and areas of responsibility for different groups – as many commentators fear (see for example Cleaver, Unell and Aldgate 1999; Hampton, Senatore and Gullotta 1998; Weir and Douglas 1999)? What is it like for professionals to work in this area of practice? We believe that it is only by bringing together critical concerns in relation to both substance misuse and child protection that these questions can be answered.

Of course, neither substance misuse nor child maltreatment are new phenomena; both have existed for centuries. What has changed, however, is the level of awareness of the impact of parental substance misuse on child welfare – one of many parental behaviours which are increasingly seen to have a significant effect on parenting capacity and child safety (Cleaver *et al.* 1999). While there is an increasingly vast literature on both substance misuse and child welfare (Harbin and Murphy 2000), what is missing is an exploration of ways in which they interact in the family context, with particular reference to the child's experience.

However, the first of many cautionary notes must be sounded here. When we talk about substance *misuse* we are referring to alcohol and drug use that causes problems on a number of levels with implications for child welfare and maltreatment. This is not to say that all substance-misusing parents maltreat their children; many do parent successfully and this must be clearly stated and recognised. However, it does not follow from such an important qualification that *all* will be able to parent successfully or without significant consequences being experienced by the children involved.

Substance misuse also increasingly features in families who are known to welfare professionals for other reasons and can be a contributory factor in domestic violence, mental health problems, offending, family breakdown and social exclusion as well as child maltreatment. The context in which behaviour takes place is also critical as is the dynamic between environment, parenting and child welfare. For all these reasons, a wide range of professionals – social workers in both adult and child and family care, probation officers, health visitors, doctors, community psychiatric nurses, teachers, drug and alcohol specialists, family centre staff and many others – need to address it as an issue which involves confronting assumptions (whether positive or negative) and feeling able to assess risks and needs with confidence. Unless this happens more effectively, children will indeed continue to remain invisible and they will be at risk.

This is not just a hunch or a groundless fear. Increasingly, research provides us with evidence of the impact of parental substance misuse on child welfare at both an emotional and a physical level and of the effects on child–parent attachment, arguably the cornerstone of healthy development across the life cycle. Research also suggests that children are falling through gaps in services and that professionals, both adult- and child-focused, feel increasingly ill-equipped to deal with this combination of issues. In addition, the 'care management' culture has made it easier to create separations than connections (Weir and Douglas 1999). As a result, families' problems are being compartmentalised and distributed across services, so that professionals rarely get a complete picture. Meanwhile, childcare professionals express concerns about a lack of knowledge about alcohol, drugs and their effects and impact; adult-care professionals express equal uncertainty about addressing parenting issues in their work and lack of confidence in assessing child welfare. Professional boundaries, territorial anxieties, client loyalty and confidentiality are also central concerns as is the problem of whether it is the actual child in the family who is kept in mind or the 'child' part of the adult that gets all the attention. These are some of the concerns that have been voiced during the course of our research and highlight the range of professional dilemmas we aim to address.

Throughout the debates that follow there will be an emphasis on a number of key themes. The dynamic that occurs between parenting capacity, child development and family and environmental factors will provide an overarching context in which all debates will be placed. The centrality of attachment theory will also be highlighted not only as a way of understanding child development and parent–child behaviour but also as a significant contributory factor to parenting styles and confidence in the parenting role. Equally crucial will be its application to the understanding of the relationship that occurs between people who misuse drugs and alcohol and their substance of choice. Issues of secrecy and denial that characterise much alcohol and drug use and the legality or illegality of the substances concerned will also recur as will the fears and fantasies experienced and the assumptions that are made by parents, children and the professionals who become involved with them about one another. Perhaps the most central theme is that provided by the image of the 'invisible' child, lurking in the background, knowing something is wrong, trying to find a voice, tell a story or get help and its connection with our main aim – to make visible the 'invisible' child within the context of a family where there is a substance problem.

Setting the scene: children in need, significant harm and child protection

In order to place what follows in context, some of the key ideas and developments in law and policy, as they relate to children and their families, need to be revisited briefly, so that central debates can be tracked and their resonance for *these* debates highlighted.

At its inception, the Children Act 1989, with its emphasis on children's rights, parental responsibility, minimum intervention and the principle that the child's welfare is the paramount consideration in law, was hailed as the beginning of a new dawn. The Children Act laid a duty on every local authority to identify 'children in need' in their area based on an assessment of the extent to which health and development might be impaired without services and introducing the concept of 'significant harm' (Home Office 1989, Section 17).

The notion of 'significant harm' is clearly of critical importance here and has been much debated, defined and interpreted since the Act was implemented (see for example Thoburn, Brandon and Lewis 1997). 'Significant harm', however, is often the result of numerous 'insignificant' harmful experiences that build up and come together to create risk or maltreatment. As Freeman (1992) points out, 'it must not be forgotten that *insignificant harm* may betoken a risk of significant harm and so cannot be overlooked' (Freeman 1992, p.103, our italics). In other words, a range of possible effects need to be considered.

> Sometimes a single, traumatic event may constitute significant harm…more often significant harm is a compilation of significant events both acute and longstanding, which interrupt, change or damage the child's physical and psychological development. Some children live in family and social circumstances where their health and development are neglected. For them it is the corrosiveness of long term emotional, physical or sexual abuse that can cause impairment to the extent of constituting significant harm. (Department of Health 1999, p.8)

This is particularly useful to bear in mind where there is parental substance misuse. A slight accident when children are left unsupervised, reliance on a young child for childcare or emotional support, or the beginnings of behavioural difficulties due to a parent's emotional unavailability, although not significantly harmful in isolation, in combination or in increased frequency, should give professionals pause for serious thought.

By the mid-1990s there were indications that although the letter of the law was being observed, the spirit in which it had been drafted had begun to be lost. Although the legislation had been aimed at all children in need, to safeguard their welfare, applying the broad definition in The Children Act 1989, Section 17 (10) proved extremely difficult in practice, with commentators observing the problems of moving from a reactive to a proactive model of intervention and exchanging 'policing' for partnership (Aldgate and Tunstill 1995; Department of Health 1994). Assessment had become focused on risk rather than need, with services targeted at children at risk of significant harm (Department of Health 2000d).

One of the crucial 'messages from research' was that childcare work had become dominated by child protection, with a focus on individual incidents of abuse, rather than holding onto a process in which child development, context and the bigger picture as a whole, was addressed (Department of Health 1995; W. Rose 2001). As a result a sense of continuity, connections, process and history was being lost (Howe 1996). Despite the guidance designed to aid assessment and planning, concern soon emerged that this was being used as a checklist, rather than as a creative tool harnessed to professional judgement in pursuit of an holistic assessment and that, once again, children in need were being overlooked in favour of children at risk (Horwath 2001; Katz 1997). In addition, concern was expressed about the quality of assessment of need, with inadequate early responses, lack of structured assessment of significant harm and a lack of systematic approaches to the gathering of information (W. Rose 2001; Social Services Inspectorate (SSI) 1997a, 1997b).

What now? Messages from research

There were a number of influences that made change imperative, with three strands of research evolving in response to concerns about the outcomes for children looked after by local authorities. The first, relating to children's developmental needs, highlighted the importance of addressing seven elements of a child's life on a continuing basis, so that they received the same attention as they would from a child's parent, under normal circumstances (Department of Health 1995; Parker et al. 1991). The emphasis was firmly on children's *needs* and increased understanding and awareness of them, providing a framework that all professionals could use for children of any age and having implications for the efficacy of continuing and holistic assessments of children (W. Rose 2001).

The second strand of research highlighted the consequences of professionals' failure to recognise parents' needs and their impact on parenting capacity. Studies revealed the way in which parents' own problems could impair their ability to respond appropriately to their children's needs and the consequences of this, which were sometimes fatal (see for example Buchanan 1996; Cleaver and Freeman 1995; Falkov 1996; Reder, Duncan and Gray 1993; Reder and Lucey 1995). This underlined the interconnectedness of children's welfare and that of their carers and opened up possibilities for joint working and family support.

Finally, there was the issue of context and environment. There was increasing recognition of the influence of circumstances in which families are bringing up children and the impact of environmental factors (see Jack 1998, 2001; Stevenson 1998), and more awareness of the link between economic disadvantage and living conditions. Research suggested that the impact on children and parenting of living in areas of high deprivation, together with the cumulative effects of disadvantage, dramatically increased the likelihood of a child entering the care system (Bebbington and Miles 1989; Social Exclusion Unit 1998). Research further highlighted the fact that issues regarding context and environment as they related to children from other races and cultures were not properly understood (Social

Exclusion Unit 1998). None of this came as a surprise, but official recognition, based on good quality evidence, moved debates forward apace.

The 'Quality Protects' initiative and the 'Assessment Framework'

Meanwhile, in the second half of the 1990s a number of reports appeared which showed that all was not as it should be in social services circles (Social Services Inspectorate 1997a, 1997b) and in response to this, on 21 September 1998, Frank Dobson launched the 'Quality Protects' programme. This initiative was part of the Labour government's family project, which aimed to end child poverty, tackle social exclusion and promote the welfare of all children so that they can fulfil their potential as citizens. One of the key objectives requiring 'that referral and assessment processes discriminate effectively between types and levels of need and produce a timely response' resulted in the evolution of the new *Framework for the Assessment of Children in Need and their Families* (Department of Health 2000a) with its three domains – child development, parenting capacity and wider family and environmental factors – reflecting the wealth of research evidence referred to above (see Figure 1.1).

What the framework represented was an holistic approach to assessment which would safeguard children's welfare more effectively through a systematic engagement with key dimensions within each domain. In addition it was hoped that it would promote more equality of services, particularly for children and families from ethnic minority groups, but also in relation to all children at any age or stage of development. Equally importantly, it aimed to encourage a move away from a 'twin track' approach that saw 'children in need' and 'child protection' as discrete activities, towards an integrated approach which was dynamic and ongoing rather than undertaken in a 'proceduralised' and 'checklist' driven manner. In theory, then, it made identifying and responding to children in need, rather than simply to children at risk, more possible, opening the way for more children to access services.

What the framework has enabled us to do in this book is to structure debates about children with substance-misusing parents and to emphasise the dynamic quality of both the parenting task and children's development, within the various environments in which this takes place. The dimensions of the three domains will be used as a series of pointers to examine issues for children of substance–misusing parents and to frame questions and responses in relation both to them and their families.

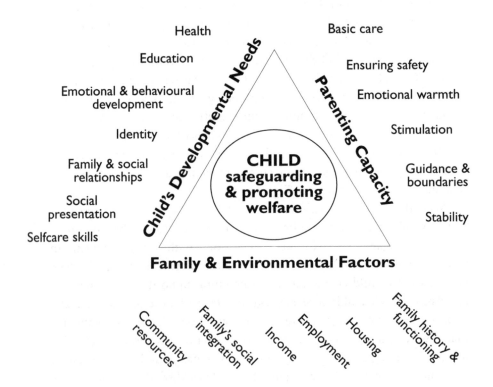

Figure 1.1 The Assessment Framework
Source: Department of Health 2000a, p.89

What will follow

The chapters are grouped into four parts. The first part of the book – Chapters 1 and 2 – provides essential context for an understanding of the dynamic between parental substance misuse and child welfare. Part two – Chapters 3 to 5 – looks at the ways in which a relationship with a substance can develop and what this might mean for parenting. The third part – Chapters 6 to 8 – concerns itself with the world of the child and the specific impact that parental substance misuse can have on child well-being. In the final chapters we examine a range of practice issues, approaches to assessment and intervention and implications for research and policy.

Looking at the content in more detail, following on from this introduction, in Chapter 2 we examine what research tells us about the links between child maltreatment and parental substance misuse. Here we shall consider the ways in which attempts have been made to establish both the scale of drug and alcohol problems among parents and the number of children who may be affected. We shall also be looking at key definitions – what do we actually mean by 'substance misuse' and how does this differ from 'use'? How is the term 'maltreatment' understood? We shall be highlighting some of the methodological problems that arise when researching the link between parental substance misuse and child maltreatment and tackling some of the contradictions and complexities of the findings. Particular attention will be paid to the links between parental substance misuse and neglect, domestic violence, mental states and mental health, child homicide and attachment problems. Issues in relation both to gender and to lone parenting will also be discussed.

In part two, we then focus on a constellation of key ideas in relation to adults' use of drugs and alcohol. In Chapter 3 we consider the way in which substance misuse has been understood and the impact of some of these ideas on attitudes and assumptions. We examine theories that attempt to explain substance misuse, both in relation to how such behaviour is categorised and how this enables us to make sense of the experiences of substance-misusing parents. Terminology will be examined, as we look at the way in which ideas about 'addiction', 'dependence' and 'withdrawal' are conceptualised, within the legal and moral context in which these debates take place, and the impact of labelling will be analysed. Issues of legality, illegality, volition and social constructionism will also be considered.

Building on these ideas, Chapter 4 explores the processes that take place in the relationship between substances and their users and the impact of these on family dynamics. In this context the interaction between the psychological and the social – parenting capacity and environment – is considered alongside theories that enable us to think more purposefully about the process that occurs between an individual and their drug of choice. Here we also consider the relevance of attachment theory as well as the dynamic that can develop in which labelling, denial and secrecy interact with one another, with obvious implications for professional intervention. We also attempt to explain and understand a progressive dependence on and attachment to a substance and the painful dilemmas, problems and conflicts which may emerge as a consequence. The impact of this both on parenting and on the capacity to care for children is examined. How and why such attachments develop, their function within individual, family and social systems and the threat posed by the prospect of losing this 'attachment' relationship are all considered, particularly in terms of the implications of such processes for assessment and intervention.

Bearing this in mind, we move on to look at the implications of these processes on the art of parenting. Set within the context of current debates relating to 'good enough' parenting, and drawing on recent research with substance-misusing parents, Chapter 5 provides an analysis of the way in which drug and alcohol problems can impact upon all the dimensions of both the parenting and environmental domains of the *Framework for the Assessment of Children in Need and their Families* (Department of Health 2000a). We examine the potential practical, psychological, emotional and social consequences as well as the way in which parents struggling with substance problems describe and manage the parenting task. The role that drugs and alcohol can play in dealing with the demands and stresses of caring for children is also analysed.

This provides a backdrop against which to enter the world of the child and the parent/child/substance/environment dynamic; this is the focus of the third part of the book beginning in Chapter 6 with the essential ingredients for child well-being. Having explored the way in which an attachment to a substance can develop, we move on to consider child–parent attachment and the centrality of attachment theory within debates about child development. The links between risk, vulnerability, resilience and protective factors within the context of parental substance misuse will be highlighted.

Chapter 7 focuses on what children, young people and adults can tell us about both the pitfalls and benefits of growing up with substance-misusing parents. We highlight the ways in which parental substance misuse can affect relationships, self-esteem and security and the various problems that can occur, in relation to attachment, separation and loss and the impact of parental substance misuse on family functioning. Role reversal, role confusion and the implications for the child as carer are also discussed, as is the potential for substance misuse to provide an unhelpful model for problem-solving.

In Chapter 8 we turn to the child development domain of the framework, focusing on the way in which parental substance misuse can affect physical and emotional welfare at a range of levels. Beginning with the hoped for outcomes, in relation to each dimension, we move on to evaluate potential threats to them posed by parental substance misuse. Short-term and longer-term consequences are considered as is the way in which additional parental problems, notably domestic violence, can exacerbate likely risks.

From here, in the final part of the book, we move on to a more specific consideration of practice issues, starting in Chapter 9 by exploring some of the dilemmas raised for social welfare professionals who encounter parents with substance problems. Based on interviews with practitioners in both adult and childcare services, emerging themes are identified relating to engagement, assessment, conflicts between the needs of parents and those of their children, and confidentiality. We address some key concerns both at an individual and an organisational level, and consider some of the interprofessional dynamics that either contribute to or militate against effective intervention and assessment.

In Chapter 10, we examine the main considerations in relation to the assessment of parenting in general and in assessing parenting where there is substance misuse in particular. We explore the impact of values, beliefs and feelings, as well as the part played by 'cultural relativism', assumptions about 'natural love' and the way in which the 'rule of optimism' can operate. The importance of child-centred practice and the role of observation in assessment are emphasised and an holistic model for assessment is presented.

Building on this, Chapter 11 considers interventions that have been seen to be effective where there are substance issues, with a particular emphasis on those which include children, families and significant others. The contribution of ecological perspectives and social support is considered and specific models are described and evaluated, notably the Stress-Coping-Health Model, the Community Reinforcement Approach and Network

Therapy. We also offer our own ideas for an holistic family-centred approach, aimed particularly at addressing the needs of children and making them more visible within intervention.

The final chapter, drawing the various strands of research and argument together, returns to debates relating to 'invisible' children and looks at ways forward in practice, policy and research. The impact of specialisation on boundaries and communication between welfare professionals is considered and ideas for improving practice through training and breaking down interprofessional barriers are suggested. We also look at ways in which new initiatives in service provision can be built on and developed, particularly in relation to services for children.

2

Parental Substance Misuse and Child Maltreatment

*To suggest that all parents who suffer from problem alcohol/drug use
...present a danger to their children is misleading...in isolation [it]
presents little risk of significant harm to children.*

(Cleaver et al. 1999, p.23)

*He fell and hurt his head today, fell and split his head open so he's getting
spoiled today... all his face was a mess and I was really frightened. And I
was stoned at the time and I felt really guilty.*

(Parent quoted in Klee, Wright and Rothwell 1998, p.14)

In this chapter we explore what research has discovered about the links
between parental substance misuse and the risk to children of various types
of child maltreatment, abuse and neglect. What happened to the parent
quoted above could happen to anyone; the difference is the degree to which
substance misuse could have either contributed to this accident or affected
the speed and efficacy of the parent's response to it.

Not all substance-misusing parents mistreat their children or come to the
notice of welfare agencies (Harbin and Murphy 2000; Mountenay 1998;
SCODA (Standing Conference on Drug Abuse) 1997). By the same token, it
cannot and must not be assumed that dependence on drugs or alcohol
necessarily and automatically reduces parents' capacity to parent effectively
or that the children's development will be damaged in some way (Barnard
1999). Many parents contain or control their drink and drug use and use
harm-reduction strategies to minimise the impact on other areas of their
lives, including their children's welfare. Even when substance misuse occurs
within a context of social and economic disadvantage, children will not

automatically suffer maltreatment. As we shall see in Chapter 6, a variety of protective factors may come into play which have a significant impact on the way in which children respond, cope and survive in the care of substance-misusing parents.

However, research does suggest that both alcohol and drug misuse creates the potential for things to go wrong (Hogan 1998; Sher 1991; Zeitlin 1994) and adds to the risks from negative family processes (Buchanan 1996; Reder and Duncan 1999; Rutter and Rutter 1993; Velleman and Orford 1999). In addition, parental substance misuse is strongly associated with neglect (Alison 2000; Bays 1990; Famularo, Kinscherff and Fenton 1992; Forrester 2000) and when combined with other parental problems – mental illness and domestic violence, for example – the dangers to children can be significantly increased.

Before we examine the research evidence, with all its methodological complexity, it is important to be clear about the way in which the terms 'substance misuse' and 'maltreatment' are to be understood and defined within the context of these debates. We also consider the issue of prevalence and how attempts have been made to establish the number of parents with substance misuse issues and how many children might be affected.

What is meant by 'substance misuse'?

Our use of the term 'substance misuse' is based on the definition provided by the Standing Conference on Drug Abuse (SCODA 1997) which highlights a number of important points:

> The terms drug use and misuse mean different things to different people. Drug *use* may be described as drug *taking*. In general misuse can be taken to mean the use of drugs which leads to harm (social, physical and psychological). (SCODA 1997, p.36, emphasis in original)

Here a useful distinction is made between 'use' and 'misuse'. What is also important is that we are not talking here about definitions based solely on quantity, but on patterns, motivations and consequences. By 'substance', however, we mean not only psychoactive drugs which alter mood, behaviour and perceptions in different ways but also alcohol, on the basis that many commentators perceive it as one among many drugs (see for example Cleaver *et al.* 1999; Robson 1999) and because its misuse in the context of child welfare can have similar implications to those of drugs. It is however worth noting that in the US literature the term 'substance misuse' is not always defined and can mean drug, alcohol or polydrug use.

At times drugs and alcohol will be discussed together. However, there are some significant differences between them in terms of impact and consequences and these will be highlighted, as and when they arise.

What is meant by child maltreatment?

As Stevenson observes,

> The word 'maltreatment' is often used to cover neglect and abuse and avoids the awkwardness of distinguishing between acts of omission (neglect) and acts of commission (abuse). (Stevenson 1998, p.5)

The term is also socially constructed – just as child abuse has been – and its meaning may change over time and place (Korbin 1991; Parton 1991). By the same token, there are a variety of cultural issues that need to be taken into account, both in terms of race and ethnicity, but also, extending beyond that to include class and position within (or outside) the prevailing social structure (Stevenson 1998).

Buchanan (1996), in her wide-ranging study of cycles of maltreatment, underlines the complexity inherent in a word that most of us assume we understand. Does maltreatment focus on 'care-giver variables' – parental pathology and intention to do harm (including emotional and psychological abuse, neglect, physical and sexual abuse) – or on the effects on the child, consistent, for example, with threshold criteria for 'significant harm'? Is a focus on neglect and abuses of all kinds too narrow, despite its usefulness in judicial and social work decisions or should a much broader definition, which embraces all elements of family dynamics, as well as extrafamilial dimensions such as social and cultural context, be used? Clearly, there is a dynamic between these two sets of ideas and to use them in harmony would seem the most productive course, in view of the fact that behaviour is inevitably affected by a range of internal and external factors, occurs in context and has a variety of consequences and outcomes for all concerned. In addition it is consistent with the *Framework for the Assessment of Children in Need and their Families* (Department of Health 2000a) discussed in Chapter 1, and highlights the importance of addressing the interaction between general socio-economic circumstances, prevailing cultures and structures, individual behaviours, parenting and child welfare. Interestingly, some commentators use the words 'maltreatment' and 'abuse' interchangeably (see for example Coleman and Cassell 1995; Reder and Duncan 1999; Sloan 1998) and this example will be followed for the purposes of this debate; however, some distinctions will be made in relation to different kinds of abuse.

Parental substance misuse: how many children are affected?

It is difficult to estimate exactly how many children in Britain might be affected by parental substance misuse since, as we have already suggested, it is characterised by denial and secrecy. This is a particularly true in relation to drug misuse, where parents often go to great lengths to keep their behaviour hidden. This may be even more the case in minority ethnic communities where figures about both drug and alcohol use are hard to assess (Brisby, Baker and Hedderwick 1997; Patel 2000). Definition is also problematic since there are a vast number of different levels of substance misuse that can occur, and patterns of use vary widely across the UK (Forrester 2001).

What is happening in the wider population can be assessed only through census data or extrapolation. The Office of Population, Censuses and Surveys (OPCS) (1996) suggests that in households headed by couples, with or without children, levels of 'alcohol dependence' occur in 27 per 1000 although this increases to 38 per 1000 in lone parent families. In relation to drugs, as far as couples with children are concerned the prevalence is 9 per 1000, rising to 24 per 1000 in families headed by lone parents. Heroin is the main drug used. Figures in relation to polydrug use remain unclear. However, as Forrester (2001) points out, these figures are likely to be an underestimate of the true situation since these kinds of statistical data rely on acknowledged drug dependency and parents who are not prepared to reveal substance use habits on census forms will remain hidden. The actual size of the parent population that misuse drugs or alcohol, therefore, is still largely based on guesswork.

The 'extrapolation' approach is exemplified by calculations undertaken by Brisby and colleagues. Based on 13.5 million parents living in Britain, with 7 per cent drinking at what they describe as 'harmful levels', they estimate that 'there are likely to be some 800,000 children in England and Wales, 85,000 children in Scotland and something under 35,000 children in Northern Ireland living in a family where a parent has an alcohol problem' (Brisby et al. 1997, p.7). There is no breakdown by ethnic origin in these figures. They do not suggest that all these children will automatically suffer harm but they do believe that 'children whose parents drink too much are children at risk' (Brisby *et al.* 1997, p.5). Another estimate suggests that, on the basis that 2 million to 3 million adults 'are "alcohol dependent" at any one time it is likely that the number of "concerned and affected others" might run to 4–6 million or more' (Orford 2001, p.21). Drawing on further research (Velleman and Orford 1999) Orford goes on to conclude: 'it follows that children currently living with excessive drinkers must exist in very large numbers indeed, probably in excess of 1 million in Britain' (Orford 2001, p.21). In relation to drug use, McKeganey, Barnard and McIntosh (2001), extrapolating from figures from the Glasgow drug action team, estimate that there may be 20,000 children living with parents with serious drug problems in Scotland alone.

Clearly there is significant divergence in these figures which relates to, among other methodological problems, how user 'dependence' or 'harm' is measured and how this is translated into 'harm' experienced by children. Whatever the true figures, there is clear evidence that this is an issue which needs to be addressed.

As we shall see, data from child protection registers can shed some light on prevalence but this will relate only to families where significant harm has been shown to be occurring. Nevertheless it is thought-provoking to consider rates of prevalence at different stages of the child protection process. Although Cleaver *et al.* (1999) do not distinguish between concerns in relation to drugs, alcohol or both, their analysis of figures suggests that substance problems featured in 20 per cent of cases at the referral stage, rising to 25 per cent at the stage at which interviews to explore suspicions of child abuse took place. This level remained the same at the case conference stage, according to English research although, in a study done in Wales, it rose to 60 per cent. At the court order stage, according to a snapshot survey by Rickford (1996), the figure rose to 70 per cent, although (as we shall see) there are considerable variations on these findings across other studies, both in the UK and in the USA.

Kearney, Levin and Rosen (2000) in their examination of the prevalence of mental health, drug and alcohol problems concluded that they occurred in at least one-third of families referred to social services departments due to childcare concerns, although in some teams the rate was even higher than this: 'social workers estimated that at least 50% and in some teams up to 90%

of parents on their caseload had either mental health, alcohol or substance misuse difficulties' (Kearney *et al.* 2000, p.8).

These figures of course relate to a constellation of problems which include substance misuse, rather than a specific set of statistics for substance misuse alone. They do however draw attention to the impact of these problems on children and the demands placed on those professionals whose task it is to protect them.

Research in context: conundrums and complications

There is a range of methodological problems that characterise research in this area, particularly in relation to sample type, study design and the often contradictory findings (Parton, Thorpe and Wattam 1997). Because the samples used are often drawn from families who already have a range of identified problems, or are known to childcare services and are the subjects of court proceedings or care orders, findings will be affected accordingly. Child protection intervention is disproportionately focused on poor families who come from the most deprived sections of society and about whom a range of assumptions tend to be made (see for example Department of Health 1995; Parton 1997). This means that there is inherent bias in studies that are based on court records or child protection registers since the constellation of factors that contribute to disadvantage significantly increase children's chances of entering the care system (Bebbington and Miles 1989; W. Rose 2001). A further problem relates to the way in which both maltreatment and substance misuse have been defined. Studies focused on 'substance misuse' may address drugs or alcohol or both and, as has already been suggested, 'misuse' can mean 'use' – especially in the case of drugs – 'problem use' or 'dependency'. All these factors affect the conclusions reached and the potential for comparisons to be made and it is often very difficult to separate out substance misuse as a risk factor, independent from all the variables that contribute to the parent–child dynamic that leads to maltreatment (Deren 1986). Velleman and Orford (1999), in their wide-ranging review of the literature on alcohol misuse and the impact on children, emphasise that it is very hard to study cause and effect in isolation. How can you tell whether substance misuse leads to child maltreatment, or whether there is simply evidence of coexistence?

It is essential, then, to explore the much wider territory of family functioning, lifespan development, and environmental factors. The context in which substance abuse takes place is of critical importance, as are any surrounding, prevailing issues in relation to parental dynamics, violence, health and social pressures. Additional problems arise in controlling for social and economic circumstances and, in relation to polydrug use, separating out the different effects of any one substance (Deren 1986; Hogan 1998).

Further difficulties are presented by some of the significant differences between alcohol use and the use of illicit substances. Here we encounter issues of social acceptance versus social condemnation, secrecy versus openness (at least to a degree) and the extent to which drug use is likely to be far more connected to criminal behaviour, health hazards and social exclusion – an issue which will be explored in more depth in Chapter 5. In addition, whereas cocaine, heroin and crack use tends to be concentrated in areas characterised by poverty and social disadvantage, alcohol and amphetamine use is likely to be more widely distributed through the population, crossing socio-economic boundaries (Gilman 2000; Hogan 1998). Problems ensuing from substance misuse are often – although not exclusively – located within a social context characterised by poverty and deprivation (Forrester 2000; Lloyd 1998) and many studies focus on disadvantaged groups with low socio-economic status and multiple problems. Once again it is the dynamic between the individual, the family and the environment, in all its facets, that will have an impact on parenting capacity either to increase or decrease the risks to the child (Jack 2001). As Garbarino (1990) observes, the links between poverty and child maltreatment are well known; the riskiness of the family however is 'not the whole story…we must go further to identify and investigate high risk environments' (Garbarino 1990, p.90). Many of the issues related to alcohol misuse and child maltreatment in affluent, middle-class families who do not easily come to the attention of welfare services will, as a result, remain invisible.

Attempts are also made to extrapolate findings from the now considerable number of studies on alcohol-misusing parents and adult children of 'alcoholics' (as they are called in the American literature) to families where there is drug misuse, especially in relation to the impact on children (see Chapter 7). The extent to which this works successfully is debatable and findings and comparisons have been inconclusive, as will be apparent (see Hogan 1998).

The final point about research findings is the extent to which American studies have relevance for the British context, in view of the differences in culture, populations and social problems. Indeed, some commentators have implied that there may be very little resonance indeed (see for example Lloyd 1998) and that such findings 'should be taken with large pinches of salt' (Hepburn 2000). Forrester (2000) warns against generalising from American research given the fact that, whereas crack and cocaine are seen as the greatest problem in relation to child maltreatment in the USA, recent British research suggests that it is alcohol and heroin that should concern us the most. Notwithstanding, it is useful to evaluate different methodologies and methods employed in research into parental substance misuse and, provided findings are taken in context and are thoughtfully analysed, potentially useful considerations do emerge. The danger, however, is that almost every negative finding can be so over-qualified, in terms of variables and factors that cannot be controlled, that no useful conclusions can be reached. Can anything usefully be said? This is the question that will now be addressed.

What follows represents a survey of some of the key studies undertaken both in the USA and in the UK, with particular emphasis on the British context, rather than a comprehensive review of all the available literature.

Parental substance misuse and child maltreatment

In the USA, parental substance misuse has long been identified as a major factor in child maltreatment (see for example Black and Mayer 1980; Deren 1986; Dore, Doris and Wright 1995; Jaudes, Ekwo and Van Voorhis 1995). Indeed, some have concluded that it is the single most common predictor of child abuses of various kinds 'approximately tripling the risk of maltreatment when other factors were controlled' (Chaffin, Kelleher and Hollenberg 1996, p.200). Some studies also suggest that it is not simply current substance misuse that may create the *potential* for child maltreatment but that a previous history of misuse may also be a significant factor (Ammerman *et al.* 1999; Famularo *et al.* 1992). Parenting skills, family life and dynamics and general child-rearing practices such as discipline, boundary setting, consistency of care and reliability, can all be adversely affected (Magura and Laudet 1996; Tyler *et al.* 1997). This may have considerable consequences for child–parent attachment patterns (as we shall see) and therefore for children's feelings of emotional safety, quite apart from the implications for physical safety. All these elements will be discussed in more detail in Chapter 5.

In Britain there have been a number of important studies in recent years which support many of the findings in the US literature (see for example Barnard and Barlow forthcoming; Bates *et al.* 1999; ChildLine 1997; Coleman and Cassell 1995; Hogan 1997; Hogan and Higgins 2001; Kearney and Ibbetson 1991; Klee *et al.* 1998; Laybourn *et al.* 1996; Sloan 1998; Velleman and Orford 1999). There is increasing interest being shown in this area, particularly as a result of recent research identifying substance misuse as a critical factor in parenting capacity (see Cleaver *et al.* 1999) and as a feature of parents whose children come to the attention of social services departments and other social welfare services (Forrester 2000; Harwin, Owen and Forrester forthcoming; Hawker 1999; Swadi 1994; Woodcock and Sheppard forthcoming).

The degree and extent of the links between substance misuse and child maltreatment, however, are far from clear, with evidence of some quite contradictory findings from the various research studies undertaken. Mayer and Black (1977) for example, using a sample of 200 parents accessing treatment services for both opiate (heroin, morphine and methadone) and alcohol problems found that, in the opiate-using parents, there was more evidence of child maltreatment than in alcohol-misusing families, although in their later study they found no differences in rates of neglect and abuse (Black and Mayer 1980). Famularo *et al.* (1992), however, found a greater link between cocaine and alcohol addiction and maltreatment than between opiate addiction and abuse. These somewhat confusing findings highlight several pitfalls already identified – definitions are (as suggested earlier) both important and misleading – and time frames may also be important, in that significant changes in society have taken place between the late 1970s and the 1990s for example so that this may also be a variable to consider.

One popular approach has been to examine records of childcare cases that have come to court where child maltreatment and abuse have been clearly found to be present, and to explore the parents' histories. Even here, however, where the methods appear similar, the findings are very diverse. In Young's (1964) study 62 per cent of parents in the sample had alcohol problems, while Fitch *et al.* (1975) found only 37 per cent could be defined in this way. Murphy *et al.* (1991), using a sample of 206 court cases over a two-year period, discovered that 43 per cent of parents abused substances (drugs and alcohol), with 7 per cent of fathers and 14 per cent of mothers being drug users. In another court-based study by Famularo *et al.* (1992), 67 per cent of the 190 parents randomly selected were abusing substances.

Other approaches have focused on parents whose children had been removed from their care due to maltreatment. In one such study, 50 per cent of fathers and 30 per cent of mothers had serious alcohol problems (Famularo *et al.* 1986), while Schetky *et al.* (1979) found parents in their very similar study had what they described as a 'significant history' of alcohol abuse. Sowder and Burt (1980) compared over 300 children of heroin users with a neighbourhood sample of the same size. They discovered rates of abuse among drug users to be 10–15 per cent higher than rates for US parents generally. In Black and Mayer's (1980) study 27 per cent of those misusing alcohol had abused their children in some way, as had 19 per cent of opiate users. The dramatic differences between some of these findings is hard to explain; what they highlight however are the complexities involved in undertaking reliable research in this complex area (Deren 1986).

In Britain, an international research study by Greenland (1987) identified abuse of alcohol and/or drugs as one of nine characteristics of parents which might indicate future abuse. This finding supported conclusions reached by Gibbons, Conroy and Bell (1995), who also found that a substantial minority of children on child protection registers had parents with histories of criminal behaviour, substance misuse or mental illness. In her 'snapshot' survey in Bolton, Rickford (1996) discovered that parental drug misuse was suspected in 70 per cent of parents whose children were subject to court orders, and in 51 per cent of those whose children were on the child protection register, what she termed 'parental substance misuse' was an issue. In half the registered cases the main problem was illicit drug misuse. A more recent study in Bolton identified a 300 per cent increase in known drug users since 1992, 46 per cent of whom had dependent children. Over 30 per cent of the children on the child protection register and 75 per cent of children subject to court proceedings had parents misusing substances at some level (Murphy and Oulds 2000). In both these studies, the stated focus was on *drug* misuse; the term 'substance misuse' was also used, although not defined. This makes it difficult to draw any conclusions from the differences in these statistics.

In his research into parental substance misuse – that is the use of drugs, alcohol or combinations of drugs – and child maltreatment in Cornwall, Sloan (1998) examined the records of 307 children from 153 families on the child protection register. He found 'significant' rates of substance use often alongside other factors (psychiatric history, history of abuse). Forrester's (2000) study, based on 50 families with 95 children on the child protection register in Southwark, revealed that parental substance misuse (both alcohol and drugs, notably heroin) was identified by social workers as a cause for concern in 52 per cent of the families and, in the main, was connected to registration for neglect. Harwin, Owen and Forrester (forthcoming) examined the care plans of 100 children subject to care orders and found that 'substance misuse was identified as a key issue in 40 per cent of the families. Alcohol was a key issue in 28 per cent...and drug misuse in 21 per cent (in 9 per cent both alcohol and drug misuse were key issues)' (cited in Forrester 2001, p.4).

Although valuable sources of information, as suggested earlier, samples drawn from child protection registers or from children subject to care orders are, of course, a very specific group, in which parents from particular backgrounds have already been identified as failing to provide adequate care, in some way. Although findings may indeed highlight a causal link between parental substance misuse and child maltreatment, in some instances, Mountenay (1998) offers a word of caution before jumping to this conclusion. She suggests that the coexistence of maltreatment, substance misuse and registration could just as easily identify a link between social workers' *attitudes* to substance misuse – especially drug use – and registration. In other words, any indication of substance misuse may lead to an overreaction on the part of professionals. This of course is just as simplistic a conclusion to draw as automatic correlation, but what it does underline is the dynamic between parental problems, child welfare and professional attitudes – a theme to which we will return.

Lewis (1997), in her study of 2000 referral calls to the National Society for the Prevention of Cruelty to Children (NSPCC), found that substance misuse featured more prominently in callers' accounts than any other type of parental behaviour, with concerns about alcohol outweighing those about drugs. Callers were not always specific about the actual substance being used, tending to refer to 'druggies', so for classification purposes, such calls were recorded as 'drugs, alcohol or both' (Lewis 1997, p.35). ChildLine (1997) examined the records of 3255 calls made to its service between 1 April 1995 and 31 April 1996 where parental alcohol misuse was an issue. Researchers then focused in detail on 2134 of these, drawn from all over the UK and incorporating all ages (children's accounts drawn from this study will be discussed in more detail in Chapter 7). Alcohol misuse was, in fact, rarely the presenting problem but tended to emerge in the context of accounts of physical and sexual abuse, domestic violence and family breakdown. It also featured in accounts of children running away from home. Three out of five children whose father had an alcohol problem, and two out of five where the mother had the problem, described accounts of physical abuse. The majority of sexual assaults were also committed by drunken parents. Children also described being neglected and emotionally abused and confessed to suicidal feelings; many children were subject to abuses of more than one kind. Once again, this represents a sample of young people who are experiencing a range of problems so considerable as to force them to call ChildLine for help. Notwithstanding, it represents a disturbing prevalence of alcohol-related parental abuse.

Maternal substance misuse

Considerable research has focused specifically on maternal substance misuse and foetal damage with the potential to lead to child maltreatment (see for example Deren 1986; Dore *et al.* 1995). Substance-misusing mothers (as we shall see in Chapter 5) come in for particular scrutiny for a number of logical and not so logical reasons, based not only on the physical and cognitive impact of substance use on foetal development but also on stereotypes about what constitutes being a 'good' mother or mother-to-be (Ford and Hepburn 1997; Klee 1998; Klee and Jackson 1998; Klee, Jackson and Lewis 2001). In studies by Kelley (1992) and Jaudes *et al.* (1995) in utero exposure to drugs was found to be connected to later maltreatment, often severe enough to warrant the child's removal from parental care. In Kelley's study, a group of cocaine-using mothers whose babies were born with withdrawal symptoms were compared with a non-using sample, matched for socio-economic status, age and race. Almost 60 per cent of the drug-exposed babies were subsequently identified as suffering from abuse or neglect, compared with 8 per cent of the control group and, by the age of 11 months, only half the drug-exposed babies were still with their mothers. What we do not know about this study is the extent of family and community support; what we do know is that drug-misusing mothers are reluctant to use antenatal services, health clinics and other supports for fear of censure. It is clear from research studies in this area that babies born drug or alcohol exposed and with withdrawal symptoms may often be hard to care for. Substance-misusing women may have a range of problems to manage, in terms of accessing substances, and behaviour may be characterised by inconsistency, irritability, lack of energy and impaired judgement. This, together with social context and the absence of family or friendship support systems, has been seen to set up a dynamic between parent and child which can result in increased risks of maltreatment (Famularo *et al.* 1992). The specific impact on both the unborn child and infant will be examined in more detail in Chapter 8. Although it is generally assumed that alcohol misuse in particular is more common among men than women, 40 per cent of the children in the ChildLine study reported maternal alcohol misuse as the problem – a far greater number than would be expected from the national picture.

Lone parenting

The issue of lone parenting and substance misuse remains significantly under-researched despite the fact that links have been made between other mental health problems, lone parenthood and a level of vulnerability in adults where child welfare can become an issue (Audit Commission 1999; OPCS 1996; Sheppard 2001). As Cleaver and colleagues discovered in their wide-ranging evaluation of the available literature, 'Lone parents show a higher rate [of alcohol dependence] than found for couples with children... These findings...suggest that children living with a lone parent are more vulnerable to the impact of parental drinking' (Cleaver *et al.* 1999, p.15). The same, they concluded, was also true of parents who misuse drugs although specific studies do not exist. In the ChildLine study, alcohol was a problem for more lone fathers than lone mothers, even though statistically there are more of the latter than the former (ChildLine 1997). In the study by Woodcock and Sheppard, which explored the implications for child welfare of the coexistence of both maternal depression and alcohol problems, lone parents made up a sizeable proportion of the sample identified (Woodcock and Sheppard forthcoming). Many studies do not, however, always indicate whether parents have partners or not, so the full picture is harder to put together.

In a study of 126 cases referred to a community alcohol team in Torbay, Hawker (1999) identified links between lone parenthood, alcohol misuse and childcare concerns. Over half the lone parents disclosed that they always drank to the point of intoxication, with a further 14 per cent indicating that this was 'sometimes' the case. In 45 per cent of cases there was social services' involvement although not necessarily for critical childcare concerns; in 38 per cent, however, there were child protection issues resulting in registration. Clear links were also found between childhood attachment problems and abuse/trauma and, in the parents' histories, multiple losses, depression and problems with self-esteem. Alcohol was identified as a coping mechanism by 90 per cent of the sample and as an escape either from the present or the past for 75 per cent. Clearly this was a very specific clinical sample where alcohol misuse was a prerequisite for services. Nonetheless, the findings are thought provoking.

Fanti (1990), in his examination of family issues relating to alcohol misuse, draws attention to the fact that, even in two-parent families, if there is one problem drinker, the other parent effectively can become a lone parent with an extra dependent family member to support. This additional source of stress can adversely affect parenting capacity and increase risks to children.

Alcohol, drugs and types of maltreatment

Attempts have been made to connect substance misuse of various kinds to different types of maltreatment or abuse although clear links are hard to make as no systematic research has been done (Cleaver *et al.* 1999). A few studies, however, appear to have been able to come to some conclusions regarding physical, sexual and emotional abuse or combinations of these, and are worth discussion. Neglect will be addressed separately.

Famularo *et al.* (1992) found that parents who abuse alcohol are more likely to abuse their children physically, although this was also determined by whether it was the mother or the father with the alcohol problem. While fathers who drink might hit their children, mothers who drink to excess are more likely to neglect their children. This is confirmed by NSPCC research undertaken by Lewis (1997), who found the greatest correlation was between fathers and physical abuse. In relation to the link between child abuse and drug abuse, Famularo *et al.* (1992) discerned a connection between cocaine abuse and child sexual abuse, and Leiffer, Shapiro and Kassem (1993) found a link between drug use in mothers and sexual abuse. Black and Mayer (1980) discovered that in one-fifth of their sample physical or sexual abuse had taken place but they did not specifically link type of abuse to either drugs or alcohol. In contrast, Lewis (1997) found that substance-misusing parents featured very rarely in cases of sexual abuse and

Forrester (2000) that they did not feature at all for registrations for this type of maltreatment. Velleman and Orford (1999), however, identified a clear link between family violence, alcohol misuse, and physical and sexual abuse, at the hands of mothers, fathers and siblings.

The emotional and psychological damage caused by inconsistency, rejection and verbal abuse that can be experienced by children with alcohol-misusing parents has also been highlighted in various studies (see for example Brisby *et al.* 1997; ChildLine 1997; Laybourn *et al.* 1996; O'Hagan 1993). Forrester's (2000) study found that 61.5 per cent of children registered for emotional abuse alone had substance-misusing parents – a percentage that rose to 66.67 per cent when combined with other categories. Forrester (2000) does point out, however, that the links between substance misuse and emotional abuse were complicated by the fact that prescribed drugs – antipsychotics and tranquillisers – featured in some of the families. This link between mental health problems, substance misuse and child welfare will be explored in more detail later.

Parental substance misuse and neglect

There is something all-encompassing about neglect – a qualitative shift in the experience of living – that needs to be considered, independently and coterminously with other types of abuse. In addition, neglect is a significant issue for these debates since it is now 'the highest category of registration on child protection registers in England' (Tanner and Turney 2000, p.337). Most importantly, in this particular context, 'Child neglect is the commonest type of abuse among substance misusing parents' (Alison 2000, p.12). Stone (1998), in his study of practitioners' perspectives on neglect, also found that 'parents who have a substance abuse problem…are thought to be over represented amongst neglecting families' (Stone 1998, p.37).

Childhood neglect and abuse also have major implications for welfare in adulthood and with parenting capacity, with links being made between these experiences and adult depression (Bifulco and Moran 1998; Sheppard 2001). The implications for this state of mind and child welfare will be explored in due course.

Neglect has been defined very simply and broadly thus: 'neglect occurs when the basic needs of children are not met *regardless of cause*' (Dubowitz *et al.* 1993, p.12, our italics). Basic needs, of course, encompass everything children require not only to survive, but also to develop emotionally, physically and intellectually and to realise their full potential. Stevenson (1998), in her wide-ranging analysis of the dilemmas presented by child neglect, draws attention to a fuller definition which focuses on the severity and the persistence with which these needs remain unmet 'resulting in significant harmful impairment of health and development or the avoidable exposure to serious danger, including cold or starvation' (Nottingham Area Child Protection Committee 1997, cited in Stevenson 1998, p.4). This, then, embraces situations in which a child lacks adequate food for good health, is exposed (through lack of appropriate supervision) to various hazards and dangers, including access to drugs, may live in adverse conditions, as a result of the physical environment, and may be denied access to medical care or treatment (Stevenson 1998, p.4). Neglect, then, is not simply about the physical environment but also includes the totality of the child's experience. It will therefore not necessarily be visible – although this is often the case – but it may be palpable in the sense that neglected children can exude a sense of being uncared for on many levels and this can communicate itself to those around them. As Stevenson observes, 'the pain of children is particularly hard to bear and that of chronically neglected children is in a class of its own' (Stevenson 1998, p.70).

Stevenson distinguishes between intermittent and chronic neglect and illustrates this with particular reference to substance misuse (Stevenson 1998, p.46). In cases where there is intermittent neglect, parents are seen as capable of providing adequate care in general but this can be punctuated by bursts of substance misuse which undermine the quality of care provided, leading to risky situations. In such instances, parenting is often seen to be very good during non-using periods and what is then required is the provision of what Stevenson describes as an alarm system, so that when there is a breakdown in parental functioning, appropriate protection can be mobilised, ideally through family and community networks. In relation to chronic neglect, however, levels of care are consistently wanting, often characterised by lack of supervision, exposure to various hazards and risks, and failure to meet basic material needs – food, clothing and clean, hygienic living conditions. These have been identified as likely casualties where there is substance misuse.

In US research, neglect is identified as the greatest concern in many studies (see for example Ammerman et al. 1999; Bays 1990; Famularo et al. 1992; Jaudes et al. 1995; Murphy et al. 1991). Black and Mayer (1980), in their study of 200 families, found that all the children in their sample of substance-misusing parents had suffered some form of neglect and, for 30 per cent, this had taken a very serious form. Murphy *et al.* (1991), who compared samples of substance-misusing and non-misusing parents who were subject to court proceedings, found that substance misuse was clearly connected with persistent and repeated neglect. Jaudes *et al.* (1995) concluded from their study that there was a very high risk for children born to drug-misusing women of neglect in the future.

British studies also confirm this link. In the NSPCC study, Lewis (1997) found that one-third of calls reporting neglect mentioned substance use, mainly by mothers. In two out of three such cases, alcohol was cited as the problem and mothers were the culprits. This confirms other findings discussed earlier which associate neglect as a type of abuse more closely associated with mothers than with fathers. However, as Lewis points out:

> the association of neglect with drinking mothers should be treated with caution. The calls are likely to reflect public opinion that 'good mothers' or…any 'respectable' woman does not drink more than the smallest amount. Heavy drinking by fathers may go unreported in neglect cases because the drinking is more socially acceptable or because fathers are not seen to be responsible for the family. (Lewis 1997, p.35)

Tanner and Turney (2000) also counsel caution in relation to issues of gender. Despite what they describe as 'the pervasive link between women as mothers and neglect…there has been little critical analysis of this connection' (Tanner and Turney 2000, p.338). The issue of gender is one to which we return in due course.

Forrester (2000, p.241) found that 'substance misusing families were very significantly over represented in neglect cases'. A substance-misusing parent or parents were identified in 62.5 per cent of cases where children had been registered for neglect and in 57.6 per cent where registration had been for either physical abuse and neglect, or emotional abuse and neglect. Heroin use was strongly related to registration for neglect but a third of such children also had alcohol-misusing parents. Crack and cocaine barely featured.

Children's accounts of life with alcohol-misusing parents suggest that many children experienced significant levels of emotional and physical neglect (Brisby *et al.* 1997; ChildLine 1997; Laybourn *et al.* 1996). These accounts will be explored in more depth in Chapter 7.

Not all studies distinguish between neglect and abuse of various kinds so it is not always possible to identify exact links or correlations with absolute precision. However, overall there seems to be clear evidence that in clinical samples, either court related, agency record related or referral related, neglect and substance misuse are often found together, although the level of this is not always clear.

Substance misuse and domestic violence

The link between domestic violence and child maltreatment and the interface between substance misuse, domestic violence and child welfare are the subject of much debate (see for example Buchanan 1996; Cleaver et al. 1999; Mullender and Morley 1994). There is a significantly increased risk of violence in the family where substance abuse is present which is clearly reflected in many studies (see for example Bays 1990; Velleman 1993; Velleman and Orford 1999) and children's accounts vividly convey the impact this has on them, as we shall see in Chapter 7. Velleman (1993) found that alcohol was a contributory factor in 80 per cent of domestic violence incidents while Brookoff et al. (1997) found that, in 92 per cent of such cases, drugs or alcohol had been used on the day of the crime. Although it must be acknowledged that the interaction between substance use and violence is by no means as simple as some findings may suggest (Fagan 1993), there are indications that violence is a significant variable in the degree to which other adult behaviours impact upon children. In other words, it may not be the drug or alcohol misuse *per se* that does the damage but the violence that accompanies it. Indeed Velleman and Orford (1999), who undertook an extensive study comparing the experiences of 164 offspring of problem drinkers and 80 comparison respondents, found 'a very significantly raised incidence of violence in families with a problem drinking parent' and this had implications for children's exposure to such violence (Velleman and Orford 1999, p.218). This was likely to be severe and regular, often extending throughout a significant period of childhood. Indeed, some commentators would argue that domestic violence is by far the most damaging of all parental behaviours in every sense (see Hester, Pearson and Harwin 2000 for a comprehensive overview of research on this area). The picture is further complicated by evidence that suggests that when parents both have mental health problems and misuse substances this significantly increases the risk of violence (Mulvey 1994), although this tends to be associated with what Weir and Douglas (1999) describe as 'acute symptoms' – for example feeling dominated by another power, or under threat from nameless forces. An additional thread that needs to be considered relates to substance misuse as a *response* to or way of managing domestic violence (Hester *et al.* 2000). This is clearly an important consideration where assessment is concerned. The dilemmas inherent in untangling the interwoven strands connected with these debates are clearly considerable as well as being highly individual; only careful exploration will shed light on their interrelationship.

Substance misuse, mental states and mental health problems

A significant amount of research now exists that relates to the risks posed to children by parental mental health problems and the prevalence of mental illness where there is child abuse, maltreatment or child death (see for example Falkov 1996; Falkov *et al.* 1998; Gopfert, Webster and Seeman 1996; Reder and Duncan 1999; Sheppard 2001; Wilczynski 1997). Children of lone parents are seen as particularly vulnerable in this context (Audit Commission 1999). The specific issues related to child homicide will be dealt with separately.

Research into the links between mental health, states of mind and substance misuse relate not only to the way in which mental health problems and substance abuse interact but also to the impact of parental substance misuse on children's mental health (Dore *et al.* 1995). This latter aspect will be more fully examined in Chapter 8. A further distinction also needs to be made between what Swadi (1994, p.237) calls 'mental state and judgment ability' and a diagnosed or apparent mental illness, such as depression. The former is characterised by problems with concentration, a chaotic approach to the parenting task, substance-induced hallucinations or catatonia, or generally not being quite connected with what is going on, while the latter is generally more clearly defined and specific.

Knowledge about the links between mental health problems and substance misuse springs from two sources – studies focusing on parenting, childcare and mental health specifically, which have thrown up substance-misuse links (see for example Sheppard 2001; Weir and Douglas 1999; Woodcock and Sheppard forthcoming) and studies focusing on parenting and substance abuse which reveal links with mental states or mental health problems of varying severity (see for example Bates *et al.* 1999; Klee *et al.* 1998; Swadi 1994; Velleman and Orford 1999).

Here then we enter the realms of 'dual diagnosis' defined in the Standing Conference on Drug Abuse guidelines as 'the concurrent existence…of drug or substance misuse and one or more mental disorders' (SCODA 1997, p.21). This can occur either as a result of substance use triggering psychiatric disorders (drug-induced psychosis, anxiety and depression, as described in Appendix 1) or substance misuse developing in response to psychiatric problems, where drugs or alcohol are used to manage distressing symptoms. US research also underlines these links, with problem drug use identified in many psychiatric patients, and many people presenting for drug treatment showing signs of mental disorder (Rounsaville *et al.* 1991; Weiss 1992). In particular opiate users seem to have high rates of anxiety, depression, phobias and mood swings (Williams, O'Connor and Kinsella 1990). Lloyd (1998) also highlights the links between drug use, depression and suicide.

Whatever the relationship, people who are coping with both mental health problems and substance use are generally perceived as particularly needy and vulnerable and therefore anyone in their care may be more at risk, particularly since, as we have already seen, both mental health and substance misuse feature as significant factors in child abuse (see for example Greenland 1987; Reder and Duncan 1999; Weir and Douglas 1999). Hogan's extensive review of the literature certainly seems to support the view that comorbid psychiatric symptoms are likely to adversely affect parenting capacity in drug users (Hogan 1998). In studies specifically focused on parenting and drug use, aggression, irritability and depression were identified as common symptoms, underlining what is often a mixture of potentially problematic states of mind and actual mental illness (Hogan 1997; Hogan and Higgins 2001; Klee *et al.* 1998).

Sheppard (2001), in his extensive study of maternal depression and childcare concerns, identified a constellation of problems both in the parenting arena and in relation to child welfare. In his sample, drawn from social services caseloads where depression had been measured using the Beck Depression Inventory, one-fifth of the women identified also had alcohol problems. When this sample was subjected to further analysis, the risks posed to children were seen to increase significantly, to the extent that Woodcock and Sheppard (forthcoming) concluded that 'alcohol dependence, when allied to clinical depression operates in a particularly pernicious and debilitating way'. What were described as 'marked deficits' in parenting compared with the 'depressed only' group were noted and parenting was characterised by a destructive and undermining attitude towards children. The overwhelming needs of the mothers concerned were seen to supersede all considerations of the welfare of the children. Living in such an environment was considered to pose very real dangers to the children concerned. The majority of this sample were also lone mothers. What has to be remembered is that this was a clinical sample of mothers already identified as having a range of complex problems including clearly identified depression.

In the study by Hawker (1999) of lone parents with alcohol problems there was evidence of diagnosed clinical mental illness in 18 per cent of his sample and, in some cases, this manifested itself in overdoses and frequent hospital admissions. This posed particular risks to some of the children concerned, depending on levels of support.

Parental substance misuse and child homicide

Debates about risk, child protection and parental substance misuse regrettably would not be complete without a consideration of the most extreme consequence of child maltreatment – filicide. Research suggests that drug and alcohol abuse has featured in child homicide both immediately before the commission of the crime and on a longer-term basis, in the run up to its commission (see for example Crimmins *et al.* 1997; Jaudes *et al.* 1995; Stroud 1997; Tyler *et al.* 1997; Wilczynski 1997).

Falkov (1996) reviewed 100 'Part 8 Review' files which have to be kept by every local authority when a child is seriously harmed or killed by a carer. It was found that 25 perpetrators and 10 partners were suffering from a psychiatric disorder, with 2 in each group having drug dependency problems. Substance misuse was also identified as an important secondary problem for 5 perpetrators and 1 partner. In her study of child homicide, based on data from England and Australia, Wilczynski (1997), who identifies substance misuse in her category of psychiatric characteristics of child killers, found that one-third of her English sample and one-tenth of her Australian sample had used substances at the time of the killing and almost twice as many had used some kind of substance in the period prior to it. A history of 'substance use' was present in 60 per cent of her sample, although this term was not clearly defined. Women, she found, were slightly more likely to have abused substances both before and at the time of the crime than men and, typically, the substance in question was a prescribed drug – usually antidepressants. In contrast, men tended to have used alcohol or illegal drugs. Children under 1 year old were at the greatest risk and children were generally killed at home.

Reder *et al.* (1993), in their analysis of child abuse tragedies involving 35 child deaths which had been the subject of inquiries, found that in 7 of the cases there was a history of drug or alcohol dependency in one or both parents. They observed that 'drug and alcohol dependency not only implied dependency conflicts but also problems with control since the parents' self control was recurrently impaired and responsibility and the locus of control externalised' (Reder *et al.* 1993, p.50).

Reder and Duncan (1999), in their follow-up study, examined 112 cases in which a child had died as a result of maltreatment using, as Falkov (1996) had, 'Part 8 Review' files. They found that 'substance misuse is even more strongly associated with child maltreatment generally and with fatal abuse in particular than the other mental health problems' (Reder and Duncan 1999, p.55). The impact of the lifestyle that accompanies illegal drug use was seen as the main factor affecting child well-being. This is a more significant correlation than that found by Falkov (1996), despite some minimal overlap in the sample, although the reasons for this are unclear.

It is of course important to bear in mind that these studies were exploring the link between mental health problems and child homicide. The degree to which substance misuse and mental health problems coexist and interact, as we have seen, is an important variable to consider in relation to all these findings. Drug and alcohol induced psychoses, for example, were responsible for some child deaths rather than substance misuse *per se* and it was often the *dynamic* between mental health, substance use and violence that contributed to an environment that proved fatal for the children concerned.

Studies of fatal child abuse and neglect in New York found that drug abuse by the main carers had directly contributed to the child's death in between just under and just over a quarter of cases (Besharov 1994; Deren 1986). In comparisons between fatal and non-fatal child abuse, drug 'addiction' in fathers or stepfathers was significantly higher in the fatal cases. In a major study in the 1980s which encompassed nine states, Alfaro (1988) found a wide variation in the extent to which substance misuse featured in at least one parent, ranging from 14 per cent to 43 per cent across the samples. The reasons for these variations, however, were not explained. What does seem apparent is that substance misuse can contribute significantly to higher levels of risk contributing to child fatalities. In other words, it is seen to play a significant part in child deaths, albeit under circumstances already suggestive of stresses and tensions.

Substance misuse, attachment problems and child maltreatment

Secure attachment between children and their parents or care-givers has long been considered the cornerstone of healthy development across the life cycle (see for example Bowlby 1988; Brandon, Schofield and Trinder 1998; Daniel and Taylor 2001; Howe *et al.* 1999). As we suggested in Chapter 1, if someone's main attachment is to a substance, this may have implications for their capacity to attach to others. Attachment theory in relation to the adult–substance dynamic will be explored further in Chapters 3 and 4 and in relation to child welfare in Chapter 6. Here we explore connections between substance misuse and attachment problems as identified in a number of studies (Brooks and Rice 1997; Klee *et al.* 1998; Laybourn *et al.* 1996). Howe *et al.* (1999) suggest that disorganised patterns of attachment, where children are in a permanent state of anxiety and distress due to their experience of a parent as emotionally unavailable and unable to meet their needs, whatever they do (see Chapter 6), are particularly common where parents have alcohol or hard drug problems. This is demonstrated in several of their case studies, although in most instances there were a variety of other problems, apart from substance misuse, that were affecting family dynamics and child conduct. Some illustrated the way in which childhood experience of parental substance abuse can go on to affect substance use, parenting and attachment in adult life and the difficulties that ensue. This links, in some respects, to theories of transgenerational transmission of attachment problems related to substance use which suggest that children of substance-misusing parents, where attachment patterns have been insecure, find intimacy and relationships difficult in adult life (Robinson and Rhoden 1998). Howe *et al.* (1999) also suggest that people with serious drug and alcohol dependence, who are unavailable in a variety of ways for periods of time, may encourage non-attached patterns in their children – the children's experience is of unresponsiveness so it becomes pointless to seek anything they need from either their parents or any other adult. These themes will inevitably recur in relation to both parenting and the child's experience.

Klee *et al.* (1998) analysed a number of studies focusing on substance-misusing parents (mainly drug users but also polydrug users where alcohol and a range of both illegal and prescription drugs were combined). They focused in particular on risk factors, protective factors (including the role of social workers), parental dysfunction, managing issues of disclosure and children's awareness of parents' behaviour. Attachment problems were identified as one example of parental dysfunction. Although parents' emotional attachment to their children was assessed as 'mostly very high', in relation to both mothers and fathers (whether biological or not), in the sense that parents talked about their love and devotion to their children (Klee *et al.* 1998, p.29), this was not always indicative of the rounded attachment required for healthy development, as described in Chapter 6. Indeed, this high level of emotional 'attachment' often resulted in a degree of intense dependency which was unhelpful to the child. In other words, the child was seen as a therapeutic presence and a source of comfort, to help the parent through a difficult time. This often led to what was termed 'role reversal' about which more will be said in Chapter 7. Highlighted here is the obvious but crucial point that 'attachment of child to parent is different than attachment of parent to child' (Flores 2001, p.68) and that, if children are used to meet the unmet needs of parents, their psychological well-being will be affected. Some mothers blamed the need to obtain supplies, in order to continue parenting, for the fact that they had become overdependent on their children. They regretted the fact that they had made assumptions about their children's capacity to cope with responsibility, resulting in incidents where children had been left alone, or left caring for smaller children at a very young age.

What is interesting here is that the level of attachment was seen from the parents' perspective although not necessarily experienced as real attachment by the child. This underlines the central importance of a working knowledge of attachment theory in understanding parent–child dynamics and the dangers of reaching conclusions based on parents' perceptions and expressed emotions, rather than observation of the child's experiences.

Robinson and Rhoden (1998), who specialise in working with children of 'alcoholics' (COAs), paint a very graphic picture of the consequences for children when parents with drink problems are unable to attach to their children:

> In active alcoholic families, infant trust is challenged from the first day of life because parents are too consumed with alcoholism to provide adequate support and nurturance to children. The inconsistency, neglect and abuse that characterise many alcoholic homes will leave children with an overriding sense of mistrust, insecurity and separation anxiety. They learn very early that they cannot count on anything. (Robinson and Rhoden 1998, p.179)

The significant period, in relation to attachment, from their analysis, is the first year; if children have received a great deal of attention from carers during this time, they are less likely to develop attachment problems by the time they are in their teens. However 'by one year of age COAs who have developed insecure attachments become uncertain that their care givers will be there when they need them' (Robinson and Rhoden 1998, p.124) and this leads to insecurity, emotional distress and a range of social and behavioural problems including the inability to form close relationships (Brooks and Rice 1997).

This very grim picture is borne out by many of the children of alcoholics whose stories feature in the US literature and a very deterministic picture is painted which needs to be seriously evaluated. The reality is that, for many children, the attachment problems related to parental substance misuse can have far-reaching consequences. This is not to say that there is nothing that can be done about it, or that children may not survive despite these circumstances, but that this is a reality for some children that cannot be ignored.

A totally negative picture?

As suggested earlier, the link between parental substance misuse and child maltreatment is not axiomatic and there is evidence to support the contention that substance-misusing parents can parent effectively and do not necessarily pose significant risks to their children. Smith and Adler (1991) for example did not find a significant link between neglect or abuse and substance misuse. Coleman and Cassell (1995), although they acknowledged that the overall picture was 'gloomy' and the outlook for children of substance-misusing parents 'poor', concluded, from their analysis of studies, that clinical experience seemed to suggest that 'some substance misusing parents can provide satisfactory childcare and a few manage to flourish despite their parents' substance misuse' (Coleman and Cassell 1995, p.189). This is not, however, exactly unequivocal, in terms of positive effects. Other findings suggest that children find parents more pleasant and amenable when using substances and that stress in families may be ameliorated by substance use, with positive results (Laybourn et al. 1996; Seilhammer, Jacob and Dunn 1992). Overall however, these arguments are neither numerous nor very convincing.

In relation to maternal substance misuse, some of the more negative findings are countered by research which suggests that appropriate and non-judgmental intervention focused on safer substance use can support such mothers to parent successfully and well (Ford and Hepburn 1997; Hepburn 2000). Provision of methadone as a substitute for heroin, attendance at drug dependency units, together with any additional strategies to stabilise use and lifestyle, were all seen as effective in enabling mothers to provide adequate care for their children (Burns, O'Driscoll and Wason 1996; Klee and Jackson 1998).

One significant factor which has emerged in the context of many of these studies is that of lifestyle. The relationship between the chaotic lifestyle often associated with drug use, in particular, and alcohol use, to a lesser extent, is a complex additional variable and creating more stability both in relation to substance use and in relation to daily life can make all the difference in terms of risks, and potential for children coming to harm (see for example Burns et al. 1996; Reder and Duncan 1999; Sloan 1998). However, as we shall see in Chapters 5 and 7, the distinction between a chaotic *lifestyle* and chaotic substance *use* is an important one and the two should not be confused or conflated.

The other variable that needs to be considered is that of treatment. If the parent is receiving or has received treatment for the substance problem, does this automatically reduce risk of maltreatment? There is, not surprisingly, no clear answer to this question. Murphy et al. (1991), for example, found very high levels of substance misuse among their sample of parents subject to court proceedings for abuse and neglect and concluded that such parents were often less likely to respond to court ordered services. Nevertheless, they concluded that if parents were able to stop substance use, the outcome could be positive, although the basis for their optimism was unclear. However, other research suggests that treatment does not necessarily solve the problem, as we shall see in Chapter 7. Unless it is clear why the substance use is occurring, in terms of its role in managing other underlying problems, simply dealing with what might be a 'symptom' of other difficulties is not a real solution. In fact it may actually make things worse, in the short term, as the underlying issues that may have been previously managed by the substance use begin to surface.

Summary

What can we make of all this conflicting and often confusing research? The most obvious point is that this is a complex area to investigate and it is hard to separate the various strands from one another and tease out the links between individual experience, family situations and social, economic and cultural contexts. As a result, no firm conclusions can be reached without a thorough exploration of a number of issues. Past substance use as well as present behaviour, levels of conflict or violence, issues of mental health, the nature of parenthood, whether lone or shared, and outside pressures are all important. Treatment for substance abuse does not necessarily or automatically make things either better or safer for children; sensitive and non-judgemental intervention, however, can make a difference to some groups. The coexistence of substance misuse and other difficulties clearly increases risk. Entering the world and family life of the person with the substance problems is probably the only reliable way of assessing the real risk to any particular child in any particular situation (Aldridge 2000).

The evidence, however, does highlight the extent to which substance misuse can have significant adverse consequences for the levels of maltreatment of all kinds that children experience. The links are clearly there in clinical samples drawn from court records, social services case records and referrals to voluntary agencies, although we know little about these links in relation to the wider community. The overall picture, then, suggests that this is a real problem of sizeable dimensions and that it is now being discovered in Britain as a significant issue in child welfare, with alcohol alongside heroin as the major cause for concern.

Part Two

Parenting and Substance Misuse in Context

3

The Dynamics of Substance Misuse

Knowledge itself has an elusive shadowy quality. You know and you don't know. You know and you won't know, because knowing in a full and honest way means acting...and accepting and changing...all of which is far too scary...the mind can't take it all in, can't do it, and so – poof – the knowledge swims off.

(Knapp 2001, p.48)

In Chapters 3 and 4 we address some important questions about the relationships that can develop between drugs and alcohol and the people who use them. We consider the ways in which an understanding of theories of 'dependency' and 'addiction' have influenced responses to such relationships and how this can be used to explore implications both for parenting and for client–worker relationships. Some key theoretical concepts that attempt to explain substance misuse, dependence, addiction and withdrawal will be explored and we shall examine how substance-misusing behaviour is categorised and the way in which this allows us to make sense of the processes and 'lived experience' of substance-misusing parents. What are the processes and commonalities that affect the relationship between users and their families, and users and professionals? For those working with substance-misusing parents, it is clearly important to gain some insight into such processes, and the way in which they develop and might be sustained, so that the potential impact on parenting capacity can be assessed more effectively. We shall also be considering the impact that chronic drug and alcohol use can have on parents, the kinds of conflicts it induces and the pressures to which it may lead, in relation to the very difficult art of parenting. Alongside these debates, we shall also be discussing some key questions about concepts used, charting the historical progression from moral explanations to medical and disease models, before moving on to wider explanations of misuse.

Many of the ideas and theories that we discuss have emanated from research into alcohol misuse, since there has been less conceptualisation in the field of drugs. Nevertheless, allowing for differences between different drugs, we argue that many theoretical ideas and concepts have a number of commonalities and these will be highlighted when they occur.

A central question, of course, is the way in which definitions, explanations and concepts can either assist or obscure effective practice. We need to look at different perceptions of drug and alcohol users and consider how issues of legality and illegality impact on how assessments are made. Do we have a shared language for people's substance misuse and, if so, what is it? What are the effects of language and labels? How much do concepts related to substance misuse help or hinder professionals and clients? Linking drug use to problematic behaviour of any kind immediately raises a series of questions concerning assumptions, myths, stereotypes and moral judgements. How can such connections be made? On what evidence are they based? Can problem substance use be defined and classified in any useful or fair way, given the complexity of the activity itself and the psychological, sociological and cultural variations in people's use? Such questions inevitably force us to revisit terms, definitions and theories.

Addiction or volition?

As we shall see in Chapters 5 and 10, attitudes towards 'addiction' affect our assessments of drug-misusing parents and can influence our approach to issues of motivation, choice and responsibility. The concept of 'addiction' is a disputed one and many of the differences in the interpretation of this term relate to the *degree* to which it implies loss of control. The idea of complete loss of control once 'addicted', however, is viewed by many as too simplistic and this is reflected in debates about the nature of addiction itself. Some commentators argue that the term itself, particularly in the popular imagination, implies behaviour which is utterly compulsive and largely outside the realm of free will, when in fact substance use is mainly the result of rational decision-making.

Many do not accept such an inclusive category as 'addiction' at all. Davies (1997), for example, argues that the 'variable patterns and types of substance use discredit the concept of a "state" or "entity" adopted by a "species" of drug addict' (Davies 1997, p.75). He suggests that drug choices and drug use are mainly determined by individual, rational decisions, even if such decisions themselves may be influenced by societal pressures. Like others, he is critical of misdefining, or attempting to identify too specifically what he calls 'sequences of purposive behaviour'. While such criticisms offer important correctives to purer 'positivist' approaches, they do not appear to reflect the reality of day-to-day experiences often described by children and parents regarding problematic misuse (Orford 2001). The danger here is in falling back onto a more relativist position, where any assessment of problematic parental relationships with substance misuse, as it impacts on children's lives, becomes too politically incorrect to consider. Where, then, does this leave the children, relatives and parents who are attempting to make sense of the problematic processes of drug misuse?

What are required are ideas that help us gain an empathic and convincing understanding of the interaction between psychological and social pressures which impose themselves in particular ways and how these may develop into patterns of 'coping'. The challenge here is to assist parents and children attempting to make sense of problematic processes of drug misuse. A more helpful notion of 'addiction', in this context, is one that can be viewed *differentially* as a wider categorisation of processes that interfere with an individual's ability to stop, or alter such an activity, once begun. This requires what Orford (2001) calls more qualified models 'which yet retain a truth to the experience of the developing attachment to a substance…where one's ability to modify that behaviour, in the face of mounting evidence that it is causing harm, is diminished' (Orford 2001, p. 346). Potential patterns of 'dependence' do exist, even if the reasons for their emergence and persistence may be both complex and variable (Bonner and Waterhouse 1996; Orford 1985 2001).

Clients and professionals, then, are faced with the difficult dilemma of establishing the reality of the relationship with the substance amidst a complexity of theories, and ambiguity surrounding competing definitions combined with the natural tendency in those struggling with drugs and other life problems, to deny a potentially increasing 'dependence'. This dilemma is most acutely identified by Knapp (2001), quoted at the beginning of the chapter.

The issue of terminology

The difficult balance between recognising the actual impact of substance-misusing behaviour and yet not making automatic assumptions about it is nowhere better illustrated than in the constant change of terminology used. The term 'addiction' is used both in common parlance and in professional journals and debates. It tends to be associated with more medicalised concepts of chronic use, although (as we have seen) the ideas behind this are far from straightforward. The term 'dependence' suggests that a person relies on drugs or alcohol, either for physical or psychological reasons, or both. Some commentators (see for example Shephard 1990) suggest that 'dependence' feels like a more common human condition than the concept of 'addiction', which is viewed as more isolating. The term 'problem drug use' tends to refer to use that results in detrimental consequences or harm to the user or others in their life. The term is defined in relation to the harm that results, rather than from the frequency or level of individual use. Such harm, by this definition, can theoretically result, then, from different levels of substance misuse and not just from those who are seen as using at high levels or who are viewed as being 'dependent' on substances (Drugscope 2001).

The social constructionist perspective

Some argue that debates about illegal drugs provide a perfect example of the way that society constructs a social problem in a particular way in order to divert attention from other more difficult or insoluble social issues. From this social constructionist perspective the way in which drug misuse is classified or described can be seen as a way of controlling problem or deviant groups (Szasz 1974). The characteristics associated with it make it 'the perfect enemy in this regard' (Christie 1986, quoted in South 1999, p.9). Some of the language of drug use also emphasises 'exceptionality' – something different from the norm and an activity that consigns some to the 'symbolic zones of danger and exclusion' (South 1999, p.10).

Terminology – particularly in the field of drugs or alcohol, where popular images of 'druggies' or 'drunks' can be so pervasive – can easily stigmatise or label. This can lead to an over-rigid view of an 'addiction' which is not representative of a parent's use of drugs or alcohol over time. It is also important to be aware of the impact of language in general, and that terms such as 'alcoholic' or 'addict', in particular, may discourage parents from disclosing or coming forward about their problem. On the other hand, it is important not to dismiss concepts which may help make sense of the more problematic patterns of use which impact on the lives of individuals and their families. There are then two sources of danger here. The first is using stigmatising or unhelpful language. The second is becoming preoccupied with language as a reflection of anxiety about discussing the real implications of problematic use, which may end up failing to identify those 'distressing and bewildering experiences of many whose life and their children's is full of contradictions' (Orford 2001, p.346).

Labels or definitions?

Whatever the finer debates about the terminology, at some point the assessment of 'problematic' substance use has to be tackled. This is where reaching a shared understanding about what is meant by any terms or labels used becomes critical and often involves a directness from professionals, in an attempt to reach common understandings. Processes of negotiation can provide a sound basis for an effective assessment.

Reaching this shared understanding, however, is a complex process (Taylor 1999). Terms and definitions have different connotations and implications, depending on whether they occur within a professional or personal context. Words describing problems with alcohol or drugs can mean different things to different people. For example, in the study undertaken by Taylor (1999), descriptive phrases such as 'does not have a classic alcohol problem' or 'consumption is above what would be medically considered excessive' were used by professionals in reports, without any common agreement or understanding having been established between author and subject. Taylor (1999) also found that clients would tend to describe behaviour only in terms of what it was not rather than what it was – what Bennett (1996) has described as excluding terms, used to emphasise what they are not like, perhaps reflecting their fear that professionals would make adverse judgements. Again Knapp (2001) illustrates this process vividly by her use in her own mind of 'worst case scenarios' to make her own drinking appear unproblematic by comparison with that of others:

My definition of alcoholism was very narrow and extremely specific. The word dripped with stigma and stereotype, none of it applicable to me. Bums on street corners clutching paper bags and muttering obscenities: women with smeared lipstick and bad hair, alone on barstools: pictures of destitution and bad genes and deeply flawed moral character – these were alcoholics and I found images of them consoling for a very long time... Not me. (Knapp 2001, p.48)

In this context, Velleman's (1992) definition of problematic alcohol misuse is very useful when assessing parents misusing substances of any kind:

If someone's drinking causes problems for him or her...for husbands, wives, children...then that drinking is problematic... There are many implications of such a simple definition. It means that whether or not someone has a drinking problem is not determined by fixed quantities...or fixed timings, but instead is a matter of negotiation by the individual with him or herself, family, friends, work place, and society as a whole. (Velleman 1992, p.3)

Such a negotiation, however, is anything but simple. It is complicated not only by issues of legality and illegality but also by the influence of conflicting and powerful moral connotations associated with various types of substance misuse. It is also affected, in our context, by the additional risks associated with the label 'bad parent'. All these factors are likely to coalesce, in ways that make it particularly difficult for parents to discuss their substance misuse openly or in a way that they feel will not expose them to adverse judgements and stigma and, most significantly, consequences in relation to their children. As a result, the nature of such a 'negotiation' for professionals is a complex one. The climate in which it occurs may involve particular tensions and pressures, necessitating skills to mediate issues of conflicting rights, while demonstrating an empathic understanding of parents' situations and needs. We shall look at such issues in more detail when discussing professionals' approaches to such difficulties in Chapter 9.

Legality and illegality

As we have already suggested, the way in which people who misuse substances are viewed is influenced both by society's ambivalent and contradictory responses towards different drugs, and the context in which they are used. Alcohol use is a particularly good example of a drug which, on the one hand is advertised in a way that associates it with a successful and positive lifestyle, while on the other is identified as at the root of moral decay and crime.

The issue of legality and illegality is, of course, a key determinant here. This can be seen directly to influence ideas about the relative addictive potential of particular drugs and their association with particular types of 'chaotic lifestyles', or indicate particular patterns of use. While the illegality of a drug *may* indicate a higher concern about its use, it does not offer a straightforward indication of the extent of potential harm. The extent of the social as well as physical harm caused by alcohol – a legal substance – is an example of this. The moral and legal connotations associated with illegal substances allows for little manoeuvre, in terms of negotiating levels of acceptable use (Davies 1997), although the move towards harm-reduction initiatives may indicate some steps in this direction (Tsui 2000). Essentially, then, although it is acceptable to talk about cutting down on drinking, it is less so to talk about cutting down on heroin intake since, by definition, it should not be being used at all. There is a major difficulty here in assessing 'problematic' use, in the context of a society that openly uses a range of drugs in various ways, for different reasons, and applies different standards, depending on those who use them.

Assessing harm

The assessment of substance-misusing parents is influenced (as we have seen) by concepts of addiction and dependence and the way in which these are shaped by moral and legal connations. It may be that some drugs *are* more potentially harmful, particularly within certain contexts, and in certain environments, but it is important to examine why this may be, rather than making assumptions either that all illegal drugs are potentially more harmful or indeed that all legal substances are potentially less so (Forrester 2000).

When thinking about the impact of substance use, it is important to consider what is meant by harm or potential harm, not simply in relation to the physical and psychological implications for the individual concerned, but also in relation to the impact on parenting capacity and child development and the dynamic between the two. Patterns of drug use, in this context, are particularly important. Some drug use may be seen to impact more or less seriously on children. This may depend on the parent's relationship with and attachment to the substance and how this affects the daily management of the child, on both practical and emotional levels. Thus a chaotic and unmanaged use of amphetamines could have a greater or lesser impact on parenting ability than a maintained methadone habit, depending on the way the substance use impacts specifically on childcare.

In other words, approaches emanating primarily from an individual health perspective tend to omit more detailed consideration of the interaction between the individual context, the substance misuse and the effects on parenting capacity. Concepts of harm (and indeed risk) have become too narrowly associated with measurable reductions in the adults' substance abuse behaviour, rather than any wider consideration of measurement of harm to the family. Historically, for example, there has been a tendency to omit the importance of family functioning when evaluating the success of the individual's 'treatment' (Feig 1998). Indeed, some in clinically related fields have suggested that models of risk assessment have not adequately accounted for particular issues within families to be considered. These include the intimate and intense nature of relationships, which can lead to irritability at a lower threshold and the issues of vulnerability and dependence (Oates 1997). In addition, concepts of risk and harm can also affect the way that services are funded as well as delivered. As Appleby (2000, p.4) observes: 'there are concerns…over funding mechanisms which will only resource programmes capable of showing a measurable decrease in alcohol consumption, rather than a reduction in the wider impact of harm associated with alcohol misuse'. In many ways, then, conceptualisations of substance misuse reflect the tension between adult and child services that we shall discuss in later chapters.

Conceptualising problem substance use

We now move on to consider some of the key ways that substance misuse has been understood from a medical, psychological and sociological perspective, acknowledging the continuing debates concerning the respective weight given to such theories, in accounting for what are called detrimental 'attachments' to substances. We shall be concentrating on those models that give prominence to both the physical and psychological processes that are seen as significant and there is some detailed discussion of 'disease' concepts of substance misuse, given their historical importance and influence on subsequent developments. However, as we discuss in Chapter 4, perspectives that shed light on the progressive and chronic attachment to substances, which some parents develop, need to account for the interaction of physical, psychological and social pressures. In reviewing some of the key explanations for problematic adult substance use, we specifically relate the implications and relevance of these to the wider family system.

From moral lassitude to 'disease'

> 'We find the contagion has spread among [the female sex] to a degree hardly possible to be conceived...unhappy mothers habituate themselves to these distilled liquors, whose children are born weak and sickly, and often look old and shrivelled as though they had been numbered many years' – as a committee of justices observed in 1722. (Barr 1998, p.189)

This comment on the relationship between an excessive use of gin, considered at the time an 'epidemic' among the poor, and the effect on child welfare illustrates the enduring nature of the debate surrounding the link between substance misuse and child welfare. To what extent do adults have control over 'problematic use'? Does the use of such substances lead to physical and psychological dependence? If so, to what extent is chronic use equated with bad or poor parenting behaviour or as a 'disease' that needs treating?

There is much debate about exactly when notions of moral lassitude and irresponsible behaviour began to be replaced by more complex notions of why people continued to abuse substances – specifically alcohol – to excess. Some have argued that ideas about 'disease-like characteristics' evolved as early as the late seventeenth and early eighteenth centuries. What is clear is that a range of theories were emerging that identified patterns of 'addiction' (although not called that) well before the development of more medical views on addiction and dependence. By the same token, there were changing notions of parenting and child welfare.

The growth of the disease model

In the second half of the nineteenth century, the disease model grew in strength and influence, specifically in relation to the use of alcohol and, in 1884, Norman Kerr succeeded in strengthening the link between drink and 'illness' by uniting the diseases of alcohol and drug addiction with that of mental health (Berridge 1979; McMurran 1994). Meanwhile, medical concepts of 'addiction' were given impetus by the increasing use of the hypodermic needle to inject drugs. This was an important factor, since many commentators argue that differing attitudes to drugs and alcohol are, in part, associated with the fears surrounding the nature of intravenous use (Gossop 2000). Significantly, the development of heroin and cocaine for medical use and fear of its subsequent misuse contributed to the development of the disease model for drugs other than alcohol.

The publication of Jellinek's *The Disease Concept of Alcoholism* in 1960 is generally held responsible for the evolution of medical and disease models in their modern-day formulation. Before then, while excessive use was viewed as troublesome or morally wrong, what had not been so clearly conceptualised was that individuals acquire a habitual and special propensity to drinking excessively (Orford 1985, 2001). The disease model, in its more medicalised and modern form, describes addiction as, at least in part, a biochemically based chronic and progressive disease with identifiable signs and symptoms. Progression is seen to lead, for a number of people, to 'dependence' and loss of control. Jellinek (1960) identified five types of 'alcoholism', two of which he equated to a disease since they involved this loss of control and an inability to abstain.

Heather and Robertson (1981) summarise Jellinek's description of emergent alcohol problems as a 'series of barriers which less serious types of problem drinkers successfully fail to surmount, leaving only the alcohol addict on the finishing line' (quoted in McMurran 1994, p.14). While facing much subsequent criticism because of its association with over-rigid medicalisation, Jellinek's framework provided one of the most detailed descriptions of the variety of drinking phenomena (Orford 2001).

Implications of the disease model

What implications does this model have when thinking about children and families? Some feel that it provides a true account of the processes that individuals and families experience and, as such, may be seen as helpful in assisting people to understand both the complexity of their experiences and to make sense of previously confusing states. Its popularity as an explanation is evident from the sheer number of people (including those in the public eye) who account for their chronic use in this way. As Edwards, Marshall and Cook (1997) remark, it is often embraced by those who see a clearer goal in viewing their problem as a disease that is incurable, with rehabilitation centred around vigilant avoidance. It can also help reduce destructive and perpetuating cycles of guilt.

The notions of disease and powerlessness are, as Collins and Keene (2000) point out, at first sight somewhat paradoxically linked to the notion of responsibility for one's own recovery, but in this model responsibility is seen to arise from acceptance. Many of these concepts (which are central to the philosophy of Alcoholics Anonymous, an organisation that offers group support to drinkers and their families) appear to suggest some key notions of motivation when dealing with chronic histories of misuse and some have been critical of the professional trend away from these, arguing that 'softer' terms shield society from the reality of the most damaging examples of abuse. 'It baffles me that it is seen as politically incorrect to describe someone as having the illness of "alcoholism". I believe the woolliness of terms like "problem drinker" helps society avoid the seriousness of the problem and causes all sorts of confusion to the relatives of alcoholics' (Cutland 1998, p.99).

'Disease', free will or responsibility?

Many argue that the idea of addiction as a disease is an inaccurate analogy and that the concept of an illness places substance misuse in a category like pneumonia, in the sense that individuals are passive recipients of something beyond their control. In this sense, it can be seen to allow people to abnegate their responsibility in relation to the impact of their 'illness' on others. By the same token, the focus on individual psychopathology and physical symptoms, independent of broader sociological and psychological processes, can be seen as unhelpful although, by some accounts, the model does allow for some psychological and attachment processes to be considered.

Gossop's (2000) reservations focus on the fact that, while historically it may have been more humane to redefine addiction as an illness, it has helped perpetuate many 'junkie myths' about passive and helpless victims, addictive personalities and lifestyles. Such explanations are seen to avoid the more complex reasons for people's drug misuse, involving a different range of social problems, the availability of certain drugs and cultural setting. Indeed Harwin (1982) suggests that this has influenced service delivery and types of approaches. She argues that approaches have, as a consequence, tended to give greater prominence to the individual with the 'disease' and only 'subsidiary status' to the family. However, many adherents (as we have seen) feel that such an account does not do justice to the literature dealing with issues for the 'alcoholic family' (see for example Brooks and Rice 1997; Brown 1988).

Stigmatising or liberating?

Although some view the disease model as 'stigmatising', others consider that this is challenged by its continued popularity. According to Miller and Kurtz (1994), it has received a bad press due to a tendency to caricature the Alcoholics Anonymous (AA) movement, with which it is so strongly associated, and is far more flexible than it seems. It is argued that the support structure offered by AA and its related organisations utilises natural recovery processes in a way which is valuable and effective. We shall see in Chapter 11 the way in which more recent approaches to family intervention have built on the concept of social support utilising some of the systems of group support and organisation that are characteristic of AA.

The value of seeing substance misuse as a disease, then, is both functional, in that it explains behaviour, and arguably an effective meta-phorical categorisation that equates with a process of feeling out of control and increasingly powerless. This may also have implications for the way in which children are assisted since, in some ways, it may be helpful for children to make sense of their parent's behaviour by viewing it as some kind of illness (see Chapter 8). However, as Velleman and Orford (1999) point out, it could be viewed as unhelpful in that it may prove demanding in its potential implications. Children may assume greater responsibility for their parents' 'condition', as a consequence.

Chick and Cantwell (1998) suggest that people in turmoil are helped by having a framework on which to peg their experiences: 'a gestalt which has some inner cohesion, [people] feel less confused and can see more easily a plan of action' (Chick and Cantwell 1998, p.10). There is something of the flavour of this in the account by the professional footballer Tony Adams of his chronic use of both drugs and alcohol and how this impacted upon his relationship with his children:

> I think Oliver and Amber were too young to realise what was going on, but Clare was affected at the time. I couldn't understand why sometimes she avoided me or ran away from me. Then Jane told me that she was frightened of me. That really hurt, went right through me. And it made me angry.

Daddy loves her, can't she understand that? ... Mostly I couldn't see that my drinking was doing damage to anyone... But that is the selfishness of the illness. (Adams with Ridley 1999, pp.286–287)

Just as it can be used with individuals, the disease model can also be applied to families who live with 'addicts' and separate groups have been developed for relatives and children (for example Families Anonymous, Al-Anon and Al-Ateen). This has implications for the dynamics of 'family recovery', with recognition of the need for support for both the partners and the children of alcoholics. While there is not normally any suggestion that addiction is a partner's fault, in viewing addiction as a 'family disease' – as many do – some pressure appears to rest with the whole family to own the problem and accept the need for recovery. Consequently, some partners may be seen to be involved in mutually dependent relationships with alcoholics because the addictive behaviour meets their own needs, in some way (Cutland 1998), although others have stressed that the concept of 'co-dependency' has often been misunderstood (Brown 1992).

When it comes to methods of intervention, disease models focus on tackling the fundamental components of the disease itself, usually on the basis of abstinence rather than controlled use. Implicit in the approach is that treating the disease needs to come first, before any other changes can be made. As Adams points out, distress at his daughter's reaction did not stop him drinking: 'only when I wanted to stop for me rather than other people was that going to happen' (Adams with Ridley 1999, p.287).

Three questions remain. To what extent does such a model help individuals to make sense of their relationship with substances and assist family members with effective strategies and coping mechanisms? Does it focus too specifically on certain characteristics of substances and individuals, in ways that distract from the influence of social problems and the way they interact with family relationships? Does it concentrate too exclusively on abstinence-only based goals?

This model does, however, remain influential, particularly in the field of alcohol use, and although Jellinek's categorisation has not remained convincing in its pure state, in certain quarters, his distinction between alcohol addiction and problem drinking is still seen as helpful (Orford 1985, 2001). In addition, the essential dichotomy established in this model – namely the distinction between those in the grips of a 'disease-like process' and those not affected in this way – is the cornerstone of later classifications and distinctions (McMurran 1994). At the same time, however, the central but enduring confusion remains between dependence which is thought to be purely 'psychological' and dependence involving an altered physiological response to the substance involved (Orford 1985). This is a theme to which we shall return.

Widening the explanation for use: the interactive dimension

The idea of a dependence syndrome, combining physiological, behavioural and social effects, was developed by Edwards and Gross (1976) and subsequently endorsed by the World Health Organisation (Edwards *et al.* 1977). Again, while developed in relation to alcohol, in many of its aspects it can be seen to have resonance for those dependent on other drugs. Such a concept envisages 'dependence' as a chain of habit, involving degrees of dependence, rather than a more hard and fast categorisation of an illness *per se*. By this means, it attempts to avoid some of the more stereotypical notions of 'alcoholism' or 'drug addiction' associated with the disease concepts, while retaining recognisable, although not rigid, stages. It emphasises the way that physical and emotional effects can interact and impact upon behaviour and it has been influential as a potential guide for professionals.

Essentially, as Davies (1997) explains, this approach involves a progressive attempt to create a framework in which pharmacological, physiological, environmental, social and phenomenological variables are all taken into account. This continuum of dependence can provide a useful baseline from which to measure the interaction of physical and psychological effects of chronic substance misuse. It also helps suggest potential developmental patterns of use and ways in which these can affect the significant routines of everyday life. It has obvious relevance, therefore, for working with substance-misusing parents and assessing the impact of their behaviour on children.

The key elements described here are drawn from the work of Edwards *et al.* (1997) and linked to both potential patterns of drinking behaviour and the implications for parents, carers and children:

- narrowing of repertoire
- salience of drinking
- increased tolerance

- withdrawal symptoms
- relief of withdrawal symptoms by further drinking
- subjective awareness of compulsion to drink.

Narrowing of repertoire

As reliance on alcohol increases, motivation to drink focuses more on relief from or avoidance of withdrawal. Patterns of drinking become narrowed, in the sense that the person may begin to drink the same whether it is a workday, weekend or holiday. External contingencies including mood or social factors are seen to make less difference in affecting this regular consumption, although such a pattern may be seen as more variable than fixed. However, as dependence increases, patterns are seen to become more fixed, whatever the competing pressures or responsibilities. So, for example, drinking within a family setting may continue on a holiday or weekday, as there is a need to maintain alcohol consumption, despite the reasons against this.

Salience of drinking

As drinking increases, the individual gives greater priority to maintaining alcohol intake and tends to rationalise continued drinking. Reasons that may have previously inhibited use in certain circumstances – 'the children are still awake' – and were once effective in controlling drinking periods, may be increasingly neutralised or given as reasons for continued drinking – 'the children are so difficult and drinking helps me cope'.

Increased tolerance

Here the person is able to sustain an alcohol intake which would incapacitate moderate drinkers, although normal functioning *is* impaired. In the later stages of dependence, individuals begin to lose their tolerance and can become incapacitated by quantities of alcohol which previously would have had less effect. Cross-tolerance will extend to certain other drugs, particularly general depressants such as barbiturates and benzodiazepines, so the person who has become tolerant to alcohol, will also have tolerance to these and vice versa. This may be particularly significant where there are issues of depression.

Withdrawal symptoms

The extent to which these occur relates to the level of dependence and varies from having little effect to severe symptoms. Symptoms include tremors, nausea, sweating and other physical symptoms, sleep disturbance, hallucinations, grand mal seizures and delirium tremens. Again the severity is seen to relate to the level of the dependence, in addition to factors within the individual. A variety of symptoms may develop in relation to drugs other than alcohol (discussed individually in Appendix 1). Withdrawal symptoms involve a complex interaction of physical and psychological factors and have significance when assessing the potential impact on parenting. So, for example, in relation to mood swings, this may vary from feelings of 'being on edge' to feelings of great agitation or depression. This, as we shall see in Chapter 5, may have particular significance for parenting. Many studies have shown that 'sobering up after heavy drinking may not necessarily reduce tension but increase irritability as a result of hangovers or withdrawal symptoms' (Laybourn *et al.* 1996, p.39). By the same token, cessation of drug use does not initially lead to a more settled situation (Aldridge 1999).

Relief of withdrawal symptoms by further drinking

Someone dependent may try to maintain a steady alcohol level in an attempt to avoid withdrawal symptoms. This is likely to be indicated by the pattern of the drinking – the time of the first drink of the day, for example – and it is important to see how this may be affected by personal and social factors. There is however a central dilemma here. Drinking regularly in order to maintain equilibrium may be the only way to cope with family responsibilities and stresses, since attempting to endure withdrawal symptoms, struggling with the impact of this on the ability to concentrate and managing home life may be too much to bear. It may seem, therefore, more appropriate to drink to relieve the effects of withdrawal. The same dilemma applies to those misusing drugs.

Subjective awareness of compulsion to drink

Those experiencing one or more of the symptoms described above, including withdrawal, may find it difficult to make sense of the complex experiences of compulsion, craving or withdrawal (Edwards *et al.* 1997). Consequently the ideas of 'loss of control' and 'craving' are easily misinterpreted or misunderstood. This points to the importance of gaining an understanding of what the individual's experience of 'compulsion' may actually mean. Is there loss of control and, if so, what are the implications of this? What level of control does the individual experience? Control may be better viewed as 'variably or intermittently impaired' rather than lost. Gaining a more realistic understanding of 'control' and 'craving' enables the emergence of a more detailed picture of the way in which behaviour may be affected and may be seen to have clear relevance for assessing pressures upon parenting capacity.

This dependence 'syndrome', then, has the potential not only to provide an accurate, albeit far from definitive, explanation for many of the processes of dependence, but also to provide a helpful structure, which enables clients and families to make sense of an experience which causes confusion and anxiety. It is not, however, without its critics. Some suggest that it remains too medically based; others that it over-stresses the biochemical issues of dependence and fails to account for cultural variations.

Edwards *et al.* (1997) attempt to balance the use of this important conceptual tool with an emphasis on the importance of gauging how this will be different for each individual. They also underline the importance of professionals' sensitivity to language and meaning as a way of interpreting each individual's unique experience:

> There should be a willingness to play phrasings backwards and forwards until there is a flash of mutual comprehension. The possibility of understanding will often be destroyed if conventional terms such as 'craving' or 'loss of control' are prematurely used...clinical work is dependent on being alert towards meanings of words and nuances of phrase which are partly idiosyncratic...but often culturally endowed. (Edwards *et al.* 1997, p.42)

Dependence, frequency of use and time spent with children

It is useful to consider the potentially 'progressive states' of this syndrome, in attempting to assess particular patterns of drinking within a family setting. It is also important to think about, as others have (Laybourn *et al.* 1996), issues of frequency and timing. When considering issues for substance-misusing parents how do these elements coincide, when parenting skills are needed most? How far are parents with a dependence on a substance able to mitigate its impact, by adjusting their use in ways that will have less significant consequences? This involves a complex assessment, in which both the parents' use and the child's particular needs, depending on age and stage of development, are considered.

In their research into the effects of parents' problem drinking on children, Laybourn and colleagues identified four different patterns of drinking that were seen to affect the ability to parent in different ways (Laybourn *et al.* 1996, p.37):

- *Constant opportunistic drinking* when parents appeared to drink at any time of day, depending on finances, stresses and so forth.

- *Nightly drinking* involving regular consumption but only in the evenings, often to avoid times when the children were around.

- *Weekly heavy drinking* involving a settled routine of heavy drinking at certain times during the week.

- *Binge drinking* involving bouts of drinking, lasting days or weeks, during which parents drank most of the time, followed by periods of sobriety.

Harnessing an understanding of the pattern of dependence to an awareness of times when the provision of parenting skills is critical, helps to chart when and how substance use interacts with crucial periods of parent–child contact. There will be some differences in relation to use of other drugs but it seems clear that some of the characteristics identified can be usefully transferred to other dependencies.

Substance misuse as learned behaviour

> Individuals discover that the use of a certain substance is in some ways effective in dealing with a set of life problems. It is the effectiveness of drugs which makes them potentially dangerous and there comes a point where even a belief in their effectiveness, in the face of much objective evidence to the contrary, is sufficient to maintain habitual or frequent use. (Shephard 1990, p.9)

The emergence of social learning theory and cognitive psychology, particularly in the 1970s and 1980s, was seen to offer new and more realistic approaches to problem drinkers and drug users, based on a different set of assumptions about the 'nature, development and resolution of problems related to addictive behaviour' (Baldwin 1990, p.68). As a consequence, self-control models of behaviour, educational approaches and a focus on skills and other behavioural interventions emerged. This was partly on the basis that the disease model's focus on abstinence could be counter-therapeutic, due to unrealistic expectations in relation to relapse, which was now more centrally recognised as being a normal part of the process of change. The development of psychologically based 'controlled' approaches to drinking represented a significant shift away from a 'disease' approach in the field of alcohol (Heather and Robertson 1981) and similar developments evolved in relation to drug use (Bennett 1989).

Those who favour psychological explanations, derived from learning theory, tend to see substance misuse as a more 'variable' condition rather than a specific category of behaviour or disease-like state. In other words, it is viewed as a mechanism used to alter, however temporarily, reactions or responses to people and events. As Shephard (1990) observes, not only do people use substances as rewards but also the effects of the drugs and associated behaviours can be rewarding in themselves and these experiences are affected by factors such as parental behaviour, peer group activity and availability. The reinforcement of behaviour provided by drugs can, of course, be seen as potentially harmful (or negative) where drugs are used to cushion individuals from difficult experiences or tasks such as parenting. As we shall suggest in Chapter 7, substance misuse can provide a potentially dangerous device for problem-solving.

In terms of behavioural theory, once dependence or use has become established it becomes more and more entrenched as repeated use can be triggered by psychological or physical cues associated with that behaviour. Strategies for dealing with these situations include detailed cognitive and behavioural techniques to help individuals unlearn previous responses and consider alternative coping mechanisms. Such approaches are often linked to models of decision-making or the difficulties associated with sustaining change – in other words, the question of motivation.

An influential and now ubiqitous contribution here is Prochaska and DiClemente's 'Transtheoretical Model of Change' (Prochaska and DiClemente 1982, 1984; Prochaska, DiClemente and Norcross 1992) and we discuss the implications of this for family approaches in Chapter 11. Despite the fact that Prochaska and DiClemente's model was described as 'transtheoretical', it is associated with learning theory in that behavioural theorists have linked learning to different levels of motivation and to subsequent strategies. This is hardly surprising as an underlying assumption of the model is that positive progress by the 'addicted' person occurs via the relearning which is gained as they move cyclically through various stages, gaining knowledge, even if not progressing in a linear manner (Prochaska *et al.* 1992). Consequently, then, despite its 'non-denominational' claim, it has strong cognitive-behavioural leanings (Orford 2001).

Approaches derived from social learning theory have been adapted in relation to issues of expectation, social cues and relapse (Marlatt and Gordon 1985). As Collins and Keene (2000) suggest, while cognitive behavioural techniques can be applied whether the aim is abstinence or controlled substance use, the theory behind them would tend to imply that any behaviour can be learnt or relearnt and therefore tends to raise questions about the necessity for abstinence and the 'irreversibility' of addiction.

Learning theory and family functioning

More specifically in relation to families, learning theories attempt to account for the way that substance misuse offers short-term advantages which appear to outweigh the long-term disadvantages (Bennett 1989). For the family as a whole these might include a distraction from other family conflicts or problems and the avoidance of separation, resulting in 'enmeshed' relationships (Yandoli, Mulleady and Robbins 1989). However, learning theory, while useful in certain situations, can be viewed as too narrow if it fails to account for the way that physiological notions of substances influence the way in which people develop attachments (in other words, the biological effect of the substances themselves) or include the impact of wider environmental influences.

Some developments in family approaches have, however, attempted to adapt concepts from social learning theory and to combine these with an emphasis on the importance of attending to the family and wider social and community support. The 'Community Reinforcement Approach' (Azrin 1976; Smith and Meyers 1995) adapted for both drug and alcohol users (Ryan *et al.* 1999), is a good example of such an approach which stresses the importance of social, family and work influences as 'reinforcers' to help clients recover. In another development, 'Network Therapy' (Galanter 1993) and the more recent 'Social Behaviour and Network Therapy' (Copello *et al.* 2001) utilise a number of behavioural and cognitive strategies with the aim of building networks 'supportive of change' (United Kingdom Alcohol

Treatment Trial Research Team 2001, p.13). All these models are discussed in more detail in Chapter 11.

Social pressures and substance misuse

Many have argued that explanations of problematic substance misuse have not given due weight to the sociological pressures which influence a dependence on, or attachment to, substances (Peele 1985). This is particularly pertinent in relation to substance-misusing parents, who may be more susceptible to the effects of poverty, lack of social support, unemployment, poor housing, discrimination or any combination of these. Although the link between poverty and drug use is complex and somewhat contradictory, problem drug users tend to be found in higher numbers in areas of social deprivation (Gilman 2000; Lloyd 1998) and as the Advisory Council on the Misuse of Drugs (1998, p.113) states: 'the strong balance of probability [suggests] that deprivation today in Britain is often likely to make a significant causal contribution to the cause, complications and intractability of damaging kinds of drug misuse'.

Within this approach, substance misuse has been viewed primarily as a coping response – albeit a problematic and self-defeating one – in the face of both social and environmental stresses. Indeed, Peele (1985), using aspects of 'control' theory, argues that society, and all the sub-societies to which people belong, create the potential climate for an addictive response from those who occupy unsatisfying and stressful positions within the social order and who feel that the available compensations and rewards are either not worthwhile or completely unobtainable.

Gilman (2000) describes a process in which social exclusion, unemployment, underemployment, low educational achievement, poor housing, family stresses, breakdown of community and fear of crime can all coalesce. This results in a level of despair and hopelessness, where people feel things have reached a point where there is very little left to lose. The option of drug use, then, rather than being debated on the basis of advantages, disadvantages and risks becomes what he terms a 'why not?' issue (Gilman 2000, p.23). In other words, the answer to the question 'Why would you use heroin and risk dependency?' is simply 'Why not?' An escape – or what seems to be an escape – from such bleak feelings is suddenly available, as this extract illustrates:

> A feeling of nothingness came over me... Then I decided that I was just not going to go on feeling like that. As long as I couldn't have the life I wanted, I'd adjust myself to shooting dope again. If I was going to be nothing, at least I'd feel the way I wanted to feel, not the way I felt naturally. (Silverstein et al. 1981, p.46)

Here we are provided with an insight into the acute pain of despair and the way a substance can provide escape, however temporary or illusive it may be. There is a clear sense that only when 'shooting dope' can this individual feel really alive and truly himself. Here one begins to gain a strong sense of the way in which such feelings can lead to a psychological attachment, while subtly but powerfully, alienation and estrangement develop in the wake of the more positive feelings induced by the substance taken.

Acute social and psychological pressures can merge, particularly when there is a history of deprivation or family trauma. Much research evidence points to the fact that a significant majority who experience chronic problems with substances also experience severe psychological and social pressures, including sexual or physical abuse. This woman describes her use of heroin as her way of coping with one such experience:

> I took heroin because James' dad...used to beat me up, but it was violent really violent. To get away from the beatings and the everyday problems of life... It gets you blank. You can blank everything else out. And all you've got then is just you. All I had then was just like me, me son and the house and I was in the house with my son and I knew that I was safe with my son. So it made me feel safe and I could handle everything. (Elliott and Watson 1998, p.41)

The way that social pressures combine with and impact upon a person's capacity to cope vividly illustrates the potential significance of social factors in influencing the perpetuation of use and sharply challenges conventional wisdom about the uniquely addictive qualities of the drugs themselves. Is it too fanciful to suggest, as David Rose (2001) does, that many who remain 'addicted' in response to traumatic psychological and sociological experiences, effectively feel themselves to be in a 'war zone' from which substance misuse appears to provide the only available 'shelter'? Here, the use of substances is seen as a natural escape route from intensely traumatic social and psychological pressures which can act as motivators for sustained use.

In considering the impact of external factors on substance-misusing parents, then, we are considering a potentially complex interaction between the personal and the social. The interplay of social systems in the child and family environment is very significant and, as Garbarino (1990) argues, can provide a kind of 'social map' for understanding connections between these elements. Thus while it is important to avoid making assumptions about the connections between poverty, substance misuse and childcare, such a perspective may throw important light on the way that limited resources and support increase the pressures on such families:

> Impoverished microsystems begin to form systematic patterns of deprivation. School and social networks will reinforce developmental delays... The greatest risks come when families lack the financial resources to purchase support services in the market place and are cut off from informal helping relationships. (Garbarino 1990, pp.89–90)

This is closely linked to the ecological perspective now incorporated into the *Framework for the Assessment of Children in Need and their Families* (Department of Health 2000a) with the welfare of the child dependent upon the interaction between developmental need, parenting capacity and environmental factors (Jack 2000). As Bronfenbrenner (1979) says:

> Whether parents can perform effectively in child rearing roles within the family depends on the role demands, stresses and supports emanating from other settings...parents' evaluations of their own capacity to function, as well as their view of the child, are related to such external factors...adequacy of childcare arrangements, the presence of friends and neighbours who can help out in emergencies, the quality of health and social services and neighbourhood safety. (Bronfenbrenner 1979, p.7)

Most significantly, many of the key elements of this model link to developments in research identifying the importance of social support and its role in enabling and sustaining change. Social support can be seen to offer potential stress buffering influences on individual and family behaviour. The extent, dependability, reciprocity, closeness and congruence – that is, the degree to which types of support match need – of the social support available can directly or indirectly affect parent, family and child functioning (Dunst and Trivette 1990).

Thus, what may be identified as poor parenting in a family where one or both partners are abusing drugs or alcohol, could instead be the result of a combination of interconnecting factors such as poor health, financial pressures, poor self-esteem and relationship problems. This alternative perspective assists in understanding, evaluating and formulating interventions which take into account the complex dynamic between personal and social factors. In other words, neither the problem nor the solution is based solely on an identification of a deficit in parenting skills, but the way that parenting capacity is influenced by a range of other factors including social support. This approach also helps in the consideration of what level and type of intervention may be most effective, influenced by what Garbarino terms a 'dual mandate – to look both *outward* to the forces that shape social contexts and *inward* to the day-to-day interaction of the child in the family' (Garbarino 1990, p.78, emphasis in original). In due course, we shall see how these ideas have influenced developments in both assessing parental substance misuse and models of intervention.

The impact of labelling

> I'm not saying that all social workers are like that but the majority of them think 'You're a drug addict, you're a bad person, no hoper, we'll stamp that on their file. They should take more care of the kids', you know blah, blah, blah. (Bates *et al.* 1999, p.72)

The way that friends, family, professionals and wider society respond to drug-misusing parents is particularly pertinent, given that drug use and parenting represent two activities associated with strong moral imperatives. We now consider how the way in which such activities are viewed can affect both the attitudes and behaviour of substance-misusing parents and their interaction with professionals and others.

The processes by which labelling occurs offer a number of insights into the ways in which reactions from others impact on the behaviour itself, increasing the potential cycle of further alienation or marginalisation, from significant others or 'society', as roles are assumed and then established. This is particularly significant given that we have identified the concept of social support as a key factor in influencing the ability or desire to control or abstain from substance misuse. Labelling theory, by offering some insights into the processes by which people can become detached from potentially supportive relationships with family, friends or wider social networks, offers clues to the ways that these may be regained. Such ideas then will underpin some of the methods of intervention that we shall review in Chapter 11.

There are a number of relevant concepts here. Bacon (1973, cited in Orford 1985, p.223) outlines a process which he calls 'disjunction in labelling'. Here, the early reaction to someone's increasing drinking (or drug use) may be accompanied by irritation, distress and criticism from those within her or his family or social circle. It may be that either this is not taken seriously by the substance user or its impact is misinterpreted (deliberately or otherwise, consciously or unconsciously). Signals may not be received, or may be deliberately ignored, causing those expressing concern to feel rebuffed and leading to a distancing between them and the person causing anxiety. What may follow is a process of labelling, albeit often covert, in which communication becomes less direct. Such labelling can develop to a point where an excessive drinker or drug taker may be excluded from relationships with family, friends or other social groups. Orford (1985, 2001) describes Bacon's account of such a process as 'dissocialization', as a result of which individuals may be attracted to other groups engaged in similar behaviour, where they feel accepted.

> An individual would show marked changes in terms of the groups to which he belonged, the movement being towards groups which tolerated more [drinking] effects, and which in other respects were less demanding... Losing control (in Bacon's view) was a process involving the actor and others. (Orford 1985, p.254)

Zinberg (1975) links this process to identity formation and self-image. He describes the way in which labelling can lead to a gradual drift towards alienation, as particular social relationships are lost and others are gained: 'they...had been declared deviant by the larger society. They had become isolated from those views of the world that permit a coherent and integrated sense of self' (Zinberg 1975, cited in Orford 1985, p.224).

An insidious and complex process can occur where the use of the substance can make one feel more like oneself, while leading to the very opposite.

> When a person takes drugs (to avoid certain feelings), he knows at some level what he is doing. When the effect of the drug wears off, the self he has to face is further reduced in stature, further damaged in his own eyes. This,

on top of his worsened external situation, provides yet another reason for wanting to escape again. (Silverstein *et al.* 1981, p.4)

A vicious circle can develop whereby individuals' perception of their 'reputation' and feelings of exclusion combines with a demoralised sense of identity and self-worth, leading to resignation about the negative labels that are attributed. In other words, one gives in to the label. Goffman (1963) interprets this process in a slightly different way. He views the acceptance of such a label or role as leading to people acting out or stressing certain characteristics associated with it. The deviant part of the identity (the drug user or alcoholic) can then become the master role, subsuming all other equally integral roles or parts of the personality, which are denied or suppressed. This can lead to a spoiling of the more complex mix of good and bad parts of an identity.

One possible outcome of all this is that individuals increase their substance use as a consequence of the labelling process. Internalising the label of 'out-of-control drug user' or 'problem drinker', for example, is seen as a crucial step in a 'deviant career'. Such internalisation is seen to occur when behaviour reflects what others anticipate and expect to see. Consequently there may be an increasing tendency to be drawn towards fulfilling the expected role, leading to what Becker (1963) has described as 'role engulfment'. This is seen to have particular consequences both for the way the labelled user acts in future and, most significantly, for the way in which he or she is viewed by family and friends, professionals or society. Less energy is invested in what may have been considered the more positive aspects of social life with less return and, as a result, a pattern of negative reinforcement can develop. Recent research findings (for example Project MATCH Research Group 1997, 1998, in the field of alcohol) have identified the significance of the way in which individuals' relationship to their social environment impacts upon substance misuse and the ability to control this. As a consequence, recent models of intervention have built upon this (see Chapter 11).

Theories which explore the impact of social reaction can provide a rich source of explanation about the ways in which dependencies may be reinforced, even though they say little about the primary reason for people's attachment to substances. The stigma attached to being labelled can therefore be seen to shape actions and behaviours in particular ways.

Labelling and the dynamics between professionals and substance-misusing parents

An understanding of the dynamics of labelling and internalisation are significant both for substance misusers themselves and professionals working with them. It can offer useful clues and pointers to the way in which characteristics of behaviour can be established and assigned, affecting motivations to change, interactions with others and how engagement is negotiated. This is particularly pertinent when considering the relationship between parenting and substance use. Judgements, expectations and anticipation of moral condemnation are likely to be central to any exploration or assessment of the potential connection between the two, significantly impacting upon the parent–worker dynamic. Clients' explanations of their behaviour are likely to be influenced by both their anxieties and their fears about professional reactions and the prospect of being subjected to investigation. As other researchers have found, initial accounts of attitude or behaviour are partly determined by the perceived response of the figure in authority (Cody and McLaughlin 1988). Those involved in what are perceived as being deviant situations may feel the need to develop strategies that keep feelings of invasion and accusation at bay. Characteristics associated with good or bad parenting can become almost unconsciously associated with notions of a substance-misusing 'identity'. Even when this is not the way in which a professional perceives the link, it may be the way the client anticipates the professional's view. For example, research into clients' experiences of child protection procedures (Cleaver and Freeman 1995) illustrated natural feelings of intrusion and being judged that clients felt when they were the subject of investigations, and highlighted the need for professionals to take into account clients' perspectives. We shall discuss the implications of such issues in more depth in Chapter 4.

Summary

To label someone an 'addict' or to make an assumption that he or she is 'dependent' on a substance is clearly unhelpful. On the other hand, without some attempt to gain a conceptual understanding of the state and experience of those with problematic 'attachments' to substances, a considered assessment of the effect and impact on the child is hardly possible. In making such assessments, as McMurran (1994) observes, models of substance misuse, in addition to fitting the observed data, need to provide an accurate representation of people's experience of the painful processes they are encountering. In addition they need to allow for some qualified speculation about how substance misuse may develop, how associated problems arise and how they may be reduced.

In assessing parenting when there is evidence of substance misuse it seems particularly important to make use of theoretical concepts that assist individuals and family members to make sense of processes of 'dependence' and 'attachment' from an empathic position, in contrast to those which offer little more than what some commentators have called a 'diagnostic label' or 'kind of magisterial sentencing' (Edwards *et al.* 1997, p.51).

4

Attachment and Reinforcement
Maintaining the Habit

When does a person cross the lines dividing social drinker, problem drinker, alcoholic? I don't know… But I do know that a line is crossed, or perhaps several and that on some barely conscious level, the drinker understands this, understands that a dark and irrevocable shift is taking place, a progression that cannot be willed away…an experience…seeping and insidious, a slow and steady deepening of the relationship, a barely perceptible shift from want to need, an ingraining that takes place over many years.

(Knapp 2001, p.48)

Habit may be based very largely upon processes that operate beyond full awareness. Indeed, in a sense…the disease-like quality of habitual excessive behaviour is due to circumstances which allow for the flourishing of strong attachment-forming processes, which in some cases are more than a match for forces of restraint, although the latter may appear much more reasonable and may be much more easily listed in a form of words.

(Orford 1985, p.279)

In this chapter we look at why some people develop and sustain intense attachments to substances. In relation to parents, this allows us to gain some significant insights into the potentially problematic tensions and dilemmas that arise in caring for children while sustaining a drug or alcohol habit.

As we have seen, the extent to which it is possible to identify specific or differentiated processes in relation to attachment to substances is a central debate in the field of addictions. How does chronic substance misuse develop and how does it impose itself on other aspects of one's life? Are there progressive implications that influence decisions, actions and, in particular, attitudes towards responsibilities for children? If the attachment to substances leads to a gradual erosion of freedom of choice, as more emphasis is given to their use, what is the nature of this erosion and what are the implications for child welfare? In essence, attachment to a substance can be seen as a way of coping, in the face of various psychological and sociological pressures. This relationship may then compete with child–parent attachment, so crucial for child well-being, and may affect family functioning and interfere with the capacity to parent. Defensive strategies, similar to those which characterise some attachment patterns, may develop in relation to the user–substance relationship (Howe *et al.* 1999). These will be discussed in detail in Chapter 6.

Problematic substance misuse of an intense kind can provide an impersonal attachment focus which distracts from and diminishes the parenting potential of an adult, and is consequently a negative factor in children's experiences. In the face of sociological and psychological pressures and as a result of the *interaction* between the substances and these pressures, unhelpful coping patterns and other problems can develop.

This is significantly different from suggesting that attachments develop solely or principally because of the 'addictive characteristics' of substances *per se* and different again from models of addiction which equate attachment with core or discrete conditions more readily associated with biological or medical explanations. Such characteristics are clearly part of the way in which attachments develop, but many people use drugs without developing problematic attachments. Differences in users' experiences of how and why they feel attached or dependent rely, to a large extent, on the part played by the particular substance and the function it is fulfilling. This will be affected by immediate circumstances, family systems and wider sociological influences.

Developing attachment

As we have seen, theories that suggest that substance misuse is mainly a rational choice hardly seem to account for the pull between the substance and the demands of parenting or explain the difficult tension between the two. If it is a simple choice, do we view parents who allow drug use to interfere with parenting as merely irresponsible? If we view chronic 'dependence' on substances as a type of 'enslavement',what are the implications for children and for effective intervention? As one commentator has observed, alcoholism 'is not a disease of the elbow. It is not muscular spasms that bring the glass to the mouth' (Herbert Kleber, quoted in Solomon 2001, p.224).

Here, then, explanations which do justice to the strength of progressive use of substances, within their sociological contexts, without resorting to over deterministic views, appear the most fruitful. Borrowing ideas from Orford's (1985, 2001) work we favour a model of attachment to substances which is essentially developmental. Thus, attachments develop as a result of sociological and psychological influences rather than due to the addictive nature of the substance *per se*. This helps to shed light not only on why some people become dependent and others do not, but also on why some people remain dependent, in progressively attached ways, but not others.

Freedom of choice (as we have seen) is not completely taken away at a particular point by the 'dependence' but the ability to control use is diminished, as attachment to the substance increases. Such models of 'attachment' allow for the complex processes engendered by social pressures, in addition to the unpredictability of internal states. On the one hand, there is always a point where a decision is made to take a drug. In this sense 'addiction' is not like a pathological disease which imposes itself upon the individual. On the other hand, the combination of psychological and social pressures can severely limit the *perception* of choice in a most fundamental and real way.

An analogy with the experience of depression may be a useful one here. Feelings of depression, when they arise, often do not appear to involve volition, in that feelings of panic, confusion and anxiety may arise suddenly, may persist for no apparent reason and there may be no foreseeable relief (Solomon 2001). This is what makes them potentially so frightening and distressing. The emotions aroused may give one the sense that one has little control and limited ability to moderate the effects, and that one is at the mercy of such feelings without a sense of being able to escape them. Therefore while, rationally speaking, individuals may be seen to have a choice about how to deal with such feelings, in reality the perception of choice is changed by the feelings engendered and the level of fear or despair evoked. It may seem that there is no clear way out. Such experiences may equate with those of parents resorting to drugs or alcohol under severe strain. As we have seen, such experiences may be the result of intense social and psychological pressures and under these circumstances it is not hard to see how patterns of attachment to substances can emerge as a way of escaping, or controlling them.

The way in which attachments develop, how behaviour can become self-defeating and conflictual and the way in which it involves elements of secrecy and denial are all aspects which we shall discuss in more detail, drawing out the potential implications, in terms of assessment, for professionals. Most significantly, such developmental processes need to be viewed as 'normal' responses to substance use rather than as pathological.

Physical dependence or emotional attachment?

Gossop (2000), when discussing withdrawing from opiates, talks about the way in which the physical effects of 'cold turkey' have been vastly exaggerated. This can be seen both to perpetuate and to mask the more central and perhaps ontological explanations for drug dependence. In a sense, then, the language of physical withdrawal almost comes to symbolise more illusive, complex and fundamental issues of worth, meaning and identity – the psychological pain at the heart of chronic use, the anxiety beyond or beneath.

In a similar vein, Davies (1997) has argued that concepts of withdrawal have failed to take account of research evidence suggesting that the intrinsic influence of such a process does not result from a biological or pharmacological process alone. He suggests that the significance of this process and how it is resisted (or not) is also affected by a variety of situational and cognitive factors, rather than emanating from the pathology of the user. In other words, developing and progressive use emerges from the stress of struggling with personal and social pressures.

Perhaps nowhere is the complexity of the interrelationship between the physical and emotional aspects of substance misuse better illustrated that in Pearson's (1987) classic study of heroin users which continues to offer many insights into assumptions, myths and ambiguities associated with drug use. In this study Pearson uses interviews to highlight some of these, drawing on accounts of people coming off heroin. Here we see a clear reflection of an inherent difficulty in disentangling the physical and psychological impact of withdrawal. Many of the examples used demonstrate that the physical problems may have been over-stressed due to the complexity and difficulty involved in describing the emotional component. Pearson (1987) describes how the numerous accounts of dependence and withdrawal contrast and conflict, with some describing the acute difficulty of managing withdrawal symptoms, and others dismissing them as akin to flu. While some explain the sheer impossibility of coming off drugs, others stress that the difficulties really arise after withdrawal, when one is left to manage emotional issues without the support of the substance.

> It's hard to explain what a turkey is like...a lot of people say this happens and that happens, but when I done my turkey it wasn't as bad as I was expecting. But it was bad, if you know what I mean...it was unbearable...like...but it wasn't as bad as I was expecting... It's not the actual coming off you know, this thing you hear 'cold turkey' and all that...most of it's in your head, you know, a mental or memory sort of thing. (Pearson 1987, pp.152–153)

Here we see the different emphasis given to the physical difficulties of giving up a drug, as opposed to accounts which downplay this aspect and describe the emotional problems. Experiences, of course, vary from person to person, due to the differing reasons for using substances and the different types of use. Consequently 'giving up' is experienced very differently, depending on whether use has been short- or long-term, and the role it has played in cushioning the self against painful emotions. For some, what is being relinquished may be an emotional attachment, rather than a physical or psychological dependence. The difference may relate not only to the level of substance misuse but also to the function that such use has served. One theory here is that an attachment to a substance develops in response to the individual's inability to form satisfactory emotional relationships (Flores 2001). A person who lacks the capacity to attach due to either personal or environmental reasons is both attracted to dependence but further impaired by it.

> Because of the potent euphoric emotional 'rush' that alcohol and drugs produce, they are powerfully reinforcing and inhibiting of the more subtle emotional persuasions in a person's life. Consequently, the vulnerable individual's attachment to chemicals serves both as an obstacle to and a substitute for interpersonal relationships. (Flores 2001, p.64)

For some, stopping substance use involves the end of a 'relationship' that may have been part of their lives for many years, integral to their identity and crucial in helping them deal with the most painful emotions and experiences. Under these circumstances, giving up is likely to prove painful and possibly traumatic. In other words, the development of entrenched and painful attachments is related, at least in part, to the role the substance may have played and the function it has fulfilled, possibly over a long period of time. It is difficult, under such circumstances, to separate the physical effects of withdrawal from the emotional effects of not having the drug any more.

Clearly, consideration of the processes of dependence and withdrawal is important, as these can be seen to have a major physical and psychological impact, particularly in relation to some types of alcohol or drug misuse. There are often significant health considerations here which can affect both individuals and their families. For professionals encountering those experiencing significant problems with substances, while it is important to take into account the potential implications of differing aspects of withdrawal, it is equally important not to underestimate the potential core 'need' to rely on substances as a method of coping.

This again raises central issues about why people become reliant on drugs in the first place. Edwards *et al.* (1997) illustrate this in stressing that many professionals, encountering clients with problematic use, find that their histories reveal either use of a variety of drugs sequentially or concurrent polydrug use. Thus, while it is important to examine each type of drug use, in terms of its potential physical effect, what is also important is to recognise the continued reliance on, or attachment to, chemical substances. This is particularly important, given that continued attachment may often reflect a problem in another aspect of life, such as, for example, the relationship between personal and structural problems. Unresolved feelings of depression combined with low levels of opportunity and high levels of poverty would provide one example of this difficult combination of circumstances.

Polydrug use is particularly difficult to understand as it can be precipitated by a range of factors. It may counteract the effects of other substances, deal with withdrawal from other drugs, or be related to current drug availability, to fashion, or to peer group pressure. As well as considering the potential impact of combinations of substances on behaviour, such switching and/or mixing, over time, suggests a reliance which, in itself, implies a continuing need to deal with pressures. Within this context, it is necessary to gain an understanding of the underlying reasons for this.

Attachment to substances as management of pain

In her interviews with a number of drug-using parents, Hogan (1997) comments that they appeared to be preoccupied not with their own pleasure, but with the goal of pain avoidance or reduction. As we have argued, emotional and psychological pressures can be seen as much more frightening than physical dependence *per se*, as they can involve central questions about self-worth and identity which can strike at the heart of one's personality. For those whose attachment to a substance may be of long standing, the extent of the psychological connectedness may be so embedded that both the anticipation and experience of pain and loss may be profound. Under such circumstances, the language of physical withdrawal can seem the most accurate way of describing – at an almost symbolic level – more illusive, complex and fundamental issues of loss, identity and meaning. In other words, the language of physical pain can become the medium in which to express more elemental emotional agony. As Gossop (2000) observes:

> the exaggerated fear [of physical withdrawal] makes more sense if it is reinterpreted as a fear of living without drugs. What terrifies [the person addicted] is not the symptoms of withdrawal, distressing though they may be, but the yawning emptiness beyond. (Gossop 2000, p.193)

This sense of emptiness is well illustrated by Williams (1972), here discussing different kinds of pain:

> It's as beings who think and feel that we are vulnerable to the onslaughts of suffering. And in mind and feeling we can suffer just as much and generally far more when our suffering is linked to no...external distress. For when linked to something objective or external our suffering seems to make some sort of sense, however bloody that sense may be. But when our suffering comes only from within our heart and mind with nothing outside to pin it on, then it seems utterly and senselessly malignant...suffering attacks us in the very centre of our identity. (Williams 1972, p.153)

As we saw in Chapter 3, feelings of sterility, despair and loss of meaning may result from the impact of a variety of social and psychological factors. In discussing the links between social exclusion and drug-using parents, Gilman (2000) points out that such voids can be psychological, social, emotional, spiritual or temporal, and that dependence on substances can, as a consequence, be used to fill such voids 'by default' (Gilman 2000, p.23).

Flores (2001), writing from a psychodynamic perspective, expresses the same point in emphasising that, for some, serious dependence can act as a necessary distraction 'from the gnawing emptiness that threatens to overtake them' (Flores 2001, p.67). The attachment to substances can be seen, then, as a way of offering protection from anxiety, insecurity, disappointment, loss, anger, frustration or any number of other emotions. In considering such protective qualities, concepts of identity, worth and value are seen as key in making sense of such a developing attachment.

Here substance misuse is seen to play a role in maintaining 'emotional homeostasis' by helping to regulate the more extreme emotions that are experienced (Leventhal and Cleary 1980, cited in Orford 1985). When it may be anticipated that this source of regulation may not be available, feelings of anxiety surface, stimulated by the potential for the emergence of negative feelings. The 'emotional memory' of what the substance offered can then be seen to provoke the desire to continue the pattern. In other words, when people discover that a particular sensation can dramatically change negative feelings, even when they know that this is only temporary, the memory of this escape from painful feelings can provide an almost instinctive desire to recapture this sensation. Such a process may be seen to be progressive. This may happen even after periods of abstinence, as long as the problems with living that provoked the search for relief are not resolved (Silverstein *et al.* 1981). It becomes easy to see how such 'problem-solving' mechanisms can develop into an entrenched habit.

Attachment and loss

It is difficult to think about attachment without considering issues of loss, as they are parts of the same process (Howe *et al.* 1999). Here it is useful to see how different kinds of losses are evoked, when separation from a substance is anticipated or experienced.

First, there is the anticipated loss of the good feelings evoked by the drug in question and what this may represent for the individual. Second, when the effect of the substance is absent, this may induce strong feelings of guilt and regret about what has been lost over the years, in terms of opportunities, relationships and so on. Parents may have to face the loss of the substance as a coping mechanism which may be keeping various emotions generated by family life and the demands of childcare at bay (this will be discussed in more detail in Chapter 5). In addition, there may be a range of accumulated losses from childhood onwards, which substance use has effectively suppressed. The gambling term 'chasing losses' seems a pertinent one here describing, as it does, the natural tendency to try to desperately recapture what has been lost, resulting in a vicious circle of more loss and regret. This complex cycle of loss, guilt and despair can help to explain the difficulty of tackling patterns of 'dependence' which can, in itself, contribute to the motivation to continue substance use. As Orford (2001) points out, many of the charges of 'bad character' among those with substance-misuse problems can at least partly be attributed to the 'dissonance' created by unresolved loss, as we shall see. The sheer accumulated process of loss may act as another explanation for the development of attachment to substances and help to explain why it is so difficult to break free.

Denial as a natural response to pain and loss

Given the variety of functions that an attachment to substances can fulfil, it is not surprising that professionals may encounter some difficulties in working purposively to achieve change where substance misuse has become an established 'coping mechanism'.

On an emotional level, for those who have experienced long histories of using substances or where the use has provided significant emotional support, facing the possibility of examining their pattern of substance misuse can be particularly stressful. The prospect of exposing 'such layers of anxiety and emotional need' may feel very intimidating. (Silverstein *et al.* 1981, p.52). Such layers can be embedded with stressful associations and painful feelings of loss and regret. Consequently, it can feel unsafe to go too near such areas. The novelist David Lodge, in talking about such memories associated with loss, describes feelings of anxiety centred around an anticipation of what he calls 'the booby traps of memory triggered at every step' (Lodge 2001, p.63). Such a description may approximate to some of the feelings experienced by people who are attempting to confront difficult and problematic experiences in their histories.

Such fears may also be combined with a range of other anxieties. Given the illegality of many of the substances in question, society's reaction to these and the moral imperatives associated with substance misuse and parenting, it is not surprising that this will often result in attempts to keep the full reality of substance use 'secret' both from oneself and others. In terms of substance-misusing parents, not only may there be concern about the personal implications of disclosing the use of substances, but also they will be wary about revealing information which they perceive may have implications for their children and their relationship with them.

It is important to consider that this may be the climate in which substance-misusing parents encounter professionals. Within this context, professionals have often acknowledged the difficulty associated with establishing a realistic but mutual understanding of the role that substance use is playing and in achieving a period of sustained intervention to effect change. What often appears to emerge, as a result of clients' anxieties, is a gap between professionals' assessments of a situation and clients' own perceptions. One potential outcome at the assessment stage is a kind of chase around definitions of what constitutes problem substance misuse and problem behaviour. In fact, what this may represent is a fear of exposure, self-discovery, being unfairly judged or labelled or the adverse consequences of professional intervention (Taylor 1999).

Taylor (1999) identifies the problem of working with denial as a critical factor in both the identification and understanding of levels of substance use and the way in which it manifests itself in the interrelationship between worker and client. Research into assessments carried out on chronic substance-misusing offenders substantiated the need for professionals to gain an understanding of the psychology of such processes, how they reflect individual attachments to the substance in question, and ways in which they may indicate more productive approaches to engagement (Taylor 1999).

What, then, are some of the explanations for such reactions? Orford (2001) suggests that the defensiveness, rationalisations and transparent excuses that so often seem to accompany such behaviour are more accurately viewed as an inevitable part of the confusion, panic and fear that are evoked as a consequence of conflicted emotions, rather than, as some would have it, the result of a weak moral response. He describes the nature of this possible conflict in some detail, outlining the way that denial or 'secrecy' can emerge from an unresolved conflict between an attachment to the substance and the pressure to relinquish this. The continued desire, on the one hand, to stay 'attached' to the substance is opposed, on the other, by the distress resulting from the behaviour it induces. If the conflicting feelings cannot be resolved, one possible outcome is a cycle of depression, confusion and panic. Behaviour can itself become unpredictable and it may be difficult to think straight, due to strong feelings of confusion. While there is a desire to reduce the feeling of conflict, such intense emotions can push an individual to seek relief, not necessarily in a constructive fashion. In other words, the cycle of use can be perpetuated as a result of this conflict, with substances providing a major alternative to dealing with decisional tension. This may continue the cycle of use as much as lead to its diminution.

Another possible response may be to hide the reality of the substance-misusing behaviour from oneself or others. Orford (2001) describes two kinds of conflicts which may emerge here. The first is *intrapsychic* conflict, making demands on the individual in question that are, rationally speaking, unwanted. The second is *interpersonal* conflict, which involves growing secrecy about the behaviour in question. Processes of denial or secrecy are viewed, here, as a way out of such conflicts:

> Such justification-promoting behaviour is probably seen to be an integral part of excessive appetite behaviour, even though it may appear quite transparent to the onlooker, and is yet another consequence of dissonance which makes its perpetrator more unpopular. (Orford 2001, p.271)

These ideas help to make sense of many of the responses evoked. In other words, excessive appetite behaviour can take on additional dimensions as a result of the conflict it produces in parents trying to deal with the dual attachments involved in substance use and parenting.

In relation to parenting there are likely to be increased pressures. These include the pressure to continue to cope with the demands of parenthood in a way that is not undermined by the use of substances. Yet, relinquishing drug misuse, while problematic in itself for the reasons we have discussed, may increase the immediate difficulties, given the anticipated withdrawal of the coping mechanism that substances offer, or are perceived as offering. As we shall see in Chapter 5, many parents express the view that substance use improves aspects of their parenting, although this could be seen as debatable. Others, however, are all too aware of the dilemma experienced (Elliott and Watson 1998; Hogan 1997; Klee 1998; McKeganey *et al.* 2001). As one parent put it:

> When I've not got it, I've got no time for them. I've got time for them but they just irritate me because I'm in pain and they just want to jump all over me and all things like that… Like kids do… But you can't do it because you're in pain. It's not that I don't want to do it but I can't do it because I'm ill. I am ill, because it's an illness. Well I think it is anyway. (Elliott and Watson 1998, p.42)

This is just one potential outcome of excessive substance misuse under certain circumstances. It is, however, useful to consider the effects of such conflicts when assessing and working with substance misusing parents. We discuss possible responses and approaches in more detail in Chapters 10 and 11.

Kearney (1996) sees the process of denial as performing three key functions – providing ways of surviving, ways of adapting and ways of buying time. He also stresses the importance of keeping in mind that denial is a natural and self-protective response to pain – something that is used by everyone in everyday life, albeit at different levels. At the same time, however, this 'mechanism' has significant implications as a survival strategy, as it influences the client's potential response to the worker. Since denial is a survival strategy, part of its rationale is to resist pressure to change. Denial, then, in its purest sense becomes a way of protecting individuals from unacceptable threat and a way of buying time to cope with that threat. Kearney discusses different types of denial, all used as protective responses. These include denial of facts ('I have not been drinking'), denial of implications ('I drink heavily but that doesn't mean that it's a problem'), denial of change ('So, I'm an alcoholic – so what?') and denial of feelings ('It doesn't bother me') (Kearney 1996, pp.12–26).

The dynamic that can result from these responses is one where the professional is anxious to effect change, and the client may have some desire to change but, simultaneously, a desire to remain the same. This is another example of the conflicted state.

What is crucial, here, is creating a climate in which the client considers there is enough emotional and practical support to feel that it worth taking the risk that things may change for the better, even if, in the short term, things feel worse. This is particularly important when working with parents, since the consequences of feeling worse, whatever that might be like, will have implications for the care and welfare of the children.

Summary

A progressive attachment to drugs or alcohol can impact on other significant relationships in the user's life and may have particular implications for parent–child attachments. Clearly this is only one way of viewing chronic or harmful misuse, and it is acknowledged that patterns of attachment are variable and dependent on the level and extent of misuse of substances.

However, some of the processes discussed attempt to elucidate ways in which a progression to 'dependence', while on the surface difficult to comprehend given the potential consequences for children involved, may be viewed, under some circumstances, as an understandable reaction to a combination of intense psychological and social pressures. Consequently, perspectives which explore parents' attachment to, and relationship with, substances may be seen to be particularly important in the way that they underline some of the acute tensions involved in maintaining a problematic dependence while caring for children.

As we have seen, a struggle between the developing 'attachment' to a substance and the attachment to children can be accompanied by many conflicting feelings and emotions. As a consequence, those in such situations may react to professionals with suspicion or defensiveness. This suggests the need to acknowledge both the potential strength of such attachments and the processes which may accompany them, as they have particular implications for both assessment and engagement.

5

The Impact of Substance Misuse on Parenting

There's no doubt in my mind that my substance misuse has affected my older children – how can you be a good father when you are that self-destructive?

(Will Self, quoted in Barber 2000)

The whole point of detox is for me and my son... I don't want him to go to school in a few years and someone to turn round and say 'your mum's a junkie'. It's not nice.

('Julie', quoted in Elliott and Watson 1998, p.39)

Most parents do not deliberately set out to harm their children or to develop behaviours which are likely to have an adverse impact upon them (Cleaver and Freeman 1995; Department of Health 2000b). However, parents have needs too – needs too long neglected by research, in terms of their impact on their children – and substance misuse (as we have suggested) may be seen as one way of either meeting them or managing the fact that they are not being met. This, in turn, may have a number of consequences for children, depending on a variety of factors. In this chapter, we are going to turn our attention to the parenting domain and the environmental factors that influence parenting capacity. This will include some overarching ideas in relation to all parenting, as a prelude to considering specific issues that are relevant where there is parental substance misuse. The effects of drugs and alcohol on the individuals who use them and the potential impact of these on parenting will be examined and the needs of substance-misusing parents will also be addressed.

The role of parenting in child welfare

Children rely on parents and carers for their very existences and there is a consensus that optimal development is achieved only as a result of parents' ability to meet their children's needs throughout their formative years (Belsky 1984; Department of Health 1995; Jones 2001; Reder and Lucey 1995; Rutter 1975, 1986, 1995a). There will inevitably be cultural variations in relation to what parents need to do to achieve this and ideas about what constitutes abuse or neglect will differ (Cleaver and Freeman 1995; Korbin 1997; Stevenson 1998). Broadly, though, there is agreement about the aims of parenting which are summed up well by Jones (2001):

> Parenting…refers to the activities and behaviours of parents which are necessary to achieve the objectives of enabling children to become autonomous. These activities and behaviours change as the child develops. Thus parenting, as an activity, is firmly yoked to child outcomes. (Jones 2001, p.256)

Highlighted here is what might be called the 'developmental dance' – fluid, responsive, sensitive interchanges between children and parents over time in which the closeness and distance between 'dancers' may be negotiated or changed, where other 'partners' may also play their part and where account must be taken of the general surroundings in which the dancing is taking place, in terms of context and atmosphere. A crucial aspect of this 'developmental dance' is parents' capacity to place children's needs before their own and to provide a holding environment in which dependency needs can be managed and met.

'Good enough' parenting

Promoting development through responsive, sensitive care has become synonymous with what is known as 'good enough' parenting. This rests on the idea, derived from Winnicott's (1964) work, that there is no such thing as a 'perfect' parent and that this is an unrealistic and unhelpful goal to strive for. Instead there is a level of care that is 'good enough'. As Bettelheim (1987) has observed:

> Perfection is not within the grasp of ordinary human beings… But it is quite possible to be a good enough parent – that is, a parent who raises his child well. To achieve this, the mistakes we make – errors often made just because of the intensity of the emotional involvement in and with our child

– must be more than compensated for by the instances in which we do right by our child. (Bettelheim 1987, p.ix)

What this actually means, however, is open to debate. 'Mistakes', 'errors' and doing 'right' are all relative terms and open to a variety of interpretations. 'Good enough', therefore, continues to be a contested issue since views differ as to what this really means and whether there is a shared understanding of what it represents as a working concept. This has particular implications for decisions in circumstances where parenting is seen as not 'good enough', leading to legal action and the possibility of the child's separation from a parent. Notions of 'good enough' also change over time and are influenced by the culture, structure and socio-political climate of the day (Parton 1997). Research into social work practice suggests wide variation of ideas about what constitutes 'good enough'. As Daniel (2000) observes:

> they [social workers] may mean that the child is receiving consistent and optimum physical and emotional care or they may mean that a child is receiving a minimal amount of care...it has been suggested that 'good enough parenting' is in fact used to represent a 'lesser' version of parenting...that social workers will accept poorer standards for children than for members of the community...and work to a 'rule of optimism' where poor parenting is given the benefit of the doubt. (Daniel 2000, pp.91–92)

Here, then, there is an obvious chasm between notions of optimal and notions of minimal, suggesting that any assessment of 'good enough' is a skilled and complex task and prey to subjectivity, bias and the triumph of hope over expectation. There is also evidence of the way in which children are discriminated against, in terms of the conditions they are expected to endure, compared with other people. Finally there is the problem of blinkered vision and the perils of the 'rose-tinted spectacle' perspective. This rule of optimism as well as other factors that can affect professional judgements will be dealt with in more detail when we consider the assessment process in Chapter 10.

Assumptions and stereotypes

Standards of 'good enough' may veer dramatically where there is evidence of drug or alcohol use and a range of values and beliefs come into play. One of the prevailing problems for this area of practice is that negative stereotypes and assumptions abound and all drug- or alcohol-using parents are seen as a homogeneous group.

Assumptions are also made about the relative harm that can be caused by drug and alcohol use. Forrester (2000) found that social workers automatically assumed that drug use was potentially more harmful than alcohol use partly because, for most, alcohol was more familiar and therefore they felt more confident in assessing its impact on childcare. One consequence of this was that drug use *per se* was seen as placing children at risk, irrespective of pattern, frequency and type of use or support systems available. It also underlined the extent to which parenting could be assessed independently of substance misuse.

This leads us to the next consideration in this area of practice, relating to perceived knowledge and expertise. In studies undertaken to explore workers' issues and dilemmas in this field it was clear that many professionals felt experienced in the field of either drugs, alcohol or childcare but rarely in all three (Adams 1999; Bates *et al.* 1999; Forrester 2000; Klee *et al.* 1998; Kroll and Taylor 2000). This led to two significant consequences. One, not surprisingly, was the level of anxiety and fear generated both in the individual and throughout the professional system. The second was the way in which these powerful emotions could be projected on to other professionals, as a way of managing lack of knowledge or understanding. In several studies considerable criticism was levelled by professionals at the practices of other individuals and agencies. Accusations typically related to overreaction, underreaction, lack of rapid response, inability to grasp the urgency of the situation, or undue focus on the adults in the situation, to the exclusion of the child (Bates *et al.* 1999; Elliott and Watson 2000).

What practitioners have to struggle with here is separating out what is bad parenting (or 'not good enough' parenting), and would be bad parenting in any circumstances, from what is bad parenting as a result of substance misuse. As one family centre worker observed, 'some parents would not be good enough parents whatever – drugs would not make them any worse'. Indeed, Bates *et al.* (1999) in their study of attitudes towards drug-misusing parents among social welfare professionals including social workers, drug dependency unit workers and health visitors, found them struggling to separate out these strands – struggles replicated throughout the systems that exist to manage substance abuse and child protection.

This brings us to what might be called collision of circumstances. In other words, parental substance misuse occurs for many reasons, in many contexts as we have seen. Poverty, social and structural disadvantage or exclusion, oppression, environment, mental health problems, domestic violence, emotional pain, anxiety, hopelessness and culture can all play their part in both its onset and maintenance and there is a strong correlation between problem drug use and social and individual deprivation (Barnard 1999; Hepburn 2000). These levels of complexity cannot be emphasised too strongly.

The parenting domain and parenting capacity

The assessment of 'good enough' parenting involves addressing some key elements, now enshrined in the *Framework for the Assessment of Children in Need and their Families* (Department of Health 2000a), which outlines six dimensions of parenting capacity. These are:

- basic care
- ensuring safety
- emotional warmth
- stimulation
- guidance and boundaries
- stability.

(Department of Health 2000a, p.17)

Alongside these are seven crucial factors in the environmental domain:

- family history and functioning
- wider family
- housing
- employment
- income
- family's social integration
- community resources.

(Department of Health 2000a, p.17)

In exploring the impact of substance misuse on parenting, both these sets of dimensions need to be considered. Provision of these, however, can and will be affected by a host of factors. As Reder and Lucey have observed: 'parenting is not a quality that someone does, or does not, possess, but is a relationship that responds to fluctuations in other relationships' (Reder and Lucey 1995, p.13). In other words, it is not a free-standing 'skill' that exists independently of context and environment. When talking about parenting skills and styles (and, indeed, about sending people to 'parenting classes') this needs to be borne in mind.

The degree to which the necessary elements of parenting can be provided, then, rests on a number of factors, not the least of which is the extent to which parents' own needs either have been met in childhood, or are being met in the present (Howe *et al.* 1999; Reder and Duncan 1999). There is, then, a dynamic occurring in relation to both past and present relationships, and between the internal and the external world. Parenting, then, is not a static activity since it requires adaptation and change, reflexivity, evaluation and analysis. It is this fluidity which needs to be understood and which will require an equally fluid response from practitioners, rather than the application of what Woodcock (forthcoming) has identified as 'static notions of parenting'. Just because a parent may be 'good' or 'bad' at parenting at some point does not mean that this will be the case for all time. Some people are better with children at different developmental stages; life cycle events may affect parents' capacity to function, circumstances may change and stresses and strains may be ameliorated or exacerbated.

The social, political, historical and cultural context of parenting is also significant and will change over time (Parton 1997). Implicit in many debates surrounding parenting are certain assumptions about its 'naturalness' – what Sheppard refers to as the 'myth of biological motherhood' (Sheppard 2000, p.41). Traditionally, it has been seen to be instinctive, innate and something that we will do spontaneously, faced with the responsibility of a child. It is also probably the only complex adult task we do for which we do not undertake any formal advanced training whatsoever. These assumptions have been seen as particularly pervasive in relation to 'mothering' since, when we talk about 'parenting', this is often what we really mean (Kearney 1994; Sheppard 2000; Woollett and Phoenix 1991). By the same token issues of culture are very significant in relation to parenting. This is not just about race and ethnicity but also to do with socio-economic culture and the individual cultures that evolve in families (Ryan 2000). All these elements have resonance for parenting in general but additional issues also arise where there is parental substance misuse. It is to these that we now turn.

Parenting, gender and culture

Women and men are treated differently when it comes to issues of childcare, child welfare and child protection (Ammerman *et al.* 1999; Buckley 2000; Daniel and Taylor 2001; O'Hagan 1997; Ryan 2000). Research into social work practice in child and family settings suggests that mothers are still expected to 'protect' children, irrespective of any prevailing circumstances, and are seen as axiomatically better and more 'appropriate' carers than fathers (Farmer and Owen 1998). In addition, rigid and essentially middle-class ideas about men, women and children are still clearly in operation, with scant regard paid to the impact of power differentials and other differences on the family dynamics (Featherstone 1997).

Alongside this are the additional assumptions about race and culture. Stereotypes still abound in relation to gender roles and relationships in black and Asian families, quite apart from the range of potential misattributions that can be attached to families of other ethnic origins (Banks 2001; Patel 2000). Banks draws attention to specific assumptions based on the 'strong, Black, African-Caribbean mother' able to cope with anything, without support, the 'quiet but able Asian mother, who is (mis)perceived as following good cultural expectations about childcare when she is not', and last, but not least 'avoidant, domineering, absent fathers' (Banks 2001, p.144). By the same token, there are assumptions made in relation to families of dual heritage and Jewish, Irish, rural or traveller communities. Assumptions about substance use in various cultures are also prevalent. As Patel (2000) points out, culture may neither provide the protective shield against the scourge of drug or alcohol use that might be (stereotypically) assumed nor, by the same token, promote it.

Culture, of course, does not simply relate to the constellation of factors associated with ethnicity. Ryan (2000) highlights the importance of paying attention to what she calls 'socio-economic' culture within families, so that assumptions based on this do not get in the way of exploring gender roles and responsibilities in relation to parenting. This relates not just to who does what in terms of work or childcare, but also to who wants whom to do what.

Does the mother really want the father to be more involved or are there risks attached to this in terms of autonomy and power? Are fathers really excluding themselves or are they being excluded? Does high involvement in childcare spring from desire or necessity due to unemployment? All these are critical questions which will need to be addressed in any exploration of parenting processes quite apart from the context of substance abuse and the role it may play.

Mothers on trial: the blame game

Many commentators have observed a tendency towards 'mother blaming' within clinical childcare practice and research (see for example Buckley 2000; Caplan and Hall-McCorquodale 1985; Chess 1982; Farmer and Owen 1995, 1998; Phares 1997; Sheppard 2001) seeing it as 'an entrenched part of intervention' (Farmer and Owen 1998, p.559). These assumptions also pervade the received view of mothers who abuse substances (Kearney 1994; Klee 1998).

Mothers continue to be seen as the caring guardians of their families' health and welfare; substance-misusing mothers challenge that ideal image and tend to provoke punitive responses. As Kearney observes: 'The image of the bad mother is a terrible, unspeakable notion; a mother using drugs is a clash of values affecting society's sense of emotional and moral security' (Kearney 1994, p.6).

Different types of judgements are made about women who are parents and abuse substances from those made about men (see for example Ettore 1992; Hepburn 2000; Klee 1998; Klee et al. 1998, 2001; Kroll 1997). Such women, in the words of Mary Hepburn, are seen as 'bottom of the pile'. When women who abuse drugs and alcohol become pregnant they are placed in a category that is even lower than this (Hepburn 2000).

Because of the negative stereotypes surrounding maternal substance misuse, many women try to remain hidden, frightened that their children will be removed if their substance use is revealed (Harbin and Murphy 2000). Pregnant users fear pre-birth case conferences and the immediate removal of their baby and these fears often keep women away from services which they assume will be judgemental, hostile and unhelpful (Ford and Hepburn 1997; Hepburn 2000; Klee et al. 2001). Because they stay away from services further negative assumptions are then made about them – after all how can any responsible mother-to-be fail to use prenatal services and be a good person? In other words, they find themselves in a double bind – damned if they do and damned if they don't. The irony is that research has shown that women show a good behaviour modification response during pregnancy so that if professionals can gain access to them there is a good chance that risk can be lessened through management of drug use, reducing consumption and controlling drug and alcohol use that may be out of control. Hepburn (2000) has found that most pregnant substance misusers desperately want to do the best for their babies and that setting achievable goals which promote self-esteem and minimise risk of failure is extremely effective. In addition seeing drug use as one of many social problems rather than out there on its own helps to place the women's lives and experiences in context so that, rather than being treated and labelled as drug or alcohol misusers, they are seen as people with special or particular needs. As we have already suggested, substance use is part of the complex pattern of economic factors, social deprivation and exclusion to which many women, by virtue simply of gender, are exposed.

In the shadows: what about fathers?

When it comes to social work intervention in families, men become shadowy figures, lurking just out of sight (Daniel and Taylor 2001; Jones 1994). They are invisible in social services' waiting rooms and in family centres; probation offices and prisons, however, are full of them as are contact centres and the offices of the Child and Family Court Advisory and Support Service (CAFCASS). Researchers who attempt to include fathers in family-focused studies have little success even with samples of two-parent families where the fathers are ostensibly more available than they are in lone-parent households (Phares 1997). Practitioners have also been found to exclude or avoid fathers even when they are part of the parenting couple and are responsible for the child abuse which has brought them to the notice of social services (Buckley 2000). In her overview of child protection research findings, Ryan (2000) found that attention rapidly appeared to shift onto the mother, excluding the father. Farmer and Owen (1995) found that by this means fathers guilty of abuse were thus enabled to 'opt out' of both responsibility and any work that was going on. The only circumstances in which fathers take centre stage are as abusers, perpetrators, deserters, cads and bounders. This suggests that a process occurs in the exclusion of men from social welfare services that needs to be examined and explored. Social welfare practice with fathers, as Daniel and Taylor (2001) observe, also needs to change dramatically.

Fathers' inaccessibility, compared with mothers, and the fact that children who come to the attention of child welfare services are almost always in the care of their mothers are often offered as explanations for the absence of fathers in childcare and child protection research (Crittenden and Ainsworth 1989; Farmer and Owen 1998; Miles 1991; Phares 1992). However, as O'Hagan (1997) points out,

> men are highly significant in child protection and are likely to exert a major influence on the quality of care provided for the child and on the degree of risk to which the child may be exposed. (O'Hagan 1997, p.27)

It is important to remember, however, that this influence could work positively as well as negatively. Exclusion could undermine any efforts being made including harm reduction strategies in relation to substance use, safer childcare practices and increased family support. Inclusion, however, has been seen to have various benefits including acting as a protective factor in terms of substance misuse. This is certainly borne out by Klee's study of drug-using parents, in which many of the substance-misusing mothers emphasise the father's role in supporting them and caring for the children (Klee *et al.* 1998).

If social workers avoid fathers the consequences can be significant for the mother, the child and the management of the case (O'Hagan 1997). Excluding the father may set up suspicions of collusion and secrecy which may exacerbate any behaviour that is causing concern. A lone mother is then essentially left to face the music. It is she who will be monitored, assessed and judged; meanwhile the partner is marginalised, just out of the agency's sight, yet very much there in the wings and able to exert influence, sensing he is being avoided or ignored. This impedes the gathering of clear and accurate information that has a direct bearing on the child's welfare. An additional and critical consequence of excluding or avoiding the father can be summed up in this way: 'if that important, official person isn't able to challenge the man who is abusing me – worse still keeps avoiding the man – what is going to happen to me? '(O'Hagan 1997, p.36).

Although the context for this is abuse, its resonance for other situations which pose a risk to children is obvious.

Parenting and substance misuse in context

Implicit in the discussion so far is that parenting is an activity requiring considerable skill and application, as well as a range of personal qualities, including patience, tolerance, understanding, consistency and physical stamina. All this can easily be undermined by a range of factors, as Rutter (1974) has observed:

> Good parenting requires certain permitting circumstances. There must be the necessary life opportunities and facilities. When these are lacking even the best parents may find it difficult to exercise these skills. (Rutter 1974, cited in Department of Health 2000b p.10)

The range of variables which can affect parenting on both an individual and a structural level are what Belsky and Vondra (1989) have identified as the multiple determinants of parenting. What they offer is an ecological model that groups these determinants into *characteristics of the parent, characteristics of the child* and *sources of stress and support in the wider environment*. These can operate at individual, historical, social and circumstantial levels. In other words, personality and characteristics, personal biography – including own childhood experiences and physical and mental health – and relationships with partners, friends and family, will all have an impact on parenting behaviour. A crucial determinant is seen to be the parents' own 'internal working model' – an inner sense of their own value derived from experiences with parents, carers and others, particularly in relation to the way in which their needs were met, and the trustworthiness and availability of attachment figures (Howe *et al.* 1999; see also Chapter 6). Different internal working models will affect parents' own attachment behaviour in relation to their children (Reder and Lucey 1995; Woodcock forthcoming). In addition certain wider issues, such as employment, finance and knowledge about child development will also play a significant part (Department of Health 2000b). As both Will Self and 'Julie', quoted at the beginning of this chapter, illustrate, parents can demonstrate considerable insight into the impact of these factors on their parenting and recognise that they are not meeting their children's needs as well as either they might, or they would wish to. Critically, parents' ability to accept responsibility for their own behaviour and acknowledge its impact on relationships and quality of life are significant factors in assessing potential for change (Reder and Lucey 1995).

Psychopharmacology is clearly beyond our scope in this book. However, in order to understand the impact of substance misuse on parenting, some understanding of the physical and psychological effects of drugs and alcohol is essential. In addition it is important to appreciate the impact of both withdrawal and the stress caused by lack of the substance or issues to do with obtaining it. In Appendix 1 we offer an overview of the main drug groups, including alcohol, together with their likely impact and after-effects. Although we tend to talk generally of substance misuse, alcohol has a different impact to drug use. Moreover, the type of drug used will also cause a number of different reactions and responses. The reason for the substance use is also a significant factor.

First, though, some core points need to be made. Not everyone who uses substance A behaves in manner B. Even if some do behave in manner B at times, it is the frequency and pattern of this behaviour – assuming it is in some way antithetical to 'good enough parenting' – that is significant, together with any additional consequences that might also have an adverse effect on safety, domestic and social harmony or lifestyle. In other words parents could drink excessively on a regular basis, but as long as they did so in a way that did not impact on their children – when they were asleep or when the parents went out or when the children were at school for example – this would not, in itself, pose a child protection problem although it may present a health risk to the adult concerned. Problems would ensue if this drinking pattern posed risks such as lack of supervision in the evenings, inability to get children to school or collect them or general domestic and social chaos. Provided there was another adult providing oversight, this might not be problematic either. Much substance misuse is episodic, not consistent or contained within a particular space. Binge drinking or drug use, however, can cause serious lapses in concentration, when safety measures and child supervision are often cast to the winds. This type of usage can be particularly difficult to assess and we will return to the problems in relation to this in due course.

The difficulty is, of course, that much substance misuse takes place in the context of stresses and strains of daily life, exacerbated by social pressures, experiences of discrimination, low self-esteem, anxiety and depression. The behaviour itself can also cause friction in partnerships and if one of the consequences is parental conflict or domestic violence, then the picture changes dramatically. Indeed, as we have already seen, violence is the most significant variable for the well-being of children and the combination of this with any other factor – whether it be substance misuse, criminal behaviour, or mental illness – increases the risk of harm to children considerably.

As has already been suggested, the same substance will affect different people in different ways and will also affect the same individual differently, depending on a number of factors. These have been identified by Cleaver *et al.* (1999) as:

- current mental state

- experience and/or tolerance of the drug

- expectations

- personality

- how the substance is taken (orally, via injecting, smoking, sniffing)

- quantity of substance taken.

These are all critical in relation to the overall impact of the substance and its effects on behaviour. As Cleaver and colleagues go on to observe:

> Only by knowing the possible behavioural outcomes for parents with these kind of problems can we begin to identify the impact which this may have on children. (Cleaver *et al.* 1999, pp.23–24)

It is the *way* that stresses interact that is of particular significance and to assess this involves gaining a detailed picture of how patterns of misuse affect parenting capacity. This, as Reder and Duncan (1999, p.6) suggest, is an *interactional* or systemic model, one characteristic of which is that risk is seen in the context of interactions between family members and the informal and the formal systems that surround them.

Substance misuse and parenting behaviour

As Swadi has observed:

> Substance misuse affects parenting capacity directly through its effects on mental state and judgment ability or, indirectly, through the parents' lifestyle or the adverse social environment in which such parents live. (Swadi 1994, p.237)

Within this context, then, attention will now be turned to the ways in which substance misuse can affect aspects of parenting, at both a direct and an indirect level. Incorporating the dimensions of parenting capacity and environmental domains mentioned earlier, we have grouped these effects into two kinds of consequences.

Practical, psychological and emotional consequences

These relate to the impact on family functioning and family relationships, including attachment and separation, parenting skills and styles, and to levels of risk, including neglect, abuse and potential hazards, as well as parents' perceptions of their children and control of emotions.

Social Consequences

These relate to the impact on living conditions and standards, work and finances, and to social life and levels of social isolation and social exclusion.

In separating consequences into these categories, we acknowledge that there is a continual interplay between them. There is also overlap between these themes and those to be highlighted in Chapters 6 and 7 in relation to children, since some of the dynamics will apply to children and parents alike (for example, the impact of role reversal and issues of denial and secrecy). Some themes will, therefore, be revisited in the context of children's lives.

Practical, psychological and emotional consequences of substance misuse on parenting

There is a constellation of practical, psychological and emotional effects that can be caused by substance misuse which have a significant impact on all the dimensions of the parenting capacity domain as well as the 'family functioning' dimension of the environmental domain. Indeed, many parents are all too aware of these effects and their consequences, in terms of what they are unable to provide for their children and the impact on their skills as parents (Barnard and Barlow forthcoming; Elliott and Watson 1998, 2000; Hogan and Higgins 2001; Klee *et al.* 1998; McKeganey *et al.* 2001). As one parent observed:

> No it [drug use] doesn't make you a better mum, it makes you worse...you look after them and everything but you're still wondering...all the money

you're spending on that, you're thinking what you could have bought for the kids.(Klee *et al.* 1998, p.17)

However, there is also another complex link between substance misuse and the provision of good parenting, in that many parents felt that usage affected parenting for the better, as these three comments illustrate.

'I'm a much more capable mother on whizz with them, I talk to them for ages'; 'I'm nicer with her'; 'I've got three kids and it makes me cope better'. (Parents quoted in Klee *et al.* 1998, pp.16–17)

Some parents reported more energy, patience, resilience and the capacity to cope more effectively, although this was in many ways related to whether the drug use was chaotic or stable (Bates *et al.* 1999). Others were conscious of the fact that they were happier using drugs although 'it's false happiness, I know that. It's a false caring for them' (McKeganey *et al.* 2001, p.11). This mother was also aware that the contrast between her drug-induced happiness and her mood when coming down was a source of considerable confusion for her children. A number of parents were conscious of the fact that chidren adapted their behaviour according to their knowledge and awareness of the parent's reactions to being either 'up' or 'down':

She knew not to go near me in the morning till I'd had me foil, then mammy would play. In the morning the sickness was the worst… I'd just be telling her to get away. Once I'd had the gear into me I'd be the best mother on earth. (Mother of 4-year-old girl in Hogan and Higgins 2001, p.22)

What has to be considered, then, in this context is the role that the substance plays in the parenting task – what Elliott and Watson (2000, p.30) refer to as 'the deep association between drugs and coping'.This may include managing the pressures and tensions of bringing up children, providing a 'reward' to compensate for the demands of childcare or helping to manage unresolved issues resurrected by being a parent. In addition, the substance may also have a role in managing relationship tensions with the other parent, partners or family, or in keeping difficult feelings, depression or other types of mental health problem at bay as well as helping to alleviate pressures and stress caused by day-to-day living (Elliott and Watson 2000). What is significant to consider, then, is the importance attached to the substance misuse, its role in behaviour and the overall effects that it has on all those in its orbit.

Substance use, childcare and risk management

For many parents, risk management was a significant issue, highlighting some of the practicalities of juggling what Elliott and Watson (1998, p.42) describe as 'two careers: being a parent and being a drug user'. Parents identified different risks for children of different ages, with safety, supervision and alternative care provision (usually by family or friends, for the more fortunate) being an issue for younger children and awareness of parental behaviour being more of a concern with older ones. An additional issue was how to manage the risks posed by drug-using friends who came to the home, coupled with the dangers of exposure to other aspects of the drug subculture. Many parents developed strategies for managing risks which involved trying hard to drink or use drugs only when the children were not around, or, if they were in the house, to do it secretly. The effectiveness of this strategy, however, varied.

> I always said I would never jag in front of him…but see if it came to it and he walked into the toilet when I was putting that in ma arm I wouldn't pull it out. (Parent quoted in McKeganey *et al.* 2001, p.10)

> He might have spotted me once or twice…when you're on drugs you always slip up. He might have seen me injecting once. He might have barged into the room once… If you're using five times daily of course you drop your guard. (Father of 8-year-old boy quoted in Hogan and Higgins 2001, p.15)

Elaborate steps were also taken to ensure that supplies were not around longer than necessary, mindful of children's curiosity and the dangers of accidental discovery. Notwithstanding, parents were realistic about the extent to which some dangers would be harder to avoid – the chance discovery of needles or methadone, the accidental ingestion of alcohol or pills. Other parents realised that, despite attempts at secrecy, the 'before' and 'after' parent was inevitably bound to cause curiosity in children whose powers of perception were rarely underestimated. As one mother observed 'he sees a difference when I've not had them and when I have had them, so that's when he's aware' (Elliott and Watson 1998, p.44). Alcohol-misusing parents were equally conscious of this (Laybourn *et al.* 1996).

Guilt, shame and remorse

Mindful of the manifest consequences for their children, guilt, shame and remorse were regularly expressed by parents. This father had been forced to reflect on the impact of his drinking:

> Father: (struggling with emotion throughout) 'I'd say it's held Donna back quite a lot (long pause). I'd do everything completely differently... In a way I've destroyed her'. (Laybourn *et al.* 1996, p.69)

This mother also had had to confront the reality of her drug misuse:

> it was one night when I'd sold all the furniture...the children were really starving and instead of running around trying to get them food I was running about, trying to get my drugs. In the end I think the shame caught up with me and the guilt. (McKeganey *et al.* 2001, pp.7–8)

The extent to which these feelings of remorse translated into change, however, varied. Remorse could also have a variety of consequences, from using more drugs to deal with the guilt, to overcompensating, spoiling the child or making supreme efforts to make things right and provide the child with everything that the parents had been denied (Aldridge 2000). Denial of the impact of substance use was, however, also common (Laybourn *et al.* 1996).

For many the onset of parenting or the realisation of the implications for parenting provided a strong motivation to change substance use behaviour (Bates *et al.* 1999; Elliott and Watson 1998; Harbin and Murphy 2000; Hepburn 2000). It also increased determination to do a good job because of the risk of the child's removal. As one parent in the study by Bates *et al.* remarked:

> Being on drugs and knowing that you're under the microscope...the way they [professionals] see parents and kids and that, it makes you more aware, it makes you try a little bit harder than normal parents. (Bates *et al.* 1999, p.76)

The substance use not only had an impact on these areas but also played a role in relation to managing them. The role of the substance use at various stages of the parenting process, then, is an important area to explore, with significant implications for assessment, as we shall see in Chapter 10.

Family functioning and relationships

> Once people start to drink or take drugs inappropriately or unsafely, the structure and functioning of the family as a system of relationships is affected. (Velleman 1996, p.235)

It is widely acknowledged that substance misuse can cause serious disruption to relationships and family dynamics (Tunnard 2002). This can operate at a number of levels. The most obvious is the impact of substance misuse on the parenting couple. Velleman draws attention to the potential for communication problems which can often result in conflict, discord, overall family distress and possible violence and abuse (Velleman 1996;Velleman and Orford 1999). Often such problems arise as a result of denial. Even when it is apparent that the substance abuse is affecting the family as a whole, as well as individual members, the person with the problem may resolutely refuse to engage in any dialogue about it, causing a range of reactions in children and generating frustration and anger in the non-using partner. Another scenario is presented by the potential for substance use to encourage things to be said that might be better left unsaid and cannot subsequently be taken back. The final consequence for communication is the way in which the topic of substance use dominates all dialogue. As Velleman (1996) observes, both the emotional quality – from intimacy and companionship to confrontation and conflict – as well as the content are affected. The ultimate consequences of this range of problems is separation or divorce, with all the distress, upheaval and uncertainty that this can involve.

As we have already suggested, there are links between substance misuse and domestic violence although they are complex, in the sense that there is a 'chicken and egg' element that is central to any debate about this issue. In other words, substance misuse can develop in women, for example, as a response to domestic violence or be a reaction to earlier traumas in life which have a violent element (Farmer and Owen 1995; Hester et al. 2000; Velleman 1993).

In studies of parental drug misuse three themes emerged as significant in terms of parenting capacity and family functioning (Hogan 1997; Hogan and Higgins 2001; Klee et al. 1998; McKeganey et al. 2001). First, the most common was that parents had less involvement with children – 'I know we were there 24 hours...but we weren't really, we were stoned' (Hogan and Higgins 2001, p.23). One mother summed this up very eloquently, admitting, 'Your whole life revolves around the gear…that's your main thought', while another confessed, 'I know I am not able to give one hundred per cent to my children… I had to have my fix… I lost out a lot on their childhood… The most important thing they missed out on was their mother. I was a junkie first and a mother second' (Hogan 1997, p.28). By the same token, there was evidence in other studies that parents showed poor awareness of children's needs and reduced sensitivity to risk of damage at all levels (Bates *et al.* 1999). This has obvious implications for parents' capacity to be emotionally available for their children. As we have already suggested, the substance itself may be used as a way of negotiating attachment issues in both child and adult relationships. In other words, substance use may be a way of keeping others at a distance, managing dependency needs that may be difficult, coping with partner dissatisfaction or dealing with conflict.

The second theme identified was increased irritability with children. This was largely connected to withdrawal or the effects of drugs or alcohol wearing off which would cause feelings of physical illness. Parents described feeling cranky and frustrated or snappy, even though some believed that the drug was making them more relaxed.

> if I was to go two days without it, I'd take it out on my kids. I would turn around and say 'it's your fault I've not got drugs'. If they moaned for the least wee thing, I'd jump down their throats. I'd not hit them but I knew in my own mind I shouldn't have been doing that. (McKeganey *et al.* 2001, p.11)

Some parents, however, did confess to hitting children and often interactions were characterised by harshness.

The third theme, already referred to, was the atmosphere of secrecy that seemed to pervade the family as a consequence of the substance use (Barnard and Barlow forthcoming; Brisby *et al.* 1997; ChildLine 1997; Laybourn *et al.* 1996). What emerges from many of the studies is a series of images of angry, irritated, scared or bewildered children being shut out of rooms or told to go away while mysterious activities take place, or accidentally stumbling upon adults doing something that is subsequently explained in a way that does not completely make sense. This creates what Barnard and Barlow (forthcoming) describe as 'a world of mirrors where nothing is as it seems', leaving children feeling confused, rejected and burdened with secret knowledge. Although parents described how they tried to hide their drug or alcohol use from the children, this served only to raise anxieties and suspicions. As a consequence, even when they were not using or drinking, children were reluctant to trust that this was so. This then affected general levels of trust between parents and children.

Rhythms of family life

Substance misuse affects the shape of the family and its everyday rhythms due to its impact on rituals and daily functioning (McKeganey et al. 2001; Velleman 1996). Special occasions are often under threat as a result of the impact of drug- or alcohol-related behaviour, roles change, and routines are upset or abandoned:

> events, like collecting a child from school or serving an evening meal become fraught with uncertainty. Anything which requires planning…often becomes an impossibility. (Brisby et al. 1997, p.10)

Although many parents resolutely denied that they were unreliable or forgetful, this is a dimension of family functioning with far-reaching consequences particularly for security, safety and overall stability.

Lifestyle and 'chaos' theory

Much has been made of the lifestyle so often associated with substance misuse, with its often 'chaotic' quality affecting many of the aspects of parenting considered so far (Barnard 1999). This 'chaotic' aspect is of course more likely to be visible in some sectors of the community than others, particularly if access to childcare, family support and help with the running of the home are available to disguise the internal emotional chaos that might be being experienced.

The impact of lifestyle rather than the substance misuse per se has been seen to have considerable consequences for parenting (Burns et al. 1996; Cleaver et al. 1999; Coleman and Cassell 1995; Hogan 1997; Sloan 1998; Swadi 1994). Particular problems arise if there are frequent changes of accommodation, if children are left with unsuitable caretakers and if routines are either irregular or non-existent. Of course, a chaotic lifestyle can mean different things to different people and what may seen chaotic to some may not do so to others. What is significant here is the level of predictability that can be assumed and relied on. In other words, even if tea is not always at 5 p.m., knowing that there is food in the house and that tea will occur within an hour or so of that time, as opposed to wondering whether it will appear at all, is what will make a difference.

Parents interviewed in many of the studies also made a distinction between chaotic substance *use* and the chaotic *effects* of substance use, emphasising that the two were not necessarily linked. Although use could be chaotic at times, this did not necessarily mean that domestic life would totally disintegrate. In other words, substance misuse and a chaotic lifestyle were not automatically linked.

'Chaotic use' of course has a wide interpretation. In the SCODA guidelines it is defined as:

> the unrestrained use of different drugs in combination…sometimes with alcohol, or bingeing…until the supply runs out or exhaustion or heavy intoxication prevents further use. Chaotic drug use implies…an adverse effect on user's health and welfare and the user may have little regard for the way their behaviour affects others. (SCODA 1997, p.35)

According to this description, chaotic use would invariably have a number of implications for child safety and lifestyle, unless protective factors were available in the form of non-using partners or others who could offer support during such periods.

A chaotic lifestyle also makes it hard for professionals and parents to keep in touch – indeed part of the chaotic response is flight from professional contact (Reder and Duncan 1999). By the same token, the impact of an alternative lifestyle, focused on activities associated with the procurement and use of substances, within a social group with this shared interest also needs to be considered. This will be discussed in more detail later.

Role reversal and role confusion

Many parents with substance problems were conscious of the fact that their children were sometimes called upon to take on adult responsibilities beyond their years and this has also been a focus of concern for many professionals (Bates *et al.* 1999; Brisby *et al.* 1997; Coleman and Cassell 1995). At times an over-intense attachment between parent and 'responsible' child could develop, leading effectively to 'role reversal', where the child became the parent and vice versa (Klee *et al.* 1998). Such relationships were characterised by a tendency to 'look to their children for emotional support'

(Reder and Lucey 1995, p.7). Examples included an 8-year-old boy who accompanied his mother, who had a drink problem, to have a termination and then supported her emotionally in its aftermath (Brisby *et al.* 1997), and a 6-year-old girl who regularly took her alcohol-dependent father to psychiatric appointments to ensure he found his way there and was on time (Coleman and Cassell 1995). This father was all too aware of the extent of the role reversal in his relationship with his daughter – 'She was the parent and I was the breadwinner. It was as simple as that. Being a drug addict is a 24 hour job, out robbing all the time, you're out all the time' (Hogan and Higgins 2001, p.10).

For other parents, it was simply a question of expedience, leading to children becoming 'over-responsible' when parental substance use prevented them from carrying out domestic or childcare duties. Some defiantly defended decisions such as keeping children at home to help with housework and childcare, despite the fact that they were missing school. Others, aware of the extent to which reliance on a child was inappropriate, expressed regret and remorse:

> Amanda used to have to babysit for Suzy when she was little while I just nipped out for ten minutes. She was only seven, never mind having to look after a six month old baby. I shouldn't have done that – anything could have happened. (Klee *et al.* 1998, p.30)

> He was doing everything for himself just like growing up at four years old…he was having to look after his wee brother he was sort of playing mummy and daddy…he'd get up in the morning and make his bottle because mummy and daddy are lying on the bed sparked from the night before. (McKeganey *et al.* 2001, p.9)

Parenting skills and styles

There is broad agreement that problems for children occur when parenting style 'fails to compensate for the inevitable deficiencies that become manifest during the course of the twenty years or so it takes to bring up a child' (Department of Health 1995, p.19). There will inevitably be bad times for some children – family problems, periods of neglect, episodes of abuse – but provided these are interspersed with periods when they are loved and cared for and things go well, the outcome could still be good. The most detrimental parenting style is an approach characterised by high criticism and low warmth in which 'negative incidents accumulate as if to remind a child that he or she is unloved' (Department of Health 1995, p.19). This creates an emotionally neglectful environment, with the potential for additional types of abuse to take place. Substance misuse and its connection with the apathy and listlessness associated either with its after-effects or ongoing effects, can result in inconsistent, inattentive and erratic parenting, characterised by confusing or contradictory messages and puzzling communication, as well as variable levels of care and conflictual relationships with children (Barnard 1999; Cleaver *et al.* 1999).

Research into the parenting attitudes and styles of substance-misusing parents yields equivocal but thought-provoking results, although it is difficult to gain a clear picture. This is due to differences in both research approaches and definitions of parenting, as well as the fact that most research is focused on mothers rather than either fathers or both parents, and is largely American. In studies of drug-misusing mothers, Colten (1980) found that the major difference between what were termed 'addicted' mothers and a control group was related to the addicted mothers' levels of self-esteem as adequate parents and their fears that their children would grow up to be addicts or criminals. Bauman and Dougherty (1983), however, using Baumrind's Parental Attitudes Questionnaire (Baumrind 1974), found no differences in parenting attitudes between a group of methadone-maintained mothers and a non-using group. They did, though, find differences in parenting styles and behaviours, with the substance- misusing mothers more inclined towards behaviour that could be seen as rejecting and avoidant and characterised by threats, control, harshness and disapproval. This is linked to findings by Wellisch and Steinberg (1980) who also found a tendency in such mothers to over-control children, excluding any outside advice or involvement. Kandel (1990) noted low levels of warmth in mothers, although, interestingly, found that drug use among fathers improved parenting in some respects, in that levels of punishment were lower and involvement in activities with children was greater. Hien and Honeyman (2000) explored the link between substance use and maternal aggression in their study of American mothers on low incomes who misused drugs. They found more severe levels of discipline and more inclination to punish. However, these tendencies were related to being involved in violent relationships and using avoidant-coping strategies.

In relation to parenting styles and behaviours in alcohol-misusing parents, some research suggests that both mothers and fathers tended to use what Baumrind (1974) has identified as an authoritarian parenting style, characterised by use of power and discipline without logic or explanation and resonant with the high criticism/low warmth style discussed above (Baumrind 1974; Krauthamer 1979). Ironically, parenting styles associated with laxity and indifference have also been noted and have also had adverse effects (Brisby et al. 1997; Laybourn et al. 1996). Most studies, however, suggest that inconsistency in styles presents the most difficulties, with parents conscious of being reasonable one minute and irrational the next and children feeling confused by sudden changes in behaviour, attitudes and concern with discipline. High levels of conflict and violence between both parents and parents and children are also seen as significant in affecting parenting styles and behaviour (ChildLine 1997; Velleman 1993, 1996; Velleman and Orford 1999).

Parenting skills and styles can be undermined by a number of factors. Low self-esteem and depression have both been shown to have an adverse impact on parenting (see for example Bifulco and Moran 1998; Sheppard 2001) and several studies, based on work with substance-misusing mothers, have found a link between these three variables (see for example Kelley 1992; William-Peterson et al. 1994). Another significant factor in parenting styles relates to learned behaviour. In other words, if individuals have been badly parented, their own parenting capacity may be affected and this may undermine their confidence in the role (Barnard 1999; Bays 1990). However, transgenerational parenting problems cannot always be explained in such simple terms and much depends on the parent's internal working model.

Neglect, maltreatment, risks and hazards

> I stopped loving my kids...my drugs were more important than my kids...
> I wasn't hitting them... I was just neglecting them. I wasn't feeding them
> regular, I wasn't washing them regular. (Klee et al. 1998, p.18)

There are various dangers associated with neglect. On a practical level, it affects the home environment, leading to poor standards of hygiene with attendant health risks, irregular supplies of food and general material deprivation (lack of appropriate clothes, furniture, bedding and other basics). Inconsistent regard for safety and levels of surveillance can also lead to a higher risk of accidents of various kinds, due to inattention (Alison 2000; Cleaver et al. 1999). In addition, substance-related accidents, as a result of parents' failure to keep supplies out of reach, have been identified as a concern among both parents and professionals (Bates *et al.* 1999; Hogan 1997). Careless disposal of syringes, bottles and needles and children's tendency to copy parents can have fatal consequences: 'I had a little girl and she died through drinking methadone', said one mother (Bates *et al.* 1999, p.26). Small children are at greater risk not only for obvious reasons but also because parents often assume that seeing drug-related behaviour, in particular, is not damaging as it would not be understood for what it was. As one mother confessed:

> I did use in front of her when she was younger thinking she didn't cop but she did. I'm not going to lie. When she was about three or four she put a piece of string round her arm and started tapping her arm, mimicking me. (Hogan and Higgins 2001, p.15)

The physical effects on parents of certain drugs may pose particular health risks or hazards. Possible loss of consciousness caused by substance misuse creates the potential for children being placed at physical risk unless there is another adult around to take over supervision. If left alone, children might find themselves in situations which they may have no way of handling – injury, illness or fire, for example. Risks also spring from being left either unattended or with unsuitable people. As one parent confessed:

> you'd want to go out...so you'd leave them with anybody. I never left them on their own...but I left them with people who weren't suitable, really. (Mother quoted in Klee *et al.* 1998, p.14)

Part of the reason for this, according to this parent, was the effect of the amphetamines she took which caused hyperactivity – 'you want people to hurry up...kids can't and you can't be bothered sitting down and talking to them, like you are supposed to' (Klee *et al.* 1998, p.14). This 'speediness' often led to things being done much too quickly, with the concomitant disregard for risk or failure to observe hazards; errors could also be caused by tiredness, as the effects wore off.

There are also risks from abuse of different kinds. These could range from dealers threatening children with violence, to ensure that a parent's drug debts were paid, to actual injury:

> My eldest son had bruises on the side of his face and I think it was my partner who had hit him, but I was too out of my face to notice. (Mother quoted in McKeganey *et al.* 2001, p.12)

This underlines the impact of substance misuse on a parent's capacity to protect children from harm. This mother's failure to notice must have conveyed a powerful message to her child. In addition, as we shall see, children who may become the focus of substance-induced paranoia or hallucinations may also be at risk of significant harm.

Although many parents took pride in the fact that they were able to provide physical care and guard against some of the obvious risks, they did not always appreciate – or perhaps feel able to acknowledge – that neglect could occur at other levels or accept that their children 'were missing out on attention, affection or emotional security' (Laybourn et al. 1996, p.52).

Criminal behaviour

The illegal status of many drugs often meant contact with an environment at best unsuitable and at worst dangerous for children (Barnard 1999; Klee 1998). Often parents confessed to turning to crime, including drug dealing, or to prostitution (with all its health risks and physical hazards) as an alternative way to finance drug use that they could not afford. This could have a number of consequences including involvement with a range of criminal behaviours which may expose the child to scenarios involving stress, the fear of and/or threat of drug-induced violent behaviour, drug-related activities or associated crimes (Hogan 1998; Hogan and Higgins 2001). The ultimate consequence for parents – imprisonment – with its implications for family breakdown, would also have far-reaching effects for the rest of the family. Whereas it was possible to shield and protect young children from exposure to such activities, the older that children became the more likely they were to become inadvertently involved in adults' behaviours and parents were all too aware of the fact that their children were increasingly likely to find them out.

Some parents, rather than cover up their behaviour, included their children in the substance-taking activity, involving them in fetching drink or pills. Others took the view that the children would not notice the comings and goings in the house, or be aware of the implications of certain behaviours (Klee 1998; Laybourn et al. 1996). Some children could also be involved in criminal activity either directly, as accessories to crimes such as shoplifting, or indirectly, by being made aware of the source of the families finances (Barnard 1999; McKeganey et al. 2001).

Distorted perceptions and emotional control

Hostile and aggressive behaviour, delusions, feelings of paranoia, self-harm and dramatic changers in mood and attitude have all been identified as aspects of chronic substance misuse (Coleman and Cassell 1995). It can also cause altered perceptions and hallucinations:

> I thought there was an aeroplane on the motorway, slammed me brakes on but there was nothing there…the second time, I was driving, I was awake but me mind must have gone. (Mother quoted in Klee *et al.* 1998, p.14)

There is also a danger of developing a distorted view of children, who can find themselves blamed for a range of circumstances that are nothing to do with them. This may be linked with unresolved issues in the parents' childhood histories or with emotional states in the present; whatever the reasons, children can be subjected to outbursts or accusations which can cause pain and distress both in the short and longer term (ChildLine 1997; Brisby *et al.* 1997; Brooks and Rice 1997). Emotional control has also been shown to be a casualty of substance misuse with frightening, confusing or violent behaviour deeply affecting children and sometimes placing them in physical danger (Laybourn *et al.* 1996; Reder and Duncan 1999).

The prevalence of low self-esteem in many chaotic drug-using parents has the potential to impact on parental mental health, particularly in relation to depression (Aldridge 2000). Klee *et al.* (1998), in their analysis of several samples of drug- and polydrug-using parents, also found a high incidence of depression and aggression. Although some parents were able to identify the risks posed by these strong feelings and either remove the children from range or self-medicate, in order to alleviate symptoms, these were not infallible sources of protection and this had significant implications for parenting.

Social consequences of substance misuse

Here we consider the wider aspects of the environmental domain in which parents and their children operate. In this context, parental substance misuse may have particular consequences for both the structural and the social aspects of the family's life.

Living conditions, work and finances

Substance misuse, particularly if the substance concerned is illegal, is often very expensive and this has obvious financial implications, except for the wealthy. It may be that drug or alcohol use has made employment more difficult to sustain; resources may be diverted away from the family budget, with food, clothing and household bills being sacrificed or housing being placed at risk (Coleman and Cassell 1995; SCODA 1997; Tunnard 2002). Conflicting demands may be especially acute in economically deprived families.

Although many parents were aware of the financial implications of substance misuse and what this may mean, in terms of what could be provided for their children, most struggled to ensure that at least provision of regular food was not affected, although attempts were not always successful (Bates *et al.* 1999).

Parents expressed considerable shame at the realisation that their children had been denied both basic necessities and some of the other material possessions which other children enjoy. They were also conscious of the way in which every aspect of domestic life could so easily spiral downwards into squalor: 'the kids are losing out, like tramps...it's dead scruffy...the kids are dead short, we don't give a shit, we're dead selfish' confessed one couple, presenting themselves for help (Klee *et al.* 1998, p.25). For others, however, maintaining standards in the home was seen as a priority, since evidence of squalor equalled risk of 'detection'. Indeed, as we have seen, some argued that substance use provided the energy to enable those very standards to be maintained, despite other demands and stresses.

Where there were adequate resources – at least one source of regular income and available and reliable childcare support – substance misuse could be sustained and supported without undue effects on finances and living conditions.

The community context: social life, social isolation and family support

> Some people may be able easily to explain to friends and neighbours that their partner has got a drinking or drug problem, but most people...find it an extraordinarily difficult thing to do: it is simply too shameful to admit. (Velleman 1996, p.236)

Even more difficult might be admitting that *you* are the one with the problem, and for many parents this was the crux of the matter. An individual's social life will often be significantly affected as a result of this shame, and the anxiety, secrecy and concealment it involves. Denial also features significantly. The substance use may lead to withdrawal from the social arena, for fear of detection or censure. Alternatively, the social world and the substance use become interwoven, so that the social circle narrows to include other users, but excludes contact with non-using friends, even though they might be a protective influence (SCODA 1997). The substance use can become what Brown (1988) has termed 'the central organising principle'. As she explains:

> In developing the concept of alcohol as the central organising principle... I outlined the development of a behavioural and thinking disorder. The primary focus becomes alcohol and the drinking behaviour while the primary cognitive focus is the denial of that behaviour...the drinking behaviour and its denial become the central organising principle for the alcoholic. (Brown 1988, p.33)

Everything becomes organised around procurement and use and the family's life is structured accordingly. Although Brown's application of this concept relates to alcohol, it has equal resonance for all substance misuse (see for example Brooks and Rice 1997).

Fear of exposure and the need for secrecy may have a range of effects on the family's social life and parents may have to manage the reactions of neighbours after inebriated gatherings, embarrassing behaviour or obvious signs of substance use in public. For many – professionals included – such behaviour induces alarm, apprehension and revulsion rather than unalloyed sympathy and concern.

In the study by Bates *et al.* (1999), the majority of parents had drug-using friends and some had *only* drug-using friends. The pattern of daily life, for some, revolved around interactions within this group and many parents were aware of the impact that this contact might have on the children. Although many took steps to ensure that drug use was never witnessed, slip-ups occurred and it was often difficult to shield children from the terminology and paraphernalia associated with the actual activity of using. Anxiety was also expressed about children overhearing discussions about AIDS or needles. There was also an awareness of the risks posed by various friends coming and going and that their behaviour may be unpredictable. Although some of these aspects were less relevant for parents who misused alcohol, there was still, in some studies, a sense of the social context of alcohol use, with the pub as the focal point for many and drinking with friends, either there or at home, the main social activity. The main difference of course, in the social context, is the extent to which drinking is socially endorsed and encouraged, in contrast to drug use.

One consequence of the social isolation that can flow from substance misuse is that families close in on themselves. Households become distanced from normal support systems, with parents too anxious to seek help in case children are taken into care (Coleman and Cassell 1995). Fear of disapproval from other family and friends can cause further retreat into a substance-using environment and culture, to the exclusion of a wider circle of social supports (Velleman 1993). There are also additional issues for families from cultures where there is a specific stigma associated with drug or alcohol misuse (Patel 2000; Tunnard 2002).

Parents' behaviour at school, influenced by inebriation, withdrawal, wariness or anxiety, may lessen opportunities to gain support from other parents. It may also reduce the chances of children being asked to other children's homes, thus impacting on the development of their social networks, with their potential for contributing essential protective factors (Coleman and Cassell 1995). Once childcare concerns are identified, however, parents can then run the risk of becoming doubly stigmatised as drug or alcohol users and as 'bad' parents. As Bates *et al.* (1999, p.79) observe, 'Most people in society distance themselves from drug users and child abusers – those that come into both categories form even more of a pariah group'.

Parents often appeared to be very aware of the dangers of their children being excluded from a proper social life, due to their behaviour. Many, as a result, made great efforts to ensure their children were accepted and linked in with community activities. One father felt intense guilt that his son's speech delay might be related to the fact that neighbouring parents were preventing their children from playing with him, due to drug use (Bates *et al.* 1999). Messages could be subtly transmitted about what could and could not be said outside the family, which often put children's loyalties to the test (Laybourn *et al.* 1996). Community rejection and exclusion from neighbourhood life often left vulnerable parents even more at risk, with drug-using mothers particularly affected (Cleaver *et al.* 1999; Hogan 1998; Klee *et al.* 2001). Velleman and Orford (1999), however, found very little evidence of the impact of social isolation on children of problem drinkers, either as children or as adults, when compared with a group of offspring of non-alcohol-misusing parents. They did, however, report more friendship difficulties, frequent feelings of embarrassment about their homes and a sense of being somehow 'apart' from others (Velleman and Orford 1999, p.145). This appears to suggest that something had taken place in the interaction between family and the outside world which had affected their sense of self.

Partners were often a source of social support as was the extended family, although for some, the opposite was true, with family rejecting the substance-using parent completely (Hogan 1997). Where there was family support, this was highly valued and became particularly crucial if there was a threat of family breakdown. This might be caused by imprisonment for substance-related crime, admission to hospital (as a result of substance-related illness or an overdose), a decision to enter a detoxification or rehabilitation facility, or the need for refuge, as a result of domestic violence.

Social exclusion

> Heavy end substance misuse is woven into social exclusion… In theory drug addiction can affect anyone without regard to race, class, gender or age. In practice drug addiction embraces a disproportionate number of the socially excluded… Put simply, addiction fills voids… Drug *use* may be an equal opportunity recruiter. Drug *addiction* is highly discriminatory. (Gilman 2000, p22–23, emphasis in original)

There is a critical dynamic between individual circumstances, social circumstances, substance misuse and the process by which individuals and families slip into the twilight category we refer to as the 'socially excluded'. This is characterised not only by poverty but also by a range of other disadvantages that all interact and merge together. These include unemployment, poor housing, 'drained' and untrusting communities where there is limited welfare capital and levels of both crime and fear. As we saw in Chapter 4, the 'voids' relate not only to the internal world but also to social and environmental contexts and to life opportunities, hopes and aspirations. Although Gilman's (2000) analysis is specifically related to drug use, there is clear resonance with chronic alcohol use, as the caseloads of social workers in deprived areas bear witness (Forrester 2000). The link between deprivation and substance use is also often confirmed by the still-favoured practice of placing families where there is substance misuse, who are often also prey to a range of other social problems, on so-called 'sink' estates (Lloyd 1998).

Caution must be exercised, however, in relation to making assumptions about the substance-misusing community, since, as Will Self and many others prove, substance misuse is no respecter of social position or class, although the implications for exclusion may be different and the voids to be filled may have different causes. There are (as we have seen) a number of strands that may significantly interact, but equally importantly, may need to be untangled. As Hogan (1998) points out:

> serious drug dependence problems are frequently associated with low socioeconomic status and socially disadvantaged living conditions. Failure to include an appropriately matched sample risks confounding parental drug use with socioeconomic status and precludes reaching meaningful conclusions about the separate effects of a drug using lifestyle and social deprivation. (Hogan 1998, p.615)

The needs of substance-misusing parents

> I wouldn't go...cause everyone who saw you there or going in there would think you were a junkie or summat...and the people who worked there might see us and think is she capable of looking after that child? (Mother quoted in Elliott and Watson 1998, p.55)

These intertwined fears of being stigmatised and judged, leading to the removal of children, tell us a great deal about why parents prefer to remain invisible to services, leading, in turn, to their children's invisibility. The needs of substance-misusing parents are not dissimilar from those of their children, as we shall see in Chapter 7. Many were 'hurting on the inside' (Laybourn et al. 1996) for a variety of reasons, not just in relation to their own issues, but also in relation to the impact of their behaviour on their children.

What parents needed most was to be considered as individuals 'in the round', for whom a range of issues may obtain which included the misuse of drugs or alcohol. This then involved looking beneath the stereotypes and labels at the person beneath. As Bates et al. (1999, p.79) confirm, 'those who misuse drugs, particularly if they are parents, are frequently treated in a stigmatic and discriminatory way'. This aspect is seen as particularly important as it affects attitudes to services and to the professionals who provide them. Addressing non-substance-related problems as well as those related to the substance use seemed to be critical in this respect (Elliott and Watson 1998; Hogan and Higgins 2001).

Barriers that parents experienced when contemplating use of services included draconian rules and regulations, agencies that were difficult to get to and having to wait a long time for appointments and assessments (Bates *et al.* 1999; Harbin and Murphy 2000). Many felt that some workers lacked appropriate knowledge, training and experience to appreciate their difficulties and that more awareness on the part of professionals of polydrug use was needed. Often parents were taking several substances at once, including alcohol, and felt there was too narrow a focus on heroin, to the exclusion of all else (Elliott and Watson 1998).

One of the greatest hurdles to overcome in order for parents to feel able to ask for and receive help, was the suspicion and fear that contact with some services could generate – a hurdle reflected in general child protection (Cleaver and Freeman 1995). There was a sense that, once substance use – particularly drug use – emerged as a fact of life, two things were likely to happen. One was overreaction by professionals, with the exception of drug dependency unit workers, who, it was felt, were more familiar with the issues. The other was an immediate assumption that substance misuse equalled inadequate parent. There was a consistently expressed fear of child removal and a belief that discovery or admission of substance use would override any consideration of individuals as parents.

Parents also needed to feel that their stories were heard and believed. In other words, if they said they could care for their children, provided their substance misuse did not become chaotic, then this needed to be acknowledged, since they might be more 'expert' in this area of assessment than anyone else. Of course, this could really work only in the context of a trusting relationship with workers, since if chaotic use did develop, it would be important to acknowledge this, so that help could be provided; this was identified as a particular hurdle (Bates *et al.* 1999). There was a feeling that trust and communication could be vastly improved by a clearer acknowledgement of the power of the professionals, what they could or might have to do, and what they could not.

Other anxieties related to 'coming out' and the exposure and censure that might follow. People finding out, the impact on family, friends and particularly on children were causes for concern as was the issue of confidentiality. Where would this information go? Who else might find out? Although parents expressed the view that more home visits would be helpful, since childcare demands might make office visits difficult, ironically some parents took the view that strangers appearing in their street would simply arouse curiosity and increase the risks of being exposed (Elliott and Watson 2000).

Parents identified a number of factors which they felt would assist them both in the parenting task and in addressing the issue of substance misuse. First, the stigma needed to be removed from access to services, particularly relevant for families from communities where particular stigma might be attached to such contact. Equally important was that parents were seen in context, both literally, via more provision of home visits (provided this was seen as helpful rather than stigmatising) and in terms of their structural, cultural and material worlds. This would increase awareness of the realities of parents' lives. Services would be welcomed that offered an inclusive approach that involved mothers, fathers and children, with informal support during difficult times and related to practical and emotional problems that might be non-substance related. Information about agency regulations, confidentiality and powers were also seen as essential for good working relationships. Some parents felt that they would be helped by more information on the impact of substance use on their children and how to guard against ill-effects as well as advice and guidance about how to talk to children about substance use and its impact on relationships (Hogan 1997; Hogan and Higgins 2001). Childcare possibilities during difficult periods, as well as flexibility, individual treatment and not being judged were also critical factors in making or breaking client–worker relationships, as was some form of follow-up service and continuing support after treatment for substance use.

Summary

There is much to be learnt from what parents can tell us in relation to how they manage life as parents, the role played by their substance misuse and the dynamic between their histories, life in the present and the social and environmental context in which they find themselves. What is equally clear is that there is a wide variation in terms of experiences and that we still know very little about the day-to-day impact of substance use on parent–child involvement in respect of both mothers and fathers who, once again, seem to have drifted out of focus. We also know that substance- misusing parents are not a homogeneous group.

Many substance-misusing parents are all too aware of the consequences of their behaviour and take appropriate steps to minimise the impact on their children. However, many may be unable or unwilling to face these consequences and this has significant implications for child well-being.

Part Three

The Effects of Parental Substance Misuse on Child Welfare

The World of the Child
Attachment, Vulnerability, Risk and Resilience

Into the dangerous world I leapt
Helpless, naked, piping loud.

(William Blake, Songs of Innocence and Experience, 1794)

We now focus on the world of the child. In this world various processes need to take place in order for healthy growth at all levels and these processes will be significantly affected by parent–child interaction. We have seen the way in which a relationship with and an attachment to a substance can develop. We now consider this in relation to parent relationships and examine the way in which these attachments might conflict with one another and the possible consequences. This will involve looking at some key aspects of child development and the ways in which children survive exigencies, depending on their vulnerability and the protective factors that may or may not exist in their individual make-up, their family and their community. Part of this discussion will inevitably revolve around the whole area of risk and risk assessment, that fraught activity which forms such an important element in all areas of social welfare practice. These themes are seen as particularly relevant to the whole area of child welfare and parenting and will recur in the chapters that follow.

The world of the child

The world of the child evolves through a dynamic interchange between the individual, the family and the outside world. This idea, originating in the work of Winnicott (1964), is reflected in the ecological model which forms the basis for the *Framework for the Assessment of Children in Need and their*

Families (Department of Health 2000a; Horwath 2001). Because, as William Blake suggests, the world at large can be full of dangers, the child's world should be a secure and loving place created through the parents' or carers' capacity to provide safety, emotional warmth, stimulation, guidance, boundaries and stability. The provision of a holding and containing environment, secure attachments and the management of separation and loss are all key elements of this. In addition, the child will develop ways in which to adapt to the evolving world around him or her by developing 'defensive strategies' (Howe *et al.* 1999).

Object relations, the holding environment and containment

Object relations theory, in relation to personality development, evolved from psychoanalytic thinking about the way in which infants make sense of their world, based on observations of mother–baby interaction (Greenberg and Mitchell 1983). The theory rests on the idea that the *object* – that is to say anything significant in the child's world that has some internal representation – assumes critical importance in organising the child's inner world (Preston-Shoot and Agass 1990). The 'object' can be an actual object, a person, or something that is experienced as part of a person – a bottle or a breast. Through experiences with these 'objects' – as good or bad, reliable or not – the baby begins to construct a sense of self from which identity will spring.

It is fairly unnerving being a baby, as Winnicott (1960) suggested when he saw the infant as internally chaotic, with a range of inner experiences that are not connected together in any way. The atmosphere in which object relations takes place, then, becomes critical in enabling the baby to organise these experiences into a coherent pattern to enable a sense of self to evolve. This is where the 'holding' environment and containment come in to the picture. Essentially, the holding environment is one where needs are met, where there is reliability, where the carer is attuned to signals, signs and communication and can mirror the infant's experiences and gestures in a way that makes the baby feel good about him/herself (Winnicott 1960). This has often been described as a 'relationship dance' (Stern 1977) involving a fluid, graceful exchange of signals and responses, in which the parent and baby come together, move apart, with the parent completely in tune with the baby.

During this process babies gain a sense of their own physical and emotional needs and start to know who they really are.

Part of this holding environment involves the actual physical holding, touching, cradling and rocking that accompanies the meeting of basic needs which shows babies that they are loved and therefore lovable. This means that when they do not need anything, they can just 'be', secure in the knowledge that there is a good object out there who will come if needed. This, then, creates a safe, nurturing environment, on both an internal and external level.

Babies are subject to very powerful feelings of anger, despair and frustration. Because of their lack of development, they find them overwhelming and incomprehensible. This is where the importance of containment within the 'holding' relationship plays an important part. Containment originated in the work of Bion (1959, 1962) and has come to be associated with the carers' ability to absorb and manage powerful feelings so that they can be discharged safely. The theory is that babies fear that these powerful feelings will destroy everything in their path and that this fear is managed by the containment provided within the holding environment. This enables strong emotions to be managed so that, despite feeling anger, babies do not come to see themselves as bad.

The capacity to provide this holding environment is dependent on the carers' ability to put themselves in the baby's position and to manage uncertainties and powerful feelings. This capacity can be stretched to snapping point, at times, by the normal exigencies of family life. If the parent is assailed by other demands, personal needs and pressures, it may be undermined still further and the ability to respond to the infant's needs may be erratic and unreliable.

Attachment

Through the provision of holding and containment, infants begin to develop a sense of self and start to see the world as a safe and reliable place. This process forms the basis for attachment relationships as infants begin to attach to the source of safety and attention to their needs.

Attachment theory originated in the work of Bowlby (1969, 1979, 1980) who saw attachment as essentially an instinctive force necessary for the infant's very survival. Howe *et al.* (1999, p.14) define it as 'any behaviour designed to get children into a close, protective relationship with their attachment figures whenever they experience anxiety'. It is hard to imagine a world without attachment theory since its significance to anyone working in the field of childcare is so central. It is in problematic early attachment relationships within families that the beginnings of emotional and psychological problems can be found (Brandon *et al.* 1998) and there are also clear links between attachment, problems in parenting and consequences for the quality of children's lives, all of which can be exacerbated by substance misuse.

Attachment between child and care-giver has long been recognised as the cornerstone of healthy psychological and emotional development, both during childhood and in later life (Bowlby 1988; Parkes 1996). Attachment *behaviour* is a child's way of obtaining reassurance and protection from an attachment figure at times of anxiety:

> attachment behaviour is activated whenever young children feel distressed and insecure and need to get into close proximity with the main care giver. Thus situations which lead to separation from or loss of the attachment figure not only cause anxiety but also entail the absence of the very person who is able to soothe the child...prolonged or repeated losses and separations of the attachment figure...might therefore subject children to sustained periods of unresolved distress. (Howe *et al.* 1999, p.13)

In addition to this physical closeness, attachment theory extends to include a child's sense of emotional closeness to a care-giver – the belief that they are present and available *psychologically* as well as physically (Howe *et al.*1999). As a consequence, 'attachment figures who are emotionally unavailable and unresponsive are just as likely to cause anxiety and distress as those who are physically absent' (Howe *et al.* 1999, p.14). As we have seen, one of the possible effects of substance misuse on parenting is difficulty with attachment at a number of levels; if the adults' primary attachment is to a substance this has implications for attachment to others (Kroll and Taylor 2000). Consequences of this for children can be low self-esteem, lack of confidence, insecurity, mistrust, confusion and self-blame, with implications for the formation of close relationships in later life (Brisby *et al.* 1997; Brooks and Rice 1997). Fragmented or disrupted attachment relationships in childhood have also been linked to problems with parenting (Rutter 1995a) and links between attachment problems and physical, sexual and emotional abuse and depression – particularly among mothers – have been well documented (Bifulco and Moran 1998; Sheppard 2001).

When Bowlby undertook his pioneering work on attachment, the attachment figure was seen to be exclusively the mother. It has taken some time for attention to be paid to fathers and attachment although there is now a body of research that demonstrates clear attachment patterns in relation to them; although patterns or attachment behaviours that promote closeness may be different, they are no less significant for that (see Daniel and Taylor 2001). It is now also recognised that infants can attach to a small number of people with equal success. These can include fathers, grandparents and carers, although they may not all have the same importance to the child, since the mother is still generally the favoured attachment object. This may, however, have less to do with intrinsic or innate capacity and more to do with social order and cultural norms. Having more than one attachment figure can have considerable benefits if, for any reason, a primary attachment figure is not either physically or emotionally available. Indeed, in such circumstances, Bell (2002) suggests that a good-quality relationship with a reliable, involved and trusted professional can play a key role by providing children with an important secondary attachment figure:

> both like and unlike the parental role in that it embodies some aspects of good parenting – such as warmth interest and guidance – but not others – such as love or constancy. The concept of secondary attachment is useful here in enabling practitioners to understand the nature of their caregiving alongside that of the parent. (Bell 2002, p.6)

Belsky and Cassidy (1994) have identified three types of attachment behaviour that may be exhibited at different times and that human beings replicate in a variety of ways throughout life. *Signalling behaviour* such as smiling, babbling and laughing show the attachment figure that the child wants to engage in some kind of communication or play. This behaviour brings the attachment figure to the child so that he or she can enjoy this exchange. *Aversive behaviour* also brings the attachment figure to the child but the aim is to stop whatever may be happening – crying, for example. Finally, *active behaviours* such as following the attachment figure will take the child to the desired person, instead of getting him or her to go to the child.

Within the attachment relationship, the child will develop 'an internal working model' of all relationships (already referred to in Chapter 5). This has been defined as 'mental representations...of...worthiness based on other people's availability and their ability and willingness to provide care and protection' (Howe *et al.* 1999, p.21). Different attachment experiences will generate or create different internal working models and through these children will gain a sense of themselves, other people and the link between the self and others. These mental representations also operate at the level of expectations and beliefs. In other words, on the basis of these mental representations of relationships, children will have expectations about the way in which they will be treated and the trustworthiness and availability of adults they encounter. In addition, the internal working model provides a way of understanding what works in terms of how needs might best be met, based on children's experiences of the people who care for them. As Bowlby (1973, p.203) observed, 'The function of these models is to simulate happenings in the real world, thereby enabling the individual to plan behaviour with all the advantages of insight and foresight' and thus provide the template for subsequent development.

Ideally, an internal working model should give a child 'a notion of who his attachment figures are,where they may be found and how they may be expected to respond' (Bowlby 1973, p.203). If someone's internal working model is insecure, it is harder to make sense of how other people behave and what is happening around him or her. Coping with anxiety and distress is also more difficult because the capacity to make sense of personal feelings and behaviour and that of others is undermined. As Howe and colleagues explain, if people's internal working model is secure they are able

> to reflect on the self, others and relationships in a relatively non defended way. This allows people to think about their own and other people's actions, feelings, beliefs and behaviours. It is a cognitive capacity used to deal with emotional issues. (Howe *et al.* 1999, p.235)

Understanding and awareness of a child's internal working model, through observation of general behaviour and relationships with others, can shed much light on the way a child sees the world and the degree of safety and security they have experienced in it so far. These ideas also contribute to an understanding of the way that adults relate both to one another and to the social welfare professionals they may encounter, particularly when issues of attachment, separation and loss are concerned. This may also help to explain particular attachment issues in relation to the use of substances, as we saw in Chapter 4. Equally important is professionals' awareness of their own attachment issues when working with families in which competing needs and vulnerabilities arise (Howe 2001). As we shall see in Chapter 9, one of the reasons for the 'invisibility' of children whose parents misuse substances may be the extent to which the worker 'attaches' to the child in the adult rather than to the actual child. This can often be connected to the way in which contact with children resurrects painful emotional memories.

Attachment patterns and defensive strategies

The child's attachment experiences and internal working model of relationships will affect attachment behaviour patterns. Behaviour is then organised accordingly, in that children adapt to the attachment relationships in which they find themselves by behaving in ways which secure them a version of what they want or need or enable them to manage, to a degree, with whatever they have. In insecure relationships, behaviour consists of what are called 'defensive strategies' – both behavioural and psychological – which help to manage or ward off feelings of anxiety and distress. As Howe (2001) observes:

> it therefore has to be understood that even children whose parents are violent and abusive develop and show attachment behaviour, albeit of a distinctive, insecure kind. It is the type and quality of attachment behaviour that is of interest and not its perceived presence or absence, strength or weakness. (Howe 2001, p.202)

The different categories of attachment patterns are almost universally based on those developed by Ainsworth *et al.* (1978) through use of the well-known 'strange situation' procedure. This procedure was designed to test levels of security between infants aged from 12 to 18 months and their main carer by activating and then assessing attachment behaviour through the use of a series of experiments in a laboratory-style setting. Infants were subjected to a degree of stress by being in a strange room, and experiencing the arrival of a stranger (with whom they were subsequently left) and the periodic departure and return of the attachment figure (see Bee 2000; Howe *et al.* 1999 for a detailed account of this experiment). As a result of this research it was possible to distinguish between secure attachments and two types of insecure attachment – detached/avoidant and resistant/ambivalent. A third type of insecure attachment – disorganised/disoriented – was subsequently identified (Main 1991; Main and Solomon 1986). In addition, some children fail to develop any kind of attachment. This can be due to institutionalisation from an early age, and experiencing numerous carers. In extreme and unusual cases, this *nonattachment* is observed in children whose primary carer has a serious mental illness or chronic substance-dependency problems (Howe 1995).

The 'strange situation' procedure, however, has its critics; Dunn (1993) draws attention to a number of issues that are worth examining in relation to it. One is a danger of assuming that what the test captures is a permanent quality of parent–child interaction, since when family circumstances change so can attachment behaviour. Although behaviour during the procedure tells us something about the present, it clearly cannot tell us about the past or predict the future, as relationships alter over time. Finally Dunn (1993) highlights the fact that children's experiences of separation will affect their response to the 'strange situation', as will their personalities.

Notwithstanding its limitations, the 'strange situation' has been used widely all over the world and findings indicate that secure attachments are the most common pattern, although there are some differences in the frequencies of some of the insecure patterns. It would appear that the same factors contribute to the establishment of secure and insecure attachments, irrespective of culture, and that internal working models are developed in the same way (Bee 2000). Because of the implications for substance-misusing parents – who (as we have seen) can exhibit many of the characteristics that can result in insecure attachments – and the consequences for their children, these patterns are worth examining in more detail.

Securely attached children will approach a carer confident of an unconditional response, certain that needs will be met and that they will be readily consoled. They will separate without anxiety and will respond positively to being reunited. Insecurely attached children who have developed a *detached/avoidant pattern* have discovered that if they are upset this seems to get them the opposite of what they want and need. Instead of comfort, they will receive a rejecting or angry reaction or a denial of what the behaviour is really about. As Howe *et al.* (1999) observe, the best 'defensive strategies', in these circumstances, involve denying distress, ceasing to show it in any way. Strong feelings are blocked out and the child strives to become emotionally totally self-contained. By these means, the child can retain some degree of closeness without activating the rejecting, denying and controlling response experienced when needs are expressed. The child, as a consequence, may feel less rejected.

A *resistant/ambivalent pattern* of attachment springs from a lack of certainty about how carers are going to respond, since they are experienced as unreliable, inconsistent and insensitive – although you want them, you know you cannot rely on them. This is immensely frustrating and leads to intense feelings of either love or hate. In order to make any kind of contact, extreme strategies are called for, using angry, demanding, attention-seeking behaviour in order to break through the emotional barriers that are being experienced.

Some children cannot develop any of the strategies discussed so far. Their emotions remain heightened and uncontained, no behaviour works to assuage their anxiety and distress. In many ways, the child is in a permanent state of emotional chaos and panic. This *disorganised/disoriented* pattern is usually generated when it is attachment figures who are the cause of the original distress. In other words, they have abused the child in some way or are emotionally totally unavailable, due to mental health problems or chronic substance misuse. Whatever they do, comfort is not forthcoming and attachment behaviour becomes a confused mixture of angry approaches, indifference, avoidance, withdrawal, dazed behaviour, confusion. At times the child may also 'freeze physically or psychologically' (Howe *et al.* 1999, p.29).

What attachment theory highlights is the complexity of assessing attachment and the danger of assuming that physical contact or proximity to someone is the same as being attached to them. In the Kimberley Carlile inquiry, although the social worker had observed a range of worrying signs and behaviours during an office interview in which he described Kimberley as looking 'withdrawn, sallow, pasty and still' (London Borough of Greenwich 1987, p.110), when the family left the office, parents and children were holding hands. From this he appeared to conclude that she was securely attached to them, recording that 'It was almost an archetype for a happy family scene... I therefore could not have been more reassured by the family dynamics than I was by this overall display on this occasion' (London Borough of Greenwich 1987, p.111). This physical manifestation of attachment seemed to counteract all the other evidence he had seen that something in this family was amiss. By the same token, professionals will often encounter children who, at a first meeting, will climb onto their laps and ask if they can come home with them. Personal charisma and skills with children cannot, of course, be ruled out but a more likely explanation is the indiscriminate attachment borne of insecurity.

Risk assessment: perils and pitfalls

Risk assessment in all its forms has taken a firm hold in most social welfare agencies and a considerable literature now exists to assist thinking about this difficult aspect of practice (see for example Cleaver *et al.* 1998; Corby 1993, 1996; Department of Health 1995; Kemshall and Pritchard 1996, 1997; Parsloe 1999; Parton 1996; Thoburn *et al.* 1997). Assessing risk in childcare has been a constant source of anxiety and concern, highlighted by public inquiries into the deaths of children in care (see Reder and Duncan 1999; Reder *et al.* 1993; any of the numerous reports and inquiries that have been carried out since the death of Maria Colwell in 1974, and now including the inquiry into the death, in February 2000, of Victoria Climbié). Although current practice, in line with the refocusing debate outlined in Chapter 1, centres on moving away from a twin-track approach that sees 'need' and 'risk' as separate rather than part of a continuum, the identification of risk still drives child protection practice on the basis that identification of high risk will ensure that children are protected and that resources are directed where most required (Parton 1996). Alongside risk to the children, of course, risk to the worker must also be considered. As a result of increasing accountability and responsibility for clients' welfare, although paradoxically this can often be coupled with a decrease in supervision and support in understanding the processes and dynamics of problematic families, social workers are quickly blamed when things go wrong. The problems and tensions inherent in keeping children safe have been brought into sharp relief in the wake of the pillorying of social workers who find themselves in this position. Trapped between a rock and a hard place,

> on the one hand they [social workers] are accused of being overprotective of children and over intrusive into family life…on the other…criticised for being naive, ineffectual and indecisive, unwilling to intervene. (Stone 1998, p.4)

Because of the complexity of managing risk and its consequences, there have been many attempts to develop guidelines and checklists to enable balanced decisions to be made and to 'get it right'. Although these have been useful to a degree, many feel that they fail to take into account the complexities of individual people's lives and the extent to which certain factors may be more significant in some situations than in others. Equally importantly some factors or combination of factors 'may have different meanings in different contexts' (Cleaver *et al.* 1998, p.3). In addition, 'the limits of attributional checklists which may inhibit professionals' thinking rather than enhance it' have been identified (Reder and Duncan 1999, p.74). This underlines the fact that any tool is only as good as the person who uses it and that mechanistic approaches can close down enquiry rather than enable a process of exploration to take place. As Reder and Duncan go on to point out:

> They [checklists] tend not to provide enough information that is specific to the dynamics of the case in question, since it is the meaning of individual attributes in the context of interpersonal functioning that gives more valid clues to the risk. (Reder and Duncan 1999, p.74)

What is interesting, however, in the context of this discussion, is the implicit belief that there is a way of measuring and predicting risk if only we can find it and that, once we do, all our problems will be over. This can be attributed to a number of causes. One that we find interesting is that risk assessment has become an organisational symbol of control, creating the illusion that we can manage risk and that there is some scientific, positivist method that will answer all our prayers. It is perhaps in the pursuit of the perfect risk assessment that a number of things are lost along the way. As Sargent (1999, p.184) observes, 'Assessing risk is a mixture of both art and science...the art of risk assessment lies both in the application of available instruments and in the use of practitioners' judgment and experience'. A sensible, simple formula indeed but harder to achieve in practice than in theory. The whole area of risk assessment, then, remains a complex and taxing one (Horwath 2001).

A core principle enshrined in the Children Act 1989 is the importance of keeping children with their families where possible, having assessed risk and put in place appropriate supports and safeguards. One of the prevailing problems has been, however, that although the former activity – risk assessment – has been pursued with vigour, the provision of the latter element – family support – has been much slower to come (Department of Health 1995; Sargent 1999). A central dilemma is also at issue here, that is the truism that the family is seen often as both the source of all problems for children and the solution to them, a belief that is certainly reflected in much government rhetoric and policy. This, combined with the increasing strains upon agencies which have resulted in preventive work being reduced and intervention after the event becoming the norm, has meant that by the time a social worker enters a family's life, matters have generally reached a critical stage. As a consequence this is likely to mean that the issues are more complex, the attitude of the family may be more defensive and the sanctions and conditions that the social worker may need to apply may be more stringent.

It is against this backdrop that we have to examine assessing risk where there is parental substance misuse, particularly in relation to the way in which different factors are evaluated and weighted, responded to or set aside. These are themes to which we shall return.

Despite the burgeoning literature on risk, historically discussions on risk and drug/alcohol problems did not address those posed by substance-misusing parents to their children in any real depth despite the fact that 'risk to whom?' was a question on many risk assessment checklists (see Kemshall and Pritchard 1996, 1997). In contrast (as we saw in Chapter 2) assessing risk in childcare work identifies parental substance misuse as a key predictive factor in child maltreatment (Greenland 1987).

In 1997, the Standing Conference on Drug Abuse published policy guidelines for inter-agency working in relation to drug-using parents (SCODA 1997: see Appendix 2). This begins by considering the issues presented by drug-using parents, before addressing the provision of services for children and families and inter-agency working. Assessment, services for drug-using families and the particular dilemmas presented by pregnancy are also explored. The guidelines themselves, specifically devised for assessing risk, provide a framework for considering the drug use itself, environmental factors, provision of basic needs, the way in which drugs are obtained, including any financial or legal implications, as well as health risks, social support and parents' perceptions of the situation. Additional guidelines are also provided for working with pregnant women who use drugs. Apart from the SCODA guidelines, many local authorities have provided their own to help with assessment where substance misuse in general is an issue, although the extent to which they are disseminated or known about varies considerably among practitioners, as we shall see in chapter 9. Indeed, as Aldridge (2000, p.2) has observed, 'it is still common to find social services departments and drug agencies that have never heard of the SCODA guidelines', even though they have been available for several years. Assessment will be considered in more detail in Chapter 10.

Risk and vulnerability

Before we look at the dynamic between risk, resilience and protective factors in detail, it seems important to emphasise some key points. Risks, in relation to children, have been defined as:

> those features in children's makeup or experience which might adversely affect their psychosocial development in some direct or indirect way. Risks increase children's *vulnerability* to adversity and stress. (Howe *et al.* 1999, p.231, emphasis in original)

Risk can of course operate at a range of levels. Living in a high crime area, limited educational opportunities, being poor, or living with parental conflict or domestic violence are all very different types of risk which operate at both an individual and a structural level. However, they are similar sorts of risk in the sense that they have the potential to affect social and psychological development. Having a substance-misusing parent may result in social isolation for the family. This will impact on the child's social network and on the capacity to form social relationships. This may have implications for interaction with teachers and schoolfriends and may further separate children from potentially supportive networks or from models of family life which would act as a counterpoint to their own. This in turn may affect identity, self-esteem, confidence and self-efficacy. Environmental and familial stresses may cause children to react aggressively or in a way that could easily become labelled as 'difficult'; this in turn may cause problematic responses from parents and a spiral of reaction and counter-reaction could follow.

As we have already suggested, angry and critical parenting constitutes another risk to good developmental outcomes for children. When we add to this dynamic the research evidence which suggests that abused children have an increased risk of developing abusive behaviours, and children of substance-misusing parents of developing a substance-misusing problem of their own (see for example Dore, Doris and Wright 1995; Velleman 1992; Velleman and Orford 1999), we can see the cyclical risk potential in addition to the actual risk factor that is present in the here and now. In other words 'spirals of negative experiences – *negative chain events* – are often experienced by those children who are most vulnerable to stress' (Howe *et al.* 1999, p. 232). Rutter (1999) identified the ways in which negative chain reactions can develop over time in response to the dynamic between individual and environmental experiences and the way people behave as a result. To put it very simply, if your experiences have been poor or are bad and you feel bad about yourself, you may behave badly to others, causing you to experience further negative experiences, although the insertion of a good experience can trigger a positive chain reaction that may break the original cycle.

However, 'the *risk variable* may not be the direct risk agent' (Howe *et al.* 1999, p.232, emphasis in original). In other words, it is not just the risk factor alone that is problematic; one risk factor rarely leads to irreparable damage. It is rather what flows from the risk factor – what Rutter (1999) defines as the risk mechanism – that becomes significant and crucial in relation to what may happen next. Social exclusion, poverty and disadvantage are risk variables and make the art of parenting more difficult but it is the problems with parenting that are more likely to cause emotional damage rather than the other factors *per se* (Rutter 1995b). So it is with parental substance misuse. Use of the substance is a risk factor but the critical variables relate to what it does to parent–child relationships, attachment, lifestyle and so on. Risk is not about any single circumstance but about the dynamic that can occur between factors placed within a particular context which includes individual, structural and environmental elements.

In their wide-ranging study of risk and protective factors among drug-using parents and their children, Klee *et al.* (1998) identified three 'sites' of risk which shed light on potential danger zones for children – the drug-induced behaviour and mental state of the parents, the physical environment (dangers of accidental access to dangerous substances) and the social environment. This last element (as we saw in Chapter 5) was seen as particularly problematic, since the potential for harm was many layered and pervasive, involving contact with drug users on a regular basis, the opportunity to observe drug-using practices, either by accident or through adults' carelessness, and the attitudes and role modelling that might be acquired. Although protective factors were present in relation to the stated desire in both fathers and mothers to protect their children from all these potential risks, the degree to which this was achieved was very variable. There were many examples in the study where age-inappropriate reliance was placed on the child's good sense, rather than the parents' good management.

Resilience and protective factors

Resilience and protective factors have been described as 'the counterparts to the constructs of vulnerability and risk' (Werner 1990, p.97). The concept of resilience has emerged in recent years as a phenomenon with a critical role to play in child welfare and child protection (Butler 1997; Fonagy et al. 1994; Rutter 1993, 1995b, 1999; Werner 1990). Over the years psychiatric and social welfare professionals have been exercised and fascinated by the apparent phenomenon of children who, despite the most dire experiences, somehow rise, phoenix-like, from the ashes and appear unscathed, coping with the stress they encounter and going on to do remarkably well. These children came to be called 'invulnerable' or 'resilient' and have in some literature also been described as 'transcendent' (see for example Robinson and Rhoden 1998). Initially the resilient child was described as 'the psychologically invulnerable child' (Brooks and Rice 1997, p.77), analogous to a doll made of steel which could be struck by a heavy object but remain undamaged. Anthony (1978) contrasts this invulnerable steel doll with both the glass doll, who will shatter as a result of stressful experiences and remain 'broken', and with the plastic doll who will be permanently dented by what happens to them. Other images employed have emphasised the flexible quality of such children, rather than simply underlining their toughness, with such children described as bouncing back or springing back into shape after being squashed by some dreadful experience (Butler 1997; Wolin and Wolin 1993). Rutter (1993, 1999), however, came to feel that some of the underlying assumptions behind these images were unhelpful because they suggested that resilience could be absolute rather than relative. He took the view that resilience can vary in the individual, depending on circumstances, and can change over time – what can be managed now may become unmanageable later. This is a view shared by many commentators in relation to children of substance-misusing parents, who see resilience or transcendence as processes rather than states of being. This has particularly important implications for assessment when it could be assumed that 'once OK always OK'. As children's needs change so will their capacity to cope with stresses in their lives. As Robinson and Rhoden observe:

> Transcendent children do not forget the pain of their pasts. They do not deny the harsh realities of their experiences but they are able to extract constructive meaning from that reality...transcendent children use the painful experiences of their childhood to cultivate the strength necessary to

transcend the experience of that childhood and find their way to satisfying adulthood. (Robinson and Rhoden 1998, p.70)

However, there are also inherent dangers in labelling a child 'resilient':

> On the surface these kids appear to be functioning exceptionally well. But professionals must be careful in making this interpretation…many cases of invulnerability may be a disguise for an inner misery that resilient children are compelled to hide. It would behove practitioners to take caution in labelling children who appear to be resilient…not discount the resilient child simply because he or she appears to be functioning better than the more vulnerable child in the family… Resilient children may be in greater need than those who can reveal their vulnerability. (Robinson and Rhoden 1998, pp.68–69)

This highlights, once again, the importance of treating children as individuals and resisting the urge to make assumptions about the extent to which they may be coping. Managing in a difficult situation at one point in time may give way to increased vulnerability and inability to cope at another. Positive labels can be as misleading and dangerous as those with negative connotations.

Ignorance and innocence, it is assumed, also protect children from the impact of a range of behaviours. Many parents behave as if children below a certain age see nothing, understand nothing and know nothing. Some parents may develop a mutual complicity with their children in which knowledge and understanding are not admitted or acknowledged, even though everyone knows what is going on (Brisby *et al.* 1997; Brooks and Rice 1997; Klee *et al.* 1998). In a study which explored children's experience of parental alcohol misuse, Laybourn *et al.* (1996) discovered that age sheltered children less than adults assumed. Although most parents who were interviewed thought that awareness developed between the ages of 8 and 10, these researchers found that even the youngest children in the sample, aged 5 and 6, were able to make connections between alcohol and changed behaviour and were conscious of the differences between their parents' drinking and that of other grown-ups. For Barnard and Barlow (forthcoming), in their study of 36 children and young people who had grown up with drug-misusing parents, 'it was clear that they [children and young people] knew far earlier and in far more detail about drugs than their parents believed to be the case'.

In addition, where a child came in terms of birth order was another interesting variable; it was found that both parents and children interviewed felt that older brothers and sisters often protected younger children from the impact of behaviour and that certain behaviour – alcohol-induced violence, for example – tended to be directed at the older child, drawing the fire away from the others. This often resulted in older children shouldering responsibility for confronting a parent's behaviour and taking on a caring role in relation to younger children. By the same token, it was found that younger children felt disqualified from saying anything: 'I always wanted to say something to him... I'm the youngest and I didn't feel it was my place' (Laybourn et al. 1996, p.77).

Rutter (1995b) identified the existence of what he called 'protective mechanisms' to describe the characteristics, processes or factors that can coat the individual sufficiently to guard them against the impact of particular risks and stresses and enable growth, in all senses of the word, to continue. As Howe et al. (1999, p.233) put it: 'stress resistant children are able to retain competence in environments of stress and adversity'.

Here we see some internal rudder which keeps the child on course, despite a stormy sea. Resilience is not just about keeping your balance, being constitutionally strong or having a buoyant personality, but also about perceptions of and approaches to difficult or problematic situations. This is something to do not just with internal resources, but with family and community as well (Rutter 1993). The following sets of characteristics are taken from Fonagy et al. (1994), Garbarino (1990), Luthar and Zigler (1991) and Rutter (1993, 1995b, 1999), as well as from studies done with children who have grown up with substance-misusing parents (see for example Brisby et al. 1997; Brooks and Rice 1997; Laybourn et al. 1996; Robinson and Rhoden 1998).

Individual protective characteristics which foster resilience include

- secure attachment
- strong self-esteem
- positively regarded temperament
- cognitive competence, good problem-solving skills
- absence of neurobiological problems
- absence of early loss and trauma

- social understanding, awareness and empathy
- internal locus of control
- goal directedness
- ability to use adults as resources
- spiritual or religious faith
- good verbal skills
- a good sense of humour.

Resilient children have been found to have a strong belief in themselves and their own power to change the way things are. They tend to have a good sense of humour, are able to be flexible and have a positive outlook. Resilient or transcendent children who find themselves in adverse family situations also appear to have the capacity to 'disidentify' with their families – detach themselves from them in some subtle way, so that they end up on the edges of family life rather than immersed in it (Rubin 1996). This capacity to distance themselves when things are problematic is seen to represent a healthy coping response. Robinson and Rhoden (1998) also suggest that this 'disidentification' frees the transcendent child to seek support, comfort and a sense of belonging elsewhere – from neighbours, teachers, friends and their parents, as well as from external arenas such as school, or community activities.

There is a suggestion that individual resilience characteristics tend not to be stereotypically gender specific, with both boys and girls being carers, risk-takers, independent and/or expressive (Werner 1990). However, as we shall see in Chapter 7, Laybourn *et al.* (1996) found there were some clear gender differences. Girls were less avoidant and more 'watchful' and protective while boys tended to act out, rebel, commit delinquent acts, and get into fights with parents or others (Brooks and Rice 1997; Laybourn *et al.* 1996; Robinson and Rhoden 1998).

Many children are resourceful and proactive in developing strategies for combating the effects of parental substance misuse and have many of the resilience characteristics identified above. These will all be explored in detail in Chapter 7.

Critically, the child's capacity to attach and, of course, the availability of someone to become attached to, has been a significant finding in relation to providing a cornerstone upon which to build individual characteristics of resilience. Indeed, Fonagy *et al.* (1994) see secure attachment as the critical predictor of many of the characteristics of the resilient child: 'There is thus a prime facie case that resilient children are securely attached children; that is secure attachment is part of the mediating process where resilience is observed' (Fonagy *et al.* 1994, p. 235). This, in turn, is linked to the idea of the secure internal working model – the way in which the human being makes sense of the world by referring to previous experiences. This enables the future, particularly regarding relationships, to be predicted in terms of reactions and counter-reactions, allowing the capacity for both insight and foresight to develop.

The critical element here is the use of the mind to organise the feelings and it is this dynamic that enables complex and distressing situations to be understood and managed. Fonagy *et al.* (1994) have termed this capacity the 'reflective function' and they argue that this positively influences resilience. In effect, it bestows considerable power on its owner, since it enables the individual to think about feelings and experiences in a way that provides possibilities for forward planning, other options, autonomy and learning from experience (Fonagy *et al.* 1994; Howe *et al.* 1999; Main 1991).

Familial characteristics include

- availability of at least one stable, nurturing caretaker
- existing family rituals, structured family activities
- low parental tension, minimal family discord
- high parental self-esteem
- consistently enforced family rules within a framework of well-balanced discipline
- adequate economic status
- treatment for substance misuse and attempts to abstain
- openness and good communication between parents and children.

These characteristics seem to reinforce the importance of the family's shape. This relates to the extent to which an organised, structured existence which has some degree of reliability and consistency, together with the capacity to discuss what is happening, has a critical impact on resilience. As we have seen, a chaotic lifestyle, where boundaries are blurred, rituals and landmarks are abandoned and roles are confused has a significant impact on family well-being. In addition, the presence of parental conflict or violence undermines resilience at a significant level, in terms of both children and the adults who could support them.

The social context in which the family operates – the richness of the family environment – is clearly a critical element in relation to protecting children and enhancing resilience (Garbarino 1990). Care and support, either from someone within the family, or a closely connected adult, are critical factors – a non-substance-using parent, for example, may not necessarily be living in the household but is able to keep things together, contain chaos and minimise disruption. Grandparents were also seen as important sources of help. Although parents recognised how helpful it might be for children to talk to someone about family problems, they themselves were, in the main, reluctant to do so. Rationales for this included assumptions about age and understanding and the belief that it was better not to talk about potentially distressing subjects. Guilt and shame on the parents' part also prevented acknowledgement of what was really happening in the family and children were reluctant to raise the subject for fear of causing further anxiety (Laybourn *et al.* 1996; Velleman and Orford 1999).

An environment characterised by social impoverishment combined with poverty poses the greatest risks of child maltreatment. Economic stability can, of course, cushion some of the effects of parental behaviour which may contribute to social impoverishment. Poverty exacerbates stress for children at a number of levels. However, it would be dangerous to assume that affluence alone would protect children from suffering. Garbarino (1990), while acknowledging that material advantage enables protective 'layers' to be purchased – for example childcare either at home or elsewhere, after-school activities or holiday play schemes – and that more affluent families are also likely to have a range of social networks upon which to call, sounds a note of caution:

> The affluent but socially impoverished environment may catch up with children and families as they face the transition to adolescence when the need for social stability increases to compensate for the increasing psychological and physiological challenges of puberty. (Garbarino 1990, p.90)

The issue of treatment and attempts to abstain has also been identified as a protective factor in drug-using parents by Klee *et al.* (1998). However, because managing, reducing or stopping substance use is usually easier said than done, the strain engendered by attempts to give up drugs or alcohol can, in fact, increase tensions and, ironically, make children more vulnerable, rather than less, at least in the short term. (Aldridge 1999, 2000). Often, despite good intentions, abstinence or cutting down is hard to sustain, especially when parents feel that drugs give them more energy and actually enable them to parent more effectively: 'the energy is unbelievable...even without kids you need energy but you need more with kids' (Klee *et al.* 1998, p.15) and, as a single mother remarked, 'when you've got kids and you're on your own...you can't say... "I'll go to bed for a couple of hours"...you've got to keep going' (Klee *et al.* 1998, p.12).

Community characteristics include

- positive, nurturing school experiences
- availability of supportive adults to serve as role models and care-givers
- cultural connection, value and identity
- socially rich environment
- community members free from 'drain' and able to give of themselves
- community resources (such as childcare, health care, good education and leisure facilities and transport).

The importance of what Garbarino (1990) calls 'the socially rich environment' has gained increasing currency with the move towards a more ecological perspective in the field of childcare (Jack 1997, 2000; Jack and Jordan 1999). Basically such an environment means that the community, in the form of its members, has enough resources to look out for its more vulnerable members, rather being being drained by fears of exploitation, becoming beholden or having increased demands made on them, as a result of acts of generosity or kindness. In contrast, the 'drained' environment is characterised by mistrust and avoidance, rather than generosity and protection. People will walk on by, rather than intervene. A community whose members are free from drain, according to Garbarino (1990), provides types of protective behaviours that can act as safety nets to children by keeping an eye out, intervening to protect a child from bullying or just offering care, when parents seem stressed or are unexpectedly not where they are expected to be. This kind of environment will have a positive impact on family well-being – or in ecological terms, the microsystem (family) will be positively affected by the dynamic with the macrosystem. This becomes particularly crucial in families where there is substance misuse, due to the risks of exclusion, labelling and social isolation.

School has been identified as a safe haven for many children experiencing stress, irrespective of academic ability. The support of teaching staff and of other children can provide vital energy for children; the risks however of stigmatisation, labelling and bullying cannot be ruled out, especially when parents have exhibited strange behaviour when drunk or under the influence of drugs. Race and culture can operate as protective factors – a clear sense of cultural identity and positive messages about who and what you are are clearly crucial if yours is not the dominant culture. However, the presence of racism and discrimination can also tip the balance in terms of stress factors and increasing vulnerability. Much depends on the way the family views outsiders and whether or not a culture of privacy and secrecy has evolved which prevents children from feeling free to talk about personal matters. Some children feel that, as a way of managing, the problems should be compartmentalised, so that outside relationships can be protected from contact with familial problems and the illusion maintained, at least for a time, that the problems are not there. Young people of a similar age are the preferred community support, with unrelated adults featuring to a lesser extent. A pair of listening ears, however, at a critical moment, was of great value.

Vulnerability: who is most at risk of significant harm?

Turning protective factors on their heads provides one type of framework for identifying which children might be most vulnerable in a household where there is parental substance misuse. In other words, the absence of protective factors that might foster resilience at individual, family and community levels would suggest a variety of degrees of vulnerability. The picture generally tends to be many layered and a more detailed consideration is therefore required.

Children are at one level intrinsically vulnerable, along a continuum depending on their age, size, race, gender and ability, as well as any combination of these factors. Prematurity, disability, serious illness, difference of any kind or being unwanted will all affect vulnerability, as will being born under stigmatising circumstances (Buchanan 1996). In addition, children may be vulnerable as a result of who they are, when, how and why they came into the world and in relation to the meaning attached to them within the family, depending on associations made between the birth and other events, or the expectations placed upon the child in terms of what they might promise, or put right (Reder *et al.* 1993). Indeed, this idea of the meaning of the child has become a central idea in much work related to child protection and abuse (Reder and Duncan 1999) and is always worth exploring in families where there are concerns. Does the meaning of the child and the parent's substance misuse connect in any way and, if so, how and why?

In terms of overall vulnerability, a number of factors come into play. These include the extent to which the child is directly involved in the parent's problem behaviour, irrespective of the seriousness of the behaviour itself. The children most at risk of significant harm are those who are the subject of rejection, aggression, violence or neglect as a result of the substance abuse or are the subject of their parents' substance-induced delusions or paranoia (Quinton and Rutter 1985). In their study of child fatalities, Reder and Duncan (1999) found that, in families where parents had substance problems and children had died or been killed, their vulnerability sprang from the fact that parents were so absorbed with their own needs that the child's were ignored. Safety and welfare were not seen as priorities, parenting was characterised by neglect and helping agencies were kept out as far as possible. Tragedy struck in the form of avoidable accidents, neglect or assault.

Because there is a higher rate of alcohol and drug dependence among lone parents than in households headed by couples (OPCS 1996), children of lone parents who abuse substances are particularly vulnerable (Audit Commission 1999; Cleaver *et al.* 1999; Hawker in preparation). Children are less likely to be affected if they have strong, sound social networks, if the parent's behaviour does not lead to a chaotic lifestyle, family discord or family breakup, and where the problems are not too severe (Rutter 1990). It also helps if, in a two-parent family, one parent is substance free, there are other adults sharing childcare or offering support somewhere in the social system, the home environment is safe – syringes, pills and bottles are kept out of reach – family activities and rituals are maintained, and finances are adequate (Laybourn *et al.* 1996; Velleman 1993). Although entering treatment can also been seen as a positive, as we have seen this can by no means be assumed.

Girls tend to be less affected by parental substance-misuse problems in the short term but if they persist they are just as likely to experience problems as boys (Tweed and Ryff 1991). This could have much to do with socialisation and the fact that girls still tend to share problems more easily with peers and others than boys, thus perhaps reducing the impact of the problem, decreasing vulnerability and mobilising protective factors (Duncombe and Marsden 1995; Nicholson 1984; Schaffer 1990). By the same token, cultural and racial differences may affect the extent to which a child feels able to confide in others regarding problems at home, or the way in which they choose to do so. Professionals who are not culturally attuned may, therefore, miss important signs and signals or make erroneous assumptions, based on race and ethnicity. As a result, they may fail to challenge behaviour or reactions, with all the dangers inherent in 'cultural relativism' (to be explored further in Chapter 10) to which this can lead (Buckley 2000; Parton 1991; Stevenson 1998). There may, however, be aspects of the cultural context that operate to provide a protective buffer against whatever may be happening at home (Bachay and Cingel 1999; Boushel 1994).

Gilligan (2001) has addressed the issue of vulnerability from the perspective of the three domains of the assessment framework. In relation to the child, vulnerability potential lies in the age, ability or disability and earlier history of the child in relation to abuse they may have experienced. In the parenting domain, serious substance misuse, in itself, is seen as a source of vulnerability, as is domestic violence and chronic mental illness. If all three factors are present then vulnerability will increase considerably. In the environment, sources of vulnerability would include living in a run-down area, where social support is weak or non-existent, and where there is poverty and social isolation. Poor relations with schools constitute an additional factor. As Gilligan (2001) observes:

> it is important to be wary of circumstances where children seem to be isolated from both support and natural surveillance of their daily care and circumstances…for example, the family who, by choice or default, are socially isolated. Social isolation cuts off potential support and removes the child from easy view and unobtrusive surveillance. (Gilligan 2001, p.183)

As we have seen, social isolation can become a consequence of parental substance misuse and professionals are often kept at a distance. As a result, children may become 'invisible', with all the risks that this can bring with it.

Summary

In an ideal world, children should inhabit a space that is both psychologically and physically safe, and where healthy growth, in every sense, can take place. However, this ideal can be significantly undermined by the impact of parental substance misuse which can affect all the elements that contribute to the construction of this 'safe place'. The cornerstone of healthy development – attachment – is (as we have seen) prey to a range of pressures which have serious knock-on effects, both in childhood and in later life. The risks posed relate not only to the impact of poor parent–child relationships but also to the effects on any relationships that the worker makes with both child and parent. This has significant implications for accurate and effective assessment and engagement, as we shall see.

The effects of parental substance abuse can be countered by a variety of 'protective factors', for example the child's personality, coping mechanisms and other people in the child's system. However, these factors will be effective only if the child has a sense of confidence and self-esteem, some experience of engaging with and surviving stressful situations and a range of problem-solving strategies. There are also a number of other issues that need to be taken into account, before we all sigh with relief about the potential for children to survive difficult circumstances.

What we still do not know with any certainty is why some children fare better than others, even when the same protective factors and sources of resilience are present (Rutter 1999). The discourses surrounding this do not constitute a precise science that enables us to label or predict with any real degree of accuracy. A cynic might be forgiven for suspecting that the identification of resilience and protective factors has been as much for the benefit of troubled and distressed professionals and researchers who needed reassurance that there was an alternative to determinism, as for the children who find themselves with parents who have problems. We have to be aware that labelling a child 'resilient' can sometimes increase their invisibility and that resilience, even when identified, is subject to fluctuation.

Of course, we have much to learn from children and young people themselves about how they respond to and cope with the impact of parental substance misuse on their worlds. It is to their accounts that we now turn.

7

Growing Up with Parental Substance Misuse

Behind the bedroom door you are sleeping... I can hear your snores rattling down the stairs to our ruined sitting room. Here among the broken chairs, the overturned Christmas tree, we are preparing to leave you. We are breaking away from you, Da. Last night you crashed through the silence, dead drunk and spinning in your own wild orbit into another year of dreams...time was, we swallowed those lines, but no longer.

(Fergal Keane 1996, p.33)

I remember seeing mummy through a hole in the door with a needle.

(Jane, aged 6, quoted in Harbin 2000, p.88)

Knowledge, understanding and insights about children's experiences of living with parents who misuse substances come from two main sources. The first is accounts from adults who have grown up with such parents and are recalling their experiences and emotions at a distance (see for example Brooks and Rice 1997; Newcomb and Rickards 1995; Robinson and Rhoden 1998; Sher 1991; Tweed and Ryff 1991;Velleman and Orford 1990, 1999; Woititz 1990). The second source springs from accounts gained from children themselves in the present or recent past (see for example Barnard and Barlow forthcoming; Brisby *et al.* 1997; ChildLine 1997; Cork 1969; Howland Thompson 1998; Laybourn *et al.* 1996). In this chapter we analyse a selection of these accounts so that we can hear from children, young people and adults – albeit at second hand – about what it is like to grow up with parents who have substance problems. Many of the themes identified in relation to parenting will inevitably be revisited here and issues raised in the previous chapter in relation to risk, resilience and protective factors will be explored.

Various methodological problems are encountered when looking at research in this area. Questions about the reliability of adults' recollections arise and have been addressed by many of the researchers concerned (see for example Sher 1991; Velleman and Orford 1985, 1999). Other factors which need to be taken into account include sample bias (whether respondents, both adult and child, are taken from clinical, community or specialist settings), how 'child of alcohol or drug user' status is established, and the way in which other factors that influence development and adult adjustment are considered. The way that children themselves are categorised also needs to be questioned, since, as Tunnard (2002. p.12) observes, 'children of all ages tend to be grouped together as if forming one homogeneous group'. Only cautious conclusions therefore can be drawn. In relation to cultural differences and their impact, some studies do not break down respondents in terms of ethnicity or race (Tunnard 2002), although this is recorded when the information is volunteered (see for example the ChildLine study, where children do not usually identify themselves by ethnic group when they call). Studies that focus on specific ethnic and racial groups do exist although do not specifically address the child's experience from their perspective (see for example Besharov 1994; Fitzgerald, Lester and Zuckerman 2000; Patel 2000). Clearly, however, any experience of prejudice, oppression or racism will compound the additional feelings for children generated by family problems that might be experienced as 'shameful' or 'secret'. What is harder to assess is the extent to which children's experiences are affected by their cultural context.

In relation to both children's and adults' accounts, there appears to be far more material in relation to parental alcohol use than to drug use. One obvious explanation for this, perhaps, is that alcohol is more accepted in our society and, although alcohol-related behaviour will be judged and labelled, it does not carry with it the same kind and level of stigma associated with illegality and the stereotype of the drug user that pervades much of public thinking. As a result, people may be more prepared to talk about the issues connected with it and allow freer access to their children for research purposes. There are likely to be far more difficulties in accessing a sample of children living with parents who misuse drugs due to fears and anxieties about the potential for welfare intervention and the child's removal. Indeed, as Barnard and Barlow discovered during the course of their two-year qualitative study involving 36 children and young people who had drug-misusing parents,

> To interview the children proved an enormously difficult and time consuming task...it is rarely possible to approach children directly without the mediation of adult gatekeepers who frequently make decisions for children over the appropriateness of their participation. (Barnard and Barlow forthcoming)

Such children, therefore, are likely to remain even more 'invisible' than the children of parents who have problems with drink. During the course of her innovative therapeutic group-work programme for children of drug-misusing parents, Harbin (2000) noted that the number of referrals did not reflect the estimated extent of the need, given what was known about the community in question, and that the majority of referrals were for children who were living apart from their parents. This suggested that, only when out of the situation, did some children feel safe enough to talk about the issues – a theory also expressed by some of the research respondents in Chapter 9.

Adults who have grown up with parental drug use are also hard to find, although, in some studies which explore experiences with alcohol-misusing parents, drugs are also a feature of the substance misuse pattern and can thereby be incorporated (see for example Brooks and Rice 1997). As a consequence, in line with the approach taken by some other commentators (for example Robinson and Rhoden 1998; Woititz 1990) the following analysis will extrapolate from findings in relation to children's accounts of parental alcohol misuse, as far as seems sensible, and specific differences will also be emphasised where appropriate.

Attachment, separation and loss

> You feel like you're always put on the second shelf. You feel like you're not number one in your parents' life and that makes you feel horrible... When you see 'em do drugs long enough you know you're not number one; you know you're always put second. And the drugs are put first... It takes a long time to get over 'cos you just can't believe it. ('Jessica', aged 15, quoted in Howland Thompson 1998, p.34)

In their work with adult children of alcoholics, Brooks and Rice found that 'two of the most compelling issues [for ACOAs]...are the pervasive losses children experience and the accompanying, often unresolved, grief'(Brooks and Rice 1997, p.108). Of particular significance were the invisible losses – the loss of a feeling of being loved, for example – which, because they are so hard to put into words and explain to anyone else, often remained a source of pain: 'I knew they loved me but they just didnae care that I was there...they were just away taking drugs and stuff', Elaine, aged 14, told researchers while Anne, aged 11, reflected back on her feelings about her mother's drug use: 'I used to think how could this have happened to me? It was just sad all the time and then I would get angry' (Barnard and Barlow forthcoming).

This sense of loss has implications for both a sense of being 'held' emotionally (see Chapter 6) and the consequences for later relationships, if losses remain unresolved (Brandon et al. 1998; Howland Thompson 1998). It also undermines resilience since secure attachment, self-esteem and the absence of loss and trauma are important individual protective factors which bolster it.

Losses can include loss of a reliable, consistent and responsive parent, loss of confidence and self-esteem, loss of a 'normal' lifestyle in which it is safe to bring friends home or go off to school (Cork 1969; Howland Thompson 1998). Parental substance misuse may also result in temporary loss of parents due to imprisonment, being accommodated by the local authority or permanent separation as a result of care proceedings (Cleaver et al. 1999; Hogan 1997). Fears about parents 'disappearing' unexpectedly – going out and never coming back – and the insecurity and uncertainty generated by these fears ('Will I be picked up from school? Will he/she still be there when I get home?') were also clearly conveyed (ChildLine 1997). Actually being abandoned was a reality for many children, as was feeling abandoned, both by the substance-misusing parent and, sometimes, by the non-substance-misusing parent, whose preoccupation with the 'misusing' partner often left less time, energy and attention for the child (Brisby et al. 1997; Velleman and Orford 1999). Awareness of the fact that drugs caused death was also an omnipresent source of anxiety and fear for some (Barnard and Barlow forthcoming). In addition there are issues in relation to loss of normal developmental stages (as we shall see in Chapter 8) and the experience of being 'lost' as individuals and, as a consequence, 'invisible' to those whose role it is to care for them (Hogan and Higgins 2001; Laybourn et al. 1996; Robinson and Rhoden 1998).

As Jessica, Elaine and Anne imply, when parents' main attachment appears to be a substance, this has implications for the child's sense of worth, so crucial for a sound internal working model. Jessica's sense of loss and rejection as well as disbelief is palpable – how could they have done this to her? By the same token a child in the ChildLine study was reported as saying to his mother, 'I didn't know if you loved me' (ChildLine 1997, p.14).

Loss of childhood was a theme in several of the studies and there are clear links here with the role of the child as carer (discussed later in this chapter). 'I don't remember much of my childhood', observed Gina, while another adult child of an alcoholic recalled watching other children playing, very much as an outsider: 'They seemed so young and I felt so old…standing inside the hallway as I worried about my mother. I was 8' (Brooks and Rice 1997, pp.108–109). Young adults in the study by Laybourn and colleagues recalled the sense of 'having missed out on vital components of childhood', particularly when they compared themselves with what they imagined to be the experiences of 'ordinary' children, or the family lives of friends (Laybourn *et al.* 1996, p.97). Children and adults also felt that they had lost opportunities for fun and laughter (Cork 1969; Velleman and Orford 1999). They felt that this sense of losing out, on a number of levels, had had a significant impact on their sense of identity.

Part of this feeling of a childhood denied was the loss of 'normal' experiences, such as birthdays, religious celebrations or special events (ChildLine 1997). As Fergal Keane's quote at the beginning of the chapter suggested, Christmas can be easily ruined, birthdays forgotten, occasions marred by outbursts or embarrassing behaviour and this sense of things being 'spoiled' was reported as significant by both children and many young adults.

Family functioning, conflict and breakdown

> Mum is fond of drink…gets grumpy and shouts a lot which makes dad angry. I think they might get separated and I don't think they want me. (Gemma, aged 13, quoted in ChildLine 1997, p.32)

> You certainly see things it [alcohol] can do to a family and people round about you and it really puts you off. (Young adult quoted in Laybourn *et al.* 1996, p.97)

All the studies reviewed here identified parental conflict, fighting and arguing as a major source of stress and anxiety and likely to undermine resilience. By the same token, the level of family support available profoundly affected both childhood experiences and adult adjustment (Newcomb and Rickards 1995). In other words, parental drug or alcohol misuse had very little adverse impact, provided the family was functioning and supportive. Substance use *per se* did not mean that everything automatically fell apart; families could be dysfunctional and unsupportive for a whole range of reasons.

Of course, 'disharmony', 'conflict', 'violence' and, indeed, 'support' are all relative terms and it is often difficult to tease out exactly how they are defined. The relationship between family conflict and disharmony and substance misuse can also be a complex one. Did the substance misuse cause the conflict or did problems in relationships cause the substance misuse? From the children's perspective, in fact, these questions are irrelevant. What they talk about is the impact of living with family stresses, irrespective of causation. Causation, however, does feature in relation to the part they feel they may have played in the family's situation. Children often expressed an acute sense of responsibility for what was happening and this had implications for their sense of power and control – if they started it, could they stop it?

One possible consequence of family disharmony in general, and violence and abuse or threats of it, in particular, is that the whole family organises itself around the substance-using member (Brooks and Rice 1997; Fanti 1990; Robinson and Rhoden 1998). Children then effectively disappear in their own right because their lives are dominated by the needs and feelings of the parents. Their actions, as a result, are governed by avoidance strategies and fear (Robinson and Rhoden 1998; Woititz 1990). Accounts suggest that children frequently denied their own feelings and that their good or bad days were determined, not by what they did or how they felt, but by how their parents were and the way in which they were behaving. Consequences of this were isolation, loneliness and a feeling that there was no one to turn to and no one to trust (ChildLine 1997). Several factors could be seen to be contributing to these feelings, not just within the immediate family but also within the wider family system and the community at large. When Roosa *et al.* (1988) administered their Children of Alcoholics Life Events Schedule (COALES), they found that children experienced significant stress, not only as a result of parental arguments and parents saying bad things about one another, but also in response to the views and behaviour of other family members, friends and neighbours. If such people also made disparaging, unkind or offensive remarks about parents, causing friction between parents and those outside the family, stress was significantly increased. These experiences inevitably made children more vulnerable (Barnard and Barlow forthcoming).

Violence, abuse and living with fear

> Ever since I can remember I've been scared. It's affected us all our lives. (Secondary school aged child quoted in Laybourn *et al.* 1996, p.56)

What children saw as their greatest problem was the violence often associated with substance misuse. Alcohol use, in particular, frequently caused aggressive behaviour and this was very frightening. Attempts to intervene by either the child or the non-using parent tended to make matters worse and, even when the violence was directed at objects, rather than at people, the consequences were devastating, with children traumatised or inconsolable for significant periods of time. Children's accounts vividly convey that one major consequence of living with substance misuse is fear – the fear of constant arguments, actual physical violence or the threat of it, either to a parent (usually the mother) or to themselves and, at times, fear of sexual abuse. Witnessing parents attempting to injure themselves, when under the influence of drink or drugs, also had a profound impact – 'Dad tried to stab himself when he was drinking and high on drugs. It was right in front of me. I was scared' (Melissa, aged 14, quoted in Howland Thompson 1998, p.34).

So did conflicts of loyalties and real fears about a parent's welfare. As Alex, aged 12, observed: 'Since mum left, dad's been drinking more and hitting me. I don't want him to get into trouble and I think if I went to live with mum he might kill himself' (ChildLine 1997, p.27).

Situations like this were often hard for children to talk about due to fears about the consequences or because of threats from parents about what would happen to them if they did: 'If I have bruises, he locks me in the house and stops me going to school. He says that if we ever tell anyone he will kill us… I'm scared…it's getting worse', said Tracy, aged 12 (ChildLine 1997, p.23).

Children were often encouraged to view outsiders with suspicion or mistrust, fearful that someone would find out about their parents' problems (particularly drug use) and that this would lead to separation or exposure (Barnard and Barlow forthcoming). This meant that professionals had to work hard to build a relationship and gain access to their confidences, mindful of these concerns. Some young people described being encouraged to see social workers as a threat, rather than a source of support and, even if they were in touch with a social worker, they stated that all they revealed were 'snippets' about what was happening at home, rather than the whole story (Laybourn *et al.* 1996). Children also reported having to lie to hospital staff about the causes of injuries or to collude with explanations provided by the abusive parent (ChildLine 1997).

A range of assaults and injuries were inflicted on children, including being thrown against furniture, sustaining cigarette burns, being stamped on, threatened with knives, slapped, hit (with hand, fist or objects), kicked, punched and throttled. Such assaults were often accompanied by verbal abuse, derogatory remarks about abilities or appearance, and comments about not being loved or wanted (ChildLine 1997). Children were clear that the emotional abuse was as painful, if not more so, than the physical. Being told by a parent that they wished they had never been born was a commonly reported experience, with devastating consequences. Taunting, unprovoked humiliation in front of others and other types of emotional abuse were described, in some instances, as 'torment' which frequently reduced the child to tears (ChildLine 1997; Laybourn *et al.* 1996).

Children were frequently baffled by the fact that they were left in the care of the violent or abusive drinking parent by the non-drinking parent, and the feelings that this engendered were powerful. Apart from disbelief and feelings of betrayal and not being cared about, children often expressed rage, anger and murderous feelings towards both the adults concerned. Feelings of vulnerability were often expressed and children were unsure whether they could really tell the non-substance-using parent about the reality of being left with the other parent. Their concern was that this might either raise the parent's anxiety level, or simply underline the fact that nothing could be done about the situation. Being confronted with the reality that one parent could not protect the child from the other often undermined confidence in, and respect for, the parent concerned (ChildLine 1997; Laybourn *et al.* 1996).

Although most of the violence was perpetrated by the substance-misusing parent – more commonly but by no means exclusively the father – the stress levels in the family, whether due to the drinking *per se* or the stressors that precipitated the drinking, would often cause violent responses in the non-substance-misusing parent, too (ChildLine 1997). Children were often very sympathetic to this parent's position, aware that the parent was trying to keep the family together and keep everything going. However, children also felt, understandably, that things were being taken out on them that were none of their making (Laybourn *et al.* 1996). As a result, some felt that they were simply adding to an already stressful situation and that there was no source of safety or support available to them. Although both substance-using and non-substance-using parents were often contrite and apologetic after incidents, children found the changes in behaviour and its unpredictability bewildering (Velleman and Orford 1999). Their contradictory feelings were also hard to manage, in that they would have to cope with angry and anxious feelings, generated by difficult parental behaviour, one minute and yet have to respond to overtures of remorse and conciliation the next.

Male children were more likely to be recipients of the violence and children reported worse experiences with fathers. Offspring accounts in Velleman and Orford's (1999) study highlight the impact of living in tense situations, the difference when the drinking parent was present and absent and the fear and hatred that drink-induced violence engendered. One respondent also highlighted the very polarised atmospheres within the home, depending on the state of play in the drinking 'game' in which the parents were seen to be engaged – 'the atmosphere was divided equally between terrible tension and a lot of genuine care' (P317 Offspring, quoted in Velleman and Orford 1999, p.130).

As outlined earlier, there are some links between substance abuse and sexual abuse. Although substance misuse does not necessarily lead to child sexual abuse, people who have been sexually abused frequently develop drink or drug problems, in order to manage the consequences of this (see for example Lloyd 1998; Newcomb and Rickards 1995). In some studies sexual abuse did not seem to feature in children's accounts at all, perhaps because disclosure was embarrassing or difficult; in others it did not emerge as significant from abuse in general. It was only in the ChildLine study, perhaps for obvious reasons due to the nature of the agency, that children disclosed troubling and frightening sexual behaviour. About 4 per cent of all children calling about sexual assaults cited drink in adult carers as an issue. Both mothers and fathers were reported as acting inappropriately, causing confusion, fear and shame at best, and suicidal feelings and fears of pregnancy, at worst. As Toni, aged 12, remarked, with remarkable empathy, 'He only does it because he's lonely but I'm frightened' (ChildLine 1997, p.34).

Family dislocation, separation and divorce

> Dad gets depressed 'cos he hasn't got a job. He drinks and shouts and hits us. Mum left. (Boy, aged 9, ChildLine 1997, p.36)

Substance misuse and its consequences often led to parental separation and children experienced a range of emotions in relation to this. They expressed fears about not being wanted by either parent, or concerns about having to pick up the pieces and support the parent with whom they had remained. The run-up to the separation is often extremely stressful and children can be left in situations that are far from ideal. It often seemed to children that parents felt able to leave them in situations that they themselves found intolerable, although it must also be acknowledged that, for some, there was no other choice. Whether children always appreciated this, however, is debatable. For some children, parental separation was clearly a relief from conflict and violence; for others, however, the impact of the breakup was as bad if not worse than the behaviour that had provoked the separation. The loss of a parent – even when their substance misuse had caused anxiety and fear – was still mourned very deeply, as was loss of a sense of family and a feeling of somehow being different as a result (Laybourn *et al.* 1996). Children also spoke of the other aspects of family dislocation that caused additional stress – changing schools, moving house and losing touch with friends – all factors that can easily undermine resilience in the face of stress and adversity.

In some cases the separation precipitated a parent's substance misuse rather than being triggered by it. Children in this situation watched parents battle with grief, loss and anger using drink and drugs to manage pain. This often left children to manage their own pain alone.

Chaos and control: adapting and surviving

> We all coped differently… I coped by believing everything my mother said was right…my dad was bad. My brother coped by rebelling but he might have rebelled anyway… My sister just kept herself to herself and studied incessantly. (Young adult, quoted in Laybourn *et al.* 1996, p.82)

The locus of control shifts in the family where a substance is a member. Issues of power and powerlessness become even more significant than usual due to the fact that the family can feel very chaotic and out of control. Children will inevitably respond to what may be a chaotic atmosphere, often finding it hard to feel in charge of their destiny and believing that they are at the mercy of forces over which they have no control. Sometimes this can lead to ways of coping that can be restrictive and over-controlling – always being extremely well behaved, for example. Equally, children can feel that they must second-guess what the parent is going to do, anticipate what they want and try to respond to it or change their behaviour, in the belief that this will stop the substance use. It is here that we see the role of 'magical thinking', particularly in younger children (Bee 2000; Brandon *et al.* 1998; Jewett 1984). This is the belief that you can either make things happen or prevent things happening through the power of your own desires and wishes. Here children's conviction of their omnipotence will encourage them to believe that they have caused behaviour in others and that they are responsible for what has happened in the family. They may often be encouraged in this belief by things that parents say to them in unguarded moments, when under the influence of drink or drugs. By using magical thinking, believing that they are to blame, they also believe they can put things right and regain control over their situation. Powerlessness may lead to over-control in this way; it can also lead to loss of control such as disruptive or angry responses or generally chaotic and aimless behaviour that mirrors the muddle that children feel.

Maintaining harmony: children's roles

Much has been written about the roles that are assumed in families in order to maintain the homeostasis where alcohol is an issue, and there may be some resonance where drugs are the chosen substance (Black 1982; Crawford and Phyfer 1988; Fanti 1990; Laybourn *et al.* 1996; Robinson and Rhoden 1998; Wegscheider-Cruse 1981). However, it is important to remember that roles get assumed or assigned, in one way or another, in every family, problematic or not, and are not necessarily occupied on a permanent basis. As roles are vacated or swapped, different people will change too, in response to this. Just because a parent has a substance-misuse problem does not mean that children will react in any prescribed way; each family has to be assessed in its own right and assumptions cannot be made.

An appreciation of roles in this context may help the worker's task, in recognising and working with them, from a position of awareness and understanding of this particular dynamic in families where substance misuse is an issue. The value of understanding the type of role that can be assumed by children with substance-misusing parents is that these 'false selves' can be seen for what they are – 'an unconscious attempt by children to deal with their parents' failure to parent and to conceal and protect important aspects of inner reality' (Robinson and Rhoden 1998, p.44). They are both survival strategies and camouflage, keeping out any attempt to help, support or intervene. The danger of these 'defensive roles' is that these 'false selves' eventually become real selves – so much a part of the child's personality that they are difficult to shift and prevent the child being who they really are (Black 1982). Taken to its ultimate conclusion, this argument suggests that roles become dysfunctional and rigid – a deterministic stance that is hard to justify, in the light of more recent studies in relation to parental alcohol misuse (see for example Tweed and Ryff 1991; Velleman and Orford 1999). Clearly this is not a helpful position to assume but seeing roles as akin to a place to be for a specific reason, at a particular time, can be useful. Being able to identify when children are trapped in roles which cause them problems may assist in intervening effectively. There is also some useful overlap between these roles and the coping strategies to be discussed later.

The following categorisation is a synthesis drawn from the work of the authors cited above.

The *hero* is often the oldest child and her/his task is to prove that the family is 'normal', by behaving and performing so well socially, at school and at home, that no one could imagine that anything could be the matter. Heroes take on responsibilities beyond their years, often unable to play or relax. Although the face that they present to the world is cheerful, confident and positive, this is generally at odds with what is happening in their internal world, where feelings of inadequacy, failure and shame battle with one another. 'Why are my achievements not good enough to stop this drinking/drug use?' 'Why, whatever I do, can't I make things right?'

The *scapegoat* draws attention away from what is really happening in the family by acting dramatically. This could include becoming delinquent, truanting, running away from home, being difficult or generally causing a stir. This ensures that the scapegoat gets a lot of attention, albeit of a negative kind, and provides an excuse for what is happening ('No wonder I drink with a child like that to contend with') as well as relocating the blame – 'If only she stopped behaving badly, dad would stop doing drugs and the family would be OK'. The scapegoat is then blamed for the substance misuse which helps to reinforce any denial of the real problem. Scapegoats often come to believe that they are bad and to blame and this can have consequences for self-esteem and confidence.

The *mascot* could just as easily be named the family entertainer or the court jester, and the mascot's motto might be 'the show must go on'. Entertainment and distraction must be provided, come what may, so that the reality of the family's problems can be avoided. It can be tiring to perform all the time and it makes it very difficult to confess to feelings of sadness and despair. Mascots are often hard to get through to, as everything is deflected by humour. Although they may be great fun, not ever taking anything seriously can be irritating and they are unlikely to be taken seriously themselves. Mascots benefit from lots of positive attention although, deep down, they fear that, if they are ever 'real', no one will want to know.

The *enabler* is the practical one who makes sure things get done – that the empties get thrown away, that everyone gets up for work or school, that bills get paid. Often closest to the person with the substance problem, enablers look after the physical environment and everyday systems that the family needs to keep going, so that order and routine are maintained and crises are averted. Although there may be periods in all families when someone does the enabling for a while, when this becomes routine the child effectively becomes the adult and vice versa. Although it can make a child feel good to be so important and to be able to manage so well, the intense sense of responsibility can be burdensome and a pattern can develop whereby the feelings of anger about the whole situation become subsumed by the preoccupation with meeting everyone's needs except one's own.

The *lost child* is so quiet and unassuming that people often forget he or she is there. Lost children effectively disappear, merging with the wallpaper, disappearing into their rooms, staying on the margins, demanding neither negative nor positive attention. Becoming invisible is a good strategy for avoiding being hurt either physically or emotionally. There is relief in the family that this child does not cause concern or make demands but the consequence for the lost child can be feelings of pain and loneliness and a sense of being invisible, unloved and unwanted, although there are benefits in escaping from some of the family problems.

The *protector* is ready to – or expected to – step between parents to diffuse tension, or worse. The degree to which children have to intervene physically varies, but accounts indicate that they often find themselves in positions where some kind of direct intervention is necessary. This can include pulling one parent, usually the father, off the mother, or protecting by means of deflection, diversion or simply getting the intended victim out of the way. One consequence of being placed in, or choosing to take on, the protective role is the risk of injury. Being a young protector can cause resentment and the role is not always easy to set aside.

The role of *mediator* can be assumed or ascribed. Children may be called upon by one parent to mediate when the other parent is in a volatile state or they will often assume the role of mediator, trying either to prevent fighting or to effect a reconciliation after arguments. The role is an important one and the pay-off can be considerable, if successful. Allied to this is the role of *confidant*. Children often feel drawn into alliances with one or both parents, acting as support, adviser and companion, staying in to keep a parent company or listening to grown-up concerns, even at a young age. Being confidant to both parents can be particularly stressful, involving intense conflict of loyalties. Inappropriate worries and concerns can be hard to manage and inevitably contribute to the development of an over-adult persona.

Coping strategies

Children of substance-misusing parents often adopt a variety of coping strategies. These have been identified as *problem focused*, which include practical and tactical interventions, both direct and indirect, and *emotion focused*, including avoidance/escape, keeping watch, internalisation and externalisation (Brooks and Rice 1997; Laybourn *et al.* 1996; Velleman and Orford 1999).

Even young children engage in *problem-focused* strategies. These included direct challenges to parents – 'telling them I was fed up with…drinking …and fighting and that' (Laybourn *et al.* 1996, p.79) – as well as more practical interventions such as hiding bottles, pouring alcohol down the sink, and taking a mother's supply of heroin to school so that she would not be tempted to use it (*The Times* 31 October 1998; Velleman and Orford 1999). Deflection was also identified in the forthcoming study by Barnard and Barlow as a means by which children could avoid a range of problems that might cause embarrassment by taking charge via the rewriting of reality and making themselves feel better in the process – 'this included pretending that they got good presents for Christmas and birthdays…and pretending they were going places with their parents'. These strategies gave some children a sense of being able to exert some control over the situation, even though, in most cases, this was illusory. For others, however, failure to effect change would, after a while, increase their sense of powerlessness – if parents would not change at their instigation then there really was no hope.

Emotion-focused strategies took a number of forms, although avoidance or escape were the most common. Keeping out of the way as far and as often as possible, refusing to speak to the parent concerned, avoiding his or her company, leaving the room and, if necessary, the house, were all common tactics. Bedrooms became sanctuaries although they were not always invasion proof; children would then resort to staying out of the house, even at a very young age, or wandering the streets all night (Laybourn *et al.* 1996).

A related coping device was 'switching off' – emotionally detaching oneself, constructing a protective shell or entering an inner world of daydreams and fantasies that took one into another place (Brooks and Rice 1997). Smoking, drinking and eating were also seen as avoidant strategies, especially in adolescents (Velleman and Orford 1999). Despite strenuous efforts, however, children and young people knew that escape was transitory and 'when I came back it was always going to be there' (Laybourn *et al.* 1996, p.80).

Keeping watch was another tactic identified by Laybourn *et al.* (1996). This was far more common among girls and young women who would make a point of staying in the home, watching and monitoring the family situation, guarding anyone vulnerable and keeping an eye on the substance use and parental behaviour. There was also a significant element of control here – it seemed much more important to know exactly what was going on (and possibly missing school and social events in the process) than either not being sure or keeping out of it altogether.

Externalising behaviour took a variety of forms, significantly determined by gender. While girls engaged in constructive externalising or displacement activities – homework, hobbies, outside interests, school work – boys' externalising behaviour tended to be confrontational, antisocial or self-destructive – 'I go and do something – get caught…it just started me being bad and all that' (Laybourn *et al.* 1996, p.81). It seemed clear that, for some young people, pent-up emotions required some dramatic outlet. The fact that parental drinking also made them feel bad about themselves made them less likely to care about the consequences (ChildLine 1997).

Some children coped by turning any feelings of grief, anger or frustration inwards, becoming distressed, withdrawn, depressed and anxious, developing eating disorders or engaging in other kinds of self-harm (Bentovim and Williams 1998; Velleman and Orford 1999).

Role reversal, role confusion and the child as carer

When a father helps a son, both laugh;
When a son helps a father, both cry.
(Yiddish proverb, courtesy of Tony Newman, Barnardo's, Wales)

Dear Mommy,
Don't worry. I went out to play. I let you sleep… Harry will be in the yard and I will be at Joanne's or Mary Anne's. Harry wore a sweatshirt… and…play jacket with just the hood on his ears. I wore my red pants with my red and white hat with hood. (Linda, aged 8, quoted in Brooks and Rice 1997, p. 110)

Linda knows exactly what her mother will want to know and where her concerns will lie, and her sense of responsibility, her maturity and her sensitivity to her mother's needs are eloquently and poignantly expressed in her note. All children help their parents in a range of ways. However, for children with substance-misusing parents this natural and instinctive helpfulness can, at times, take on new dimensions.

Becoming a young carer, as research has shown in other contexts, can sometimes effectively hijack childhood, and places adult burdens on children's shoulders (Aldridge and Becker 1993; Becker, Aldridge and Dearden 1998). Developmental stages are often not resolved and children have to grow up quickly and take responsibility for a parent who may often be unwell or incapacitated. In other words, 'These young carers…are to some extent guardians of their own welfare and…their own parent's parent' (Aldridge and Becker 1993, p.45). In addition, the fact that they are 'young carers' often prevents them from being seen as 'children in need' with the attendant danger of falling through the net in relation to services (Dearden and Becker 2001).

Some, however, have warned against a trend which portrays all children who take on some caring responsibilities as heroic 'young carers' who sacrifice all, while the fact that their parents may provide them with a great deal is ignored (Keith and Morris 1995). There are of course inevitable issues that arise from this, in terms of what we really want to know about the reality of children's lives, and arguments are often put forward that caring duties provide children with a sense of satisfaction and self-worth.

Studies vary in relation to the extent to which role reversal is identified as an issue for children of substance-misusing parents. Laybourn *et al.* (1996), who interviewed 28 children and young adults, found that very few fell into the 'young carer' category. Caring responsibilities were episodic and often just amounted to the kinds of tasks that many children might be called upon to perform in a family context – looking after a brother or sister or helping with housework. However, they did occasionally care for parents in other ways which included dealing with debts and managing finances as well as aspects of physical care. 'When my mum's drunk… I always walk her and help her', recalled one primary school child, while another secondary school boy occasionally had to sleep with his mother when she had DTs – 'I used to go into bed with her…so that she could get a sleep instead of getting up and walking about and seeing things' (Laybourn *et al.* 1996, pp.64–65).

In contrast, the ChildLine (1997) study, based on 3255 records of calls from children and young people whose parents or carers were affected by alcohol, found that many children in the sample said that they were the main carer:

> The roles had been reversed and they felt responsible for looking after the parent(s) and frequently also their brothers and sisters. This was particularly so when their mother had a drink problem or they lived alone with their father. (ChildLine 1997, p.38)

Many children had to carry out anxiety-provoking, inappropriate and often very intimate tasks for parents: 'She has no control and falls over all the time. She pees on the settee and me and my brother have to clean up after her. She fits, too' (Debbie, aged 13, quoted in ChildLine 1997, p.39). Cork's (1969) study of 115 Canadian children also found that many children were taking on caring responsibilities, especially in relation to looking after brothers and sisters and doing household tasks. In their study of the impact of drug use on parenting, Hogan and Higgins (2001) found that both parents and professionals felt that children were often placed in positions where they were taking on caring responsibilities and becoming adults very young.

Once assumed, the role of parental child can be hard to relinquish and this can cause a range of problems. When the parent's alcohol problem is resolved and they want to resume their parental responsibilities, children may be reluctant to forgo the freedoms that being a 'grown-up' afforded them (Brisby *et al.* 1997). Children may feel unable to let go of the parent for whom they have taken such responsibility and this can prevent the normal processes of separation and individuation from occurring (Robinson and Rhoden 1998).

Some research indicates that role *confusion* rather than role reversal can occur in families where substance misuse is a feature (Laybourn *et al.* 1996). Here, parents' behaviour causes such embarrassment or is seen to be so stupid, childish or out of control that the child loses all respect for them. Children then come to feel that the parent has forfeited any right to have authority over them and the balance of power shifts as a consequence: 'You behave badly, so don't try telling me what to do'. Laybourn *et al.* (1996) describe observing families where intergenerational boundaries had completely broken down and parents and children taunted one another as though they were all the same age. In other families there were clear examples of role reversal where, at times, the child would take on the role of critical parent and the parent the role of guilty child. Often such children would appear to behave just like children until the parents' problem behaviour occurred, whereupon they would become very assertive and parental. In response, parents would become sneaky in their behaviour and dread being told off. This kind of role confusion and reversal often left children unsure about who they were and what was going on. It often also led to strong feelings of disgust and, at times, hatred towards the substance-misusing parent (ChildLine 1997). Adverse reactions could also be experienced from the extended family towards substance-misusing parents who appeared to have abnegated their responsibilities, particularly if this contravened cultural beliefs (Spicer and Fleming 2000).

A model for problem-solving

> preschool children were asked how adults involved in a conflict should resolve their differences without violence. Three of the children reported that they should 'drink' or 'smoke' something. One boy said that when his dad yells, he drinks something 'to be quiet'. A girl described her parents sitting down to smoke cigarettes after an argument 'then they felt better'. (Brooks and Rice 1997, p.99)

This account highlights something powerful about the way in which children learn how alcohol and drugs can be used as a coping device to deal with negative feelings. For many people, a substance is the only means by which they can manage family responsibilities but it is hard to hide it from children completely and it can provide a potentially dangerous model for problem-solving (Aldridge 1999, 2000). The relationship with the substance can become the one seen as the most reliable, particularly if it also becomes associated with the belief that other aspects of functioning will also be enhanced – what Sher (1991) calls 'alcohol expectancies'. This is, however, a highly contentious and much debated area since the relationship between parents' behaviour, theories about intergenerational transmission, the impact of peers and environment, and a host of other individual variables is very complex (Lloyd 1998).

It is perhaps not surprising, nevertheless, that many young people who grow up with a substance-misusing parent or parents often develop a substance-use pattern of their own (Baumrind 1983; Biederman *et al.* 2000; Cadoret 1992; Lloyd 1998; Sheehan, Oppenheimer and Taylor 1988; Wisely *et al.* 1997; Zeitlin 1994). Sheehan *et al.* (1988) found that 41 per cent of the 150 opiate users interviewed said they had a parent with either a drug or an alcohol problem while Wisely *et al.* (1997) found that over 50 per cent of their sample of 24 young heroin users said that someone in their family had a substance-misuse problem. In most cases it was a parent although sometimes it was a sibling. There is also extensive US research which connects parental substance misuse with drug and alcohol problems in offspring and theories have been put forward which link this to both genetic and environmental factors (see for example Chassin and Belz 2000; Lloyd 1998 for a full discussion of this). In interviews with staff working with young people being treated for drug problems, it was significant that a high proportion of residents had grown up with parents who had abused drugs, alcohol or both and that this had been a learnt solution to problem-solving (Kroll and Taylor 2000). As Aldridge's (2000) study of young people's drug habits suggests, the problem-solving model presented by parents can be a powerful influence:

> The majority of parents I work with where multi-generational drug use is a factor, describe how unhelpful their own parents' coping strategies were. Such parents were seen to model for their children unhelpful coping strategies based on ways of using alcohol or drugs. Allied to this form of coping are hedonistic approaches to discipline, frustration and unhappiness that can leave young children unprepared for problem solving. (Aldridge 2000, p.4)

Do all children of substance-misusing parents develop substance-misuse problems of their own? Velleman and Orford (1999) were interested in testing 'Parental Modelling Theory' and their respondents provided them with some interesting findings. In their comparison of a control group and what they called an 'offspring' of drinking parents group, they found that those in the latter were more likely to be involved in heavy, risky or problematic drug use – 'drug' here meaning tobacco, alcohol, drugs or all three – but the difference between the groups was not as great as expected. Equally interesting was that the modelling did not occur,as expected, along gender lines, with sons copying drinking fathers and daughters copying mothers. Sons were seen as at more risk, irrespective of which parent drank. Modelling behaviour also seemed linked to the quality of the child–drinking parent relationship – the more positive this was, the more likely the modelling behaviour would be. They found the strongest link to be with modelling in women who saw themselves as like their fathers and had good relationships with them. Here is P290 Offspring on the subject:

> 'F [father] was someone to look up to – I always admired him. I always felt I had to keep up to his image of me – that was a bit difficult'…because the father was a drinker it made her look at it [drinking] too lightly. She said if a man didn't drink at all it would put her off him. (quoted in Velleman and Orford 1999, pp.171–172).

> Some children were all too aware, however, of the power of modelling and expressed the fear that substance misuse, like measles, might be 'catching'. A sense of inevitability could take hold and children found it hard to believe that they had choices about what and who they become (Robinson and Rhoden 1998). As Roy, aged 16, told ChildLine: 'I've been involved with drinking, drugs, fighting. I'm desperate to change. I don't want to be like dad' (ChildLine 1997, p.33).

> All the young men interviewed in the study by Laybourn *et al.* had followed what they saw as the family tradition of heavy drinking. Some had also started using drugs and two had developed substance problems that had resulted in criminal activity, leading to imprisonment. One respondent observed, 'It must be in the blood' while another felt that his own drinking was 'partly learned behaviour' and that, given the high levels of alcohol consumption he had been used to seeing as a child, he saw his own as minor by comparison even though 'I know I was heavily into the drink' (Laybourn *et al.* 1996, p.96).

Elephant? What elephant? Denial, distortion and secrecy

> I was already, at nine years old, used to covering up, pretending that life inside our house was as pretty as the outside. (Somers, quoted in Robinson and Rhoden 1998, p.130)

> I've always wanted to tell one of them [friends] about my dad being an alcoholic. But I just find it dead hard to keep it inside me but I feel it's something I want to keep within ma family. (Child respondent, quoted in Laybourn *et al.* 1996, p.72)

Secrecy and denial, with the resultant confusion, tensions and anxieties that arise, are clearly issues for the children of substance-misusing parents. The dynamic of denial, distortion, confusion and secrecy can result in the substance use becoming the 'central organising principle' of the family, with all the family members operating around it, and in relation to it (Brown 1988; Robinson and Rhoden 1998; Woititz 1990) and 'whose rhythm is drawn from meeting the needs of a drug habit' (Barnard and Barlow forthcoming). From the child's point of view, a 'don't talk' rule is imposed and children are encouraged, from an early age, not to 'tell'. If challenged, the child's perceptions of the realities of the family are called into question (Brooks and Rice 1997):

> children know that the household revolves round something other than themselves but they are not allowed to know what it is and they are not allowed to ask what it is... this persists even once children have worked out that drug dependency is at the heart of their family dynamic. (Barnard and Barlow forthcoming)

What can evolve, then, is 'a conspiracy of silence' where shame and fear of consequences effectively cut families off from both wider family and community (Laybourn *et al.* 1996, p.71). This has obvious implications in that children are effectively silenced and isolated from potential sources of support which might foster resilience. Drug misuse, in particular, connects children and parents to a subculture in which secrecy is essential, due to anxieties about police raids, imprisonment and the consequences of criminal activity (Brisby *et al.* 1997; Hogan 1997; Hogan and Higgins 2001). As Fixy, aged 15, observed:

> There were so many things I had to keep quiet so I just didn't bother to say anything in case I let something slip out that I shouldn't have done so whenever they started talking about things I'd just say I didn't know. (quoted in Barnard and Barlow forthcoming)

The longer this culture of denial and secrecy persists, the harder it is to penetrate, with children admitting to becoming mistrustful of outsiders, reluctant to confide and fearful of attempts to help, support or simply ask questions. Knowing but being forced into denying what you know, as Barnard and Barlow have argued, makes it difficult for the 'knowing' self to discuss that which is being denied. Hogan's (1997) study also suggests that parental secrecy breeds secrecy in children about more than just the drug use because of the atmosphere of furtiveness created in the home, due to locked doors and other types of suspicious behaviour. The experience of constantly feeling shut out and excluded, literally and metaphorically, contributed to children's sense of being unwanted, rejected and unimportant (Barnard and Barlow forthcoming; Hogan and Higgins 2001). Ironically, although they worked hard to keep the 'secret', children also felt aggrieved because people did not try to discover the 'secret' or make attempts to find out what was wrong, although they acknowledged how difficult this would be (Robinson and Rhoden 1998).

Here we encounter 'the elephant in the living room' – a huge, significant, but secret presence which takes up a lot of space, uses considerable resources, and requires both a great deal of attention and the adjustment of all those in its vicinity (Hastings and Typpo 1984).

> A child would never overlook an elephant in the living room ('Hey there is an elephant in the living room. Doesn't anyone else see it?'). When adults behave as if there is no elephant, the child experiences a distorted reality. (Brooks and Rice 1997, p.93)

Confusion about the elephant increases as does the child's uncertainty about the reliability of his or her own perceptions: 'It must be me; there must be something wrong with the way I see things – I can no longer trust my own judgement'. The world, therefore, becomes an uncertain place, as children cease to know whether what they are seeing or experiencing is real or not – what Barnard and Barlow describe as 'a world of mirrors where nothing is as it seems'. If children suggest their parent is drunk or drugged, they may be told they are wrong because the adults may not want to hear what they are saying. Instead, children are offered explanations – 'dad is not drunk/ drugged, he is just tired/upset' – which instinctively they know do not make sense – 'but I can see he is drunk/drugged! Why can't you admit it?' As Judy Brow, an experienced family drugs programme worker observes, in relation to maternal heroin use:

> By the time a user's child is three or four they will already have adapted to their mother's habit. They learn that they can't tell the truth – because mum doesn't want to hear that things are wrong. They learn to look after their mother but not to rely on her. (Brow, quoted in Sellar 1990, p.31)

There is an instinctive reluctance to accept such a view, with all its deterministic implications. However, it does highlight a potential reality for some children, in terms of their adaptation to the consequences of substance misuse.

Eventually, denial may get passed through the children in the family, with older children beginning to deny the perceptions of their brothers and sisters, to ensure that the painful reality does not escape into consciousness (Robinson and Rhoden 1998). Alongside this is the issue of the child's management of the anxiety that is provoked by the 'elephant' which might be paraphrased like this: 'I don't like this elephant, but no one else ever admits it's there, so what do I do with my fear?' This in turn can lead to what Brooks and Rice (1997) refer to as the 'don't feel' rule which often means that children are discouraged not just from feeling but also from talking about feelings. Effectively, then, the three 'dont's' – don't trust, don't feel, don't talk – are

> what keep the secret [of the substance misuse] in the family…'don't trust' and 'don't talk' messages tell children they can't go outside the family for help – no one outside the system can be trusted. (Brooks and Rice 1997, p.100)

As one parent observed, 'That was a big thing that I done… I never taught her to be able to share honestly about her feelings or anything… I just taught her to hide things' (Barnard and Barlow forthcoming).

The issue of secrecy looms particularly large for ethnic minority groups, when it comes to accessing services. Seeking help outside the community can be problematic for a range of cultural reasons, since admitting to substance problems may lead to exposure and censure. A range of assumptions are often made based on cultural stereotyping – certain groups are not 'supposed' to have such problems and so it is hard for them to be heard by others, including those providing services. It is still assumed, for example, that the Irish will drink, but that Muslims will not, that some groups, if they have these problems, will look after their own, and that strong religious beliefs will act as some kind of protective mantle against the scourge of substance misuse (Awiah *et al.* 1992; Brisby *et al.* 1997; Patel 2000). These beliefs can lead either to the realities of children's lives being ignored or to assumptions being made about the way in which the extended family will swoop in and save them if need be.

Implications for friendships: embarrassment and exposure

> It was difficult to bring people home because you weren't sure if he would be drunk or sober. There was always a tension when you went home to see what it would be like. (Mo Mowlam, quoted in Wilson 1999)

> Kids at school would tease me... I didn't want anyone to come to my house... It was torture living with him. (Robinson and Rhoden 1998, p.64)

Many children spoke of embarrassing incidents, involving encounters between friends and a parent under the influence of drink or drugs. Inviting friends home was often viewed as hazardous, due to anxieties about the state a parent may be in or the way he or she may behave, combined with the importance of keeping the substance use a secret (Brisby *et al.* 1997; Cork 1969; Velleman and Orford 1999).

Friends were often discouraged from visiting, after witnessing arguments or violence; some children made conscious decisions not to discuss home life with them. Parents' behaviour would be covered up or lied about and sometimes parents would not be mentioned at all (Barnard and Barlow forthcoming). Others, in contrast, actively used friends as confidants and seemed able to sense when other children were experiencing similar problems and make links with them (Laybourn *et al.* 1996). Although in some cases, friendships were terminated due to embarrassment caused by parental behaviour, for others the fact that friends had witnessed this opened a door for confidences. It was a relief that they knew, without an announcement having to be made, and made support easier. In this context, because friends were the most likely 'outsiders' to get to know about the problem, they could also access help, either informally, by telling their parents who would then offer support or, in some cases, contacting outside agencies. ChildLine (1997) reported that many children called due to their concerns about friends who were having problems with parents' drinking.

However, bullying and taunting as a result of parental substance misuse was also common – 'a girl at school called mum a slag and a drunk and I hit her and broke her nose' (Sandy, aged 14, ChildLine 1997, p. 37). Children were also targeted as a result of their dirty, unkempt appearance due to neglect or scarce resources: 'All my clothes are too small. I lost my girlfriend because she said I smell. Others call me names and make fun of me' (Paul, aged 14, ChildLine 1997, p.37). Such experiences, for some children, led to increasing withdrawal from contact with peers, resulting in social isolation and loneliness and increasing their vulnerability (Barnard and Barlow forthcoming; Hogan and Higgins 2001; Robinson and Rhoden 1998).

Distrust generated by difficult parental relationships, unpredictable behaviour and attachment problems together with the denial/secrecy/confusion dynamic often leads to young people having problems forming intimate relationships, unless they are able to separate themselves from the family and develop their own identities (Newcomb and Rickards 1995; Robinson and Rhoden 1998). This 'struggle for intimacy' (Woititz 1990) seemed to be related to lack of personal skills as a result of skewed family dynamics, and established coping strategies that made adapting difficult. Where dependency needs were not met in childhood, these could emerge in an extreme form in adulthood to the extent that huge demands were made on any partner. This has emerged as particularly significant for men since, although family support can offset this effect for women, men appear more vulnerable in this regard, irrespective of protective factors. Family support, then, is clearly highlighted as a significant variable for adult adjustment (Newcomb and Rickards 1995).

Benefits of parental substance misuse

> Every time they're drunk they say 'Come here' and give me cuddles. And I sit on their knee and they hold me tight and they don't let me go. (Child respondent in Laybourn *et al.* 1996, p.48)

For some children with a substance-misusing parent or parents, there were significant benefits, albeit usually of a short-term nature. Not all studies touch on this, focusing on the far more prevalent negative consequences, and some studies are based on problem-focused referrals which would be unlikely to generate anything other than difficult and painful accounts. A key variable in relation to any positives, however, was the issue of family conflict or disharmony – if this element was absent then the potential for positive long-term outcomes for some children was increased (Velleman and Orford 1999).

The child quoted above was one of a handful in the Laybourn et al. (1996) study who approved of the fact that parents became more demonstrative and affectionate when drunk. Other children in this study, however, were not fooled by what they saw as maudlin shows of affection. They often experienced them as embarrassing or suffocating and saw them as meeting the parents' needs rather than theirs. Looking back, some young adults mistrusted what they had come to see as false affection which would not have been there without chemical assistance. However, there was a sense of being loved and some children really derived pleasure from that, despite the fact that the love might have been inconsistent. Some children appreciated the fact that discipline was more often lax when parents were under the influence of a substance and that, as a result, they had more freedom, attitudes were more benevolent and parents could be more generous (for example with pocket money). On the other hand, such laxity could also convey the sense that parents did not really care what children did, where they went or what happened to them. Some children found intoxicated behaviour funny and entertaining and others appreciated the fact that parents were often significantly more cheerful, which had positive consequences. Drinking parties were remembered positively, although often these memories were tainted by the unfortunate scenes that ensued (Spicer and Fleming 2000).

As we have already seen, children often gained a sense of status and self-worth from taking on caring responsibilities, although generally this reached a stage when it became burdensome and felt inappropriate. Some children did not seem to be affected by parental behaviour at all. They appeared to be successful both academically and socially, presented as cheerful and positive in interview and were no problem to their parents. As Laybourn et al. (1996) were quick to point out, however, this did not necessarily mean that these children had been entirely unaffected by their parents' drinking, but, they had managed to deal with the consequences or to rise above them. Other positive consequences identified in retrospect by adult respondents were increased maturity, autonomy and independence, general resilience, and increased communication and social skills (Velleman and Orford 1999). Some young adults felt that they had developed greater sensitivity and insight into others' problems and people felt able to turn to them in a crisis. In two families in the Laybourn study, high academic achievement was seen as a direct result of deliberately diverting energy into school, in an attempt to manage parental drinking. Finally some children felt that the problems in the family caused by alcohol or for which alcohol had been seen as a solution had brought everybody closer together.

What children said they needed

> That's how I'd feel all the time: I'd feel alone. Drugs were more important than me. I didn't come first in my mother's life...she was more worried about drugs. (Felicia, aged 17, quoted in Howland Thompson 1998, p.34)

> Ma Mum got hurt on the outside and we got hurt on the inside. (Child quoted in Laybourn *et al.* 1996, p.55)

The 'hurt on the inside' was clearly the element requiring the most pressing response. This emotional pain – the result of persistent undermining of confidence, criticism, and verbal attacks and threats – had a significant impact on the internal world of the child, particularly in relation to self-esteem. Isolation and lack of support were also identified as contributing to that 'hurt'. Feeling safe, wanted and important – central concerns for Felicia – were also critical, as was protection from violence and conflict and freedom from fear.

Another theme that emerged was the degree to which children affected by parental substance misuse were a 'hidden' group – invisible to professionals unless the child or adult came to the attention of welfare services for some other reason. Even then, the needs of the child often remained unseen or secondary to those of the adult concerned. Because of children's innate sense of loyalty, their awareness of what people think of drinkers and 'druggies' and fears about professional intervention, they were often trapped in a position where they could not ask for help or acknowledge their fears to outsiders, remaining weighed down by what Barnard and Barlow have termed 'silent knowledge'. At the same time, they could not manage the situation in which they found themselves. Construction of the 'false selves', referred to earlier, provided real barriers to accessing help and here it seemed important for professionals to be patient enough to see these for what they are and to peer under them with gentleness (Robinson and Rhoden 1998; Woititz 1990). At its most basic, there was a need for someone simply to notice that something was wrong.

What becomes increasingly clear is that actually telling anyone what was going on at home, while the child is still living there, is a real issue. It was crucial for any confidant to be clear about issues of confidentiality, so that children know what would happen to the information they gave and that they will not be punished, judged or blamed for talking about parents' behaviour. Children often expressed real fears about being separated from family and 'taken away' somewhere. They also implied that, when they had summoned up the courage to try to tell someone about what was happening at home, they had not always felt listened to, understood or taken seriously and this had a significant impact in terms of trust and self-esteem. All these points have important practice implications which we shall address in more depth in Chapters 9 and 10.

Practical help and physical protection featured more in some studies than in others. Witnessing violence, however, and how to manage it were persistent worries and the impact of family disharmony was seen as often more of a problem than the substance misuse. Many children felt that it would help to have someone to talk to or to be able to talk openly about the problem within the family. Some also expressed a desire to meet other children in similar circumstances, to share experiences. Others would have welcomed a break, some time away. Younger children simply wanted someone 'to tell mummy to stop drinking' (Brisby *et al.* 1997, p.14). Valuable ways of supporting children under stress included freeing them from guilt about parents' substance use, helping them regain some sense of control over their environment, giving them space to be children, if this was hard within the family, and reassuring them that people can 'get better' (Brisby *et al.* 1997; Robinson and Rhoden 1998).

It is generally assumed that, since it is the substance misuse that causes problems for children, once this is 'treated' or parents are helped to manage their substance use, the problems will go away and all will be well. What is apparent, however, was that children need continued support, even after treatment, due to unresolved feelings, adjustments to new roles, rules and behaviours, new fears and anxieties. 'Although their parent may receive help, they [the children] frequently do not' (Brisby *et al.* 1997, p.14). Children, as a consequence, can feel abandoned once again.

Summary

When parents have substance-misuse problems, children have a range of ways of adapting and coping with what happens in their lives, although some of these modes of adaptation can prove to be unhelpful and can be hard to shake off. For some, depending on a range of factors, the experience of growing up with substance misuse, despite its difficulties, may not inevitably lead to disastrous consequences. In relation to parental alcohol misuse, many people emerge intact, even when periods of childhood are stressful and difficult (see for example Ackerman 1987; Tweed and Ryff 1991; Velleman and Orford 1993, 1999; Werner 1986). The position in relation to drug use, however, remains less clear (Harbin and Murphy 2000; Hogan 1998) although it is apparent that there are increasing numbers of children growing up with drug-misusing parents whose needs remain unmet because they are effectively silenced. This has obvious potential implications (Barnard and Barlow forthcoming).

Childhood can be a minefield, even in the best regulated homes, and it is all too apparent that additional mines litter the paths of children with substance-misusing parents. Listening to what children have to say and being prepared to hear about their particular reality is the only reliable way of gaining any insight into what they are coping with and how they are managing. Equally crucial is creating an environment in which children of drug-misusing parents, in particular, can feel safe enough to come forward, as their voices are still rarely heard.

8

Parental Substance Misuse
and Child Development

He treated us as if we were invisible. The focus of his attention was the drink and was to get drunk.

(Child respondent quoted in Laybourn et al. 1996, p.51)

It's awful in the long run... when you grow up you have to deal with a lot more problems... it's so hard to think that your mom would do that to you... the drugs just take over.

(Brandy, aged 16, quoted in Howland Thompson 1998, p.35)

In this chapter we examine the degree to which parental substance misuse can affect physical and emotional welfare at a range of levels. This is not just about risks of *abuse* posed by drug or alcohol misuse, but about the risks to children's needs generally and the overall significance for child well-being if they are undermined or neglected. While there is no suggestion that all children of parents who misuse substances are automatically going to experience developmental problems, this type of behaviour can affect the extent to which children's needs, across the developmental domain, are met. For the two young people quoted above, their experiences clearly cast a long shadow. For others the effects may be less damaging and painful although for others still the impact might be much worse. It is important not to pathologise or label children but it is equally important to identify those who are at risk and need help and support (Cleaver *et al.* 1999; Department of Health 2000b).

To untangle the various strands that interact to affect child development when children live with parents who misuse substances is a complex task (see for example Dore *et al.* 1995; Velleman and Orford 1999; Zeitlin 1994). The substance use may have an impact on adult behaviour in general, on parenting in particular and on parent–child interaction. The effects on children will depend on who they are, as people in their own right. Their characteristics, personalities, coping mechanisms and outside support systems will all have a bearing on how they feel, how they manage and what they do in response to their situation. The context in which children develop, both in terms of family functioning and environmental factors, will also be significant. In other words, children are all different, and the way in which they respond will vary.

Child development and the developmental domain

Child development has always been regarded as a process in which a number of things happen simultaneously along a continuum and various milestones need to be reached in order for children to achieve their potential (Department of Health 2000b). A baby, for example, has to learn to feed, to attach, attract people's attention, move, make sounds, play and cope with separations, while the tasks of adolescence revolve around separation of a different kind, identity formation, managing educational demands which lead towards the world of work and independence (Masten and Coatsworth 1998). Theorists have also identified developmental stages, tensions or tasks that have to be resolved or achieved before a child can move on developmentally (Erikson 1995; Freud 1901; Piaget 1969) as well as oscillating processes that take place from infancy onwards which have an impact on psychological welfare (Klein 1963, cited in Mitchell 1986). It is self-evident that development is affected by social context, culture and familial expectations which in turn are affected by race, religion and ethnicity. The impact of financial circumstances and access to education, community resources and support are also significant. In view of the fact that many child development frameworks not only are eurocentric in origin but also fail to acknowledge social or environmental factors, theories which also incorporate the realities of children's lives in the twenty-first century need to be integrated within classic discourses (Banks 2001; Bee 2000; Department of Health 2000b).

Within the child development domain of the *Framework for the Assessment of Children in Need and their Families*, six dimensions of child development have been identified (Department of Health 2000a, p.17). These will now be considered in relation to the possible impact upon them of parental substance misuse and they will be clustered as follows:

- health
- education and cognitive ability
- emotional and behavioural development
- identity and social presentation
- family and social relationships
- self-care skills.

It is generally recognised that the effects on children of any type of behaviour to which they are exposed will be influenced by both their chronological age and their stage of development particularly as these aspects will have implications for their degree of vulnerability or resilience and the risks that may be involved. For this reason, and adopting the useful structure provided by Cleaver *et al.* (1999), each dimension will include a broad exploration of the needs of babies, children and young people. What needs to be borne in mind throughout are all the protective factors discussed in Chapter 6 – in the individual, the family and the community – that might sustain and support children and offset negative consequences posed by these risks.

Health

This dimension refers to all aspects of health, growth and development and will begin at the beginning – pre-birth. The unborn child needs a calm environment, ideally inside a calm mother who experiences minimal stress, is not subjected to physical dangers, and who has the advantages of economic stability, a clean environment, adequate diet and good health care. In addition the baby should not be exposed to unnecessary drugs, toxins or medicines – smoking, alcohol and drugs should be avoided and even taking aspirins or painkillers is discouraged. All the family and environmental factors discussed in Chapter 6 have critical relevance for what is to follow in terms of the welfare of the child.

From birth onwards a period of steady physical growth can be expected. However, babies and small children are fragile and need safe surroundings, where infection and exposure to everyday hazards are avoided, a rapid response to illness is sought and appropriate nourishment and physical care

are provided (Cleaver *et al.* 1999). Physical or learning difficulties or disabilities which were identified or anticipated in utero require appropriate assessment and, if necessary intervention.

Children need to be protected from physical danger, to be fed and clothed appropriately and prevented from finding themselves in risky situations and with people who might harm them. As physical confidence and coordination increases with age, accidents can be more frequent as greater risks are taken and the boundaries of what can be done are tested. Language and communication would normally be expected to be confident and competent. Children with disabilities in this area should now be able to communicate using alternative means and children with physical or learning disabilities should continue to get access to appropriate services when required and receive continued support to enable them to realise their full potential.

With the onset of puberty and adolescence and reactions to this, health 'blips' can occur relating to dieting in both boys and girls – a practice which brings health problems with it (poor circulation, anaemia, vitamin and mineral deficiency). Young people often need a great deal of support to cope with the changes in body shape, appearance and functioning and to feel good about the implications of this stage of development. Other health hazards are related to the risk-taking and experimentation that is characteristic of this age group although the extent of this will vary from culture to culture (Bee 2000; Hendry 1999). During this period young people may experiment with sexual encounters in response to the hormonal changes that they will experience and this will inevitably include the risk of sexually transmitted diseases. By the same token, experimentation of other kinds might also take place – smoking, drinking and forays into the world of drugs are not uncommon and can have a number of obvious consequences for health, depending on degree and frequency of use.

Risks posed to health by parental substance misuse

Particular issues arise in relation to substance abuse and the unborn child, as we began to see in previous chapters. There is considerable research to suggest that alcohol and drug use, depending on its frequency and severity, can have an adverse impact on the health and development of the growing baby (Avis 1993; Dore *et al.* 1995; Juliana and Goodman 1997; Zeitlin 1994). The type of substance, the stage of pregnancy, the way the substance is used or taken, the extent of the substance use and its duration both over time and in terms of intensity, are all significant (Gerada 1996; Hepburn 2000). The unborn child is at his or her most vulnerable during the 4–12-week period of pregnancy; substances taken at a later stage tend to cause neonatal addiction and affect growth (Julien 1995).

Cocaine and heroin do the most damage because they can cause a range of problems including detached placenta, low birth weight, stillbirth, premature birth, microcephaly and addiction (Fitzgerald *et al.* 2000; Gerada 1996; Julien 1995). Sudden infant death syndrome is between five and ten times more likely to occur in babies who have been exposed to cocaine (Dore *et al.* 1995). Intravenous drug use can cause HIV transmission across the placenta or the contraction of hepatitis C. It is also worth bearing in mind that many people who use stimulants may also be involved in a range of other risky behaviours including the use of alcohol, sedatives and opiates. Polydrug use is particularly common among women with, for example, crack cocaine and alcohol frequently used together (Dore *et al.* 1995; Zuckerman 1994). The combination of substances can therefore be a critical factor in foetal health and complicate the potential harm that can be caused.

In relation to alcohol, the most extreme effect on the unborn child is foetal alcohol syndrome which can cause physiological differences and varying degrees of impairment, learning disability, concentration problems and heart defects (Bays 1990; Zeitlin 1994; see also Appendix 1). It is one of the three most common causes of brain damage in infants and the only one that is avoidable (Dore *et al.* 1995). A lesser condition known as foetal alcohol effect has also been identified which can cause feeding problems, irritability, tremors, occasional seizures and the increased risk of sudden infant death syndrome (Julien 1995). Some studies suggest a link between spontaneous abortion and alcohol use but this is refuted by others (Cleaver *et al.*1999). However, the Royal College of Physicians (1995) found a link between spontaneous abortion, neonatal deaths and excessive drinking on the part of *either* parent, indicating that the father's drinking pattern can also have a bearing on the health and welfare of the unborn child. Indeed, there is evidence that heavy alcohol use by fathers can cause low birth weight and increased risk of heart defects (Plant 1997).

Although it is generally agreed that the more alcohol is consumed the greater is the impact on the unborn child, even this has to be qualified to some degree. Regular moderate use of substances is often less harmful than 'bingeing' as the sudden arrival of the substance in the baby's system followed by the subsequent withdrawal can place him or her at more risk (Ford and Hepburn 1997).

Once born, infant health can be affected by parental substance misuse at a number of levels. Babies can be born with withdrawal symptoms – high-pitched crying, disturbed sleep, breathing problems, feeding problems, vomiting and diarrhoea (Coleman and Cassell 1995). This can make them hard to care for and thus may affect bonding and attachment, as well as trying the patience of even the most forbearing and experienced parent. Problems that flow from this may predispose children to maltreatment (Herrenkohl and Herrenkohl 1979). Health can also be affected by parents' impaired concentration, as we have already seen; children may be placed at risk if they are not watched carefully or their environment is unsafe in some way – for example if syringes, pills or bottles are too accessible. Fear of official intervention and discovery of the substance misuse (for example, if the child is unwell and medical attention is sought) must also constitute a factor in child health.

As Chapter 5 illustrated, being left alone or unsupervised while parents are intoxicated or under the influence of drugs places children potentially at risk. The parent's need for the substance may supersede the needs of others and children may be left with unsuitable carers while drugs or alcohol are obtained (Alison 2000; Swadi 1994). Problems with drugs and alcohol may lead to parents neglecting their own and their children's physical care and levels of hygiene and cleanliness may suffer. This may be exacerbated by the extent to which family resources may be used to buy drink or drugs. Poverty significantly undermines health.

Children may exhibit psychosomatic responses to the anxieties of living with substance-misusing parents (for example, stomach aches, headaches, allergic reactions, asthma, bedwetting and sleep problems) which may be compounded if there is violence in the family (Lewis and Bucholz 1991). Some health problems may not get picked up via school medical services due to absenteeism as a result of parents' problems (Cleaver et al. 1999).

Parental substance misuse (as we have seen) can have the effect of rendering parents emotionally unavailable at times and this will have some impact on all children, irrespective of their age. Health needs, whether physical or mental, may not get picked up and appropriate support and advice may not be forthcoming. For young people going through puberty and adolescence, the support and understanding that they may require to cope with the physical and emotional changes they are experiencing may not be there. Of course, many young people would rather eat grit than turn to a parent during this time, but parents at least need to make themselves available as well as exercise tolerance and patience with some of the behavioural responses connected with puberty.

Since substance misuse can sometimes be accompanied by violence in the home, the physical risks to children and young people may increase, especially once they reach an age when they might feel more inclined to engage with parents' behaviour, express views, complain or become involved in parental quarrels. They may also fear for their own safety (as we saw in Chapter 6) particularly if the non-drinking parent is unable to offer protection and if the substance-misusing parent prone to violence is left in sole charge of the children.

Young people may not get the support and advice they need when dealing with the various pressures they may be under in relation to both sexual activity and substance use. If help is not at hand to enable them to develop appropriate skills to manage decision-making as well as the capacity to say 'no' or assert themselves in a variety of situations, they may be at increased risk on a number of fronts. In addition, although the links are complex, there is evidence that problem alcohol or drug use by parents is associated with the same behaviour in their children.

Education and cognitive ability

This dimension covers learning and skills development at all levels and is affected by a complex interrelationship of factors. Cognitive ability develops in response to surroundings and most importantly people. Babies respond to faces, voices and other sounds; they make sounds of their own which soon become babbles and then words. Movement begins with wriggling, rolling over, then sitting, crawling and walking. Grasping things, dropping things, playing 'boo', looking at picture books, and developing a sense of play and pretend all reflect children's increasing interest in everything around them (Fahlberg 1982, 1991; Sheridan 1986). Parents' participation in interaction, stimulation, make-believe and fantasy games are important as ways of learning. A 1-year-old on the road to discovery is both a joy and a real management problem.

Children benefit from the stimulation and challenges of learning, and play, make-believe, representation by drawing and making things all help children to learn about and understand their world (Piaget 1969). Language development, the beginnings of the notion of reading and conversation feature significantly as does the word 'why?' and they become increasingly enthusiastic about gaining knowledge. They start to learn from other children and converse and play with them. Sharing and taking turns are preoccupations; imagination, conscience and experimentation become increasingly important (Erikson 1995).

In time, children become aware that some aspects of things remain the same even if appearance changes – ice is made of water even though it does not look like water – and can mentally reverse a process or action (Piaget 1969). In addition, they develop the ability to deduce new relationships from sets of earlier ones. During this stage of development, there is little room for ambiguity – things must be one way or the other and the child will take what is said to her/him very literally – euphemisms are taken at face value. A 3-year-old, told that 'Granny has gone to heaven', will look skywards to see if Granny can be spotted. Children will often try to make sense of what they do not understand with the cognitive abilities that they have and, as a result, will often come to illogical conclusions (illogical, that is, to adults) that often cause anxiety.

Young people, during puberty and adolescence, demonstrate increased capacity for logical thought and the ability to formulate hypotheses, cope with abstract ideas and manage metaphor and analogy (Piaget 1969). The capacity to reflect on one's own thoughts develops during this period, as does the acquisition of skills associated with being able to think in advance about options and possibilities, imagining oneself in different roles, contemplating future possibilities and planning ahead. In addition, systematic problem-solving skills and the application of logic and hypothetico- deductive reasoning become key cognitive instruments (Piaget 1969). The degree to which these skills emerge or are refined will vary enormously depending on experience or exposure to situations, expertise and environment (Bee 2000).

School places various pressures upon children at different stages, although it should also be a source of stimulation and fun where social skills can be developed and where learning the meaning of rules and boundaries can be consolidated. Children ought to derive a sense of satisfaction from the mastery of skills such as reading, writing and counting. The child wants to learn to do things well, to learn from others and perhaps become competitive and there is more of a conscious awareness of putting problem-solving skills and language skills to work. The positive resolution of this stage is the discovery that mastery yields rewards and results; the negative resolution is a sense of failure and inferiority (Erikson 1995).

Children need continued encouragement and support to get them through what has become an increasingly competitive and results-driven secondary school experience. Homework is a regular occurrence and patience, encouragement and goodwill are required; equally important is a safe, quiet place to work. Educational problems need to be spotted and reacted to appropriately; frustration and fear of failure are not uncommon; nor is the desire to put off tonight what has to be done by tomorrow morning. Bullying – as victim or perpetrator – is not unusual and the signs of this need to be spotted at an early stage. Examinations and expectations can continue to cause considerable pressures.

Risks posed to cognitive and educational ability by parental substance misuse

The major effects relate to the level of stimulation offered to the developing child and the impact on concentration and attainment. There is evidence that alcohol use during pregnancy can affect infant development, slowing down both physical growth and cognitive development, and that the same is true in relation to drug use. However, there is some debate about what is due to prenatal exposure and what to environmental factors, although babies exposed to methadone rather than heroin in utero fare better (Burns *et al.* 1996; Fitzgerald *et al.* 2000; Tyler *et al.* 1997). On an interpersonal level, substance-misusing mothers have been shown to be less responsive to the child's signals, less willing to engage in the meaningful play that is so crucial to educational and cognitive development in babies and more likely to respond in a manner that is curt rather than facilitative (Baumrind 1974; Bays 1990; Juliana and Goodman 1997; Kandel 1990). Inconsistency, neglect and an impoverished environment are also key considerations in terms of stimulation, as is a chaotic lifestyle and the capacity to respond appropriately in order to stimulate the developing child. Parents need the motivation and energy to deal with the demands and challenges of an inquisitive and alert child and levels of these can be adversely affected by the stresses and structural pressures which either precipitate substance misuse or are the result of it (Harbin and Murphy 2000; Klee *et al.* 1998).

Children of parents with chronic alcohol problems are likely to have more problems at school in terms of learning difficulties, reading problems, poor concentration and generally low performance (Velleman and Orford 1999). Children of drug-misusing parents may suffer from limited parental involvement with schooling which has been shown to affect performance adversely. Although often committed in principle, research suggests that such parents often have difficulty in maintaining contact with teachers and following through with strategies to assist with attendance, completion of and involvement in homework and boundary setting for behaviour (Hogan and Higgins 2001). Children are also more likely to have problems at school (learning difficulties, disruptive behaviour) and high rates of absenteeism (Hogan 1998) with a significant proportion experiencing 'serious academic difficulties' (Hogan and Higgins 2001, p.18). However, whether this is to do with the earlier impact of the substance in utero or the emotional effects of the behaviour of parents and impact on the family is hard to establish (Alison 2000). Stress may cause problematic behaviour at school which may lead to exclusion. This in turn will affect educational attainment and the acquisition of qualifications which may have long-term consequences. Effects are likely to be compounded if substance misuse, mental health problems and/or violence coexist.

Young people may start missing school in order to care for a parent who may be unwell, look after younger brothers or sisters, protect family members from the violent consequences of substance misuse or monitor drinking or drug-taking. Anxiety and fear about parents' welfare often cause children to miss school in order to keep watch over them (Barnard and Barlow forthcoming). For some children with family problems, school can also provide a sanctuary and a source of good feelings. For others, there is no space in the mind for school-related issues because the child's thoughts and consciousness are permanently filled with family preoccupations (Brooks and Rice 1997) and they are too weighed down by substance-related 'baggage' (Hogan and Higgins 2001, p.19).

The use of euphemisms to describe or explain parents' behaviour when in fact they are drunk or suffering the effects of drug use can serve only to confuse or mystify younger children. As we saw in Chapter 7, denial of the reality of what children see – often from the best possible motives – causes them to lose trust in their own perceptions.

Emotional and behavioural development

This dimension relates to the child's capacity to manage feelings, behave appropriately in a range of situations, cope with separation, changes and stress and form relationships – all issues that have been highlighted by children and young people themselves. The cornerstone of this dimension (as we saw in Chapter 6) is the development of attachment, including children's ability to internalise the attachment object and develop a sense of security and the confidence to explore their environment.

Although small children begin to understand why parents have to leave them at times and develop more confidence in the fact that they will return, fears are very prevalent – fear of the dark, of monsters and so on. The greatest fear, however, is of being abandoned (Fahlberg 1991). There is an increasing wish for independence, coupled with anxiety about losing hold of the carer completely. Although children confidently run off in the park, they keep looking back to make sure their attachment object is still there. There is also the tension between wanting to be big and wanting to remain a baby which manifests itself in the development of the expression of anger, and feeling overwhelmed by emotion. These normal reactions need to be contained and safely discharged if the child is not to feel guilty about them. Frustration can result from being prevented from doing things, and there are lots of instructions to remember – don't pick your nose, don't hit/throw/pinch/eat with your fingers, and so on.

Preschool children should have developed a sense of adults as trustworthy people, to be relied on for comfort and support. Because of the day-to-day impact of the social world outside the family and at school, children may regress at times to an earlier stage, if under pressure, retreating to babyhood by thumb sucking and using baby language. Energy levels are high and more is tackled than can be realistically accomplished. Tantrums are not uncommon. As time goes on, however, concentration improves and difficulties are responded to by sulks instead (Fahlberg 1991; Sheridan 1986).

Children of primary school age have probably been able to internalise the rules and boundaries set by the family and behaviour is no longer dependent on the actual presence of an adult – they can sometimes apply their own sanctions and know what is right and wrong. When things go wrong, aggressive talk is not uncommon and occasionally threats are made though rarely acted upon (Cleaver et al. 1999).

As emotional and behavioural development becomes more complex, children can exhibit a tremendous range of emotions all within a short space of time, some of which can appear inexplicable – roaring with helpless laughter for no apparent reason, for example. They can be physically very active and restless, can tire easily and are subject to irrational fears – snakes, monsters, ghosts – rather reminiscent of an earlier stage of development, almost as though children at this point need to regress, in order to go forward (Fahlberg 1991). Attempts are made at answering back, being assertive, challenging rules. When things get too much actions can sometimes speak louder than words and hitting out and throwing things may be behaviours that reappear. In early adolescence, verbal assaults begin to replace physical attacks and young people can become more withdrawn, less demonstrative, more reflective and irritable (Bee 2000). Worries and fears tend to focus on friendships, appearance, school and exams. Differences in appearance, spots, hair and weight can all cause anxiety and distress. Emotional and/or behavioural problems such as delinquency and truancy may evolve, in response to feeling uncontained and unheard, or simply to attract attention. Because this age group tends to be more volatile, their reactions to parental problems are likely to be more intense.

During adolescence *externalizing* and *internalizing* behaviours may emerge (Brandon *et al.* 1998). Although only a small minority will experience severe disturbance, these behaviours can be worrying and need a prompt response. The most concerning internalizing behaviour is depression which increases considerably between the ages of 15 and19. Although many young people can appear down and unhappy and may say they feel depressed, depression itself is associated with not only this low feeling but also more intense feelings of negativity about the world and the future, feelings of worthlessness, self-blame, powerlessness and helplessness. They may be unable to work or enjoy themselves, and may have difficulty eating, sleeping and generally functioning (Rutter and Rutter 1993). Depression is a common feature of suicide and suicide rates increase for this age group. More young men than young women succeed in their attempts; attempted suicide rates are higher in young women (Brandon *et al.* 1998). Eating disorders, mainly in young women but increasingly a cause for concern in young men, represent another type of internalising behaviour. This can be an emotional response to a whole host of difficulties, as well as posing a health risk.

Externalising behaviour includes antisocial acts, ranging from petty crime and minor acts of delinquency to the more serious versions of both these. Conduct disorders, such as general behavioural difficulties, aggression, bullying or threatening behaviour, may present themselves both at school or college and at home (Bee 2000; Velleman and Orford 1999). Young people can be frequently described as 'out of control' and there can be many reasons for this; the meaning of the behaviour is the significant element that needs to be explored, on the basis that all behaviour is communication. Externalising behaviours can of course be influenced by peer group pressure, family boundaries and individual circumstances. Since some kind of acting out is very common among young people, it is important to establish the psychosocial context in which the behaviour takes place (Brandon *et al.* 1998).

Risks posed to emotional and behavioural development by parental substance misuse

As we already know, parents' preoccupation with the substance, its acquisition and ingestion, to the exclusion of other priorities, will have a range of consequences for children's sense of emotional security, and an unavailable, preoccupied or emotionally and physically detached parent will evoke separation anxiety. Separation can become more anxiety provoking if partings are unplanned or parents do not return either as expected or in a worrying or puzzling state (Rutter and Rutter 1993). Children of alcohol-misusing parents can suffer higher rates of separation from and loss of parents due to imprisonment, hospitalisation, random absences and the child's removal from home for various reasons (Robinson and Rhoden 1998). A similar picture emerges from some studies of children of drug-misusing parents (Gabel 1992; Hogan 1997, 1998), further compounded by children's awareness that drugs can cause death (Barnard and Barlow forthcoming). If children are suffering from in utero exposure to substance misuse, they may be harder to care for and not provide a satisfying experience for the parent. This may set up a problematic dynamic which may affect responsiveness to children's signals (Svedin, Wodsby and Sydsjo 1996).

When parents' behaviour is unusual, worrying or frightening, small children find it hard to put their fears and anxieties into words and these therefore manifest themselves in other ways, somewhat akin to the signs of post-traumatic stress disorder such as rocking, problems with sleeping and bedwetting (Juliana and Goodman 1997). Inconsistency and lack of routine can increase fears, distress and uncertainty and carers can be experienced as untrustworthy and unreliable. Children may become clingy, withdrawn and unnaturally quiet or react by developing conduct disorders and behaviour that is out of control (Brooks and Rice 1997; Cleaver *et al.* 1999). The desire to retreat is strong and escape into fantasy and make-believe is not uncommon (Jewett 1984). Generally girls and boys react differently to parental problems, as we have already suggested, with boys externalising and girls internalising their distress. In relation to parental drinking problems, however, both boys and girls tend to react by acting out – an interesting departure from the norm (Velleman 1993, Velleman and Orford 1999). Academic problems, restlessness and inability to concentrate have also been noted (Velleman and Orford 1999; West and Prinz 1987).

Emotional and behavioural development can be significantly affected by the pressure to grow up fast and take on adult responsibilities. As a consequence, bits of childhood can be lost. It is by no means the case that all children with a substance-misusing parent become carers; often there is another parent who is substance free or other people in the social network who can help. However, when caring responsibilities do fall to a young person – and (as we know) they vary in degree – this can often cause conflict. Young people are often torn between their desire to care and the fact that their own needs may be subjugated to those of the parent and are therefore not being met. This can lead to feelings of guilt and resentment. By the same token, the concerns for the parent may become so all-consuming that the young people deny that they have any needs or feelings, so that this conflict can be avoided (Aldridge and Becker 1993; Barnett and Parker 1998; Becker *et al.* 1998).

Young adults may continue to feel that they are in some way to blame for their parents' difficulties and feel responsible for what has happened. Feelings of worthlessness, powerlessness and a sense of despair and hopelessness about the future could well tip young people towards suicidal feelings and behaviour. Equally, attempts to regain power in situations where individuals do not feel they have any may lead to eating disorders of various kinds. Externalising behaviours in response to family problems clearly can give rise to a range of risks. Research suggests that children of parents with drug problems are particularly at risk of delinquent and antisocial behaviour (Dore *et al.* 1995; Moffitt 1993).

Identity and social presentation

Identity is about the child's sense of self as a separate individual and as valued and special – all prerequisites for a positive sense of self-worth and self-esteem. Social presentation relates to children's awareness of their impact on the outside world and the way in which they are perceived by others. These two dimensions are closely interlinked.

From very early on, small children exhibit clear personal characteristics that make them special and different from one another – likes and dislikes are expressed, requests are queried. By the age of 2, they are relatively confident in their abilities, expect to be liked by adults and see them as safe and trustworthy (Smith and Cowie 1991). They have a clear sense of behaviour that is likely to cause adults to be enchanted or displeased, and the ability to differentiate the self from the world around them. Children at this age fall into what Piaget (1969) terms the 'sensorimotor stage', in which they also learn that action A causes consequence B and they achieve object permanency – the sense that things still exist even if you cannot see them.

Children of 3 and 4 will be clear about their gender and may have an understanding and appreciation of their race and culture, depending on the family's approach and attitude (Bee 2000). A sense both of family and of history start to develop – their past interests them. They become increasingly aware of their good and bad selves, as a result of what adults convey to them and, ideally, a process of integration should be taking place, culminating in the realisation that they are intrinsically good people who occasionally do naughty things (Fahlberg 1991). The development of a conscience also enables them to make judgements about the relative naughtiness of others.

By primary school age, most children have developed appropriate social skills, depending on their learning abilities. They can communicate effectively, whether verbally or via other means, and can manage a range of different types of interaction – at school, home, with friends, in public places – although they may regress at times in response to stress (Daniel, Wassell and Gilligan 1999). They are much more aware of what is going on around them and want to know what grown-ups are talking about. A sense of humour and interest in jokes develop as does an opinion on every subject. This period is also a stage in which the child feels very much the centre of their own universe and egocentric thinking as well as magical thinking are prevalent (Bee 2000; Jewett 1984; see also Chapter 7). Children feel responsible for events – 'If only I had eaten my beans, Mum would not have gone funny after tea'– and that they have the power to prevent something from happening – 'If that cloud has not moved by the time I count ten, then Dad won't drink so much tonight'. Children, by this stage, have a sense of how they are the same as or different from others, not just individually in terms of appearance or ability but also in relation to family life and how parents behave. It is important to be like everyone else and for parents not to behave in a manner that will mark them out as different or become a source of embarrassment.

With the onset of puberty, although ties with the family generally remain strong, family values tend to be questioned, as the young person becomes more exposed to alternative ways of viewing the world. The influence of the peer group can often lead young people to rebel against the beliefs and cultural expectations of their family of origin and this can result in conflict. Young adolescents should now be socially adept at adapting to a range of different situations and have enhanced social awareness in relation to the behaviour of others (Bee 2000). Appearance becomes more important as does the acquisition of appropriate clothes, hairstyle and adornments and young people become sensitive to personal comments or criticisms. The fascination or, in some cases, horror at the impact of puberty becomes a preoccupation for many. By this point, children and young people have a clear sense of and feel comfortable with their racial and ethnic identity, although the impact of racism on black children and children of dual heritage may have significant consequences for this (Tizard and Phoenix 1993). By the same token, secrecy or lack of information about roots, ethnicity or family members may affect sense of self; knowledge about the past as well as feelings about it also play a key role here (Brandon et al. 1998).

The level of egocentrism in young adolescents, reminiscent of that exhibited by very young children of 2 or 3, is typically linked to a sense of invulnerability which, in turn, may lead to high-risk behaviour (Bee 2000; Blos 1967).

Reports of early adolescence as a time of unrelenting turbulence and rebellion have been greatly exaggerated (Brandon et al. 1998; Daniel et al. 1999). Provided the young person has a secure base and clear boundaries and feels loved and respected, most storms can be weathered. Those likely to be most vulnerable are those who lack a clear sense of belonging.

Identity formation remains a critical developmental task and may not be accomplished until early adulthood (Erikson 1995). There are a number of strands that comprise identity so that individual, sexual, ethnic and gender identity all interlock in various ways. Sexuality is of course one of the potentially scary aspects of growing up – scary for the grower and for the grown – and, for this reason, is often avoided in discussion between young people and parents or carers. There are a whole range of socio-cultural issues that influence when and if sexual activity takes place, although interest and motivation in relation to sex rises markedly in all cultures (Rutter and Rutter 1993). Poverty, social disadvantage and family disorganisation are all associated with earlier engagement in sexual activities and there are important gender differences – boys of 15 are still more likely to have had sex than girls of the same age (Hendry 1999).

This analysis relates to heterosexual sex; little is known about gay and lesbian sexual behaviour in adolescence due, in part, to the homophobia that still characterises these issues especially in relation to sex/health education at school. Many gay and lesbian young people feel isolated, marginalised and unhappy, obliged to join in heterosexual sex story-swapping to avoid detection (Daniel *et al.* 1999).

Sexual identity is of course intimately connected with gender identity and various roles may be tried out before a good 'fit' is established. Issues about what it is to be a man or a woman are explored via sexual feelings, roles and behaviours. Peer pressure also becomes an issue and this communicates information about what girls and boys are supposed to do or be like in order either to earn certain labels or to avoid them (Daniel *et al.* 1999; Hendry 1999).

As adolescence progresses, young people begin to define themselves more in terms of abstractions, beliefs, philosophies and moral standpoints than in terms of appearance; sense of self alters in response to cognitive sophistication (Bee 2000). Because their sense of identity becomes a little unstuck during puberty, a new one has to be found – hence the role confusion that is part of the developmental struggle (Erikson 1995). This may involve a re-examination of previously held views, choices and roles, resulting in commitment to particular views, beliefs and ideologies.

An inevitable part of the process is a period of 'crisis', although levels of this will vary. Indeed, the notion of the 'adolescent crisis' has become almost a given in western culture, where there is a lot of time for this process, since the gap between puberty and adulthood is so long. It can, however, be affected or eroded by a number of factors – for example employment or parenthood. Crisis theory has been challenged by those who consider that young people do not re-evaluate everything simultaneously but that anxieties peak at different times (Coleman and Hendry 1999). In other cultures where there are clear initiation rites and ceremonies to indicate the passage from child to adult, crises may be less common as these can smooth the passage towards a new identity (Bee 2000).

Additional issues in relation to identity formation relate to the continuing development of a racial or ethnic identity, a commitment to a particular cultural group and an acceptance of its values and attitudes (or not, as the case may be) as well as some capacity to evaluate the group in which they find themselves (Bee 2000). This process will not be the same for all people of different ethnic origins; much depends on the extent to which the culture is in the minority and how closely it links with the dominant culture, as well as prevailing social attitudes (Phinney and Devich-Navarro 1997).

Risks posed to identity and social presentation by parental substance misuse
If parents are unavailable to provide positive reinforcement of who and what their children are, celebrate their skills and express confidence in their potential, or are inconsistent in their responses, it is easy for children to feel rejected, uncertain and undermined. Children who may, in fact, be loved but have parents unable to show it, can come to see themselves as unlovable with obvious implications for their internal working model (Fahlberg 1991; Howe *et al.* 1999). In addition, children may take on or have thrust upon them too much responsibility or may become the subject of parental delusions and fantasies (Cleaver *et al.* 1999).

Self-esteem can be badly affected by parental substance misuse as the child feels unwanted, and this can lead to guilt – a sense that in some way the child is to blame because of some inherent badness (Brooks and Rice 1997). This view is challenged, however, by West and Prinz (1987), who found that problems with identity, self-esteem and guilt could not be directly attributed to parents' problems. Laybourn *et al.* (1996) found that very few younger children saw themselves as being to blame, as they tended to see the drinking problem like an illness rather than connected with the way they behaved. This 'illness' interpretation also made it easier to cope with the consequences. Much also depended on the parents' capacity to provide reassurance that the substance problem was about them and not about the child.

In the process of constructing a clear identity, a perennial concern for young people is that they will turn out like the parent who has the problem

(ChildLine 1997; Laybourn *et al.* 1996). Being the same gender as the parent with the problem can be more psychologically distressing than if the young person is the opposite sex on the basis that 'I'm a girl, Mum's a girl, is this how girls are or how I will be?' (see for example Rutter and Quinton 1984). However, as illustrated in Chapter 7, this is not always the case.

Because of the processes involved in identity formation, support, consistency and reliability all help to sustain the young person during a period in which much may be going on. The absence of parental support, on both a physical and emotional level, may leave young people adrift and far more reliant on peers. Although parents may not be direct confidants in relation to sexual orientation and identity, awareness and understanding of a young person's struggles, confusion and anxiety is important and lack of this may leave them vulnerable.

Parents' substance-related behaviour – or fear of it – will cause shame and embarrassment as children's desire to be ordinary and like everyone else is strong. The realisation that magical thinking may not work and that children are unable to control what is happening around them can have a significant impact, leading to feelings of helplessness and despair (Jewett 1984).

Social presentation can be adversely affected by witnessing parental behaviour, particularly if violence or bullying are features of the substance misuse. This behaviour may be replicated in situations of vulnerability, conflict or stress or adopted by the young person as a means of problem-solving (Gray 1993; Hester *et al.* 2000). This can lead to a variety of difficulties in social situations with the attendant risk of isolation, exclusion from school or clubs and possible conflict with the law (ChildLine 1997). Once again, if finances are stretched because of substance misuse, standards of cleanliness and hygiene may be affected and children may experience the consequences of neglect. Young people may resort to illegal means of funding their appearance, in an effort to avoid ridicule, loss of face, bullying and alienation from friends (ChildLine 1997; Swadi 1994). Parents who are weighed down by their own problems may not be able to continue to provide boundaries. Dress and behaviour may not be moderated appropriately and young people may resort to extremes of self-presentation as a response to feeling rejected or alienated (Cleaver *et al.* 1999).

Family and social relationships

This dimension relates to relationships with immediate family, friends and other significant people, the way in which outside friendships are responded to within the family and the child's capacity to separate their own needs from others and develop the capacity for empathy. This is also about sharing, belonging and feeling confident to go into the world and develop a social self.

Infants and toddlers have not yet developed the capacity to play with other children although they will play alongside them. Exposure to other children in order to develop the capacity to share is, however, important. Equally important is the capacity to play alone. Small children need space and time to think; children who are anxious and insecure find it very hard to entertain themselves.

Most 3- and 4-year-olds start to develop a social life, are able to relate to other children at a conversational as well as playful level, and develop a sense of concern and empathy for others. Sharing, helping and comforting skills evolve (Smith and Cowie 1991). Imitation plays a significant part in developing a sense of the social self – children frequently act out domestic scenes and imitate adult behaviours and expressions (Piaget 1969). By this stage, children very much want to do things for themselves and are very determined.

As children grow older, there is increasing awareness of what the family looks like to the outside world. Family relationships are valued and physical closeness is actively sought; children enjoy talking to parents about their world, although verbal expression of feelings might be less common. Separation becomes less anxiety provoking and friends start to take on increasing importance as well as providing a source of support (Dunn 1993; Dunn and McGuire 1992). School experiences encourage the child's capacity to function as a member of a group and increasingly children develop the capacity to appreciate that their behaviour may have consequences for others and that it is possible to put yourself in someone else's shoes. A competitive spirit may emerge.

By secondary school age family relationships should provide a safe jumping-off point to invest more in social relationships. The influence of these two sources of self-actualisation may either complement or compete with one another and the response of the parent of any young person entering adolescence become crucial at this time. Autonomy and independence are the goals that are sought in early adolescence although the pursuit is not without its complications. Blos (1962, 1967) saw this period as 'a second individuation process' rather akin to that experienced at the end of the third year, in which the child or young person strives for independence but is easily frustrated and resorts to tears and tantrums when things go wrong. This makes the parents' task quite a challenging one as the 14-year-old becomes a 3-year-old in a matter of seconds. There is a need for patience, tolerance, containment and an acceptance of the person's need to retreat to an earlier stage of development, if required.

Although myths about the 'generation gap' and communication problems abound, relationships with parents tend to remain strong, although discussing sex and sexuality tends to be difficult. When differences do occur they are usually about relatively minor day-to-day things (clothes, make-up, tidiness, cleanliness), about custom/conformity (suitable apparel for school, for example) and choice (as in clothes as a personal statement and expression of identity). Confidence in sexual orientation should increase during this time and the first love affair – and its demise – will represent a significant emotional experience (Hendry 1999).

The importance of peers does inevitably increase in adolescence but does not necessarily supplant the influence of parents. In fact, attachment relationships with family form the foundation for other attachments, although this can have negative as well as positive consequences since 'a young person whose family relationships are characterised by conflict may have lots of arguments with friends' (Daniel et al. 1999, p.243). It is also important to remember that many young people may have had awful family relationships or none at all to speak of and, despite this, they form good relationships with others. This can be because somewhere along the line they have had a good experience of an adult–child relationship – and this has helped develop enough self-esteem on which to build.

Risks posed to family and social relationships by parental substance misuse

These risks are very similar to the risks posed to emotional and behavioural development, as both dimensions have, at their centre, issues of attachment, security and trust. Additional risks relate to the dangers of copying substance-using behaviour, either as simple imitative behaviour in small children, or as either a problem-solver or a means of escape for young people (Aldridge 2000). If violence is also a feature, young men may copy abusive behaviour in their own relationships (Moffitt 1993). Being exposed to unsuitable adults who may be part of the adults' substance subculture may also present a range of risks particularly if criminal activity is involved (Hogan 1997; McKeganey *et al.* 2001). By the same token, as the capacity to empathise evolves, children develop more awareness of a parent's need for care or help and feel they have to respond accordingly (Brisby *et al.* 1997).

Awareness of the fact that the family is visible to the outside world has particular consequences for the children of substance-misusing parents and they 'may feel under pressure to avoid or minimise contact with the outside world which might bring drinking and its shameful associations to the attention of others' (Laybourn *et al.* 1996, p.71). The potential for the embarrassing and the unexpected makes young people understandably wary of allowing others to see what is happening in their family. This has consequences in terms of outside friendships – with implications for social support –and can lead to the danger of increasing isolation (Barnard and Barlow forthcoming). Shutting oneself away, withdrawing emotionally or putting headphones on and keeping them there might come to feel like the safest options.

Other responses might include spending more and more time away from home, not necessarily in the right company, with the attendant risks that this may involve (Velleman and Orford 1999). Young people may also just leave home, in order to escape, on the basis that anywhere, including the streets, would be better. Indeed, the most common reason for running away among young people was the neglect they experienced as a result of parental substance misuse and the incidence increases where there is also domestic violence (Wade and Biehal 1998).

Self-care skills

The final dimension relates to all the skills required for independence, from the purely practical to the more complex. From the age of about 5, children begin to do much more for themselves. They will want to dress and undress unassisted and will help with everyday tasks like shopping, cleaning and making meals. They are able to help look after brothers and sisters or help care for parents who are disabled or ill. More is expected in terms of behaviour as children get older. This may include taking responsibility for more domestic tasks and caring for brothers and sisters in more complex ways. As time goes on, children and young people become increasingly competent and can identify concerns and anxieties, using family and friends to explore difficulties or provide advice. Although self-care skills will become increasingly sophisticated, they will vary considerably in relation to exposure to various tasks – shopping, cooking, hygiene, washing clothes and so on – and ability to manage finances. The availability of adult advice will provide a necessary safety net.

Risks posed to self-care skills by parental substance misuse

The main risks relate to the temptation to allow even small children increasing responsibilities in relation to household tasks, childcare and parent care, depending on the nature of the support systems available. Parents' inconsistent behaviour (as we saw in Chapter 7) and the children's need for some control might also lead to children becoming co-parents or simply parenting their parents (Robinson and Rhoden 1998). Young people may neglect their own needs, and concern and a sense of duty and responsibility may lead to the belief that levels of vigilance are required which may then affect school attendance and restrict social life. A variety of other opportunities – leaving home to go to university perhaps – may feel too dangerous to risk (Cleaver *et al.* 1999).

Summary

An analysis of the possible risks posed to child development by parental substance misuse highlights the way in which children's needs can be undermined or neglected at a range of levels. It also underlines a number of important issues. The centrality of attachment as a critical factor in a number of dimensions is reinforced, as is the role of domestic violence as a key variable in exacerbating likely risks. Prenatal exposure is shown to have a number of consequences for later development, with the role of both maternal and paternal substance misuse, in this context, seen as significant. Physical and mental health may be at risk from neglect, emotional unresponsiveness, lack of security and an unsafe environment, while the dangers of a 'lost' childhood due to the burden of adult cares are clear. Future life chances in terms of emotional stability, educational attainment and sense of self-worth can also be placed in jeopardy. The value of identifying which aspects of child development are being affected is, however, useful only if it identifies 'which children need help and the level of concern, which aspects of development are being adversely affected and how, what services are needed to help both the child and the family' (Cleaver *et al.* 1999, p.98).

However, as Chapter 6 has shown, there are factors in the individual, the family and the environment that can act as a protective layer against some of the adverse consequences outlined here. Some children will survive, come what may. The crucial task for welfare professionals is to ensure that they can identify the extent to which children's needs are not being met and the consequences for their welfare and development, ideally before they reach a stage when they are actually at risk of significant harm. In Chapter 9 we shall look at some of the practice dilemmas involved in this process and some of the complexities involved in identifying levels of concern and appropriate responses.

Part Four

Practice and Policy Implications

9

Mind the Gap

Dilemmas for Practice

Concern about the crossover between the two issues (child protection and parental substance misuse) was not some 'rumour from abroad', but a current reality for our staff and the systems for which they work.

(Murphy and Oulds 2000, p.114)

This chapter explores some of the dilemmas raised for social welfare professionals who work with substance-misusing parents. Based on interviews with a wide range of practitioners, a variety of issues will be discussed and linked to those emerging from other studies. We shall also consider the way in which some professionals have sought to resolve the dilemmas they encounter. This will then be used as a basis for beginning to look at constructive ways forward.

As we have seen, there is a convincing amount of evidence which suggests that children living at home with a parent with a serious alcohol or drug problem may encounter a range of barriers to satisfactory development and that adverse experiences are often chronic, rather than temporary (Velleman and Orford 1999). In addition, a significant number of children referred to social welfare services or subject to care or child protection proceedings have parents who misuse substances. This presents professionals with a range of challenges in relation to engagement, assessment, confidentiality, inter-agency working and gaining access to children's perspectives. In addition, there is the danger of either making unfounded connections and assumptions between chronic substance misuse and problems in parenting or of under-reacting and failing to identify the maltreatment that a significant minority of children experience.

We interviewed forty social welfare professionals, drawn from both the voluntary and the statutory sectors in London and the south-west of England, between 1999 and 2001 – a period that saw the introduction of the new *Framework for the Assessment of Children in Need and their Families* (Department of Health 2000a). Respondents included statutory social workers in both adult mental health services and child and family care, probation officers, voluntary sector drug and alcohol workers, community psychiatric nurses, and staff at family centres and at residential units for young people with drug problems. The group was comprised mainly of front-line practitioners, although a number of managers also participated. Less formal team discussions also took place in which some of the emerging themes were shared and debated.

What we have highlighted here are the main issues that came to the fore for the majority of the professionals to whom we spoke and their resonance with some of those identified by parents in Chapter 5.

The problem of engagement: access denied

A persistent theme that emerged for all professionals interviewed was that of gaining and sustaining trust in an area of work where parents were often frightened about the implications of their substance use, fearing legal intervention and removal of their children. Many of the difficulties identified centred around resistance and denial. Gaining an understanding of these issues was a key step towards proper engagement and assessment.

For those agencies where the adult was the primary client, this particularly manifested itself in fears of alienating the client and losing contact. As one commented, 'we do not want to be a sledgehammer…we want to help the person…if we refer them to social services because of our concerns, we may lose that therapeutic relationship with the parents'. Another referred to the difficulties inherent in such a process of referral: 'you have the problem of explaining that you are contacting social services…which can alienate clients'.

It was often difficult to gain realistic and consistent information about the parents' lifestyle, given clients' fears and anxieties about disclosure. There were many examples of parents who were themselves struggling to acknowledge the effects of their substance misuse and its potential impact and professionals gave graphic accounts of how this impeded the assessment process. As one observed, 'denial can be so strong that the parent won't move on the issue at all…often if it's about emotional abuse, it's harder for the parents to take on board the impact that their abuse is having on the child.' There were consistent problems with engagement, which were also affected by clients' fears about what action the agency might take and anxieties about what may happen to information disclosed. This influenced how often, when and where clients were seen and contributed to workers' sense of starting to make progress and then losing any ground that might have been gained. This worker's experience with a mother was not uncommon: 'She never sustains appointments…she drives me to distraction…you have some really good sessions, then I don't see her for three weeks'. Even when home visits were requested and arranged, success was far from guaranteed: 'often clients would arrange to be out'.

Gaining a real understanding of the impact of substance misuse proved to be a recurring dilemma because of inconsistent contact and frustrating gaps between meetings. Although there was general agreement that 'it's important to get alongside the parent because you want to know the truth', there was an acute awareness among many professionals, particularly those involved in the assessment of childcare, that parents had 'more reasons than usual' for being guarded about the information that they shared. 'Most clients are resistant or minimise, in these situations. Very few will say this is a problem and it affects my childcare', remarked one.

Here we see the way in which the fears, suspicions, fantasies and anxieties identified by parents and explored in Chapter 5 impact on the potential for professional engagement, reflecting practitioners' concerns highlighted in other studies (Bates *et al.* 1999; Elliot and Watson 1998, 2000). The importance of recognising this reality was seen as particularly significant. As professionals testified, secrecy and denial seemed central and pervasive characteristics of both the relationship between parents and children, and between parents and professionals. In some ways an atmosphere of secrecy and distrust in the home could often be mirrored in relationships between clients and workers. What appeared to emerge here was a problematic dynamic. Professionals were attempting to help, conscious that the first step in the process needed to be proper engagement. However, they were being viewed by parents as intrusive and potentially threatening, in terms of their child protection role. Although parents often seemed to want to sort things out, their natural fears frequently got in the way of real disclosure.

Given that reluctance and resistance are key issues, strategies for dealing with these were of major significance. In her research tracking the way in which 72 child abuse referrals to a social work team were processed through the system, Buckley (2000) highlights some crucial dynamics which determined the way in which decisions and assessments were reached. Although not specifically related to substance-using parents, many of her points seem directly transferable to problems of engagement in this area of practice, particularly the extent to which cases were engaged with or filtered out based on the dynamic that occurred between the professional and the family involved. Decisions were not based solely on the objective nature of the reported incident or area of concern. 'The context in which the concern was identified…was significant in determining the likely disposal of reported concerns' (Buckley 2000, p.255). This dynamic significantly influenced the way in which cases were negotiated, remained open or were closed.

In her study, key contextual influences included the reputation of the family, pessimism about their capacity for change, a fear of making judgements about parenting, in the light of overwhelming poverty, and anxiety about the potential impact of child protection procedures. Such factors could lead to either a tendency to reframe information too positively or a disinclination to search for (or refine) information which may change such a perception. Anxieties about making judgements where there were cultural differences were also evident, leading to an avoidance of such issues. Here we see the way in which the 'rule of optimism' and 'cultural relativism' (to be explored in detail in Chapter 10) can operate (Parton 1991, p.55). Buckley (2000) also found that

> as case careers moved forward…relationships between practitioners and parents were frequently *negotiated*, rather than imposed, implying the utilisation of control on each side…It became clear that, for a number of cases, the impetus for termination had been determined not by the way in which child abuse concerns abated, but the reluctance of clients…and the withdrawal of their co-operation. (Buckley 2000, p.259, emphasis in original)

Many of our respondents' accounts also illustrated the way in which families would 'close off' social work contact at points where it was perceived to be too threatening. Practitioners' frustration was evident as was, at times, their relief at being spared difficult encounters with reluctant and sometimes hostile parents. However, many were mindful of the way in which these situations reflected a curious power dynamic and were made uncomfortable by what seemed to be decision-making by default. These processes will be explored further when we consider the dynamics of assessment.

Differences between agencies: adults' needs, children's needs

Many of the dilemmas experienced by the professionals we interviewed reflected the particular orientation of the agency involved. Voluntary drug and alcohol agencies, statutory social services' children and families' teams and adult-focused services often had different starting points. Assessment, communication, the use of information, confidentiality, inter-agency liaison and levels of responsibility for assessing risk to children were all affected.

All the professionals interviewed acknowledged that they were involved in making some level of assessment of the impact of substance use on parenting, although in many cases this may have been intuitive or non-explicit. The function of the agency was one fairly obvious factor that influenced assessment. Thus the primary focus of the agency, core tasks, organisational pressures and constraints impacted upon the *breadth* of the assessment. As one person commented: 'The lack of resources means that you only do your bit of the work…the gap is trying to fit it all together'.

Shortage of resources often pushed workers to focus on particular aspects of a situation, as a way of avoiding becoming overwhelmed by 'multi-problem' families: 'If you have cases with grey areas/ambiguity regarding the family using drugs or alcohol and/or with mental health issues, often that family is thrown around services and people may be reluctant to pick it up, due to the volume of work that it takes.' This clearly came across as a critical practice issue and militated against gaining a holistic picture of the family.

A number of statutory drug workers acknowledged limitations in their assessment of children, due to their primary focus on the adult. This was coupled with a feeling that they had little sense of the parents' wider world, due to the pattern of contact, and only occasionally saw them with their children. In fact, in some cases, parents were discouraged from bringing children to office appointments due to inadequate facilities and the fact that their presence might affect open discussion with parents about their drug use.

There were also marked differences in the extent to which workers in adult services felt responsible for making an assessment of risk to children. Some identified a child protection role, albeit of a different nature to that of statutory childcare social services, which involved making some intuitive assessment about the ability to parent, based on the workers' knowledge of type of substance and pattern of use. In contrast, others working in criminal justice or adult mental health settings, while aware of the importance of assessment of risk which, in general terms, took account of the potential harm to children, tended to make a demarcation between this and any assessment of 'parenting capacity'. This was an area seen as exclusively the domain of social services. One professional commented:

> I don't know about parenting…for me if drugs and alcohol are around that is going to be damaging for the children, but I wouldn't feel qualified to assess 'good enough parenting'. I deal with risk of re-offending, risk of harm – the 'good enough parenting' judgement isn't mine to make.

Another added: 'I have never worked in childcare…don't have in-depth knowledge of the Children Act. I am clear about not doing something that I don't know anything about.'

Like others, these professionals expressed quite a detailed understanding of the potential effects of substance misuse on parenting, talked about issues of risk and expressed a view that they would refer to other, more appropriate, agencies if they identified any potential harm to children. What was evident was the boundary that they established around their role, which excluded assessing parenting. This was seen as a more precise, complex or specialist activity that needed to be undertaken by others. In other words, professionals were acknowledging the limitations of their ability to assess in the area of parenting capacity. This raises questions about the level of assessment of drug-related risk or client need that is expected and necessary at this stage. It also draws attention to different types of assessment of risk, emanating from the differing orientations of the agencies in question. As we discussed in Chapter 3, in the case of assessing adults with substance-misuse problems, the assessment of risk may be based more on risk and harm to others and to the user themselves, rather than on specific risks related to caring for children.

What emerged from many of the interviews was uncertainty about the knowledge base required to intervene when the identified recipient of services was an adult with a substance problem who had children. Some practitioners felt that the boundaries imposed on their assessment, in terms of agency protocols and function, were legitimate although many were clearly uncomfortable working in a culture which encouraged what was often seen as a blinkered approach. Professionals were honest about the gaps in their knowledge and the impact of this on confidence; staff from non-childcare agencies felt that they lacked experience and training in child protection issues and childcare workers felt vulnerable in relation to knowledge about drugs and alcohol.

Workers often struggled to identify exactly where their area of responsibility ended and that of others' began. In other words, there were issues for non-statutory adult workers about how far they needed to assess risk posed by substance misuse to children and deciding at which point to refer on. The majority of drug and alcohol workers were aware that their responsibility was to assess whether or not a referral to social services should be made rather than to assess 'risk' or 'need'. However, this was often more complex than it might seem. It was also difficult to know whether it was possible to make an informal approach to check out whether concerns were justified without triggering the might of the child protection machinery. This very much depended on inter-agency relations, a theme to which we shall return. Childcare workers were often wary about assessing risk posed by levels of substance misuse, fearing either over- or under-reacting. Clearly the prevailing climate of high client turnover, shortages of both staff and general resources and levels of knowledge affected decisions, as did the organisational climate in which risk and need were managed.

The differences in approaches to assessment, including assessment of risk, appeared particularly significant due to their profound implications for work undertaken on the issues of substance use and parenting. These differences also affected the degree to which the issue was either recognised but not worked with (that is to say simply 'held') or the point when, once a threshold of concern had been reached, a referral was made to social services or another agency.

Decisions about referrals and responses to them were also affected by both individual and wider organisational inter-agency relationships. So, for example, one children and families social worker expressed surprise at the relatively infrequent enquiries from other non-childcare agencies to 'check out' potential areas of concern, regarding substance-misusing parents. By the same token, one criminal justice worker alluded to the difference in the referral process when there was a pre-established working arrangement. In such cases there was greater possibility of a better exchange of information, as opposed to a more procedural or bureaucratic 'investigation'. In relation to the latter, sometimes it could feel as if a professional would either have to prove beyond any doubt or significantly amplify concern about the child, in order to convince another agency or team to accept the case. A child, then, would have to be at risk rather than in need in order to receive a service, contrary to the philosophy underpinning the *Framework for the Assessment of Children in Need and their Families* (Department of Health 2000a).

The way in which inter-agency dynamics impact upon these referral processes has been illustrated by other research studies. Scott's (1997) study of the interaction between child protection teams and other agencies identified the fact that the most noticeable characteristic of the relationship between 'core' agencies and other agencies was neither conflict nor cooperation but lack of interaction. An earlier study identifying the reasons for such problematic communication attributed this to the following factors: delays in passing on information, competing professional objectives, unrealistic expectations of powers or responsibilities, disputes about control or management or procedural inexperience (Waterhouse and Carnie 1991). Most significantly, Scott's (1997) study demonstrates how *organisational* perceptions and misperceptions shape particular approaches to cases, in relation to assessment, referral and intervention procedures. First, communication between professionals is likely to be characterised by greater conflict and the possible displacement of this on to other agencies, due to the high level of anxiety engendered by attempts to protect vulnerable children from harm (Scott 1997). Second, inter-agency communication is affected by the complexity of issues associated with confidentiality and the exchange of information. This is, of course, a critical component in terms of assessment, as the comprehensiveness and accuracy of this are dependent on information from a variety of agencies.

As a result of this, what can emerge are gatekeeping disputes which Scott (1997) suggests can be seen in the resistance of an overloaded or understaffed child protection service to accept referrals. These can manifest themselves in a number of ways, some of which may have potentially damaging consequences in relation to assessment and the progress of the case. In effect what can emerge is a vicious circle in relation to the referral process.

The agency that was involved initially may 'hold' the case too long, as a result of a perception that a child protection agency will not accept it. This can eventually lead to a false view about what constitutes a 'threshold of concern' or a view that referrals can only be made when a child is 'at risk' rather than 'in need'. Alternatively, and as a result of a perception that the case will be resisted, 'the referrer may emphasise the more negative aspects of the case in an attempt to have it accepted' (Scott 1997, p.77). The ultimate impact of this may be that the child protection service may then be inclined to discount what they perceive as an 'overly negative distortion of the situation being presented by the referring agency' (Scott 1997, p.77). Scott observes how easy it is for perceptions of such processes to become fixed, affected by the reputation of a particular agency, even when procedures and practice may have moved on. This highlights the importance of referring agencies checking out the reality of differing responses to referrals.

In our sample a number of children and families social workers expressed significant and repeated concerns about the division between services for children and those for adults. Some felt that there was not only a different agenda but also, at times, a polarisation that significantly affected the assessment process. Some thought that workers appeared to avoid asking their adult patients or clients crucial questions concerning their children, even when there was a clear need, given the circumstances of the carers' situation. Others felt that specialist drug workers were too exclusively focused on the needs of their adult clients and that concerns about sustaining trust and not breaching confidentiality appeared, at times, to override the principle that the child's welfare was the paramount consideration. As one observed: 'we try to focus on the child…other agencies try to pull us off this focus…being in two camps either supporting the child or the adult affects our ability to work together to find a common cause'. This central dilemma is recognised in the guidelines for working with drug-misusing parents (see Appendix 2): 'child-centred services may not understand or feel confident in dealing with drug users, while specialist drug services may not understand the needs of children or child protection procedures' (SCODA 1997, p.4). In the eyes of some childcare social workers there was often a failure to grasp the necessity of gaining information and acting on it and, where necessary, in high-risk cases, breaching confidentiality, in the interests of the child.

A major dilemma was the different timescales within which workers tended to operate and this highlighted a particularly acute example of the potential split in services due to differing perspectives. Some adult-focused workers viewed the dependent substance-misusing behaviour as a chronic condition which, having taken years to develop, may take years to relinquish, and where relapse, for example, was seen as a stage to recovery. Child welfare workers, on the other hand, were more acutely aware of the damage that could occur to children in terms of development and welfare while the adult's struggle with drugs or alcohol was being tackled, quite apart from the need to ensure their physical and emotional safety. While the long-term goals for both adult and child were not mutually exclusive, the timescales for different professionals raised significant and fundamental differences. One worker summed this up perfectly: 'the time scale for a child is very different from that of an adult…and we can't afford to wait that long'. This difficulty manifested itself explicitly for children and family social workers in the judgement made about the time allowed to assess the capacity for change against the current risk.

A key task, then, was seen as balancing an assessment of the parents' capacity to change with the risk to the child. As a childcare worker explained:

> There is always going to be an element of risk working with families that have this sort of problem [substance misuse] and especially when you are dealing with very young babies or younger children. From my point of view as a social worker I think the biggest dilemma is that you want to move the plan on…you want to give the carer the opportunity to really move forward and to have that time to do well…you want to go ahead, on the one hand, but you want the child protected as much as possible.

Given that we have already alluded to the potential problem of concentrating on adults' needs at the cost of children's, how are these apparently competing needs to be reconciled? In our research, a number of professionals referred to agencies that had managed to resolve these conflicts more successfully. Many talked about clarity of communication and joint working. Others talked about the way that particular agencies, despite the pressures experienced, had somehow managed to support the adult yet, at the same time, support the work the childcare services were undertaking with the children. Another commented on a 'style' of approach that balanced work with the adult with retaining awareness of central issues for the child:

> They are very up front about their work with adults and adopt ways of not being deflected from concerns regarding the child, despite feeling sorry for the adults…they are up front about our function and purpose and support this.

Practice with children: engagement, low visibility and parents' needs

Professionals identified a range of issues that arose for them in relation to their contact and practice with children. One theme centred around an awareness of the effects of parental substance misuse, the pressures it caused in families and the impact on children's behaviour and development. Workers could see that children appeared withdrawn and were clearly troubled and distressed both by the manifestations of parents' use and the feelings engendered in the children concerned. In one graphic account, a family centre worker described a child whose apparent withdrawal from the world seemed to echo that of his mother's retreat as a response to chronic alcohol misuse. He seemed to have simply 'given up on life' and the implications for potential emotional abuse as well as his mental health were clearly of concern. The mother's depression and view of the outside world was seen to influence the child's and, at times, they would both spend the day under the duvet in the living room. It was difficult to engage with the child, particularly when the mother's own problems appeared overwhelming, and there was a perceived need to support the parent as carer for the child. Another professional commented on a similar pattern of behaviour which was viewed as 'a type of emeshment with the parent'. The pervasive influence of problems at home had left the child feeling responsible for them. In other words the child's anxieties concerning the parent's problems manifested themselves in her reluctance to detach herself from the situation, when they saw how the parent was struggling to cope at home. Another example of such behaviour was illustrated by a child who sat in front of the video all day with the curtains drawn as a way of cutting off from the feelings of anxiety within the home.

One recurring problem was gaining access to and communicating with children. One child protection social worker said that children often revealed the impact on their lives only much later, usually once they were no longer in the middle of the situation and when issues of safety and loyalty were not so critical. A drug worker from the statutory sector also stressed the importance of keeping in mind how hard it is for children is to be heard – 'there is very little a child can do to access services independently, because of the interaction in the family'.

Other professionals also acknowledged these difficulties. Many observed that it was easier to make sense of children's experience as a reaction to the problems caused by their parents' drug or alcohol use, in retrospect. While the children were actually in the situation, it was more difficult to pick up what may have been going on for them.

Such responses made actual communication with children difficult particularly in an environment where (as was observed) parents' needs proved a major source of anxiety and where there may often have been difficulties in gaining regular access to children. Perhaps this in part explained an observation made by a children and families worker: 'agencies can work with families for an awfully long time without seeing the focus as the children'. Others commented on children's 'protectiveness' towards their parents. This was noted on a number of occasions, often accompanied by both amazement and respect for children's support and loyalty, at least on the face of it, despite the problems experienced by the children themselves. One professional summed this up by referring to the difficulty for some children of 'stepping outside the pattern of family life'. Another, in commenting on the difficulties of engaging with a teenager, described 'a bond with mum which has overridden everything'. It was often difficult to get a clear sense of a child's response to the situation at home as this could veer from acceptance of the situation and a caring attitude to the parent to apparently unfocused anger. Another professional felt that the child's pattern of inconsistent behaviour was possibly linked to his experience of parenting which was very good one minute and chronically bad the next. The child's anger created a real barrier to engagement.

While the complex dynamic between parent and child was seen by some to impinge on gaining information about the child's situation, further difficulties were created by the relationship between parents and professionals. As one statutory alcohol and drugs worker explained, the use of alcohol and drugs can act to suppress parents' anxieties about children and consequently it can be difficult to gain an accurate sense of what is going on until defences are lowered. The dangers of this lack of information were seen as very significant: 'you don't get evidence of where the child is at or what the child is saying until further into the proceedings…so that I feel that children are often extremely damaged by the time you get to child protection proceedings…you don't get to the child until too late'.

A community psychiatric nurse working in a substance misuse team commented that it was very difficult gaining a sense of the actual 'drug-taking behaviour' to which children were being exposed and, again, there was the issue of becoming distracted from the children's needs, when dealing with parents in crisis: 'Sometimes they attend with the children and sometimes they don't. When they do attend it's difficult to know whose needs to focus on.' Another talked about the importance of not making assumptions that older children would cope better. The difficulty of recognising the impact on older children has been highlighted in research which suggests that both the focus on prenatal exposure, infants and toddlers, and the fact that adolescents tend to be at school, working or elsewhere when the parents seek treatment has led to their being ignored (Hampton *et al.* 1998; Tunnard 2002).

Most significantly, perhaps, many professionals alluded to the inconsistent picture that they got due to the lack of sustained observational evidence of how the children were coping. One children and families social worker stressed the importance of gaining observational evidence from other settings – for example playgroups, nurseries, schools. It was generally felt that such evidence may be more productively gathered from workers with more direct knowledge of the child (for example family centre staff) and there was an awareness of the importance of thinking of strategies to offset this potential 'invisibility' of children. Some commented that they were only too painfully aware that 'we pay lip service to the emotional impact on children in such circumstances'. They felt that a range of methods of assessment were needed in order to break down the barriers that precluded more detailed insight into the realities of the behavioural impact within the home setting. Such strategies are discussed in more detail in Chapter 10.

Apart from the sheer difficulty of gaining sustained contact with children, then, there were problems in understanding and making sense of their experience. Working in a climate where parents' problems were often chronic, the difficulty of focusing on the child in such an environment and the potential impact that the substance itself played in affecting the parents' attitude and responses were also seen as problematic. Many workers were also all too aware that they were unlikely to get any sense of what life was like for children unless or until they had been removed from parental care. Often attempting to engage with children was seen as either too threatening for parents or pointless unless the worker could offer some kind of concrete help or respite from the problems. Some were able to acknowledge that they avoided such engagement precisely because they felt they had nothing to offer.

Communicating across agencies and the issue of confidentiality

Although it was generally acknowledged that the child's welfare was the paramount consideration in law (Children Act 1989), how and when information was communicated across agencies was a key issue for many professionals. This was seen to affect significantly the quality of assessment and the timeliness of intervention, particularly in cases of high risk. Many considered that there were a range of inter-agency responses from different groups, reflecting various occupational, philosophical, organisational and procedural arrangements. These were seen to have a profound impact on the ability of agencies to work together effectively and, again, to reflect some splits between the primary focus of the agencies involved.

Some childcare social workers felt that the attitudes of professionals in other agencies towards sharing information was influenced by a reluctance to be seen in a bad light by adult clients and that this often resulted in the adoption of what they saw as an inappropriate advocacy or rescuing role. This manifested itself in a tendency to focus on parenting the client, rather than exploring their parenting capacity.

> Often agencies support the adult to the extent that they are losing sight of the child. Some agencies sit in on meetings stating that they can't say anything because their work with the client is confidential. Fundamentally, that doesn't help the person with the [substance-misuse] problem.

From a different perspective, several statutory drug workers identified a confidentiality dilemma linked to issues of trust and engagement.

> Women in particular are worried about judgemental attitudes...and fear losing their children...so that you are trying to reassure them about confidentiality which links to trust...sometimes they can be reserved about telling you about childcare issues – on the other hand sometimes you are used as their confidante which can be difficult.

Other professionals including, in particular, a number of childcare social workers, felt that the procedural arrangements for sharing inter-agency information were too slow and restrictive. On a number of occasions the difficulty of gaining the appropriate information from general practitioners was mentioned, some of whom would only respond following a formal written request. There was the additional problem of doctors' availability when such formal protocols were in place. As one respondent observed:

GPs will do it [share information] but require procedural arrangements that are too slow…the mechanism does not seem to be there for a very fast response and speed does influence the decisions that we make.

One professional described what was perceived as a split in confidentiality issues between statutory and voluntary agencies. It was felt that at times there was something of a divide here between some statutory and some voluntary agencies, particularly street drug agencies. In such cases communication was more difficult and issues of confidentiality more conflictual. Another person interviewed from the statutory sector commented that different agencies had different philosophical approaches towards client confidentiality, which affected the type and degree of information shared.

Some agencies have an overdeveloped sense of confidentiality and some have an overdeveloped sense of political correctness. My being honest can sometimes be seen as a breach of confidentiality.

This seemed to reflect an over-adherence to procedures at the expense of the consequences for other agencies and more vulnerable individuals.

There seemed to be a number of issues here. The way in which issues of confidentiality and inter-agency liason impacted upon the work with the parent or child was a clear preoccupation and source of frustration for many. Then there were issues in relation to barriers to clearer and more concordant approaches to inter-agency working and confidentiality that recognised the needs of the child as paramount. Overall, no clear pattern emerged. There were difficulties expressed between different social care professionals working for the same authority (for example those in mental health and social services teams) and differences and variations across voluntary and statutory agencies.

Different approaches to assessment

Professionals varied both in their approaches to assessment and their use of particular frameworks and guidelines to assist with this task in relation to substance-misusing parents. A number of children and families workers referred to the way they had adapted child assessment frameworks such as the 'orange book'. (The 'orange book' is the commonly used name for *Protecting Children: A Guide for Social Workers Undertaking a Comprehensive Assessment* (Department of Health 1988). This guide aimed to provide a framework to enable practitioners to make longer-term plans to protect children and assist families, once an initial investigation of abuse had been undertaken. It has now been replaced by the new *Framework for the Assessment of Children in Need and their Families.)* Others were aware of more specific materials regarding substance-misusing parents, although there was generally limited use of these. In many cases, such workers had partnership arrangements with a drug or alcohol agency and would use them to help make assessments. There were a number who were unaware that their own agencies had guidelines for working with substance-misusing parents (as distinct from the SCODA guidelines already referred to) despite the fact that they were included in child protection manuals available in all local authority offices.

Some who were aware of either particular frameworks or inter-agency guidelines discussed the extent to which these assisted in gaining an accurate picture of the family in question or enabled a better sharing of information. One worker commented that the SCODA guidelines (see Appendix 2) were helpful in deciding whether a referral to the children and families team should be made and another that they were a valuable reminder of some of the core issues. However, some considered that they were too generalised to be of particular use and that, since the key task lay in gaining an understanding of the *links* between misuse of substances, other life pressures and parenting, guidelines were limited in helping with this.

The extent to which guidelines were considered to be helpful varied when it came to considering the impact of the substance misuse on family functioning in general and child welfare in particular. Although they were 'baseline reminders' of the key issues to consider, the degree to which they could assist in more fundamental ways was debatable. In particular their potential for helping to make connections between patterns of use and parenting and helping to overcome issues of denial or resistance was questionable. Potential ways of addressing such problems will be explored in Chapter 10.

One statutory drugs worker described what he called a 'lifestyle' approach to assessing substance-misusing parents. He used a model which involved thinking oneself into the particular ways that substance misuse may impact on day-to-day issues involving parenting. While guidelines may help as an aide-memoire, his approach was actually based on gaining access to the main tensions between parenting and drug misuse. Discussions about family activities, play between parent and child, how they spent time together, and how school work was supported would often generate information that helped make connections between substance misuse and children's behaviour, particularly in relation to the impact of parents' moods, ability to maintain routines and so on.

Such discussions helped gain a clearer sense of not only the child's experience within the home, but also the level of attachment between parent and child. This approach acknowledged parents' struggles with anxiety and guilt about their children's development and attempted to build up a more realistic picture from these key interactions, while recognising the part the substance may be playing in the ambiguous response from the parent concerned.

> Client's concerns are often already raised…but…they may not be able to engage [with you] or articulate these concerns, at the start of contact. Drug or alcohol use may be smoothing over the edges…it can be an emotional anaesthetic…it may be dampening down the unease they have about their parenting…My aim was to gain clients' trust in order for them to begin to express their suppressed concerns about their own parenting. Here it was not just about engaging with the client but engaging them on the issue of substance misuse and parenting.

Different agencies were often seen to hold different briefs in relation to assessment. There were descriptions of some instances where particular agencies appeared to rely on their own assessment procedures almost to the exclusion of those of others. This resulted in ignoring or overriding accumulated knowledge of a family from another agency which had been involved for a longer period. One family centre worker described a case where an assessment had been made about the parents' complex pattern of alcohol use, within a neighbourhood setting, which appeared to have been largely ignored by a children and families team on the basis of their own more limited 'snapshot' assessment. However, as a result of this experience the family centre staff initiated greater collaboration at the point of referral and more concordance about the type of assessment tools used.

Joining 'snapshots'

The importance of piecing together different types of information from different sources in a timely and consistent way has already been highlighted. There were, however, a number of difficulties in relation to this.

Many professionals were concerned about the limitations and frustrations of undertaking what they termed 'snapshot' assessments:

> you only get a snapshot of people's lives…once they leave here you don't get any real idea of what they are doing…some things you have to take at face value…some things you have to challenge, some things you piece together because of what others see or hear.

There were also problems identified at each stage of intervention that made it difficult to gain an holistic or joined-up assessment of the impact of substance misuse on family life and parenting.

Some commented on the inconsistent and fragmented way that information was gained. This may have been due to minimising the substance-misuse problem, and/or the fact that the substance in question was being used erratically. Consequently, information about the pattern of substance misuse could be absent (withheld), inconsistent or intermittent. Often there were examples of professionals encountering a roller-coaster effect. In other words, clients' description of their pattern of use sometimes appeared to move from crisis to stability in an unrealistic way. Both the absence of constant information about the link between the substance use and parental functioning and the pattern of 'acute episodes' gave professionals cause for concern that they were not seeing the whole picture. As a result emotional abuse, in particular, was not being consistently addressed. This was seen as extremely difficult to establish since a parent may have been chronically misusing drugs or alcohol for many years without their children coming to the attention of agencies. Some child protection workers raised the question of society's tolerance of such low-level abuse and a tendency for professionals to concentrate on acute episodes. This can give an inaccurate representation of the way that substance misuse impacts upon the adults' ability to parent.

Another issue seen to affect the problems of gaining honest information about the pattern of use related to the approach taken by the agency. This could arise from laudable attempts to engage and encourage change in the adult. Some recognised a real dilemma here, in that many parents had histories of being seen as 'failures' in most aspects of their lives. Consequently an ethos of encouragement rather than criticism had been established in the agency based on an approach that linked improvements in self-esteem to an increase in parenting capacity. However, this could, as a result, place too much emphasis on the adults' rehabilitation as a precursor to better parenting. As this worker commented, 'We have had to look at how we colluded with the parents' drinking cycle...perhaps we have unconsciously colluded with the adult as we have focused on them achieving changes.'

Workers from both adult and child-centred services underlined the difficult balancing act required when developing a helping alliance with the parent while retaining a child-centred focus – a theme which echoed findings from other research (Feig 1998; Glaser 1995). It was generally acknowledged that communication about concerns needed to be clear, direct and honest even when this might be painful to receive and strenuously resisted by both the parent(s) and the worker. Struggles and dilemmas included the fact that drug or alcohol use may have become a long-term coping mechanism for managing other problems. In addition the tension between the parents' desire to return to a 'real' relationship with their children that was not affected by substance use and the difficulty of achieving this had to be confronted (Elliott and Watson 2000). Equally important was recognition of the impact that simple changes could make to the lifestyle of substance-misusing parents by improving a child's routine, for example, or establishing earlier bedtimes, more regular attendance at school and so on (Heal 2000).

Summary

Substance misuse and child protection systems have, historically, developed separately and have traditionally held different orientations (Ashton 1999; Murphy and Oulds 2000). Such differences fundamentally affect both the way in which agencies interact and how professionals work together and a number of different barriers to collaboration have been identified. One is the issue of what could be called 'different professional missions' (Colby and Murrell 1998, p.193). From the child welfare perspective, the clients are the children and their protection takes priority over the parents' needs, because children cannot protect themselves. From the substance-misuse treatment perspective, the substance users are the clients and their treatment is the primary target of intervention (Colby and Murrell 1998).

It seems clear that a variety of inter-agency and inter-professional dynamics affect practice in families where parents misuse substances. What is now well recognised is that these tensions are both organisational and individual and often reflect historical undercurrents as well as replicating the dynamics of the complex family systems that are often encountered (Buckley 2000; Reder *et al.* 1993; Reder and Lucey 1995). What is also apparent is that practice often occurs within a system that is often preoccupied with events. This mitigates against types of assessments that are able to reveal 'the ongoing parental climate or atmosphere' (Daniel 2000, p.92). This has particular significance for children of substance-misusing parents, given concern about children experiencing levels of emotional harm or neglect, which are particularly difficult to identify or address.

Differing orientations among agencies reflect differing priorities and these can manifest themselves in the way in which work is undertaken. The way information is shared, how protocols regarding confidentiality are managed and perceived, and levels of responsibility for child protection issues can all differ considerably. Decisions about when a child becomes an identified cause for concern are variable and affected by a range of factors, including a climate of competing cases and limited budgets in organisations often beset by staff shortages, worker stress, poor management and inadequate supervision. There is also the central difficulty of gaining information about the pattern of substance misuse and the particular impact on the child.

Parents' fears of stigmatisation and the dynamic of secrecy between parents and children lead to significant problems regarding engagement and inquiry. This has been highlighted in Chapter 5 with regard to parents and in Chapter 7 in relation to children. There are specific dilemmas in engaging children and professionals have highlighted a number of significant issues that prevent a real assessment of both their situation and their needs. Given the significant emotional pressures in which the work takes place and the constant shortage of resources, the organisational context in which such assessments occur is bound to impact adversely. It is likely, then, that it is the combination of all these factors that leads to what professionals in our sample described in metaphors which graphically conveyed experiences of incompleteness, inconsistency and abrupt changes.

Our study clearly reflected many of the dilemmas identified in other areas of social welfare practice. Engagement with distrustful families, problems in creating an environment where disclosure was possible and fears and fantasies about powers and precipitous action were all recurring themes. There were anxieties and insecurities for both childcare workers and adult-based professionals about their levels of knowledge and the degree to which they felt equipped to assess behaviours which were outside their immediate realm of expertise. Practice in relation to children raised a number of dilemmas in relation to access, confidentiality, impotence and the pain caused by encounters with children for whom there seemed only limited options. Concerns about the limitations of 'snapshots' and how these could usefully be put alongside one another were also evident.

This study provided us with considerable insight into critical aspects of assessment and intervention where substance misuse is an issue in families. The potential for more holistic and effective approaches to both these processes will form the focus of Chapters 10 and 11.

10

Towards an Holistic Approach to Assessment

To ask the question whether drug addicts make good parents is to pose a question which, while offensive in its formulation, is serious in its import.

(Barnard 1999, p.1109)

From the initial assessment right through to the courts in extreme cases, the complexity of the parent/child relationship is still assessed in a simplistic and linear manner based on short term observations of parental drug use...they [assessment procedures] tend to focus exclusively on acute episodes rather than the everyday life of parent and child. Moreover they do not mention alcohol which is the major substance of concern.

(Aldridge 1999, p.8)

When it comes to assessing parenting, in the context of substance misuse, there is a clear dilemma about the extent to which it can be assessed independent of the drug or alcohol issue. In this chapter, we move on to a more practical engagement with some of the issues discussed so far, specifically concerning how we assess and intervene effectively in families where substance misuse is an issue. What should be done when and by whom? Who is 'qualified' to assess parenting and evaluate risk to children? How can we effectively engage with children themselves so that we can enter the child's world and know something about what it is like to be there? Why is it that children so consistently get 'lost', fall through gaps in services or remain 'invisible'? Why is it so hard to share our interventions and ideas and work together? How do we – or can we – move away from the snapshot approach based on these 'acute episodes' towards a more holistic, fluid and above all *real* engagement with parent–child dynamics and the context in which they take place – in other words, use the assessment framework in the spirit in which it was conceived?

This chapter attempts to chart a path through this territory by exploring the most significant issues for assessment in relation to substance misuse, as a prelude to looking at intervention in Chapter 11. This is inevitably an artificial separation since, as Rose and Aldgate (2000) point out, assessment and intervention are part of an intertwined, evolving process. Information of various kinds is collected, sifted, synthesised and analysed, informed by what Milner and O'Byrne (1998, p.5) term 'respectful uncertainty and a research mentality' which is in turn harnessed to a clear value base. The role that assessment might play as intervention must also be borne in mind.

Some useful guidelines will be offered in relation to assessment and then particular attention will be turned to approaches to establishing the wishes and feelings of children. What we shall not be offering is a model that supposedly 'works'; what works for some may not work for all, since all individuals and families are unique. For the purposes of this debate it is not the generalities of assessment that concern us but rather the specifics, within the context of substance misuse and there are a number of significant issues that deserve attention.

Assessing parenting

In the context of parental substance misuse, the aims of assessment are to ensure the child's safety, to reduce, manage or make safe the substance use and to determine whether a child is in need or at risk (Bates *et al.* 1999; SCODA 1997). As we saw in Chapter 6, this need–risk continuum has long been the focus of much debate (see for example Cleaver *et al.* 1998, 1999; Department of Health 1995; Parton 1991, 1996; Parton *et al.* 1997). Concerns have been expressed about the preoccupation with risk to the detriment of need, resulting in many children falling through the net and failing to get the services they require. In addition, the focus has increasingly been on 'acts' rather than actors, the 'what?' rather than the 'why?' of behaviour (Howe 1996, p.88). As Daniel (2000, p.92) observes, what gets missed as a result is the 'parental climate or atmosphere' in which the behaviour takes place which (as we saw in Chapter 5) is a significant element in families where there is substance misuse.

The complexities inherent in the assessment of parenting in general have long been the focus of much study and debate (see for example Belsky and Vondra 1989; Bettelheim 1987; Reder and Lucey 1995; Winnicott 1964). However, the debate has now moved centre stage since the inception of the new *Framework for the Assessment of Children in Need and their Families* and an increased awareness of the impact of parental problems on children. As we have already seen, parental behaviour is now no longer considered only in light of whether it is either 'good enough' or not. Rather it is considered to be multiply determined by a constellation of factors which impact and interact on and with each other (Belsky and Vondra 1989; Reder and Lucey 1995; Woodcock forthcoming). Determining how these factors influence each other is a complex and demanding task in itself. However, the more recent debates have focused on the additional problem of how social work assessments are influenced by the constructions of parenting held by social workers themselves (Daniel 2000; Holland 2000; Woodcock forthcoming). Further contributions have been provided by feminist analyses of parenting, 'caring' and assessment (see for example Turney 2000) as well as the role of 'mother blaming' (see Chapter 5). Additional debates have also centred on the extent to which assessment and intervention are linked with knowledge and placed within the context of an understanding of the dynamic nature of the parenting task (Buckley 2000) as well as the reflexive nature of assessment (see for example Sheppard 1998). This relates to the interactive dynamic between the worker, the people worked with, the worker's analysis, knowledge, research and procedures.

This notion of reflexivity underlines the fact that assessment is not just a 'technical' activity but also involves various underlying factors which influence practice. Personal beliefs and values about what is 'good' or 'good enough' come into play and these are often influenced by workers' own experiences of being parented or being parents themselves. Daniel's (2000) study clearly illustrates this. Accounts from some social workers made it clear that in undertaking assessments they were, in part, being guided by where their own children were developmentally, and the nature of their own family life. By the same token, it would be logical to assume that workers who are not parents may have an idealised notion of what parenting should be like and how they might do it if they were to parent. Alternatively, they may feel 'disqualified' to judge because they do not have children and may make a number of allowances for parenting behaviour which may or may not be appropriate. In relation to substance misuse, research has highlighted the implications of workers' fear, fantasies, stereotypes and prejudices for assessment and intervention in this area of work (Adams 1999; Bates *et al.* 1999; Kearney 1994; Klee 1998). Moreover, as Bates *et al.* (1999) point out, where there is drug misuse, the picture is further complicated by the illegality of the behaviour and the fact that such parents are often considered to be 'a pariah group' (Bates *et al.* 1999, p.79). Differing approaches are also required depending on whether the substance abuse is already identified as an issue, in contrast to situations where there is suspicion but no acknowledgement or concrete evidence.

Issues in assessment

As we saw in Chapter 9, what appears clear is that everyone, irrespective of his or her involvement, is making some kind of assessment of parenting capacity at some level once they are aware that someone who is misusing drugs or alcohol has children. The extent to which this transfers itself into a referral to social services, for example, may differ from one agency to another suggesting that different thresholds may be being applied. In addition there are issues to do with levels of confidence in relation to 'specialist' knowledge. In an ideal world, professionals should come together, each holding pieces of a complex jigsaw puzzle which is effectively the 'picture' of the family in question. What actually happens, however, may often be very different. A competition between the people involved about who knows best or most may result in a power play about status, rather than an holistic assessment. The dynamics of the family may become replicated in the professional system and cause unhelpful interactions that prevent the jigsaw from being completed (Reder and Duncan 1999; Reder *et al.* 1993). Equally possible is the potential for collusion, with all the professionals reassuring one another that things are all right really. Another option is a dynamic which is aimed at avoiding taking on a complex family by parcelling up their problems and distributing them around the professional network. As Buckley (2000, p.258) discovered, 'case conferences were frequently dominated by unacknowledged tensions which bore little relevance to the welfare or protection of the children concerned'.

There are also critical issues to do with client loyalty, as we have seen. For workers in adult services, commitment to helping their identified client – the adult in the family – may lead them either to underestimate the impact of behaviour on the children or to avoid exploring what life for the children might be like. This can result in adult-focused workers 'protecting' parents from child-focused intervention, based on their belief that childcare workers overreact and fail to appreciate the parents' point of view, and that their intervention is likely to lead to a deterioration in their client's well-being. Suspicion works in the other direction, too, with childcare workers evaluating information from drug and alcohol workers in a less than positive light, believing that crucial or potentially damning information might be being withheld or diluted. As Cleaver *et al.* (1999, p.100) observe, 'Professionals tend to focus on the needs of their specific client group... This may result in polarised views which effectively block joint working.'

Working Together to Safeguard Children (Department of Health 1999) highlights various factors, identified from research, that can affect the assessment process. Although these are discussed in relation to child protection, they clearly have resonance for any engagement between social welfare professionals and families. The following synthesis is taken from *Working Together*, the study by Cleaver *et al.* (1998) for the NSPCC and the work undertaken by Cleaver *et al.* (1999).

The validity and status accorded to information from different sources was identified as a crucial issue in relation to evidence and the weight attached to it. Information from high-profile referrers, family, friends and neighbours all had to be evaluated equally and fairly. By the same token information from children needed to be accorded more attention, alongside the way they looked and behaved. The effects on children of parents' problems were not appreciated and, as a result, children often got lost in the assessment process.

Parental behaviour was also seen as a critical factor with levels of cooperation or lack of it often leading to misunderstanding, misinterpretation and the formation of unhelpful assumptions. These, in turn, tended to cause significant information, including crucial observations, to be missed or ignored. As Cleaver *et al.* (1998, p.4) pointed out, 'attention is focused on the most visible or pressing problems and other warning signs are not appreciated'. Often uncooperative or evasive behaviour on the part of the parent was assumed to be an attempt to cover up child abuse whereas in fact it was often in order to hide other problems, including substance misuse.

Closely linked to this was parents' anxiety about losing children and their reluctance to admit problems, due to fear of a punitive response. Professionals' tendency to avoid confrontations where they were aware that parents had various problems militated against thorough investigation or assessment and fear of families with aggressive reputations caused workers to back off and avoid confessing their fears or asking for help (Cleaver *et al.* 1998). The fact that social workers often lacked knowledge and understanding about the parental problem in question and its likely impact on both parents and the family, prevented the parents' perspective from being appreciated. This in turn got in the way of establishing any meaningful and open level of communication. In addition, assumptions tended to be made by social workers that explanations and information had been understood, when in fact this was often not the case. Entering the world of families where there is substance abuse generates feelings on both the side of the worker and the family members. Most notable of these, on the families' side, are anxiety, suspicion, mistrust and fear as well as resistance and denial (Bates *et al.* 1999; Cleaver and Freeman 1995; Farmer and Owen 1998). Characteristically the hope of help and the fear of intervention and where it might lead often provide an uneasy mix.

Final points relate to the quality of information gathered and how or whether it was used if the child was not in fact seen to be 'at risk'. Recording, checking of facts and the basis for decisions were all identified as areas of concern, as was the fact that families where there was no risk were rarely referred to preventive services.

Substance misuse: values, beliefs and feelings

We have seen the way in which parenting can fall victim to a range of racist and gendered assumptions, quite apart from those generated by substance misuse itself. It is also generally accepted that personal values and histories, stereotypes and other 'baggage' often get in the way of being able to see clearly what is happening and why, which in turn may affect both intervention and processes between professionals (Adams 1999; Buckley 2000; Reder *et al.* 1993). The way in which prejudice and personal beliefs affect practice and the gap between these and research knowledge has also been identified as a cause for concern (Daniel 2000). In addition Adams (1999) has drawn attention to the fact that, although social workers might state that they are not prejudiced against parents who misuse substances, what they actually believe and feel may be different. This highlights how difficult it can be to express concerns about substance-misusing parents without fear of being branded 'politically incorrect'. Awareness of the way in which all these elements affect assessment and who gets access to services is clearly an important component of good practice, as is the way in which such dynamics can often prevent the child from being seen.

Workers may also feel aware of their lack of knowledge including the ways in which different substances might impact on parenting. As Forrester (2000) found in his study, workers had very different approaches to rating their concerns about alcohol and heroin and one possible explanation for this was

> that social workers are more concerned about heroin because of differences in our culture's attitudes towards heroin and alcohol. Their personal familiarity with alcohol use may lead social workers to see it as a contributory factor within wider social problems, while their lack of knowledge of heroin may lead them to see heroin as *the* problem rather than a pattern of concerning behaviour. (Forrester 2000, p.243)

Workers, hoping to be helpful and useful, may also feel stuck and overwhelmed, as they attempt to sort out what behaviour belongs to what. Is this to do with the substance misuse or is this a general childcare issue? Working with families where children may be at risk also evokes strong feelings and they have to be both harnessed usefully and managed effectively if a real working relationship is to be established (Reder and Lucey 1995).

The influence of the rule of optimism, cultural relativism and 'natural love'

This brings us to a number of additional dynamics (touched on in Chapter 5) that can occur between worker and client in relation to the process of change and the progress made in relation to it. The first of these has been identified by Dingwall (1986; Dingwall, Eekelaar and Murray 1983) as the 'rule of optimism'. Parton describes this as an approach which 'meant that the most favourable interpretation was put upon the behaviour of the parents and that anything that may question this was discounted or redefined' (Parton 1991, p.55). This is akin to what Prins (1999) has described as 'unauthenticated optimism' – a wish to see things moving forward, or improving, despite any evidence to suggest this is happening – although Parton's definition suggests an active move to reframe information in a potentially dangerous fashion. Here, then, there is a temptation to accord the status of a giant leap forward to the slightest signs of progress or improvement, even though the evidence may be flimsy or even non-existent except in the worker's imagination. While the temptation is clear, particularly when working with complex situations, where very little movement has been discernible, the dangers of being over-positive are obvious. A parent may be less intoxicated on this visit than on the last; this does not mean that the drinking is under control or that the causes of the drinking have been addressed. A parent may have sought treatment for a drug problem; again, celebration would be premature, since, as Aldridge (1999) points out, treatment can, initially, often exacerbate risk rather than reduce it. Although it is clearly important to build on strengths and acknowledge improvement in parenting skills and behaviour, it is also imperative that signs of change for the better do not tempt workers to avoid looking further at other factors which may counterbalance this view (Buckley 2000).

In his analysis of this tendency, Parton sees it as linked to two further 'devices' – cultural relativism and what he calls 'natural love' (Parton 1991, p.55). Cultural relativism refers to a variety of processes that come into play in relation to culture – in all senses of the term (see Chapter 5) – and ethnicity. This includes applying different standards to people based on assumptions, due to lack of knowledge, awareness or understanding, that behaviour is 'cultural', rather than exploring its potential for being abusive or harmful in some way. Parton (1991) analysed this tendency with specific reference to the Jasmine Beckford tragedy where it appeared that a white middle-class social worker felt unable or was unwilling to challenge the child-rearing practices or parenting behaviours of a black working-class family (London Borough of Brent 1985). There was an implicit assumption that the social worker had no right to criticise, since these behaviours could be cultural and any imposition of other standards would be perceived as racist.

Cultural relativism was also highlighted by the inquiry into the death of Victoria Climbié where it became apparent that a range of behaviours were attributed to cultural norms rather than troubling child–carer dynamics. Another example of this is in Buckley's (2000) study of social work practice where she found that very different standards were applied to discipline and living conditions in families who were not part of the indigenous population. Equally problematic in this context is what Banks refers to as 'a preoccupation with the exotic and unusual' to the exclusion of other relevant factors (Banks 2001, p.148).

Alongside cultural relativism sits what Parton (1991) terms 'natural love' – the belief that all parents love their children and that relationships between parents and children are instinctive and, well, natural. If this is someone's position, as Parton observes, it makes it very difficult to see anything which challenges this view, since it goes to the root of all that is natural in human behaviour. What we know, of course, is that some parents do not or cannot love their children, for all kinds of complex reasons – what the child represents, unresolved issues from the parents' own childhood, for example – and that, even when they do, love may not be enough to protect them (Reder *et al.* 1993). The dangers of idealising parenthood have to be recognised.

Importantly for this discussion, this constellation of devices may have particular implications in families where there is substance misuse. First, it may cause an overemphasis on the substance use and all that surrounds it, to the exclusion of what is happening to the children, particularly if assumptions about 'natural love' are also coming into play. Second, it may have implications for the way the 'drug' or 'alcohol' culture in which the family may operate is perceived. If, for example, there is a cultural assumption about lifestyle in relation to drug use (the idea, perhaps, that all drug users are a bit chaotic, come and go at irregular times and are different from 'us') this might raise issues about whether standards are tolerated in the drug community that would not be acceptable in families where this is not an issue. Furthermore, if cultural assumptions are made in relation to race and ethnicity, in addition to assumptions about the 'drug' or 'drink' culture, this will compound the situation further. This suggests that all aspects of a family's culture need to be explored, so that assumptions are not made at any level.

The picture is further complicated by what might be called 'baseline parenting'. This relates to the overall nature of the client group and community in which the worker operates. In other words, if the worker is involved with an overwhelmingly impoverished community of families experiencing multiple stresses and deprivation, as is likely to be the case in large inner cities or in some rural areas, in theory all the children could be assessed as being 'in need' if the strict definition is applied. However, clearly the inclusion of all such children in service provision would be impossible, so the threshold for 'need', 'risk' or indeed 'significant harm' becomes raised, either consciously or unconsciously, and the baseline for what is 'good enough' is lowered. There is a danger, then, that social workers become accustomed to some families 'bumping along the bottom', and where poverty, neglect and general stress in the family appear so interwoven and intractable, there may be a reluctance to make things any worse by imposing yet another damning judgement on the family (Stevenson 1998, p.255).

Power dynamics

The potential for parents and children to feel discriminated against in the assessment and investigation process is well documented (see for example Cleaver and Freeman 1995). Buckley's (2000) research, however, highlighted another parallel dynamic (illustrated in Chapter 9) in which parents were seen effectively to control intervention rather than the other way round. This was done by closing off contact, not being available for visits or failing to keep appointments or take advantage of services offered. The consequence was that professional willingness and commitment to continue to battle with unwilling recipients of services was effectively undermined. This has particular resonance for substance-misusing parents who (as we have seen) may have more reason that most to remain hidden, unavailable and distant from interventions which might expose behaviours that could precipitate feared or unknown responses. Although people may have a range of fantasies about worker power, workers must engage with the real power that parents and children have. What must be acknowledged, however, is the potential for this power to block engagement, and it is important to assist front-line workers to deal with such 'blocks'.

Inter-agency dynamics: working together

As we have seen, the potential split between agencies supporting the adult, on the one hand, and the child, on the other, can be played out over confidentiality, motivation and loyalty. There can also be questions of timing, reflecting differing perspectives. Substance misuse is often viewed as a chronic condition, and certain frameworks for assessment and intervention that adopt this perspective would not expect change to be rapid. Childcare professionals, however, are assessing 'parenting behaviour' and child welfare. They will come with different assessment models and a different timescale within which to see change occur. Bridges can be built when professionals have a more detailed understanding of the differing rationales that lie behind methods of work. Joint assessments are an ideal to be aimed for but, even when this is not possible, shared knowledge about aims and methods of working can encourage more innovative approaches as well as dispelling myths. Often there can be false assumptions about what another agency may or may not be doing and it is important that these are addressed. The climate of an organisation can be a powerful influence on attitudes towards other agencies. As we know, this can affect perceptions of referrals and the status they are accorded. In addition, it can affect the way in which previous assessments by other agencies are either validated or ignored, based on misunderstandings about different types of assessment and levels of expertise. Given the tensions of dealing with families where substance misuse is a significant problem, maintaining effective joint working is anything but easy. As we have seen, many of the issues involve strong feelings, are complex and can be potentially conflictual. Organisations can also have a 'transmitted history' (Scott 1997, p.74) which may have more to do with past relationships than current reality. If potential difficulties are to be surmounted a sufficiently high level of cooperation needs to exist to facilitate a climate where sharing of knowledge, expertise, assessment models and ways of working can take place. As Murphy and Oulds (2000) point out, inter-agency collaboration is evolutionary in nature – in other words, its progression is at least partly dependent upon ongoing initiatives that encourage shared clarification, and understanding of others' roles and tasks. Such progression, in this context, involves substance misuse and childcare professionals gaining a more detailed understanding of one another, in order to achieve a more holistic assessment.

Child-centred practice in family assessment

Gaining access to children's feelings about and responses to parental substance misuse is (as we have seen) not without its problems; children are often very loyal to their parents, irrespective of their actions (Harbin 2000). Moreover, as many of our research respondents found, children would disclose what had really been going on only when they were no longer living at home. Ironically, it is easy for children to get lost during the assessment process despite the fact that they are supposed to be at its centre (see Buckley 2000; SCODA 1997). Research has also shown that 'not enough attention is paid to what children say, how they look and how they behave' (Cleaver *et al.* 1998, p.4). As Shemmings and Shemmings (2001, p.124) point out, 'practitioners can find it difficult to involve children in the assessment processes' and there are various possible explanations for this. One of the main reasons is that workers risk confronting children's pain at close quarters, receiving it in its most raw and unbearable form. As Kroll (1995) observes:

> Working with children is painful. It is often about loss, anger, rejection, neglect and sadness; it is often about limited options and second rate solutions. It touches private life in tender places, it is unbearable and makes us feel helpless, sad and angry. Many workers admit to keeping children at a distance in an attempt to avoid feeling these feelings, to protect themselves from the pain and to preserve a sense of competence. (Kroll 1995, p.91)

In addition, the ethnic and cultural contexts in which children live will affect the extent to which they feel able to talk to professionals or are indeed given permission to do so. In addition attitudes towards children's entitlement to views of their own or being seen in their own right will vary from one family to another and negotiation and planning will be crucial (Banks 2001; Brandon *et al.* 1998).

As much of the research outlined in Chapter 7 made clear, children need to be seen, heard and engaged with on a real level if they are to feel confident about being helped by professionals. Workers then need to find ways of engaging with difficult feelings via training, support and supervision. Research shows that children are very good at making their needs and wants known if the right climate is created for discussion to take place and provided workers take the time to listen (Butler and Williamson 1995).

In her study exploring the views of 27 children involved in child protection investigations, Bell (2002) found that what children and young people most appreciated was having a trusting relationship with someone available, reliable and concerned who listened, treated them with respect and was not judgemental. The ability to set boundaries that created a safe place rather then being motivated by control was also important. The combination of emotional support with practical help was valued, as was a sense of humour. Being talked down to or patronised, feeling controlled and being subjected to pressurising, invasive lines of questioning were seen as unhelpful, as were constant changes of worker which often left children feeling 'bereft, forgotten and confused' (Bell 2002, p.5).

Essential ingredients, then, for child-centred practice, are establishing rapport, creating a safe place where discussion can take place and ensuring that the child knows that the worker has heard what the child has said and is clear what he or she is and is not going to do with it (Bannister 2001; Kroll

1995). Many practitioners find that seeing children initially on their own territory, but with the option of meetings in a neutral place, provides a good balance and that kit-bags of materials to facilitate communication, depending on age, inclination and ability, are very helpful (see Brandon *et al.* 1998 for suggested contents for these). In addition a child-centred philosophy, where the same principles used in adult work are applied to children in relation to respect, empathy, warmth, readiness to engage with difficult issues and a right to be heard, is important, as is a 'theoretical reservoir' in relation to knowledge of how children work and their developmental issues (Kroll 1995).

How then do we go about finding out how things really are for children particularly while they are still in the family setting? This will in some respects depend on their age and understanding but even so, age or youthfulness should not necessarily be a barrier, since play, drawing or enactment can be used to tell a useful story (see Bannister 2001; Brandon *et al.* 1998; Kroll 1994 for some useful ideas for communicating with children). Both Swadi (1994) and Camden and Islington Area Child Protection Committees (ACPC) (1999) also provide some useful areas to explore and questions that can be asked of children and these will be highlighted when we consider the holistic approach to assessment in more detail.

It is often fruitful to ask children and young people to take the practitioner through a typical day, step by step, from first thing in the morning ('and then what happens?') and try to explore what makes a difference to the day – what parents do and what children do and who else plays a part. Often enacting scenes from daily life, either through use of figures, puppets or animals or through role play, will enable the child to talk about aspects of routine that are problematic, enjoyable or confusing.

As well as creating an environment where children feel able to talk, it is also important to give them permission *not* to say anything, mindful of the fact that mistrust and suspicion may be issues. Speculating about how *you* might feel in their situation or what your concerns and anxieties might be, if you were them, can be a useful way forward, as long as options remain open and disagreement encouraged. This will actually involve allowing yourself to imagine this or know something about it through observation (see below) and this is where the emotional experience of observation can be useful. Indeed, the *Child's World* training pack (Department of Health 2000c) includes some case studies which encourage workers to place themselves in the shoes of children of different ages living with a substance-misusing parent (see Module Two 'Children's Diaries: Assessing Children's Needs', pp.23–24). This can provide useful insights into the child's experience which can then be used as a basis for speculation. Talking about how other children whose parents use drink or drugs said they felt or using research evidence to inform this area might also be useful as long as children are given permission to feel differently.

Disclosure

As we saw in Chapter 7, disclosure was a critical issue for many children growing up with substance-misusing parents. Fears centred around confidentiality, being taken away from home, parents being punished or simply making everything worse, quite apart from saying difficult, negative or critical things about people that the children love (or feel they should love). Confidentiality, in particular, needs to be addressed at an early stage so that children know what will happen to what they say and under what circumstances. Much can be learnt from ideas in relation to approaches to disclosure from other areas of practice, such as sexual abuse and domestic violence (see for example Hester *et al.* 2000).

As research has shown, in many households where there is substance misuse, domestic violence, mental health problems and/or some kind of child abuse or maltreatment may also be issues. Potentially, then, children may be being asked to reveal a constellation of difficult things happening in their lives. It may be that domestic violence is the presenting issue and it will be only after careful exploration that a drug or alcohol link may emerge. By the same token, children will respond differently in response to what is happening at home. There is no set pattern of behaviour that might suggest the child is living with substance misuse but it is always worth considering whether this is an issue where there is evidence of concerning behaviour. As we saw in Chapter 7, many children and young people are very successful at maintaining a good level of functioning, despite family difficulties. There may still, however, be tell-tale signs and these need to be picked up. Children also have mixed feelings about anyone 'finding out' and yet desperately want someone to know. Disclosure, as a result, may often take some time and have a 'one step forward, two steps back' quality.

In this context sometimes straight talking is the most effective route to disclosure. Certainly, in the domestic violence context, research suggests that this can be more beneficial than 'indirect or polite questions' (Hester *et al.* 2000, p.137). This has much to do with getting over the barrier that the topic is 'taboo', or too terrible for an adult to approach directly. Because of the cloak of secrecy and denial that is often thrown over substance misuse, breaking through the wall of denial in a direct way can be very liberating. If the worker is able to validate the existence of the 'elephant in the living room' the relief can be enormous – 'Yes, someone else can see it! Maybe my perceptions are valid after all'. Most children want to be heard and to be believed, particularly if they are operating in a system where this is not happening.

Role of observation in assessment

The role of observation as a source of additional information, at both a factual and an emotional level, and its relevance for social work practice in child and family work has been stressed by many commentators (see for example Bridge and Miles 1996; Fawcett 1996; Kroll 1994, 1995; Le Riche and Tanner 1998; Tanner and Turney 2000). The training materials accompanying the framework for the assessment of children in need and their families devotes a section to the skills of observation, reinforced by the main textbook (Horwath 2001) and underlined in the practice guidance (Department of Health 2000b). Despite this, however, this aspect of practice has not consistently been utilised as a major assessment tool in many mainstream child and family settings. Although family centre workers are obviously ideally placed to use this as a major source of assessment information, many field childcare workers feel they have little enough time to do what they have to do at a basic level, and that observation of families is a luxury they can ill afford. We recognise that this is a real practical problem; ironically, however, a period of observation can end up actually saving time due to the depth and wealth of material that it provides.

In relation to assessment in families where there is substance misuse, a critical task for the worker is the ability to 'enter the world of substance-misusing families' and to start to know something of what it is like to be there not only for the parents but also for the children (Aldridge 1999, p.9). Parents may tell you that their substance use does not affect their capacity to play, to respond appropriately, that their children always come first or that, when they are not using, they are great parents. All parents will often have a highly subjective view of the way they operate as parents;

substance-misusing parents will be no exception. As we saw in Chapter 5, parents often felt they were *better* parents when using substances, although the objective reality could be very different. By the same token, children's accounts in Chapter 7 suggested that behaviours could vary enormously and that some could be very difficult to manage; parents could be wonderful, when sober, and terrifying when drunk.

Observation of families could be a useful way of gaining a different quality of information. Obviously there are a range of factors to consider here to do with issues already discussed: worker objectivity and subjectivity, values, cultural differences and the fact that one observation alone might not provide a rounded or fair picture. Training in this particular skill would seem to be an essential prerequisite; by the same token, decisions about which professionals in a network are best placed to undertake this element of assessment also need to be considered.

Family centre workers and those in drug or alcohol agencies that offer a family-focused service would be ideally placed to negotiate with parents, so that periods of observed interaction could be undertaken. If trust could be established sufficiently for workers to be allowed actually to see what is really going on, then more purposeful assessment and intervention might be possible.

Learning from experience: approaches to assessment

For some time child maltreatment and substance misuse were assessed separately, often by different people who did not necessarily come together at any point (Hampton *et al.* 1998; Harbin and Murphy 2000). As the impact of substance misuse on parenting and child welfare became more obvious, via research particularly in the USA, however, attention turned to assessment in general and assessment of risk in particular, in the context of substance misuse and child protection. Various approaches were explored including adapting devices that screened for substance misuse for families referred for child maltreatment (Dore *et al.* 1995). A specific contribution was provided by Olsen, Allen and Azzi-Lessing (1996) who devised a Risk Inventory for Substance Abuse-Affected Families (Olsen *et al.* 1996, p.835) that brought together an exploration of substance misuse and the capacity for parents to meet their children's needs, which were considered in the context of environment and influenced by the ecological approach. This approach has clear resonance with the framework for assessment that is now used in

Britain with children in need and their families (Department of Health 2000a).

In Britain, the first set of assessment guidelines, in relation to *drug*-misusing parents, were produced by SCODA in 1987. It was hoped that they would assist practitioners to retain a more child-centred focus, despite the fact that such a focus was not explicit within the guidelines themselves, in that there was no mention of establishing the child's views, perceptions or perceived level of need or support. Swadi (1994) built on both these original SCODA guidelines and the approach to parenting assessment advocated by Reder and Lucey (1995). This approach rests on the interactional or dynamic nature of the task, closely linked with Belsky and Vondra's (1989) multiple determinants of parenting.

Swadi's (1994) approach to assessment, devised for use by child psychiatrists and a multidisciplinary team, was based on an interview with parent or parents ideally at home but alternatively at the clinic, an interview with the child (depending on age), involving use of play if appropriate, and an interview with child and parent(s) together to observe interaction. What he provided was a way of thinking about the 'what' rather than the 'how' of assessment, recognising that all professionals have their preferred approaches, methods and styles (Swadi 1994, p.237). Eight areas were explored (to be considered below) culminating in an evaluation of the information gathered. What was original about his contribution was the fact that the child's perceptions were sought 'to gain some idea about how the children view the world of a substance misusing parent and where they see themselves fitting in' (Swadi 1994, p.243).

SCODA and the Local Government Drugs Forum (LGDF) updated and revised their guidelines in 1997, identifying seven areas for exploration (see Appendix 2). Once again, the aim was to categorise the key elements that needed to be considered in order to make a judgement about whether a child was at risk or in need. It provided a template to shape a consideration of the intersection between drug use and parenting and to consider both risks and protective factors within each category. The guidelines' limitations are that, while clearly making links with the child's experience, their perspective seems a little over-focused on the adult user and, obviously, focused on the use of drugs rather than alcohol. Exploration of alcohol use as a way of *managing* drug use is, however, encouraged in the preamble (SCODA 1997, p.9). In addition, no attention is paid to variable effects on children depending on development and attachment patterns. Aldridge (1999,

2000), in his analysis of assessment in general and the SCODA guidelines in particular, draws attention to a number of significant problems which echoed those expressed by many of the professionals we interviewed. These include the difficulty of asking questions that elicit responses from parents about the detailed realities of their lives and those of their children, including play and shared activities, and the tendency to make assessments based on 'acute episodes', risking failure to pick up issues of neglect and emotional abuse. In addition, the lack of child-centredness is far from helpful in adult-focused settings where workers are, in any event, less accustomed to considering children's needs. In other words, such an omission encourages children to remain invisible. Aldridge (1999) emphasises the fact that gaining information about behaviours and activities, by asking 'What kinds of things do you do together?' or 'What do you do at the weekends or after school?' can be far more revealing than more general answers to questions about feelings or those that encourage statements of love and affection. Most parents will say that they love their children; how this expresses itself in everyday behaviour and how the *child* experiences this may be a different matter. Statements are all very well but what is really required is observable 'evidence' of this love in action. Where there is an issue about whether parents are more attached to the substance than their child, this 'proof' become particularly crucial. As Aldridge goes on to observe:

> assessors need to become involved in the everyday living arrangements of the substance misusing parents and their child's life...they need to ask questions about the parents' role in designing the child's world...are the child's emotional and developmental needs being met and, if so, how can the parent demonstrate this? (Aldridge 1999, p.11)

More recently, some local authorities, increasingly aware of the issues surrounding parental substance misuse, have developed guidelines of their own which address alcohol and drug use. Camden and Islington ACPC (1999) guidelines are a good example of these, particularly in relation to assessing alcohol misuse where the child's view is an integral part of the process and the consequences for children as well as for carers are explored. A further contribution comes from Murphy and Harbin (2000), who developed a way of thinking about assessment which acknowledges the 'twin track' nature of the task – assessing parenting and assessing substance misuse, and the fact that they would normally be undertaken by practitioners in different systems. They argue that these two processes need to come together so that measurement of substance misuse and its impact on the child can be held onto simultaneously. Incorporating the new *Framework for the Assessment of Children in Need and their Families* (Department of Health 2000a), they emphasise the fact that 'the additional element of substance misuse may exaggerate or highlight several dimensions in each domain of the assessment triangle' and that these should be 'singled out for special consideration' (Murphy and Harbin 2000, p.5). To this end they suggest that workers 'measure the use of substances as a separate element and then track the effects of this use through the other three domains' (Murphy and Harbin 2000, p.5). This would seem to be a helpful way of integrating specific concerns about substances within an existing model for assessment.

Grasping the nettle: an holistic approach to assessment

What follows is an adaptation of Swadi's (1994) model, incorporating the sources cited above and the dimensions of the three domains of the assessment framework. Issues of race and culture will of course need to be integrated at every stage of the assessment process, with due regard to assumptions, myths and stereotypes that prevail in relation to families from different ethnic backgrounds as well as to substance-misusing parents. The aim of assessment in this context, as Swadi (1994) points out, is not to determine whether someone is 'addicted' to something but to establish the extent to which substance use or misuse is affecting parenting capacity, within the cultural context in which parenting is taking place. This may need to be stressed to the parents as they will often assume that the worker is looking for evidence that they are 'addicts' or 'drunks' rather than exploring the dynamic between parental behaviour and childcare (see Chapter 3). This can inevitably lead to miscommunication on a grand scale. Some examples of potentially useful questions are included, although these are by no means exhaustive. Rather than being used as a basis of an inquisition, they are offered as an aide-memoire in relation to useful matters to explore, in order to create a dialogue with parents and children, along the lines of the 'exchange' model of assessment (Milner and O'Byrne 1998, p.29). Clearly there will be times when procedural imperatives will require specific answers to specific questions, and it is recognised that no one model of information gathering will suit everyone.

As with any approach, how it is used depends on the skills of those who use it, although it is important to stress that any assessment tools encourage certain perspectives by the manner by which they are framed. Given that we are dealing with parental anxiety about substance use, parenting and the real or imagined powers of the assessor, assessment tools in this context need to consider a combination of a framework harnessed to style and method of interviewing. This, then, is not just about type of question but an understanding of the dynamics of denial and resistance, as well as the impact of 'attachment' to the substance (see Chapter 4). Many questions are extremely sensitive and difficult to ask, except in the context of a relationship where it has been possible to establish a considerable degree of trust. This serves only to illustrate the intricate skills base required to undertake assessment in relation to these areas.

Child's perception of the situation

Both Swadi (1994) and Camden and Islington ACPC (1999) have made an important contribution to this critical aspect of the assessment process which has two essential strands. First, it is aimed at entering the child's world and trying to find out what it feels like to live there, and second, it tries to establish whether the child needs information and/or support in managing his or her situation. The approach to gaining information from children needs, of course, to be appropriate to age and stage of development.

Questions will be aimed at exploring what children do on a daily basis, whether they feel safe, where they turn for comfort, help and protection. What is it like when their parent is under the influence of a substance? What is it like when they are not? Do they have fears, anxieties, hopes about their parents' behaviour? What would they most like to be different or stay the same? Whom do they think is most affected by the substance misuse and how can they tell? Other issues to explore relate to the extent to which children may have caring responsibilities, either willingly assumed or imposed, and whether there is violence in the home. Are there things that happen that make them scared? The child's level of awareness of the substance misuse and a willingness to provide information and answer questions will also be important, as will establishing what the child may need in terms of support and who might be an acceptable source of this – friend, family member, concerned 'other' or a professional outside the family. In addition, an assessment of the extent to which the child is reaching developmental milestones should be made (see Chapter 8). The way the child makes the worker feel may also provide an important layer of information about the way in which the child may be feeling.

Accommodation, home, social support and environmental factors

At its most basic, exploration of this area is fundamentally about shelter, stability and safety. This is also about the 'feel' of the home, not just what it provides at a material level. Houses awash with the trappings of affluence can still feel cold and unsafe, with occupants isolated from friends, family and community. It is important to establish whether the housing is stable, safe, secure, whether the family has moved around a lot and if so whether this is due to debts, eviction, harassment, discrimination or drug- or alcohol-related problems. The whereabouts of extended family and what kinds of support they are offering is important as is their knowledge about the substance misuse and their attitude towards it. Equally important are community links, friends and networks for both parents and children and their variety or singularity since this (as we saw in Chapter 5) has implications for social exclusion.

Dunst and Trivette (1990) suggest that exploring aspects of an individual's network, from a psychosocial perspective, can be particularly useful in determining sources of both emotional and practical support. This includes establishing the kinds of feelings and thoughts that people have about family and friends, the degree of help and emotional care they provide, the frequency of contact and the degree of stability in those relationships. Their physical proximity to others in the support network is also important. In addition, establishing the way in which people believe that those in their networks and their community feel about them is also crucial.

Any exploration of community and networks, however, also needs to include links with the drinking or drug-using community and it is important to establish the extent to which these contacts impinge on the lives of the family as a whole and the children in particular. Are there a number of people coming and going and are the children adequately protected from the possible consequences of any adverse behaviour they might exhibit? Do children get left either with unsuitable carers or totally unsupervised while parents are elsewhere either physically or as a result of the effects of substance use? Are supplies of alcohol and drugs kept out of reach? In addition, there are issues of finance to consider in relation to sources of income, stability of employment, the payment of rent and bills and the dangers of utilities being cut off or of eviction.

Meeting children's developmental needs and provision of basic necessities

This area encompasses some obvious basics – provision of food, clothing, heat and a healthy, clean, safe living environment – as well as many of the dimensions of the developmental and parenting capacity domains. The issue is how substance misuse might be affecting the provision of children's basic physical, developmental and emotional needs. Here questions need to be asked about the detail of children's education, leisure and emotional lives – school and nursery attendance, how free time is spent, whether activities are age appropriate. In addition, levels of supervision and other behavioural issues need to be considered – staying out late, discipline problems and any involvement in the substance misuse either as active participants or as messengers or 'runners' – obtaining supplies, for example. The emotional needs of the children also need to be addressed in relation to the quality of parent–child interaction, the consistency of care and affection provided and general support with problems, homework, and all the worries, great or small, that all children will experience.

Other essential information includes establishing whether the provision of basic needs is dependent on the parent(s) being substance free and any changes in levels of care as a result of the substance use. The consequences for children in relation to taking on caring responsibilities will also need to be considered and their age appropriateness, duration and level explored.

Patterns of parental substance misuse

Effectively this is about the who, when, what, why, how and how often of substance misuse. Any assessment necessitates a detailed consideration of the effect of the particular type of substance, taking into consideration quantity, amount, pattern and type of use. The use of particular assessment tools may be useful here. For example the Maudsley Addiction Profile (Marsden *et al.* 1998) measures use in relation to physical, psychological and social factors, including potential conflict within relationships. More generally there is some evidence to suggest that techniques that enquire about levels of use in more detail, over shorter periods of time, perhaps utilising diaries, provide greater accuracy than those which ask people to summarise their drinking over longer periods (Ely *et al.* 2000).

Assessing the pattern of use also involves an understanding of the effects of both intoxification and withdrawal. Most significantly it entails assessing the link between the physical and psychological consequences of substances and their impact on parenting. So, for example, a pattern of chronic alcohol misuse involving severe disinhibition, impaired judgement, irritability, preoccupation while intoxicated or the depressive quality of the hangover, may indicate heightened risk.

It is also important to examine how one's own views on differing substances contain implicit ideas about 'addiction' or 'dependence' and how these might impact upon the assessment. Do we have pictures in our minds about the way that someone with a dependence on alcohol would behave in the home? If so is this different from our conceptions of someone on heroin (Forrester 2000)? Do we make assumed connections between the type of drug used and the likely pattern of use, as well as routes to and from chronic to more managed use? While holding on to the notions of more emeshed attachments to drugs, it is important to remain open to the complexity of patterns of use and the variety of different ways in which these impact upon children. Approaches which allow for more complex and varied patterns of substance use allow us to gain a broader perspective of its impact (Cohen 1990; Ditton 1990; Laybourn *et al.* 1996). As we have seen, the level of attachment to a substance involves a complex interaction between the individual and his or her social environment. Patterns of individual use reflect this complexity and do not necessarily adhere to fixed notions of compulsive everyday use (Davies 1997). The individual pattern may depend on the drug in question as well as availability. Some studies have suggested that use of heroin, for example, reveals a more cyclical pattern and Davies suggests that many users are influenced by a 'cost–benefit analysis' (Davies 1997, p.43). In other words, reduction of use can occur when it leads to too many difficulties in terms of money, supply, fear of arrest and so on. However, this is not the case for some whose habit is such that most major risks have become irrelevant. What is significant is that problematic patterns of use that impact on children may be more variable and complex than are first assumed.

Such considerations may help to counterbalance assessments that become too preoccupied with events rather than including the more significantly indicative atmosphere within the home. This has particular significance for children of substance-misusing parents, given the generally identified concern about levels of emotional harm or neglect which are particularly difficult to assess and identify or address. They may also assist professionals in establishing substance-using patterns more clearly over time as they affect children's development.

A critical skill here, as Murphy and Harbin (2000) point out, is being able to distinguish between recreational, experimental and problematic misuse through painstaking exploration of the using patterns and motivations. This may be closely linked (as we have seen) to feelings about parenting or about the child, confidence as a parent, managing stress or dependency, environmental factors, loss, loneliness or depression or indeed any combination of these. Are both parents using substances or is one parent, carer or closely involved adult substance-free? Are various substances being combined and, if so what, when and how? How discreet is the substance use? In other words, do the children witness the behaviour or have they stumbled upon it by accident? How is the behaviour hidden or contained so that the children are not affected? Have there ever been accidents as a result of substance use and are the parents able to acknowledge risks and accept responsibility?

Whether the substance use is chaotic or stable will also be important since this may mean there are dramatic differences in parents' behaviour which come and go without warning and this has particular implications for children, as we have already seen. This also has consequences for child safety, including risks of accidental ingestion, danger from syringes and infection.

Swadi (1994) also suggests that parents are asked about substance-related criminal activity, convictions, whether there have been periods of imprisonment and what happened to the children. In addition, attempts at giving up substances, or managing use, any treatment undertaken and its results are also fruitful avenues to pursue, particularly since this can highlight strengths, areas to build on and unexplored possibilities.

Effects on parental mental state

As we saw in Chapter 2, there are often links between substance misuse and a variety of mental health problems of lesser or greater severity. In exploring this area, the aim is to tease out these links as well as exploring any help, treatment or support that the parent is or has been receiving. It is also important to know about any medication that is being used to manage mental health problems since this may be being misused. Tracking the sequence of feelings, emotions and responses in terms of substance use and its role in managing depression, for example, would be helpful. Does the substance use make the condition better or worse? How does the mental health problem affect parenting and what is the role of the substance in this?

How substances are obtained

One of the aims here is to establish the extent to which the substance use may have become the 'organising principle' of the family system (Brooks and Rice 1997; Brown 1988). In other words, the amount of time, energy, money and organisation directed towards the substance-related activity and the consequences for the children need to be explored. It is important to try to establish who gets supplies and where the money come from to pay for them. The type of activities that may be involved – for example prostitution, dealing, other kinds of crime – and their associated risks need to be discussed as openly as possible. Who looks after the children when supplies are being sought or while the supporting activities are being undertaken? Are children ever taken to inappropriate places connected with substance use where they may be placed at risk? Is the home used for dealing, drinking parties, or as a base for the substance-misusing group to which the parent(s) may be attached? Does the substance misuse lead to financial problems that mean the children have to go without basics? Does the substance come first, so that other financial obligations are not met?

Parents' perceptions of the situation

This aspect of assessment is aimed at exploring levels of awareness, insight and responsibility in relation to substance misuse and its impact on parenting and child welfare. It also addresses issues of denial and the extent to which there might be motivation to address the substance misuse and explore the potential for change and support. This will include questions about the extent to which there is an acknowledgement of the substance misuse and the degree to which it might be affecting the family in general and the children in particular. Insight into the reasons behind use would also be an important factor, as would the extent to which parents are able to place their children's needs before their own. If there is an acknowledgement that parenting capacity is being affected by substance misuse, what do parents think they might need to do differently? What do they think might help in that process and from whom would help be most acceptable? If there is no acknowledgement, how might they demonstrate that concerns about the children's well-being are unfounded?

Putting the pieces together: evaluating the assessment

The fundamental dilemma in the assessment process is how to come to appropriate conclusions about families where there is substance misuse. In other words

> what types/levels/complexities of substance misuse, in what kind of family systems, will lead to significant harm or impairment to which types of children? Conversely, what types of substance misuse…will lead to minimal harm to children? Furthermore what types of professional intervention will help reduce this harmful impact on children? (Murphy and Harbin 2000, p.6)

Putting the pieces together in order to answer these questions will inevitably involve a range of processes. The views of all interested parties – including family members who will have theories about what is happening – will need to be sought so that the situation can be viewed from a variety of perspectives. A chronology of significant events, current information, observations and other assessments will all come together. The professional judgement reached will also be informed by an 'evidence-based' approach (Rose and Aldgate 2000, p.21). This ensures that what research and theory tell us about substance misuse, parenting and child welfare is brought into the synthesis and analysis of material collected and is put together via a reflexive, dynamic process. Available evidence, its reliability and ways in which it might require further testing need to be evaluated. Whether the assessment is being influenced by how articulate or cooperative the parents are and by their attitude will also need to be considered, as will the impact of professionals' values and assumptions. Critical questions will also need to be asked in relation to the level of need, risk or harm to the children. Who else is worried and why? What are the family's strengths and weaknesses? What kind of support and help might work best and where might it be found both in the community and within statutory and voluntary services? How might all the professionals involved work together most effectively and who should do what? Knowledge, professional judgement, consultation, open-mindedness, flexibility, humility, teamwork, sharing of ideas and a range of complex skills will all play their part.

Summary

Assessment in relation to parental substance misuse needs to be framed in relation to the differing needs of families as well as the research evidence that tells us about what potentially can go wrong for children. It is therefore evidence based in this respect but involves a dimension of reflexivity and self-examination in relation to attitudes, values and prejudices. In addition, the capacity to view a situation through a variety of different lenses and to allow oneself the luxury of not knowing and learning from someone else is critical. Communication between professionals needs to be made open and competing loyalties and demands from the child in the adult and the real child need to be addressed. In addition, the child's perspective needs to be brought more firmly into the entire assessment process so that workers can gain a sense of what children's lives are really like. This needs to involve strategies that, rather than putting children on the spot and forcing them to 'tell tales', enable them to tell a story. The use of observation and skills in communicating with children are clearly central to achieving this aim.

Family members are a vital source of information about what is happening to them and respecting their contribution to the information-gathering process can only assist in helping to devise appropriate interventions. Some of these will be considered in the next chapter.

11

From Assessment to Intervention
A Family Perspective

The recovery personnel of prime significance are the associates, the significant others... Perhaps medical or welfare or religious or law enforcement personnel are essential at this stage or that stage...but the crucial persons for recovery are the daily life associates through time...community. It is that moulding through time, persons and society which is the core of treatment.

(Bacon 1973, cited in Orford 2001, p.324)

If we wish to understand the drinking problem, we need to understand the family context within which it has developed. If we want to intervene effectively, we need to take this context into account. If we intervene in isolation, we cannot expect to see positive therapeutic change.

(Steinglass1987, cited in Robinson and Hassle 2001, p.12)

In considering issues of assessment we have stressed the importance of a holistic approach. We know that intervention needs to operate at a range of levels, if the needs of substance misusers and the people in their orbit are to be addressed and if child well-being is to be safeguarded. This chapter examines some approaches to intervention that attempt to include children, families and significant others when working with substance-misuse problems. This is not a comprehensive review but rather a discussion of some of the key debates. We also offer some of our own ideas for an holistic family-centred approach, exploring ways in which models or techniques from both childcare and adult settings may be harnessed with a view to addressing the needs of children and making them more visible within interventions.

We begin by exploring some of the blocks and barriers to working more centrally with family members before outlining some of the general themes underpinning holistic interventions. We then examine key perspectives that have emerged in recent years which have influenced approaches where there is substance misuse. Various models have evolved which attempt to respond to the needs of substance misusers and their families, although they do this from differing perspectives and in different ways. Some specifically address issues for children, others work with the family as a whole, while others still utilise social factors as a way of supporting change for the substance misuser. There are also those that concentrate specifically on the partner or other family members of substance misusers, focusing on strategies to reduce the stress and problems caused by the substance-misusing behaviour. Interventions, therefore, can occur at a number of levels and the extent to which they succeed in dealing both directly or indirectly with children's issues varies (Robinson and Hassle 2001).

Obstacles to working holistically

There are a number of explanations for the focus on the substance-misusing individual to the relative exclusion of the family or others in close proximity. Traditionally, as we saw in Chapter 3, models of assessing and treating substance misuse tend to emanate from the perspective of the individual and are predominantly health focused. There is a presumption – fairly logical on one level – that addressing the parent's substance misuse will result in reduction of harm to children and any others affected. However, as we have seen, this can be an oversimplistic assumption. Furthermore the movement towards specialisation in service delivery, where there is an increased tendency to break down problems into component parts and to allocate these to different services, has made the potential for more integrated inter-professional responses less likely. While professionals may come together at certain points, it is less clear that there is much encouragement for joint intervention initiatives. However, there are clearly significant steps being made to address this in certain quarters by innovative professionals working in this field. Examples include the development of new family support programmes (Appleby 2000) and a number of initiatives aiming to provide more integrated services (see for example Robinson and Hassle 2001). Such trends in service delivery are accompanied by the ever-present complexity of working with a range of family members or other associated individuals.

On the most basic level, many professionals experience discomfort about working with a family outside an office or clinic environment or when family members or other professionals are present. This may be due to a number of factors. Entering a family's territory generates anxieties about being out of control of the environment. In addition there are natural fears about verbal or physical attack in some potentially volatile situations. If there are other professionals present fears may also be related to exposing one's practice.

There are also particular issues about the potential working dynamic in relation to intervention. Who is seen as the client and who is seen as the problem? In some cases of chronic substance misuse, involving child abuse or neglect, one parent may be acting erratically or violently. This may not be the person with whom the professional has most contact. Alternatively, the parent or carer may represent only one element in a complicated family dynamic. Such natural tensions and dynamics are often features of such situations and these necessitate very good levels of inter-professional communication and planning. Roles and functions can easily become confused, blurred or even conflicting, particularly when levels of distress and responsibility are high, as we have seen in Chapter 9. Professionals can feel deterred from intervening more holistically due to ethical concerns about the involvement of different family members or reservations about inquiring into the behaviour of an unconsenting third party. Issues of confidentiality become more complex. Added to this, the increasing trend towards a risk and blame culture in which social care professionals operate has discouraged the development of models which appear less clear cut and possibly less amenable to bureaucratic systems of supervision (Parton 1996). This is reflected in trends in the field of childcare where, as Jack (1997) points out, there has been less support for social workers to take risks in developing more supportive approaches in working with families. Given the pressures and dilemmas professionals face, it seems hardly surprising that developments in family approaches have been so limited.

Different ideological positions about who may be responsible for the substance-misuse problem can also inhibit the development of more holistic approaches. One of the issues has been concern that interventions which stress the need to tackle broader changes within the family equate with the notion that non-substance-abusing members are, at least in part, responsible for the substance misuser's behaviour. This can lead to such interventions being viewed as controversial, given the reality that both children and women are often direct victims of abuse or violence as a result of such misuse (Copello *et al.* 2000). This is clearly a central debate. It seems crucial, therefore, to distinguish between the importance of gaining an understanding of the complex dynamics of a family, and excusing morally unjustifiable behaviour, or apportioning responsibility to non-substance-misusing members.

Barber (1995) suggests that such views are derived from a misunderstanding of the concepts of influence and responsibility in that, while it is clearly untrue that a partner is responsible for another's drinking, it does not follow that that person is unable to influence that behaviour. It may be seen as somewhat ironic, then, that ideological concern about family-centred approaches may have led to some reluctance to reappraise more holistic interventions and their potential for meeting the needs of children and partners. Velleman (1992, Velleman and Orford 1999) points out that families are, in fact, notoriously resistant to change and, consequently, for approaches to be effective, they need to take into account the ways in which families function and how this impacts upon children.

Themes in holistic interventions: the ecological perspective and social support

What happens in families is not easily separated from the context in which it occurs. To put it another way, in general people develop and solve problems involving substances within their relationships with others. All the approaches we consider recognise the importance of relationships with others in this context, be they with children, partners or the community. Two sets of ideas which help illustrate the interactive nature of the individual, the family and the wider community and which inform many of the particular interventions that we discuss are the ecological perspective and social support.

As we already know, the ecological perspective has gained increased currency in the field of child welfare (Garbarino 1977; Jack 1997, 2001) and is now an integral part of the new *Framework for the Assessment of Children in Need and their Families* (Department of Health 2000a) with all childcare professionals required to take it into account in their work.

The ecological model highlights a number of important issues which bear reiteration here. Underpinning it is the way in which structural inequality influences outcomes for families and the necessity for social welfare professionals to engage with the various systems that affect the people with whom they work (Jack and Jack 2000). It also underlines the powerful influences of social interactions in the community which can, of course, be both a source of support and a source of stress. The ecological model also emphasises the second general theme considered here, namely social support, which takes on added significance as a result of the way in which it can be seen to mediate the influence of substance misuse on the family in general and on children in particular.

What do we mean, though, by social support? It was not until the mid-1970s that empirical research into social support networks and their influence on health and illness began to emerge (Jack 1997). A number of different types of support were identified, the most common being emotional support, social integration and practical support (Cutrona and Russell 1990, cited in Jack 1997). However, while on the surface the term can seem to indicate positive help from those in the community, in fact it seeks to explain a more complex set of processes which do not automatically offer support. In other words, the extent to which social support is beneficial is dependent on a range of variables and, as Jack (1997) observes, it is important to realise that social networks are not automatically beneficial but can 'be stressful as well as supportive.' (Jack 1997, p.110). With this in mind, many of the models that we discuss include strategies for minimising the negative influences of social contexts in addition to utilising those more supportive elements.

In discussing social support it is also important to clarify the use of the term in the differing contexts of child development and treatment for substance misuse. Dunst and Trivette (1990) define social support within the context of childcare as the social network influences that parents experience as part of their child-rearing efforts.

In the field of addiction the role of social support in sustaining reductions in drug or alcohol use has long been recognised. However, the way in which social influences affect substance misuse is interpreted in a number of ways. It can be defined very broadly as all the possible influences, both positive and negative, within the substance misusers' families and wider environment which impact on their ability or willingness to continue with the substance-misusing behaviour. However, social support has also been more narrowly defined as those types of strategies that are offered to substance misusers or family members, from organisations such as Alcoholics Anonymous, often within a group setting. Here social support is seen to emerge from particular types of group processes or structures. Generally speaking there has been an increased emphasis on the role of social factors and social support, even if the particular interpretation of this differs.

Within the field of addiction, community-based models have received some impetus in the area of both alcohol and drug misuse. With regard to alcohol, the significance of social support has been identified in programmes such as the twelve-step model used by Alcoholics Anonymous and validated by the Project MATCH trials (Orford 2001). In relation to drugs, social support has been identified as a key factor among those cocaine users who have successfully maintained abstinence (Shaffer and Jones 1989, cited in Ryan *et al.* 1999). More broadly, recent reviews from the literature on the treatment of alcohol problems indicate that, where the measurement of intense treatments is concerned, effective interventions tend to include attending to social and interpersonal factors (United Kingdom Alcohol Treatment Trial Research Team 2001).

In the area of childcare, the importance of social support mechanisms which can act as buffers against stressful life events has been emphasised, with supportive networks or lack of them seen as significantly influencing adults' capacity to parent (Cleaver *et al.* 1999; Jack 2000, 2001). A number of research studies suggest that certain aspects of social support, which relate to the family's ability to function, have been identified as the most significant, having stress-buffering and health-promoting influences on individual and family behaviour. These include the extent, dependability, reciprocity, closeness and the congruence (that is the degree to which types of support match need) of the social support available. Such a model of social support does not suggest particular types of intervention, but acts as a framework to help establish how personal and environmental factors affect parents' ability to meet the needs of children (Dunst and Trivette 1990).

It is important to keep in mind the different types of social support in the following discussion of models of intervention. In Network Therapy, social support is very much tailored to supporting change in the substance misuser. The Stress-Coping-Health Model, in contrast, views the importance of social support mainly from the perspective of the user's partner. In the holistic model that we present, the balance between stress, support, the competing pressures of substance misuse and the role of parenting are emphasised. Strategies or approaches aimed at enhancing social support operate in different ways, depending on the interpretation of the concept and the basis on which it operates.

Gaining a clear picture of the systems within which people live and the nature of the support mechanisms available can feel like a complex process. Often the significance of relationships is not obvious; connections and influences are not always apparent. As a result, some of the models we discuss use a diagrammatic way of illustrating either the complexity of family dynamics or a particular social support network or both. Tools which help elicit such information seem particularly important in the context of the role of substance misuse within the family. As Warren (1993) pointed out:

> An ecological metaphor can lead social workers to see the client not as an isolated entity for study, but as part of a complex ecological system. Such a view helps to focus on the sources of...support...in the intimate and extended environment. (Warren 1993, p.40)

With regard to effective interventions for children, this can often occur indirectly on a number of levels, as a result of contact with different members of the family. This is not to argue that more specific and direct provision to children is not required. The research evidence clearly indicates that it is. However, it is not always possible to deal directly with children, for a variety of reasons. This can be due to the way that services are currently organised, conflicts within the family which may prevent the possibility of getting the whole family together and difficulties gaining direct access to children due to this. It is generally considered that efforts to assist children need to be accompanied by strategies to reduce the problem use itself (Hill, Laybourn and Brown 1996). Ideas emanating from the ecological perspective and social support can help to illustrate these differing points of intervention.

Coping perspectives

This approach focuses on the partner or carer without the substance-misuse problem. This may be due to the fact that even minimal cooperation from the person misusing the substance has proved impossible, or because such contact is inappropriate for other reasons. Alternatively it may be due to recognition of the need to place more emphasis on the impact on those who are on the receiving end of the substance-misusing behaviour.

Orford (1998) outlines three working assumptions that underpin this perspective. First, a serious drink problem is highly stressful for those having to cope with it. Second, they are often unprepared for the stress and problems that result. Third, coping with the substance use will involve many struggles and dilemmas resulting from the difficult processes that arise (including many of those discussed in Chapter 3). What is emphasised, therefore, is the need for a detailed understanding of such stresses as a precursor to helping relatives or others to develop better ways of coping. Pressures that relatives identify include the substance misuser disappearing from home for long periods, the effects on the family's social life, and the impact of secrecy. Those experienced by children include parents being moody or critical, constant arguments, having a restricted social life and, to a lesser extent, violence in the home (Copello *et al.* 2000; Orford 1998).

Proponents of coping perspectives resist the idea that substance misuse may be symptomatic of problems in the family and are critical of some types of systemic models which may be seen to pathologise others in the family. Instead they focus on the underlying needs of the 'victims' of substance misuse and the importance of accounting for the social and psychological stresses which impact on partners and families. At the same time, however, such approaches do acknowledge, to an extent, the dynamic nature of responses to substance-misusing behaviour, and suggest that some coping responses are more effective in ameliorating the above pressures and stresses than others. There is also a recognition that better coping mechanisms may well impact positively on the substance misuser's attitude and willingness to engage with treatment.

More effective coping responses from partners may act indirectly as an intervention for the substance misuser in both encouraging entry into treatment and impacting on the level of the substance misuse (Barber and Crisp 1995, cited in Copello *et al.* 2000). Significantly, such coping strategies can be helped or hindered by the social support received from family members, friends, neighbours, professionals and others in the wider community (Orford 1998) although, as we have seen, social support can have both positive and negative influences on change.

Stress-Coping-Health Model

The Stress-Coping-Health Model is a particularly well-developed approach within this tradition (Copello *et al.* 2000; Orford 1998; Orford *et al.* 1998a, 1998b, 1998c). This is currently being piloted and evaluated with primary care professionals in health care settings and would appear to have a very useful structure that could be adapted more widely. The model's strength lies in its clear conceptual structure and framework. It includes a detailed examination and description of the basic characteristics involved in each coping response. These are broadly characterised as tolerating the substance-misusing behaviour, becoming engaged in trying to change it, and withdrawing from it. This 'typology' of responses was developed from research examining the 'structures' underlying family members' reports of the way in which they coped with a drug or alcohol problem (Orford *et al.* 1998b). The stages of the intervention describe strategies for exploring three key areas – the stress experienced by relatives or family members, their particular coping responses and the social support available. A five-step approach is then undertaken in an attempt to improve the coping response, making it more effective and less stressful.

Initially, this involves using counselling skills in order to establish trust and gain an understanding of the relatives' particular stresses. Significantly the focus is on the family members' experiences of stress as opposed to details of the drug or alcohol use. Accurate information is then provided about the effects of substance dependency in order to correct misconceptions and to reduce a sense of isolation about the uniqueness of such stress. This links to the importance of offering a conceptual understanding of the issues of dependence. A central part of the model is identifying ways of coping. This involves discussing difficulties in communicating, dilemmas and types of responses.

Problems in communicating are seen to arise due to the substance misuser's use of, or relationship to, drinking or drug-taking; some of the implications of this attachment were discussed in Chapter 4. The next step involves a review of aspects of the partner's social environment with the aim of increasing positive support, while reducing unhelpful aspects. At this stage more open communication within the family is encouraged. A diagrammatic representation of the relative's social support mechanism is suggested here in order to provide a clearer picture of the influence of the social support network. Finally, the need for further help for the user, the family member, the family as a whole or other family members is explored.

The model stresses the importance of counselling skills at each stage and rests on the comparative effectiveness of brief interventions.

What seems particularly useful in this model is the manner in which those in the community are viewed as both potentially supportive or unsupportive. In other words, it allows for the complex nature of the influence of networks and operates with clients to alter the balance for the better.

Although the model has been designed to assist adults with coping strategies, it would seem to have the potential for some development in relation to coping mechanisms that could include the child. Situations which are seen to impact on the health of others in the family implicitly recognise the nature of stressful dynamics within it. Under these circumstances such coping strategies could be fruitfully extended to children. This could be as part of the partner's coping mechanism or that of the child:

> Spouses could be encouraged to talk with their children at home: problems could be discussed, different options as to how best to cope could be thought through, and action plans could be developed. Alternatively, the child could be enabled to access help in his or her own right. (Velleman and Orford 1999, p.261)

Community Reinforcement Approach

This approach was originally developed for problem drinkers but has been extended to other types of substance misuse. While much more prevalent in the USA, there has been some adaptation of the model by drug and alcohol services in the UK (Ryan et al. 1999). Although some forms of this model stress abstinence as a prerequisite for change, the version we discuss allows for more flexible goals.

The approach combines aspects of learning theory, the influence of social factors and ways in which changing dependence is influenced by concepts of identity. Altering problem substance misuse is seen, in part, to involve a necessary break from the negative aspects of a role which can become associated with to those who misuse drugs or alcohol. As we saw in the discussion on labelling theory, this may involve the internalisation of negative labels and feelings of being stigmatised. Most significantly in this model, however, concepts of self are seen to be related to social factors which can either reinforce a move away from 'dependence' or encourage further involvement, as the identity of the user becomes more associated with such activity. In a sense a vicious circle of decreasing social return can be seen to emerge from progressive attachment to a substance. This can limit the available energy for relationships and other activities, which become neglected and potentially more problem related. As a consequence there is a decreased incentive to attend to these. Feelings of worthlessness may feed into this and be confirmed by the negative labels applied by others in the social environment.

The model offers a number of interventions which focus on social, recreational and relationship factors as a way of reinforcing clients' motivation to control or stop their substance misuse (Smith and Meyers 1995). On an individual level it may include counselling to explore the antecedents and consequences of the drinking or drug-taking. One of the main aims of this is to help elucidate the negative side of the activity in terms of energy or cost and the social implications of this. Some programmes in the USA have also included coping skills for non-substance-using partners.

The model attempts to focus on ways in which new social and/or vocational activities can be developed. This is referred to as 'structure building' (Shaffer and Jones 1989, cited in Ryan et al. 1999). This is viewed as a complex process as it involves issues of confidence and self-esteem, as well as the opportunity to change social relationships and consider new opportunities (Valliant 1983). It is also difficult as it may involve developing new aspects of one's personality or rediscovering characteristics that have been subsumed through entrenched use of drugs or alcohol over time. Breaking away from an established 'dependence' is seen to involve a crucial social dimension which links directly to core issues of identity. Re-establishing involvement with family, friends, work or community, if this has been lost, involves a process of regaining a sense of worth and value within such groups or relationships. Consequently such reattachments involve emotional journeys as well as the more practical ones associated with regaining employment and so on. This process has been illustrated by Biernacki's (1986) research into people recovering from heroin use. He stresses its importance as a means to reduce or end dependence 'either geographically or symbolically' – in other words, emphasising both practical and emotional elements (cited in Orford 2001, p.324).

Interventions in this model might also include detoxification services, counselling for marital problems and advice and support with employment. In the version of this model adapted by the community alcohol and drug services in Trafford, Greater Manchester (Ryan et al. 1999), social support factors are added to the existing alcohol treatments available for dependent drinkers and other drug users. The package of services is delivered by people from the different agencies involved. Volunteers are used to offer support in the home and to access local leisure and social facilities, a measure which aims to help people to regain the social skills which they feel have been lost (Ryan *et al.* 1999).

This model acknowledges the interconnection of social and personal factors in influencing the problem behaviour and Barber (1995) underlines the way in which the approach involves a thorough assessment of the substance misuser's microsystem. It remains an example of an approach which both recognises and highlights the interactive nature of the wider social system on behaviour and behaviour change (Harwin 1982). In many ways the structure of the model is not unlike an example of effective inter-agency collaboration or a case management approach. Clearly one central question here will be how successfully the individual is able to retain an overall sense of the programme.

Network Therapy

Network Therapy, as its name implies, is another approach that stresses the importance of the influence of other people in bringing about change in the drinking or drug-taking behaviour, using the substance misuser's wider social network in addition to selected family or friends (Galanter 1993, 1999). Here, the primary focus is upon achieving change for the substance misuser rather than for concerned members of the family or significant others. In fact those selected to support ongoing change are seen as part of the therapist's team, rather than being the subjects of treatment themselves (Copello *et al.* 2001). As developed in the USA, the model's primary aim is abstinence but versions of this model include moderation as a goal.

Network Therapy rests on the notion that individuals change behaviour as a result of interactions and as part of the group's influence upon the individual. Particular group processes are seen, then, as both influencing and overcoming barriers to change. Some of these ideas appear either to borrow from or to build upon the way in which group support has been utilised within twelve-step programmes associated with Alcoholics Anonymous. Supportive group networks are seen to have the potential to reverse some of the more negative processes of labelling and alienation, which may occur as a result of developing attachment to or dependence on a substance.

Acceptance by a group is seen as a way of helping to overcome the negative cycle of feelings of low self-esteem and rejection.

> He or she is now accepted rather than rejected, despite a history of being at odds with family members and friends. Feelings of cohesiveness emerge among the network members. The patient feels well-being rather than malaise in the company of social people… Gradually, they come to accept that their distress can be relieved by means of a change of attitude, as denial and rationalisation are confronted in a supportive way. (Galanter 1999, p.25)

Being included rather than excluded helps to overcome the secrecy and defensiveness which may have developed as coping mechanisms for those experiencing alcohol or drug problems. The cohesive nature of group support and its social impact is seen to ameliorate the stresses and conflicts that result from attachment to drugs or alcohol (Galanter 1993, 1999).

Proponents of Network Therapy appear to place a rather uncritical faith in the assumed efficacy of such group processes, despite the possibility that change could simply be linked with a pressure to conform to the 'group will' (Orford 2001, p.326). Indeed, extreme examples of group processes of this kind may be found in some of the more controversial drug and alcohol programmes in rehabilitation hostels which involve a hierarchical structure, where residents are seen to progress through different stages.

Issues of power, boundary setting and confidentiality in models such as Network Therapy which utilise family or friends as co-therapists are complex and need particular attention. In addition, there may be difficulties in using models which emphasise the role of supportive networks without recognising that the insufficiency or absence of these may itself be a significant factor in drug or alcohol misuse. There may be issues for those who have no friends or family willing to participate and isolation, coupled with the lack of any recognisable social support, may be a common experience.

Social Behaviour and Network Therapy

Social Behaviour and Network Therapy (SBNT) is a more recent approach, developed in the UK. In the light of evidence that a key component of successful intervention appears to be the contribution of social and interpersonal factors, this model is currently being evaluated in order to identify its potential effectiveness in reducing alcohol misuse (United Kingdom Alcohol Treatment Trial Research Team 2001).

While encompassing some of the theoretical assumptions of Network Therapy, it also adapts ideas from other methods of intervention including the Community Reinforcement Approach and coping models such as the Stress-Coping-Health Model (Copello *et al.* 2001). Like Network Therapy and other interventions we have discussed, it is based on the hypothesis that overcoming dependencies (specifically alcohol in this model) is influenced by both positive and negative factors in the substance misuser's environment. Unlike Network Therapy, the overall goal can be moderation *or* abstinence.

In this approach social support mechanisms are used to influence change in the drinking behaviour and clients are assisted in establishing a network of people who may offer support, where this may not be readily apparent or available. This may involve steps to help a client who may feel isolated to develop the necessary skills in order to approach people and begin to develop a supportive network. In identifying the network, it is suggested that a diagrammatic representation of significant others may be used, helping to clarify aspects of social support. This stage has parallels to aspects of the Stress-Coping-Health Model where available social support is explored, while tactics are developed for increasing positives and reducing more negative influences. This is seen to be one of the worker's main tasks in the process.

> The therapist is trained to focus attention during the sessions on positive support and away from potential disagreements or conflict, e.g. a network member's criticism can be reframed as a concern and the group can be invited to consider ways of turning the concern into positive support. (Copello *et al.* 2001, p.9)

However, the main difference here is that the social support is explored as a way of encouraging change in the problem user, in contrast to focusing on the needs and stresses of his or her partner.

As developed in the United Kingdom Alcohol Treatment Trial (2001), SBNT consists of eight sessions conducted over a twelve-week period and is divided into three main phases. The first involves the identification of the network. The second consists of work undertaken with the client in order to assist them in either building a network or engaging it, with the aim of marshalling support in order to sustain and maintain change. For some the problem behaviour may have resulted in strained relationships and, consequently, the contact may involve looking at ways to address this. The third phase involves consolidation of the work and preparation for the future. The actual work itself can be undertaken in joint sessions with the client and members of the network or undertaken unilaterally via the client with the substance-misuse problem. In addition, once agreed, work can continue with members of the network even when the person drinking has ceased attending. The importance of choosing the right people as supportive members is stressed as they are expected to commit themselves to offering support and be available at times of high risk or relapse. Those included in the social network may be family members, friends or work colleagues or others deemed to be significant in the person's life. Certain categories of people, however, are considered inappropriate. These include those who have an existing drug or alcohol problem, or have undue influence because of their relationship with the person concerned (for example a manager at work) and anyone under 16.

The model illustrates not only the significance of supportive networks, but also the importance of identifying where and why these may be lacking. Consequently it emphasises the skills and strategies needed in order to mitigate problem relationships and build more supportive ones. Given that in cases of very problematic substance misuse it is more likely that relationships will be strained, this appears to be a crucial nettle to grasp as the bolstering or conflictual nature of support is clearly not independent of the substance misuser's social skills or his or her ability to form and sustain relationships.

Towards a family-centred model for intervention

Here we explore some of our own ideas for a model that seeks to make children more visible while having an impact on parents' motivation to change. It is designed to be appropriate in a range of settings, irrespective of whether the child or the adult is the central focus. Based on theoretical frameworks, skills and techniques drawn from both adult services and childcare practice, we consider that it forms the basis of an approach which might meet the needs of the whole family more effectively. The central aims are the resolution of the substance problem, while acknowledging the needs of children. This is not necessarily dependent on abstinence on the part of the drug or alcohol user but on the management of substance use, with due consideration given to harm-reduction strategies and the protection of children.

The proposed approach combines the use of the transtheoretical model and motivational interviewing within the context of a systemic understanding of the family's functioning. Genograms and ecomaps, both associated with the ecological model, are used to gain detailed information about the family and the world of its members and to place the children firmly on the agenda by making them more visible, even if they are not actually seen as part of the intervention. Issues of attachment both between child and carers and between user and substance can be explored, alongside the impact of the substance as a family 'member'. Social support and the role played by the substance in coping with past difficulties, the management of relationships or social factors can also be considered.

This combination of ideas is not without precedent (see for example Brooks and Rice 1997; Robinson and Rhoden 1998). Family work approaches have also been used in voluntary sector agencies (see for example Vetere 1987, 1998) and Yandoli et al. (1989) used family therapy in addiction treatment and intervention in a hospital drug dependency centre. They found genograms particularly useful 'for turning up drug problems in other family members such as problem drinking or tranquilliser use' (Yandoli et al. 1989, p.55).

The chosen components of the approach have been selected for their efficacy in addressing the variety of issues presented by substance misuse, family functioning and social support. The transtheoretical model developed by Prochaska and DiClemente (1982; Prochaska et al. 1992) as discussed in Chapter 3, together with motivational interviewing, are seen as particularly effective in enhancing clients' movement towards positive change.

Because motivation became central in the field of addictions during the 1980s and 1990s, Prochaska and DiClemente's transtheoretical model has gained influence as a framework for intervention. It assumes that 'addicts' pass through five stages of change — pre-contemplation, contemplation, preparation to change, action and maintenance, and that their 'addiction' differs at every point (Prochaska et al. 1992; Sutton 1996). Most progress occurs via a spiralling pattern, in which people sometimes relapse, and through this process they learn from their mistakes. Consequently they will approach the stage differently the next time they encounter it. People are not seen to progress in an ordered or linear manner as this is viewed as comparatively rare in the context of 'addictive' behaviour.

Motivational interviewing, devised by Miller and Rollnick (1991), emphasises the ambivalence experienced by substance misusers. It is a therapeutic technique requiring sophisticated interpersonal skills which offers a number of suggested interventions. The principal aims are to 'develop a perceived discrepancy or dissonance between the [client's] current behaviour and stated goals [which includes] the provision of accurate feedback, the removal of barriers to facilitate the treatment process and working through the decisional benefits and costs with the emphasis on positive incentives' (Davidson 1996, p.181). Using this technique helps the worker focus on the internal struggle of the client as they consider changing behaviour. Motivational interviewing is more task focused than traditional client-centred counselling and attempts to balance client self-determination with a more directive orientation for the worker; in Miller's words it is confrontational but not in the usual sense (see Miller and Rollnick 1991 for a detailed exposition of this).

Systems theory (as we have seen) has been criticised for both pathologising and blaming some family members for the behaviour of others, and for reinforcing power and gender imbalances (see for example Orford 1998). Our interpretation of such a model, however, emphasises the importance of different levels of responsibility within the family, avoiding any attempt to shift blame onto those who may be seen to be on the receiving end of the behaviour in question. The application of systemic ideas provides a potentially important framework through which to view both the dynamics of substance use and its impact on others, particularly children. Seeing the substance as a central part of the family system which may have an impact on everyone else provides an interesting perspective from which to analyse what is going on.

Family systems theory is a complex body of knowledge and we can offer only a very limited account of it here (see Barker 1992; Burnham 1986; Gorell Barnes 1998 for a more detailed analysis). There are, however, elements that we see as critical. The interconnectedness of family members and the way in which the behaviour of one member can impact on others has been reflected in accounts from both children and parents. Because of this, a systemic perspective which examines these interrelationships, the way in which relationships change, behaviour adapts and roles are assumed, in relation to the substance-misusing behaviour, may usefully address some of the issues that families confront. By the same token, change in one part of the system will have consequences for everyone else.

Two practice tools associated with systemic thinking are genograms and ecomaps. The genogram is essentially a family tree that includes additional social information – a symbolic and visible representation of a family's composition which shows the extended family network, ages and occupations of all the members, births, deaths, marriages, divorces, migrations, and dates of significant events (see Burnham 1986 for a detailed account). It expands horizontally to depict the current generation and vertically to chart generations through time and can be adapted to reflect all kinds of families whatever their composition. Partnerships are depicted by a horizontal line; children in the family are linked by a vertical line from this horizontal and are ranged horizontally beneath (Warren 1993).

The ecomap originally developed by Warren (1993), starts with the genogram at its centre. Around this, a series of circles are ranged to symbolise different aspects of the family 'ecosystem' – work, friends, school and so on – with links made between these and the relevant family member. Size of circle denotes significance; closeness and distance of circles to family system denotes degree of attachment. In a family where substance misuse is an issue, not only would the substance concerned be included in the genogram, but also associated aspects connected both with it and the user would be depicted in the ecomap – drinking/drug-using friends, source of substance, probation officer, general practitioner/clinic. Sources of both support and tension in the ecosystem could then be identified.

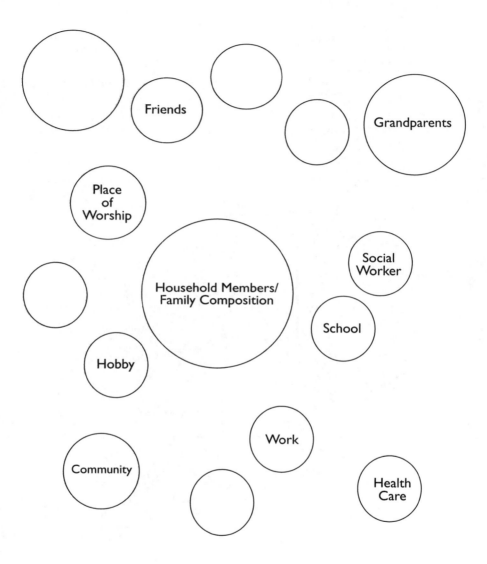

Figure 11.1 Guide to Ecomap Structure.

Genogram Symbols

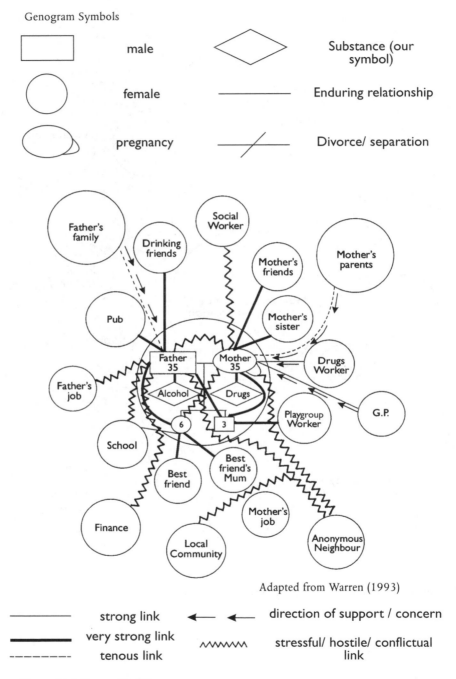

Adapted from Warren (1993)

Figure 11.2 Example of Ecomap

Figure 11.2 illustrates the relationships and links in a family where the father uses alcohol and the mother uses drugs. The couple are expecting their third child in three months and an anonymous neighbour has telephoned social services to express concern about the care of the children, who are perceived as neglected – 'she's always out of her head and he's always in the pub'.

The mother feels some antagonism towards the social worker as she is already working with a drugs counsellor to manage her drug use more safely in view of her pregnancy, and is also seeing her GP for depression. The father's drinking is placing a strain on the marital relationship, as are the close links with drinking friends in the local pub. It is also threatening his job and causing financial problems. Both parents feel angry with the anonymous neighbour and there is a great deal of local gossip going on in relation to this, causing some conflict within the local community. They also feel as though they are being pointed at and there have been some angry exchanges with other parents in the school playground.

Both children have supportive links with the wider community and both are attached to their father. Mother and daughter are going through a difficult period at present, as the daughter is concerned about her mother and feels she has to keep an eye on her all the time. Mother and son remain close, although the latter wants the new baby to 'go and live with granny'.

Mother feels she has to work longer hours in order to support the family and this is taking its toll on her health. Her main sources of support are two close friends who also use drugs, and her sister who does not. Both paternal and maternal grandparents want to help but are kept at a distance due to friction in the past.

An ecomap may serve a number of additional functions. First, the process of working with this visual representation in a collaborative way may lead to an understanding and acceptance of the tensions or dilemmas to be overcome, helping to tip the motivational balance. As Warren puts it, 'the connections, the themes and the quality of the family's life seem to jump off the page and this leads to a more holistic and integrative perception' (Warren 1993, p.4). Second, as he goes on to point out, 'it portrays an overview of the family in their situation in a way which makes more visible the points of conflict to be mediated, bridges to be built and resources to be sought and mobilised' (Warren 1993, p.40). In this way it may help the client move from contemplation towards a more action-centred strategy.

The ecosystem could be explored in terms of parts of it that might be strengthened in order to address the reduction of harm related to the substance misuse, as well as gaps in the ecosystem that could be filled by community resources or agency support. This could be done by providing more childcare support, a referral to a family centre for both parenting support and playgroup facilities, and perhaps some external support with substance misuse via drug or alcohol services. This might create the space for both parent and child while change is being considered and in such a way that fears to do with child removal are lessened and a more honest appraisal of the issues can be established, since this is one of the major obstacles in this area of practice (Cleaver and Freeman 1995).

Both genograms and ecomaps can be used successfully with either just the individual identified as the client or including other members of the family and/or other professionals who may be involved. The professional network and its role in the system is particularly important (as we have seen) since it may be part of the problem as well as part of the solution (the criminal justice system in all its manifestations might be the most obvious example of this, as would the child protection system). This approach could also enable clients to think systemically and holistically, locating change and options in a wider context. The tools suggested would enable experimentation with different constellations of elements of the systems and hypothesising about the effects of change may be safely explored. What effect would giving up drugs and alcohol have on your relationship with your partner/child? If you 'evicted' the substance what might life be like? What do you think your children would say/do/feel? What might the risks be and to whom? What gap would it leave? What might fill it? What do you fear its absence might reveal? Making significant changes to long-standing behaviour can feel threatening. Trying out change in a safe environment, making visible some of the invisible blocks, obstacles and rewards might make it a little less so.

Clearly this approach has not been tried or tested, unlike the other approaches we have discussed. However, we suggest that it may have some significant benefits. It would make visible and 'out there' a number of important issues which it is often hard to get at through other means. These include identifying the substance and its system as part of the wider family network and illustrating the extent to which the substance impacts on other family members, particularly children.

It would also serve as an additional and more graphic way of gaining access to what has been called 'the pattern of denial' (Taylor 1999) – discussed in Chapters 3 and 4 – which is likely to feature, at some level, in substance-misusing parents' perception of the effects of their behaviour on their children. Bringing the substance into the genogram, into the house, into the living room might move parents towards the possibility of breaking through this denial or pattern of attachment to the substance and, in turn, help them to validate their children's perceptions of what is really happening in their family. In addition it may help identify a number of strategies that could ameliorate the impact of parental substance misuse within the home.

This holistic approach is also consistent with current debates in child protection about how best to mobilise 'protective factors' both in the individual and the wider system to minimise risk of harm or damage (Howe *et al*. 1999; Rutter 1990, 1999; see also Chapter 5). In relation to children of substance misusers, factors such as an external support system which assists with the development of coping skills, a supportive adult relationship and the encouragement of the development of the skill of 'planfulness' – the tendency to use planning in relation to important life decisions – are significant in helping to break negative chain reactions and improve resilience (Velleman and Orford 1999).

Child-centred practice in family intervention

With regard to more direct services for children, there are a range of views about the most fruitful way forward. These relate to problems in identifying specific consequences for children who have substance-misusing parents since the type of problems to which children are vulnerable varies. A range of mediating factors exist and the individual responses of children will differ (Velleman and Orford 1999). Because of these factors, some argue that responses are better deployed as and when difficulties arise rather than attempting to identify particular outcomes and associated treatments too precisely. Engaging children in need of services also affects the way in which services are made available and accessible and are delivered. Some commentators, therefore, while supporting the development of specialist provision for the more acute and particular problems that children may experience, stress the importance of a wider point of access to a more general range of services (Laybourn *et al*. 1996). These, it is argued, can play a pivotal role, if they can increase awareness of the particular clues which indicate that parental substance misuse is a specific issue for children.

The qualitative study undertaken by Hill *et al*. (1996), based on interviews with children themselves, echoed the need for a network of services which reflected not only their differing perspectives, but also a recognition of the diverse ways in which children might want or be able to respond to assistance, depending on age, gender, family circumstances and personal coping styles (Hill *et al.* 1996, p.165).

The services needed for children can be categorised into two main types. On the one hand, general, unobtrusive facilities where help can be gained without the nature of the problem being visible to others are clearly extremely useful. Examples of this include teenage counselling agencies, one-to-one befriending services, preventive work in schools and youth clubs, drop-in centres for young people, family services, anonymous help-lines and educational initiatives. On the other hand, more specialist services offering individual counselling, group work, family mediation and an out-of-hours crisis service are also required. Clearly there is an important balance to be struck here between diversity and specialist treatment. As we discussed in Chapter 9, more child-centred approaches are dependent as much on ways in which organisations respond and collaborate as on the development of particular models or techniques.

At present there is limited provision specifically for children of substance-misusing parents. While there appear to be a number of burgeoning developments here, as Harbin (2000, p.81) observes, there appears to be 'no systematic support…involving a clear understanding of children's needs or perceptions or of their relationship to their parent's drug use'.

There are a number of factors which make direct work with children difficult, as we have already seen. There is the problem of making services attractive and accessible to children, given the likely impact of secrecy, loyalty and denial within the family. The issue of parental consent is crucial here, given that parents are the primary gatekeepers of the services children receive (Barnard and Barlow forthcoming; Gensheimer, Rosa and Ayers 1990, cited in Velleman and Orford 1999). Even where a good level of trust exists between professionals and parents, children's feelings of loyalty towards their parents can make it difficult for them to engage with issues, particularly when they feel in the midst of experiences which can be both confusing and problematic. As a result children may need considerable support to talk about their parents' substance misuse and behaviour (Barnard and Barlow forthcoming). Young children, in particular, may need a type of 'psychological permission' which involves more than merely tacit or verbal approval from the carer, but rather a dialogue which helps them overcome natural inhibitions when discussing potentially conflicting emotions with relative strangers (Laybourn *et al.* 1996, p.121).

Types of programmes aimed specifically at children of drug-misusing parents reflect some of the key issues that we know impact on children's lives. Both individual and group programmes often revolve around a number of central issues which are seen to reflect the problems and needs of children in such circumstances. Such interventions aim both to help children make sense of the impact of substance misuse for them and to encourage contact with others who have experienced similar difficulties, either via activities which may offer some outlet or escape, or more personal peer group support.

Enabling children to make sense of a parent's drug or alcohol misuse may initially involve looking at ways in which such use is seen within the family. Is it viewed as an illness? If so, what does the child understand by this? Is this is a helpful way for the child to make sense of the behaviour or does it have other consequences, in terms of guilt and responsibility? By exploring children's views of the situation and how it affects them, the feelings related to anxieties, fears, expectations and pressures can be explored more fully. Helping children to express feelings is especially important, as emotions may often be very mixed, particularly as children's own needs are likely to be denied. There may well be particular issues with regard to children's experiences of loss and separation. The consequences of substance-misusing behaviour by the parent may also result in loss of self-esteem or problems of identity for the children involved (Robinson and Dunne 1999; see also Chapter 8).

Helping children to develop better coping strategies is generally viewed as an important objective of any intervention. This may involve helping them find more effective ways of responding to situations at home and to lessen the negative impact on them, as individuals, and on other aspects of their lives such as school and friends. Robinson and Hassle (2001, p.33) also emphasise the importance of the development 'of a sense of self which is not bound up in family problems'. In more severe cases of parental substance misuse, this may involve assisting the child to employ tactics for dealing with situations of personal care and safety, although clearly this is dependent on the level of risk within the home. In this context it is also important that children are not made to feel responsible for managing such situations.

A second main aim is to provide children with appropriate access to services which can offer support, encouragement and opportunities away from the immediate environment (Robinson and Dunne 1999). Specific group-work initiatives can be valuable particularly where they are able to offer support from other children who have been in a similar position. The study by Hill *et al.* (1996) emphasised the importance of the social support offered by others in such settings. Al-Ateen (part of Alcoholics Anonymous) which supports teenaged children of alcoholics, was viewed as particularly valuable by a number of children interviewed as it allowed them to gain insights from other 'survivors' and to develop coping skills. Other group initiatives have also highlighted the importance of peer support in helping to reduce feelings of shame and guilt in a supportive environment.

However, there may well be problems relating to both referral and attendance when specific groups are set up for children. Parents may be wary of a group which deals with issues of substance misuse, however sensitively, fearing that such issues cannot be contained or that children may obtain information or ideas detrimental to their welfare via their peers. Parents may also be anxious about what children may reveal about the home situation. All these factors make decisions about the appropriate age range of children in such groups and the content of sessions even more crucial (Harbin 2000).

Despite the potential difficulties, professionals have outlined a number of ways in which such problems can be mitigated. Planning and clarity about confidentiality and parental involvement are all crucial. Initial meetings with key family members and joint sessions with children are essential in helping to overcome understandable fears about disclosure, as well as other anxieties and misconceptions that can arise about what may occur in such settings (Robinson and Dunne 1999). The NSPCC Kilburn Project/Caversham Children's Centre group-work initiative, for example, made a point of providing detailed information to both parents and children about the groups they run including what some of children's initial reactions may be. This both helps to allay fears and anxieties about issues of confidentiality and reassures parents who may be more easily able to anticipate the child's reactions to discussing sensitive issues in a group (see Robinson and Dunne 1999 for detailed examples of these group-work initiatives). Harbin (2000), reviewing one interesting example of a therapeutic group run for children, stresses the importance of both a thorough assessment of the child beforehand and the provision of further individual work afterwards, if required, in order to follow up particular issues that may be raised.

To date specific group-work programmes for children have been slow to develop and clearly more needs to be done, particularly in view of the fact that research indicates that even a comparatively short group programme can have a significant impact and provide a catalyst for further progress (Robinson and Dunne 1999).

Research into children's needs has emphasised the importance of listening to children, working with them and avoiding responses which reinforce a sense of helplessness (Hill *et al.* 1996; Laybourn *et al.* 1996). As Hill and colleagues point out, children are 'active participants in the situation' and service developments 'should aim to work with children and young people and not just for them' (Hill *et al.* 1996, p.165).

Summary

In discussing methods of intervention we have been at pains to identify approaches that place the child more centre stage, whether these be aimed at the primary user or others in the family. More holistic approaches suggest that change needs to occur throughout the family and, as a consequence, are more likely to be sustained and enduring. This may mean working with the family together, or using different types of interventions with different members.

This is not to suggest that attempts at involving children more directly in family interventions should not be pursued. It is, however, to acknowledge that progress in this area may be best served by adopting a more child-centred approach across the range of different services, in addition to the development of specialised provision. While many of the interventions discussed here are seen to have a secondary impact on children, this may lead to a turning point within the family, or the development of more effective ways of coping for the parent supporting the child. Alternatively or additionally it may enable professionals to see the impact on children more clearly, leading to more timely provision of direct services to them.

What we argue for here are approaches that highlight the impact of parental behaviour on the children concerned. This has particular implications (as we saw in Chapter 9) for the way in which agencies work jointly with the families of substance misusers. We have no illusions about the complexity of the task. Where a number of potentially different services are involved there is the danger of a fragmented approach to intervention, which loses a sense of how a family functions. In this way it is easy to get distracted from the impact on the child. However, this does not mean that assessments cannot be more holistic across agencies or that interventions cannot attempt to include a wider perspective. What is paramount is a higher level of cooperation and understanding which involves knowledge of and discussion about intervention for the family as a whole.

12

The Way Forward?

Successful inter-organisational activity is no arid management exercise.
The challenge is to create the right climate for collaboration, to recognise
the different contributions that participants can make.

(Hudson 2000, p.254)

I didn't want to tell anyone because I was afraid of what social services
might do.

(Child quoted in Brisby et al. 1997, p.14)

In this book we set out to explore what we see as important questions about parental substance misuse and child welfare. It has become clear that there are significant links between substance misuse and child maltreatment of different kinds as well as a variety of other problems, including domestic violence, mental health difficulties and criminal behaviour. In addition, the way in which people are labelled, stigmatised and judged as a result of their conduct has enabled us to understand the various processes that contribute to the development and maintenance of alcohol and drug misuse. In turn this has shed light on client–worker relations and the ways in which denial, secrecy, avoidance and fear have all been identified as playing their part in attitudes to accessing services and real engagement with professional intervention.

We have discovered that although it may be possible to misuse drugs and alcohol and parent effectively, more commonly the task of parenting can be easily undermined. The role played by the substance, issues of dependence and attachment and the way that these impact upon the dependency needs and attachment patterns between parent and child are all critical factors that affect this skilled and demanding activity. We have seen that looking at the substance as a family member can provide a vivid metaphor that helps to convey something of the child's experience as well as that of the family as a whole. The dynamic between parenting capacity, child development and ecological factors has also been highlighted as significant, as has the impact of poverty, social exclusion, lack of family support and wider cultural and structural issues.

What has also become clear is that for most children living with chronic substance-misusing parents, life can be very painful, difficult, frightening or dangerous due to the way in which family life and functioning and parenting capacity can be affected. Feelings of being 'invisible' and worthless, premature maturity and loss, on a range of levels, have all been identified as features of the lives of the children who grew up with parental alcohol and drug misuse. We have, however, also seen the role that social support, protective factors and resilience can play in both enabling some children to cope and assisting some parents to manage their 'dual roles as drug users and as parents' (Elliott and Watson 2000, p.30). However (as we have said before) just because some manage and survive, this does not mean that all will.

In addition, we have discovered both from research and from practitioners in person the complexity of making assessments in the context of substance misuse and child welfare and the difficulty of gaining access to the child's experience. Methods of intervention have also been considered regarding the extent to which they address the needs of families as a whole, rather than just the person with the drug or alcohol problem.

In exploring the professional domain from a range of perspectives a number of issues have emerged. Ironically, the increased specialisation and sophistication of the social welfare network has created a climate in which it is easier to create separations than connections, as we suggested in the introduction (Weir and Douglas 1999). This can lead to professionals focusing on their client to the exclusion of other family members and being reluctant to engage with behaviour that may exacerbate stresses or cause additional and potentially more intensive intervention. One consequence is that the 'child' in the adult is often attended to more assiduously than the real child in the family. Professionals will inevitably advocate vigorously for their identified clients. It is easy to see how, as a result, hierarchies of need, competing demands and conflicts of interest can all contribute to denial and mistrust between those in different agencies, often reflecting unhelpful aspects in the client–worker dynamic. Professional 'distancing' can often lead to the exclusion, either by accident or design, of key professionals who hold essential pieces of information that could contribute to major aspects of decision-making. As Forrester (2000) has observed, the low involvement of drug and alcohol workers in case conferences should be viewed with considerable concern. All these factors may lead to real barriers to effective working and increase risk (Cleaver *et al.* 1999).

The organisation of social work around specific client groups – older people, people with disabilities, children and families, mental health – has had a number of significant consequences. While this arrangement has advantages, in terms of developing skills and expertise in specific areas of practice, the disadvantages are also becoming clear (Cleaver *et al.* 1999; Kearney *et al.* 2000; Tunnard 2002; Weir and Douglas 1999). Specialisation has reinforced boundaries between services for children and families and mental health, just at the point when the overlap between these areas has become recognised. As a consequence, services for parents with drug and alcohol problems and their children are fragmented – a view that is shared not only by parents themselves but also by statutory and voluntary professionals working in these fields. This has various implications. It may mean that parents and their children may have to go to a range of services to get their needs met; services may differ in ideology, approach and protocols. Key considerations here are what might be called 'cause and effect' and time scales. In other words, assumptions are made that if the substance problem is 'cured' or controlled, the case can be closed. This flies in the face of research evidence that emphasises the complexity of substance misuse and its often chronic and enduring nature, whereas childcare social workers tend to think of it as a short-term problem (Forrester 2000). It is therefore only through a better understanding of motivation, dependence, management or abstention and relapse that real engagement with the problems can be achieved and a longer-term resolution found. It is here that a range of professionals can play their part.

Improving practice

There are a number of areas that need to be addressed to improve our practice with substance-misusing parents and their children so that we can work more effectively with the significant crossover between drug and alcohol problems and child welfare. Moreover, practice needs to be informed by the views of the people who use services so that stigmatisation, labelling and discrimination can be reduced.

Training

The value of inter-agency training has long been recognised in childcare (Cleaver *et al.* 1998, 1999; Department of Health 1999) and debates about the impact of parents' problems on child welfare have heightened awareness of the importance of acquiring relevant knowledge about specialist areas such as substance abuse and mental health (Cleaver *et al.* 1998; Kearney *et al.* 2000). Despite an expressed need for training, however, Kearney *et al.* (2000) discovered that unless it was mandatory, the response from practitioners was very poor. This has implications for the way in which training is prioritised. Our view is that social welfare training such as the new degree-level qualification for social workers, the post-qualifying childcare award and adult mental health training should include specific modules on substance misuse and its impact on child welfare, as well as other parental problems that adversely affect children.

As we have seen, lack of specialist knowledge about drugs and alcohol was a significant factor in undermining workers' confidence in their ability to assess risk as well as contributing to assumptions about the relative harm posed by different types of substance. Thus heroin use of any kind was seen as instinctively more risky than alcohol use, irrespective of pattern and frequency. This, then, is not just about accessing specialist knowledge to gain information but also about undertaking training to 'unlearn' or shed unhelpful assumptions and to challenge some of the subjective judgements that are based on them (Cleaver *et al.* 1998).

Of course it is relatively easy to suggest training as a way forward but the nature of the training and how it is undertaken is also important. Clearly inter-agency training has several advantages. Groups of professionals learn from one another about respective roles and responsibilities. Areas of crossover and joint working can be modelled and explored. If such training is both delivered and undertaken jointly then this also sends a positive message, rather than have childcare trainers 'teaching' drug and alcohol workers how to spot abuse. This avoids what Murphy and Oulds (2000, p.120) describe as a 'lopsided' experience with concentration placed more on one system than the other. 'What works' in training also has to be considered and includes 'cross agency identification of professional development needs' (Kearney *et al.* 2000, p.46). Approaches to undertaking observation and its role in the assessment of parent–child interaction and family dynamics would form a useful part of any training programme for all professionals. Agencies and organisations also need to be wholehearted and committed to enabling staff to undertake training so that practice can be enhanced and professionals supported in the taxing and demanding work that they do.

There are specific issues regarding the development of skills in communicating with children, not just for childcare staff but also for those in adult services (Cleaver *et al.* 1999). We have seen that even for some child and family workers there is a lack of confidence about how and when to engage with children and the way in which issues of confidentiality, divided loyalties and disclosure should be managed. By the same token assumptions are made about attachment, levels of resilience and children's capacities to cope that need to be challenged if children's needs are to be safeguarded and they are not to be placed at risk. There is also the issue of time, with practitioners often too hard pressed to feel able to spend enough of it with children. As Bell (2002) has shown, there is clear evidence that an engaged and trusted worker can be an important secondary attachment figure when primary carers are emotionally unavailable and that, if we listen to children, they tell us what they need in terms of time, information and choices. She argues that due to the increase in the social care system of managerialism and the impact of the cost-effectiveness agenda, the human rights perspective that should inform services has been eroded. Unless this problem is tackled children will not receive the quality of service they deserve and workers' desire to provide it will continue to be undermined.

Tackling organisational barriers

Joint training with its potential to improve communication and break down barriers will clearly go some way to improving inter-agency working. As Barnard (1999, p.1110) advocates, 'we need to break down the divide that exists between provision of child and adult services that obtains in many areas' and follow Tunnard's (2002, p.28) advice by 'resisting a fragmented approach'. However this will not, in itself, solve all the problems.

Shared protocols, guidelines that are drawn up in partnership, information and guidance specifically written for non-specialists, jointly run projects and research initiatives that include a range of practitioners and clients of services in both planning and execution, all have the potential to improve understanding and appreciation of differing goals, issues and priorities.

Issues of confidentiality (as we have seen) also need to be addressed, since differing ideas about this issue across disciplines is a recognised barrier to effective working (Cleaver *et al.* 1999; Harbin and Murphy 2000; Kearney *et al.* 2000).

Listening to children and their parents: service provision

Listening to what children and parents tell us about what they need, what would help, and the way services could be organised is an important part of working together. There will inevitably be people for whom there will never be a perfect or ideal service and who may never be satisfied. However, there are some specific changes that could be made that might improve the way that services are perceived and the way that intervention is undertaken.

Services should address family needs rather than just those of the drug or alcohol user. People need to be seen in context, with substance misuse as one of many issues with which they may be struggling. Appreciating the totality of their lives rather than simply dealing with the perceived 'problem' will achieve a number of aims. It will enable people to be regarded as individuals in their own right and in relation to all the roles they play not just as 'druggies' or as 'drunks'. This may in turn reduce the degree to which they feel stigmatised and discriminated against. It will also enable strengths as well as shortcomings to be identified (Hogan and Higgins 2001).

As McKeganey *et al.* (2001) point out, most residential services for drug users do not enable people to stay with their children. As a result separation between parent and child is often added to the problems that may have already developed as a result of substance use. The absence of such provision is also a disincentive to people who might otherwise seek help. Residential services are, of course, expensive but not nearly as costly as the potential effects of failing to provide a timely and appropriate response. In addition, services must recognise that substance misuse is not the preserve of one sector of the community. They should therefore ensure that other groups are made aware of their existence and that the services are developed so that they are accessible, irrespective of the class, background or ethnicity of the family.

Practice and policy initiatives

Services need to work together to respond appropriately to parents with substance problems, their partners and families and their children, with a commitment to be 'parent-friendly, child-centred and family-sensitive' (Hogan and Higgins 2001, p.35). Examples of this include what Kearney *et al.* (2000) call models of 'interface' practice or 'crossover' posts where mental health or drug and alcohol specialists are attached to family centres or children and family teams or where family centre workers are placed in drug and alcohol or mental health settings. This type of response helps to break down inter-professional barriers, provide specialist consultation and intervention and contribute to a more rounded response to people's problems.

There are very specific problems associated with services for black and Asian families and families from other minority ethnic groups, making them even more invisible than others with chronic substance-misuse problems and leaving their children exposed to various risks. Practitioners should be mindful of cultural and religious considerations in relation to drug and alcohol use as well as the implications for parents, their children and the wider family of exposing such use and the possible community response (Kearney *et al.* 2000; Patel 2000). They also need to offer discretion and accessibility in terms of location, agency name and language. There are also issues in relation to service provision that enable class barriers to be breached so that children and substance-misusing parents from whatever background can be offered help and support.

This suggests there is an argument for the development of new holistic services that have the potential to offer intervention to all family members. One example of this is provided by the NSPCC in partnership with the Alcohol Recovery Project in north London (Robinson and Hassle 2001). Here the aim is to treat the alcohol-using parent(s), as well as to provide systemic family intervention, services to children and young people, family support and information, training and consultancy. There are some obvious benefits from such a service, not only in terms of its potential for preventive work, with an associated reduction in statutory intervention and care proceedings, but also in relation to the sense it could convey to families that they are being helped 'in the round' and will not have to go to several different locations for support. Clearly this service is alcohol specific; it does however provide a useful template for drug-focused services.

In terms of statutory provision, services for young offenders and children with disabilities, as well as community mental health teams, provide successful models for multidisciplinary intervention composed, as they are, of a range of professionals (see for example Molyneux 2001). A comparable family-focused team would include child and family professionals, drug and alcohol specialists, approved mental health social workers, community psychiatric nurses, domestic violence experts, specialist counsellors for children and young people and family support workers. By bringing together a wide range of adult- and child-focused professionals, holistic models of assessment and intervention could be developed that harness both sets of expertise (as we illustrated in Chapter 11). Rather than identifying these services as substance specific, these teams could simply replace child and family services as we know them. Their composition simply reflects what we already know from research about the coexistence and interrelatedness of a constellation of social welfare problems that could all be usefully addressed together. Working together would become the norm and, above all, families would be provided with an holistic service.

McKeganey *et al.* (2001) also consider that a very specific facility should be provided for the children of drug-misusing parents. Because of the risks to which such children may be exposed, they advocate the provision of what they call 'safe havens' for children. In such havens children would be provided with time away from family pressures in a safe place, where play, fun and educational support are available within the context of a stable and structured routine. Access to professional assistance if child development was an issue would also be an important component. Because of the dangers of stigmatisation, the authors imply that such facilities would be open to all children under stress. Although aware that suggesting such a service will be seen as 'pie in the sky', they nonetheless feel that nothing less is required if children's needs are to be met and cycles of adversity are to be broken (McKeganey *et al.* 2001, p.19). Whatever services for children are developed, however, what is crucial is that they feel safe and approachable so that vulnerable children and young people can access them and be provided with support that promotes disclosure (Barnard and Barlow forthcoming)

At a policy level, the issues presented by substance misuse and parenting, within the context in which this takes place, need to be brought much more to the forefront so that provision of existing services can be addressed and new initiatives can be evaluated. The development of appropriate and, above all, helpful guidelines about risk and confidentiality would form an obvious part of this as would increased education about the effects of alcohol misuse in particular.

Research initiatives

There is still a great deal we do not know about parental substance misuse, its prevalence and its impact on children. This applies to both clinical and non-clinical contexts, to the experiences of children growing up with both alcohol- and drug-misusing parents, in the short term and in the long term, and to the experiences of children from minority ethnic groups.

Further research into children's experiences, particularly where there is drug misuse, is essential. Although there is now a body of information about children's lives as they are affected by parental alcohol misuse, the voices of the children of drug users remain largely unheard in the British context, although important studies have been done recently (Barnard and Barlow, forthcoming) and are under way (Taylor in preparation). We also need to know much more about how many children are affected, the environments in which they grow up and both the short- and long-term implications for well-being. This would involve both exploratory research and longitudinal studies that cross socio-economic, cultural and ethnic boundaries. It is only through hearing the voices of children and young people that the totality of their experience can be considered. We also have much to learn from them about what contributes to resilience and vulnerability and which protective factors can ameliorate the impact of the constellation of factors that can potentially impact on children's development. We also need to know and understand the reality of the lives they lead.

Alongside this, research should continue to focus on practice issues particularly in view of studies that suggest that substance misuse now features significantly in child protection cases (Harwin *et al.* forthcoming). This would provide more information from a wide range of professionals about the ways in which they assess and intervene and differences in approach depending on whether drugs or alcohol is the issue. There are significant implications for child protection services and for the assessment of children 'in need' that warrant further examination so that children do not fall between gaps in agency provision.

Any existing or new initiatives that address the needs of substance-misusing parents and their children will require thorough evaluation so that we can develop some understanding of what might work for some people and thus build up an evidence base on which good practice can be founded. Part of any such evaluation will need to harness experience and knowledge gained from parents and their children so that they can make a real contribution to service development and delivery. This might include the provision of mentor schemes and group support for children, parents and other family members.

Conclusion

Debates about parental substance misuse and child maltreatment raise some important questions about the nature of attachment and dependency and the effects not just on the active participants but on those reliant on them. Substance misuse is a factor in general crime, in domestic violence, in child maltreatment, in health and in family breakdown. It also now features significantly in child protection cases. It can have considerable adverse consequences for children and often casts a long shadow, leading to problems in adulthood unless protective factors can be mobilised. There is clear evidence that parenting – a demanding and skilled activity at the best of times – can be seriously undermined by substance misuse and that children's psychological and physical safety can be put at risk. Practitioners' concerns reflect discomfort with snapshot approaches that prevent a real picture from emerging and highlight the divisions between child and adult services. This increases the danger of children remaining invisible within the professional network.

There are clear messages from research findings, as well as from the dilemmas that practitioners have highlighted, that we need to reconsider the way in which we intervene in families where there is substance misuse. What is required is a more holistic approach to assessment and intervention that brings together knowledge and skills from both child and adult services and ensures the effective protection of children. It is perhaps only by allowing ourselves really to know what life is like for children whose parents misuse substances that a full assessment is possible. This clearly involves making a space in one's mind for the children in the family and asking the right questions of parents about what they do together and when the pressure points tend to occur. This, then, is not about blame, castigation and unit or gram counting but about entering the world of the family and really knowing what it might be like to live there.

Drugs and Alcohol

Classifications and Effects

The following classification draws on those produced by Barber (1995), Cleaver *et al.* (1999), Drugscope (2001) and Robson (1999), integrating alcohol within it. It does not attempt to provide a comprehensive review of the effects of drugs or cover the complete range of non-medical drugs. The impact of substances is dependent not only on the level and intensity of use, but also on whether such use is short or long term. The particular characteristics and circumstances of individuals who use substances also influence the way people react. The unpredictable nature of their impact is magnified significantly by the mixing of different drugs. Detailed and comprehensive information about the effects of drug and polydrug use is to be found in *Drug Abuse Briefing* (Drugscope 2001), which is regularly updated to include new developments and research. It is available directly from Drugscope Publications (tel. 020 7928 1211; website www.drugscope.org.uk; email service@drugscope.org.uk).

Impact of mixing drugs

While we discuss some individual examples of this under each drug, Drugscope (2001) points to some very useful general factors to keep in mind which we reproduce here in full:

> The combination of one drug on top of another on mind and body can produce complex effects, as yet little understood. As a general rule, it is probable that drugs of a similar nature and action upon the body, ie two stimulants or two depressants, will have an additive effect, resulting in greater stimulation or depression, depending on the drug types. Taking therefore, speed (amphetamine) on top of cocaine will increase feelings of

energy and activity, as well as paranoia, aggression and anxiety, not to mention a heavy drawn-out recovery period to contend with later. Mixing drugs which bring on opposite effects, such as speed and heroin or speed and alcohol, has more unpredictable consequences, depending on such factors such as the user's mood, individual reaction to either drug, the order in which the drugs are taken, and how much of each is taken. Amphetamine taken while drunk, for example, may make one individual feel more awake and in control, or make another feel more drunk and aggressive, exaggerating their drunken behaviour. Combinations with hallucinogens are more complex still, with mood, situational circumstances and personality playing an even greater role in drug effects. Stimulants may add to the intensity of hallucinations or visual distortions, often prolonging the experience. Depressants on the other hand may lessen the degree of intensity, or may enhance feelings of confusion and bring on mood swings. (Drugscope 2001, p.22)

Analgesics/opiates

Analgesics/opiates include heroin, methadone, morphine and distalgesics. Heroin can be inhaled or injected; methadone is generally available on prescription as a heroin substitute and occurs in linctus form and in pill form. Heroin use generally produces a rush of pleasure, followed by feelings of immense well-being and gives rise to an almost dreamlike state of unreality. 'Emotions are suppressed and the user is insulated from all cares and worries. The user's head may droop and eyes close. The body feels heavy and warm' (Sloan 1998, p.10). 'Pleasurable feelings are associated with the fact that opiates induce relaxed detachment from the impact of pain and anxiety' (Drugscope 2001, p.32).

This group of substances, taken at high levels, may cause psychological and physical dependency although some suggest that the latter is not as significant as the former for long-term users (Drugscope 2001).

For some the intense cravings accompanying the need for such drugs may result in the reorganisation of daily life to ensure that a regular supply of the drug is obtained. This may, in some circumstances, have implications for the users' own lives or the welfare of others in their care which may, at times, take on secondary importance to the procuring of supplies (Robson 1999). Although it is difficult to use opiates without becoming dependent on them, some people do manage this (Drugscope 2001). Robson cites the example of an individual who might build drug use into a social ritual which is completely separate from personal or family life and has more to do with the social scene than with any personality trait or personal problems (Robson 1999, p.189).

Methadone induces milder reactions and no 'rush' because generally it is not injected. Some people do however grind up the pills and inject that way. Those on a successful methadone maintenance script may show very few signs of drug-related behaviour and function effectively in all areas of their lives. One dose goes on working for 24 hours and encourages a more stable lifestyle. However, methadone is not a 'cure' for heroin misuse; it, too, is addictive and is often sold on the streets and traded in the same way as other drugs. As the number of people entering treatment rises there are also increasing numbers reported as overdosing on prescribed methadone (Drugscope 2001). To prescribe methadone to someone who was not yet addicted to heroin would, according to Robson (1999), create a new addict; prescriptions should be determined on the basis of stages of withdrawal until a stabilising dose has been determined.

Withdrawal from analgesics and opiates includes a range of very unpleasant physical symptoms – vomiting, cramps, sleeplessness, acute flu-like symptoms and intense cravings for the drug. Symptoms will peak about 72 hours after the last ingestion of the substance although a range of unpleasant feelings may persist – anxiety, sleep problems and cravings are the most common of these (Cleaver et al. 1999).

Heroin users often supplement their use with other drugs. A mixture of heroin and cocaine (a 'speedball') may combine the depressant effects of one with the stimulant effects of the other. The risks from this include dangers to the heart and kidneys and that of overdosing. Heroin use is also supplemented at times with depressants and alcohol. Such combinations can be unpredictable and again, in high quantities, may involve the risk of overdose (Drugscope 2001).

Stimulants

Stimulants (amphetamines, cocaine and 'crack' – a cocaine derivative) all produce feelings of well-being, euphoria, confidence and intense happiness. The use of cocaine can reduce inhibitions and grandiose ideas and plans can take shape; people are far more talkative, and feel more powerful and more competent (Cleaver et al. 1999).

Large doses or a 'spree' of quickly repeated doses over a period of hours can lead to an extreme state of agitation, anxiety, paranoia and perhaps hallucinations... The after-effects of cocaine use include fatigue and depression, but are less noticeable than the corresponding effects after amphetamine use. (Drugscope 2001, p.129)

Impulsiveness, lack of inhibition and impaired judgement, however, can lead to catastrophe; hallucinations or psychotic episodes or delusions similar to those seen in schizophrenia can occur and often dangerously aggressive behaviour can erupt without warning (Robson 1999).

While the effects of cocaine and crack are intense but short term, the impact of amphetamines lasts for hours. Like cocaine, the overall effect is one of optimism, sharpened perception and concentration. However, there is a far less pleasant side to amphetamine use.

With some people...especially as the body's energy stores become depleted, the predominant feelings may be anxiety, irritability, and restlessness... High doses, especially if frequently repeated over a few days, can produce delirium, panic, hallucinations and feelings of persecution. (Drugscope 2001, p.21)

Appetite and the need for sleep are both significantly reduced, but in fact are merely postponed. Consequently 'prolonged stimulant use debilitates the user and lowers resistance to disease' (Drugscope 2001, p.22).

When injected the effects of amphetamines are much more powerful than if taken in pill form or snorted, and are seen as more potent than those of cocaine.

Other types of stimulants include khat, pemoline and appetite suppressants. Khat or qat, a plant of East African origin, comes in leaf form and is usually chewed or made into tea. Effects are the same as any amphetamine-like stimulant; dependency is unusual and unwanted effects mild. Pemoline – P9 – is used in the treatment of hyperactive children instead of amphetamines, although it is no longer available on prescription because of its adverse effects on the liver and bone marrow. Appetite suppressants have amphetamine-like effects and can be traded like any other drug.

Ironically in order to deal with some of the unwanted effects of stimulants – irritability, suspiciousness, an uncomfortable 'wired' feeling, heightened levels of aggression – people will turn to opiates, sedatives or alcohol for relief from these unpleasant sensations.

Cocaine is frequently used with other drugs including alcohol and cannabis and some may combine it with amphetamines, ecstasy and even heroin. The most usual combination is with alcohol and some report that users of cocaine increase their subsequent use of alcohol. Some research suggests that the combined use of these two drugs prolongs the effects.

Cocaine is particularly dangerous if taken with some hypertensive drugs and certain antidepressants (Drugscope 2001).

People who use stimulants who have mental health problems might experience 'florid episodes' leading to hospitalisation (Coleman and Cassell 1995; Robson 1999). 'The mood-elevating effects of synthetic stimulants can lead to psychological dependence…and as tolerance develops to amphetamines, so frequent users are tempted to increase the dose' (Drugscope 2001, p.22).

As with heroin, withdrawal symptoms are uncomfortable and unpleasant – depression, a washed-out feeling, cravings, sleep problems. Feelings of despair and anxiety may become sufficiently intense to cause self-harm or thoughts of suicide.

Depressants include alcohol, tranquillisers, sedatives and solvents. All these substances affect behaviour in different ways depending on what is being used and why.

Alcohol, despite being associated with merrymaking and celebration, has a depressant effect on the central nervous system. It relieves tension and anxiety but can also cause impaired physical and mental functioning. Drunken driving is one obvious example of such impaired functioning in action.

Alcohol also crosses the placenta so expectant mothers who drink excessively may have babies born with foetal alcohol syndrome. Such babies are likely to be small and floppy with flattened features and varying degrees of brain damage.

Depending on the quantity of alcohol consumed, individuals may experience loss of concentration, slurred speech, feelings of well-being, fits of laughter, coordination problems, loss of inhibitions and self-control, and aggressive behaviour. Chronic effects can include liver damage, alcoholic hepatitis, cirrhosis, digestive tract problems, some cancers and malnutrition, quite apart from raised blood pressure and risk of strokes. Large binges can prove fatal. Much depends on who is consuming the alcohol in terms of their tolerance to it, why they are doing so (mood, circumstance) and the setting in which it takes place. On an emotional level, as alcohol is a depressant, it is likely to exacerbate bleak or low feelings, despite the fact that it is generally used to alleviate them.

Despite the very obvious dangers of alcohol, it is very rarely associated with the hue and cry that drug scandals produce. However, for every death from ecstasy, suggests Robson, 'hundreds of young people will be maimed and some killed as a direct result of alcohol intoxication, yet this outrageous daily carnage is almost entirely ignored' (Robson 1999, p.53).

Tranquillisers induce feelings of calm and relaxation when taken in small doses; in larger quantities or when combined with alcohol loss of consciousness can occur. Indeed this particular mixture can be extremely dangerous, as the effects of the alcohol are heightened and the risk of overdose increased.

Withdrawal symptoms from alcohol can range from a mild hangover to fits, hallucinations, tremors, sweating profusely and vomiting. Withdrawal symptoms from tranquillisers, barbiturates and sedatives are similar to those described for heroin and opiates.

Alcohol is seen as the drug that is most commonly used in combination with other substances. It has particular consequences for those drugs which depress the central nervous system as when 'taken with benzodiazepines or barbiturates, for example, it produces a very drunken like state, which can result in unconsciousness and possibly overdose' (Drugscope 2001, p.62).

Hallucinogenic/psychedelic drugs

Hallucinogenic/psychedelic drugs include LSD, cannabis, magic mushrooms, and the 'party drug' ecstasy. The defining characteristic of these types of drugs 'is that they can have significant and profound effects on sensory perceptions, emotions and thought processes without clouding the mind' (Robson 1999, p.109). Setting, mood and expectations play a significant part in relation to the experience that results from taking this group of drugs.

Cannabis is the mildest version of this group. It is generally smoked although it can be made into a tea or used in cooking. When eaten, the amount taken is hard to regulate and people get far more 'stoned' than they may have intended. Effects include feelings of calm, a sense of being very relaxed and heightened awareness. Memory and concentration are sometimes impaired and all sense of time evaporates. Cannabis is now recognised as having positive effects in the treatment of some illnesses due to its pain-killing properties and its capacity to reduce nausea and vomiting. Medical evidence suggests that it is effective in the treatment of multiple sclerosis and other neurological disorders, cancer and AIDS. It is also effective in the treatment of opiate dependency.

In relation to the other common psychedelics and hallucinogens – LSD for example – Robson (1999) describes a typical experience in this way:

> after an initial sharpening of perception, visual distortion and a sense of detachment, apprehension, elation or fear are the first signs of take off. Thoughts begin to follow strange pathways, sparking off rapid shifts in mood...the familiar and hackneyed become novel, fascinating or terrifying... Memories long suppressed spring into consciousness...objects sometimes seem to loom immense or shrink away, with loss of perspective. (Robson 1999, p.122)

These effects can last for 12 hours or more. Adverse reactions can include hallucinations of an unwanted kind, paranoia and panic attacks – phenomena associated with a 'bad trip'. Prolonged psychological disturbances occur in some cases as do flashbacks which may last for seconds or hours. Withdrawal symptoms include mild cravings, sleep problems and anxiety. Death from overdoses are rare although can result from accidents caused by mistaken beliefs.

Party drugs were a mid-1980s phenomenon associated with acid house parties and raves and are now very much part of the club scene. The most common is MDMA or ecstasy, which comes in the form of pills, powder and capsules of various colours, shapes and sizes which bear a range of names – Disco biscuits, California Sunrise and M25 being just three examples. As they are hallucinogenic but with amphetamine-like qualities, the overall effects tend to be a mixture of intense stimulation and sensory distortion. Users tend to feel empathy and goodwill towards all humankind. Although it tends to be associated with teenage clubbers, a smaller group of users will be found among older adults who may be seeking an alternative lifestyle. Of course, there are also people who will try anything that happens to be available. Unwanted effects include drowsiness, clumsiness, fear, anxiety, panic attacks, depression and loss of concentration, leading to accidents. Occasionally the psychological reactions can be prolonged and serious and include psychotic episodes, although it is hard to separate the effects of the drug itself from other possible additional factors in these cases, including polydrug use and mental health problems. There have also been a number of much-publicised deaths directly associated with the effects of taking ecstasy. One prominent theory is that this may be related to heatstroke and dehydration, as ecstasy produces similar symptoms, but there is no conclusive evidence to show why particular young people have died (Drugscope 2001).

Ecstasy is regularly mixed with a number of other drugs such as amphetamines, cocaine or cannabis to enhance or prolong the effect (Drugscope 2001). As alcohol tends to dehydrate the body it is not generally used in combination with ecstasy for obvious reasons.

Tranquillisers and sleeping pills

Tranquillisers and sleeping pills include barbiturates and benzodiazepines. Barbiturates such as tuinal and seconal are most commonly prescribed in the treatment of epilepsy and chronic and intractable insomnia. Unofficial uses include managing opiate withdrawal symptoms, and coping with alcohol withdrawal. They are not readily accessible on the streets but may be traded informally if on prescription. Benzodiazepines such as temazepam (valium) and diazepam, on the other hand, are readily available. They are prescribed widely for anxiety, depression and sleeplessness and have no adverse effects except when combined with alcohol.

Summary

What this overview highlights are the vast range of emotions and reactions – both positive and negative – that different kinds of substance misuse can provoke (different types of drugs for example) and the implications for children of living with parents who may be euphoric, benign and indulgent at one end of the spectrum and depressed, aggressive, out of touch with reality, or comatose at the other. The potential for aggressive or violent behaviour is a fairly consistent theme throughout the drug categories, as are changes of mood and altered perceptions.

Information and knowledge about use of and withdrawal from the effects of various substances brings into focus the range of possibilities that need to be borne in mind when working with substance-misusing parents. The implications for a thorough assessment of the family system as a whole and not just the individual are clear. Equally important is the assessment of the pattern of substance use – when, why, how, with whom and where the drug is taken – and awareness not only of how individuals are when they are using it but also how they are when they are not. It is also important to find out from the users themselves exactly how certain substances make them feel and explore the way that negative reactions and withdrawal, in particular, are managed.

As Sloan concludes:

> the effects of substance misuse on a family is probably complex and varied…it is necessary not to make any assumptions about the family or the role of substance misuse [but]…to gain an overall view of the family and to understand the substance abuse in the context of the individual family and its impact on the childcare experienced by the children. (Sloan 1998, p.39).

SCODA Guidelines

These guidelines are for professionals assessing risk when working with drug-using parents; they were developed by the Standing Conference on Drug Abuse.

Parental drug use

1 Is there a drug-free parent, supportive partner or relative?

2 Is the drug use by the parent experimental? Recreational? Chaotic? Dependent?

3 Does the user move between categories at different times? Does the drug use also involve alcohol?

4 Are levels of childcare different when a parent is using drugs and when not using?

5 Is there any evidence of coexistence of mental health problems alongside the drug use? If there is, do the drugs cause these problems, or have these problems led to the drug use?

Accommodation and the home environment

6 Is the accommodation adequate for children?

7 Are the parents ensuring that the rent and bills are paid?

8 Does the family remain in one area or move frequently? If the latter, why?

9 Are other drug users sharing the accommodation? If they are, are relationships with them harmonious, or is there conflict?

10 Is the family living in a drug-using community?

11 If parents are using drugs, do children witness the taking of the drugs, or other substances?

12 Could other aspects of the drug use constitute a risk to children (e.g. conflict with or between dealers, exposure to criminal activities related to drug use)?

Provision of basic needs

13 Is there adequate food, clothing and warmth for the children?

14 Are the children attending school regularly?

15 Are children engaged in age-appropriate activities?

16 Are the children's emotional needs being adequately met?

17 Are there any indications that any of the children are taking on a parenting role within the family (e.g. caring for other children, excessive household responsibilities, etc.)?

Procurement of drugs

18 Are the children left alone while their parents are procuring drugs?

19 Because of their parents' drug use are the children being taken to places where they could be 'at risk'?

20 How much are the drugs costing?

21 How is the money obtained?

22 Is this causing financial problems?

23 Are the premises being used to sell drugs?

24 Are the parents allowing their premises to be used by other drug users?

Health risks

25 If drugs and/or injecting equipment are kept on the premises, are they kept securely?

26 Are the children aware of where the drugs are kept?

27 If parents are intravenous drug users:

- Do they share injecting equipment?

- Do they use a needle exchange system?

- How do they dispose of syringes?

- Are parents aware of the health risks of injecting or using drugs?

28 If parents are on a substitute-prescribing programme, such as methadone:

- Are parents aware of the dangers of children accessing this medication?

- Do they take adequate precautions to ensure that this does not happen?

29 Are parents aware of, and in touch with, local specialist agencies who can advise on issues such as needle exchanges, substitute prescribing programmes, detox and rehabilitation facilities? If they are in touch with agencies, how regular is the contact?

Family social network and support systems

30 Do parents and children associate primarily with:

- Other drug users?

- Non-users?

- Both?

31 Are relatives aware of the drug use? Are they supportive?

32 Will parents accept help from the relatives and other professional or non-statutory agencies?

33 The degree of social isolation should be considered particularly for those parents living in remote areas where resources may not be available and they may experience social stigmatisation.

Parents' perception of the situation

34 Do the parents see their drug use as harmful to themselves or to their children?

35 Do the parents place their own needs before the needs of the children?

36 Are the parents aware of the legislative and procedural context applying to their circumstances (e.g. child protection procedures, statutory powers)?

Source: SCODA (1997, pp.42-43)
Reproduced by kind permission of Drugscope.

References

Ackerman, R. (1987) *Same House, Different Homes: Why Children of Alcoholics are Not All the Same.* Pompano Beach, FL: Health Communications.

Adams, P. (1999) 'Towards a family support approach with drug-using parents: the importance of social work attitudes and knowledge.' *Child Abuse Review 8,* 15–28.

Adams, T. with Ridley, I. (1999) *Addicted.* London: Collins Willow.

Advisory Council on the Misuse of Drugs (1998) *Drug Misuse and the Environment.* London: The Stationery Office.

Ainsworth, M.D.S., Blehar, M., Aters, E. and Wall, S. (1978) *Patterns of Attachment: A Psychological Study of the Strange Situation.* Hillsdale, NJ: Lawrence Erlbaum.

Alcohol Concern (2000) *Alcohol and the Family Conference Report.* Alcohol Concern/National Family and Parenting Institute.

Aldgate, J. and Tunstill, J. (1995) *Making Sense of Section 17.* London: HMSO.

Aldridge, J. and Becker, S. (1993) *Children Who Care: Inside the World of Young Carers.* Loughborough: Loughborough University Press.

Aldridge, T. (1999) 'Family values: rethinking children's needs living with drug abusing parents.' *Druglink March/April,* 8–11

Aldridge, T. (2000) 'Family values: rethinking children's needs living with drug abusing parents.' Paper presented at the Substance Misuse and Child Protection Conference, June.

Alfaro, J. (1988) 'What can we learn from child abuse fatalities? A synthesis of nine studies.' In D.J. Besharov (ed) *Protecting Children from Abuse and Neglect: Policy and Practice.* Springfield, IL: Charles C. Thomas.

Alison, L. (2000) 'What are the risks to children of parental substance misuse?' In F. Harbin and M. Murphy (eds) *Substance Misuse and Child Care: How to Understand, Assist and Intervene when Drugs Affect Parenting.* Lyme Regis: Russell House.

Ammerman, R.T., Kolko, D.J., Kirisci, L. and Dawes, M.A. (1999) 'Child abuse potential in parents with histories of substance misuse disorder.' *Child Abuse and Neglect 23,*12, 1225–1238.

Anthony, E.J. (1978) 'A new scientific region to explore.' In E.J. Anthony, C. Koupernik and C. Chiland (eds) *The Child and his Family: Vulnerable Children* vol.4. New York: John Wiley.

Appleby, A. (2000) *Alcohol and the Family Conference Report.* London: Alcohol Concern/National Family and Parenting Institute.

Ashton, M. (1999) 'Between two stools: Children, drugs policy and professional practice.' In A. Marlow and G. Pearson (eds) *Young People, Drugs and Community Safety.* Lyme Regis: Russell House Publishing.

Audit Commission (1999) *Children in Mind: Child and Adolescent Mental Health Services.* London: HMSO.

Avis, H. (1993) *Drugs and Life,* 2nd edn. Dubuque, IA: Brown and Benchmark.

Awiah, J., But, S., Dorn, N., Patel, K. and Pearson, G. (1992) *Race, Gender and Drug Services,* ISDD Research Monographs 6. London: Institute for the Study of Drug Dependence.

Azrin, N.H. (1976) 'Improvements in the community reinforcement approach to alcoholism.' *Behaviour Research and Therapy 14,* 339–348.

Bachay, J. and Cingel, P. (1999) 'Restructuring resilience: emerging voices.' *Affilia Journal of Women and Social Work 14,* 2, 162–175.

Bacon, S. (1973) 'The process of addiction to alcohol: social aspects.' *Quarterly Journal of Studies of Alcohol 34,* 1–27.

Baldwin, S. (1990) 'Helping problem drinkers: some new developments.' In S. Collins (ed) *Alcohol Social Work and Helping.* London: Tavistock/Routledge.

Banks, N. (2001) 'Assessing children and families who belong to minority ethnic groups.' In J. Horwath (ed) *The Child's World: Assessing Children in Need.* London: Jessica Kingsley Publishers.

Bannister, A. (2001) 'Entering the child's world: communicating with children to assess their needs.' In J. Horwath (ed) *The Child's World: Assessing Children in Need.* London: Jessica Kingsley Publishers.

Barber, J.G. (1995) *Social Work with Addictions.* London: British Association of Social Workers and Macmillan.

Barber, J.G. and Crisp, B.R. (1995) 'The "pressures to change" approach to working with partners of heavy drinkers.' *Addiction 90,* 269–276.

Barber, L. (2000) 'Self control.' *Observer* Magazine 11 June.

Barker, P. (1992) *Basic Family Therapy,* 3rd edn. Oxford: Blackwell Scientific.

Barnard, M. (1999) 'Forbidden questions: Drug dependent parents and the welfare of their children.' *Addiction 94,* 8, 1109–1111.

Barnard, M. and Barlow, J. (forthcoming) 'Discovering parental drug dependence: silence and disclosure.' *Children and Society.*

Barnett, B. and Parker, G. (1998) 'The parentified child: early competence or childhood deprivation.' *Child Psychology and Psychiatry Review 3,* 4, 146–155.

Barr, A (1998) *Drink: A Social History.* London: Pimlico.

Bates, T., Buchanan, J., Corby, B. and Young, L. (1999) *Drug Use, Parenting and Child Protection: Towards an Effective Interagency Response.* Liverpool: University of Central Lancashire.

Bauman, P.S. and Dougherty, F.E. (1983) 'Drug-addicted mothers' parenting and their children's development.' *The International Journal of the Addictions 18,* 291–302.

Baumrind, D. (1974) *Parental Attitudes Questionnaire.* Berkeley, CA: Institute of Human Development, University of California.

Baumrind, D. (1983) 'Specious causal attributions in the social sciences: the reformulated stepping-stone theory of heroin use, an exemplar.' *Journal of Personality and Social Psychology 45,* 1289–98.

Bays, J. (1990) 'Substance abuse and child abuse: impact of addiction on the child.' *Paediatric Clinics of North America 37,* 4, 881–904.

Bebbington, A. and Miles, J. (1989) 'The background of children who enter local authority care.' *British Journal of Social Work 19,* 5, 349–368.

Becker, H. (1963) *Outsiders.* New York: Free Press.

Becker, S., Aldridge, J. and Dearden, C. (1998) *Young Carers and their Families.* Oxford: Blackwell.

Bee, H. (2000) *The Developing Child,* 9th edn. Needham Heights, MA: Allyn and Bacon.

Bell, M. (2002) 'Promoting children's rights through the use of relationship.' *Child and Family Social Work 7,* 1–11.

Belsky, J. (1984) 'The determinants of parenting: a process model.' *Child Development 55,* 83–96.

Belsky, J. and Cassidy, J. (1994) 'Attachment: theory and practice.' In M. Rutter and D. Hay (eds) *Development through Life: A Handbook for Clinicians.* Oxford: Blackwell Science.

Belsky, J. and Vondra, J. (1989) 'Lessons from child abuse: the determinants of parenting.' In D. Cicchetti and V. Carlson (eds) *Child Maltreatment: Theory and Research on the Causes and Consequences of Child Abuse and Neglect.* Cambridge: Cambridge University Press.

Bennett, G. (1989) *Treating Drug Abusers.* London: Routledge.

Bennett, M. (1996) 'When life is just poured away.' *Guardian* 17 September.

Bentovim, A. and Williams, B. (1998) 'Children and adolescents: victims who become perpetrators.' *Advances in Psychiatric Treatment 4,* 101–107.

Berridge, V. (1979) 'Morality and medical science: concepts of narcotic addiction in Britain, 1820–1926.' *Annals of Science 36,* 67–85.

Besharov, D.J. (ed) (1994) *When Drug Addicts have Children: Reorienting Child Welfare's Response.* Washington, DC: Child Welfare League of America.

Bettelheim, B. (1987) *A Good Enough Parent.* London: Thames and Hudson.

Biederman, J., Faraone, S.V., Monuteaux, M.C. and Feighner, J.A. (2000) 'Patterns of alcohol and drug use in adolescents can be predicted by parental substance use disorders.' *Pediatrics 106,* 4, 792–797.

Biernacki, B. (1986) *Pathways from Heroin Addiction: Recovery without Treatment.* Philadelphia, PA: Temple University Press.

Bifulco, A. and Moran, P. (1998) *Wednesday's Child: Research into Women's Experience of Neglect and Abuse in Childhood, and Adult Depression.* London: Routledge.

Bion, W. (1959) 'Attacks on linking.' *International Journal of Psychoanalysis 40,* 308–315.

Bion, W. (1962) *Learning from Experience.* London: Heinemann.

Black, C. (1982) *It Will Never Happen to Me!* Denver, CO: MAC Publications.

Black, R. and Meyer, J. (1980) 'Parents with special problems: alcoholism and opiate addiction.' *Child Abuse and Neglect 4,* 45–64.

Blos, P. (1962) *On Adolescence: A Psychoanalytic Interpretation.* New York: Free Press.

Blos, P. (1967) 'The second individuation process of adolescence.' *Psychoanalytic Study of the Child 22,* 162–186.

Bonner, A. and Waterhouse, J. (eds) (1996) *Addictive Behaviour: Molecules to Mankind.* London: Macmillan.

Boushel, M. (1994) 'The protective environment of children – towards a framework for anti-oppressive cross cultural and cross national understanding.' *British Journal of Social Work 24,* 2, 173–190.

Bowlby, J. (1969) *Attachment.* London: Hogarth Press.

Bowlby, J. (1973) *Attachment and Loss, vol. III: Separation, Anxiety and Anger.* London: Hogarth Press.

Bowlby, J. (1979) *The Making and Breaking of Affectional Bonds.* London: Tavistock.

Bowlby, J. (1980) *Attachment and Loss, vol. II: Loss, Sadness and Depression.* London: Hogarth Press.

Bowlby, J. (1988) *A Secure Base: Clinical Applications of Attachment Theory.* London: Routledge.

Brandon, M., Schofield, G. and Trinder, L. (1998) *Social Work with Children.* London: Macmillan.

Bridge, G. and Miles, G. (1996) *On the Outside Looking In: Collected Essays on Young Child Observation in Social Work Training.* London: Central Council for Education and Training in Social Work.

Brisby, T., Baker, S. and Hedderwick, T. (1997) *Under the Influence: Coping with Parents who Drink too Much – A Report on the Needs of Children of Problem Drinking Parents.* London: Alcohol Concern.

Bronfenbrenner, U. (1979) *The Ecology of Human Development: Experiments by Nature and Design.* Cambridge, MA: Harvard University Press.

Brookoff, D., O'Brien, K.K., Cook, C.S., Thompson, T.D. and Williams, C. (1997) 'Characteristics of participants in domestic violence – Assessment at the scene of domestic assault.' *Journal of the American Medical Association 277*, 17, 1369–1373.

Brooks, C.S. and Rice, K.F. (1997) *Families in Recovery: Coming Full Circle.* Baltimore, MD: Paul H. Brookes.

Brown, S. (1988) *Treating Adult Children of Alcoholics: A Developmental Perspective.* New York: John Wiley.

Brown, S. (1992) *Safe Passage: Recovery for Adult Children of Alcoholics.* New York: John Wiley.

Buchanan, A. (1996) *Cycles of Child Maltreatment: Facts, Fallacies and Interventions.* Chichester: John Wiley.

Buckley, H. (2000) 'Child protection: an unreflective practice.' *Social Work Education 19*, 3, 253–263.

Burnham, J.B. (1986) *Family Therapy.* London: Routledge.

Burns, E.C., O'Driscoll, M. and Wason, G. (1996) 'The health and development of children whose mothers are on methadone maintenance.' *Child Abuse Review 5*, 113–122.

Butler, I. and Williamson, H. (1995) *Children Speak.* London: NSPCC/Longman.

Butler, K. (1997) 'The anatomy of resilience.' *Family Therapy Networker 21*, 2, 22–31.

Cadoret, R.J. (1992) 'Genetic and environmental factors in the initiation of drug use and the transition to abuse.' In M.D. Glantz and R.W. Pickens (eds) *Vulnerability to Drug Abuse.* Washington, DC: American Psychological Association.

Camden and Islington Area Child Protection Committees (ACPC) (1999) *Policy, Procedures and Guidance for Working with Drug and Alcohol Misusing Parents.* London: Camden and Islington ACPC.

Caplan, P.J. and Hall-McCorquodale, I. (1985) 'Mother blaming in major clinical journals.' *American Journal of Orthopsychiatry 55*, 345–353.

Chaffin, M., Kelleher, K. and Hollenberg, J. (1996) 'Onset of physical abuse and neglect: psychiatric, substance abuse and social factors from prospective community data.' *Child Abuse and Neglect 20*, 3, 191–203.

Chassin, L. and Belz, A. (2000) 'Substance use and abuse outcomes in children of alcoholics: from adolescence to young adulthood.' In H.E. Fitzgerald, B.M. Lester and B.S. Zuckerman (eds) *Children of Addiction : Research, Health and Public Policy Issues* New York and London: RoutledgeFalmer.

Chess, S. (1982) 'The "Blame the Mother" ideology.' *International Journal of Mental Health 11*, 95–107.

Chick, J. and Cantwell, R. (1998) 'Dependence: concepts and definitions.' In J. Chick and R. Cantwell, *Seminars in Drug and Alcohol Misuse*. London: Gaskell (Royal College of Psychiatrists).

ChildLine (1997) *Beyond the Limit: Children who Live with Parental Alcohol Misuse*. London: ChildLine.

Christie, N. (1986) 'Suitable enemies.' In H. Bianchi and R. Van Swaanigan (eds) *Abolitionism: Towards a Non-repressive Approach to Crime*. Amsterdam: Free University Press.

Cleaver, H. and Freeman, P. (1995) *Parental Perspectives in Cases of Suspected Child Abuse*. London: HMSO.

Cleaver, H., Unell, I. and Aldgate, J. (1999) *Children's Needs – Parenting Capacity: The Impact of Parental Mental Illness, Problem Alcohol and Drug Use and Domestic Violence on Children's Development*. London: The Stationery Office.

Cleaver, H., Wattam, C., Cawson, R. and Gordon, R. (1998) *Assessing Risk in Child Protection*. London: NSPCC.

Cody, M. and McLaughlin, L. (1988) 'Accounts on trial.' In C. Antaki (ed) *Analysing Everyday Explanation*. London: Sage.

Coleman, J.C and Hendry, L.B. (1999) *Thr Nature of Adolescence*, 2nd edn. London: Routledge.

Coleman, R. and Cassell, D. (1995) 'Parents who misuse drugs and alcohol.' In P. Reder and C. Lucey (eds) *Assessment of Parenting: Psychiatrci and Psychological Contributions*. London: Routledge.

Cohen, P. (1990) *Drugs as a Social Construct*. Amsterdam: Universiteit van Amsterdam.

Colby, S.M. and Murrell, W. (1998) 'Child welfare and substance abuse services: from barriers to collaboration.' In R.L. Hampton, V. Senatore and T.P. Gullotta (eds) *Substance Abuse, Family Violence and Child Welfare*. Thousand Oaks, CA: Sage.

Coleman, R. and Cassell, D. (1995) 'Parents who misuse drugs and alcohol.' In P. Reder and C. Lucey (eds) *Assessment of Parenting: Psychiatric and Psychological Contributions*. London: Routledge.

Coleman, J. and Hendry, L.B. (1999) *The Nature of Adolescence*, 2nd edn. London: Routledge.

Collins, S. and Keene, J. (2000) *Alcohol, Social Work and Community Care*. Birmingham: Venture Press.

Colten, M.E. (1980) *A Comparison of Heroin-addicted and Non-addicted Mothers: Their Attitudes, Beliefs and Parenting Experiences*. London: National Institute on Drug Research Services Research Report, Heroin Addicted Parents and their Children DHSS publication no. (Adm) 81–1028.

Copello, A., Orford, J., Hodgson, R., Tober, G. and Barrett, C. (2001) 'Social behaviour and network therapy: basic principles and early experiences.' *Addictive Behaviours 26*, 1–22.

Copello, A., Orford, J., Velleman, R., Templeton, L. and Krishnan, M. (2000) 'Methods for reducing alcohol and drug related family harm in non-specialist settings.' *Journal of Mental Health 9*, 3, 329–343.

Corby, B. (1993) *Child Abuse: Towards a Knowledge Base*. Buckingham: Open University Press.

Corby, B. (1996) 'Risk assessment in child protection work.' In H. Kemshall and J. Pritchard (eds) *Good Practice in Risk Assessment and Risk Management*, vol. 1. London: Jessica Kingsley Publishers.

Cork, M. (1969) *The Forgotten Children: A Study of Children with Alcoholic Parents.* Toronto: Alcoholism and Drug Research Foundation.

Crawford, R.J. and Phyfer, A.Q. (1988) 'Adult children of alcoholics: a counselling model.' *Journal of College Student Development 29,* 105–111.

Crimmins, S., Langley, S., Brownstein, H.H. and Spunt, B. (1997) 'Convicted women who have killed children: a self-psychology perspective.' *Journal of Interpersonal Violence 12,* 49–69.

Crittenden, P.M. and Ainsworth, M.D.S. (1989) 'Child maltreatment and attachment.' In D. Cicchetti and V. Carlson (eds) *Handbook of Child Maltreatment: Clinical and Theoretical Perspectives.* New York: Cambridge University Press.

Cutland, L. (1998) 'A codependency perspective.' In R. Velleman, A. Copello and J. Maslin (eds) *Living with Drink: Women who Live with Problem Drinkers.* London: Longman.

Cutrona, C.E. and Russell, D.W. (1990) 'Type of social support and specific stress: towards a theory of optimal matching.' In B.R. Sarason, G.R. Pierce and I.G. Sarason (eds) *Social Support: An Interactional View.* New York: Wiley.

Daniel, B. (2000) 'Judgments about parenting: what do social workers think they are doing?' *Child Abuse Review 9,* 91–107.

Daniel, B. and Taylor, J. (2001) *Engaging with Fathers: Practice Issues for Health and Social Care.* London: Jessica Kingsley Publishers.

Daniel, B., Wassell, S. and Gilligan, R. (1999) *Child Development for Child Care and Protection Workers.* London: Jessica Kingsley Publishers.

Davidson, R. (1996) 'Motivational issues in the treatment of addictive behaviour.' In G. Edwards and C. Dare (eds) *Psychotherapy, Psychological Treatments and the Addictions.* Cambridge: Cambridge University Press.

Davies, J.B. (1997) *The Myth of Addiction,* 2nd edn. Amsterdam: Harwood Academic.

Dearden, C. and Becker, S. (2001) 'Young carers: needs, rights and assessments.' In J. Horwath (ed) *The Child's World: Assessing Children in Need.* London: Jessica Kingsley Publishers.

Department of Health (1988) *Protecting Children: A Guide for Social Workers undertaking a Comprehensive Assessment.* London: HMSO.

Department of Health (1994) *Children Act Report 1993.* London: HMSO.

Department of Health (1995) *Child Protection: Messages from Research.* London: HMSO.

Department of Health (1999) *Working Together to Safeguard Children: A Guide to Inter-agency Working to Safeguard and Promote the Welfare of Children.* London: The Stationery Office.

Department of Health (2000a) *Framework for the Assessment of Children in Need and their Families.* London: The Stationery Office.

Department of Health (2000b) *Assessing Children in Need and their Families: Practice Guidance.* London: The Stationery Office.

Department of Health (2000c) *The Child's World: Assessing Children in Need – Trainer and Modules.* Sheffield: NSPCC and University of Sheffield.

Department of Health (2000d) *Studies Informing the Development of the Framework for the Assessment of Children in Need and their Families.* London: The Stationery Office.

Deren, S. (1986) 'Children of substance abusers: a review of the literature.' *Journal of Substance Abuse Treatment 3,* 77–94.

Dingwall, R. (1986) 'The Jasmine Beckford affair.' *Modern Law Review 49,* 4, 488–518.

Dingwall, R., Eekelaar, J. and Murray, T. (1983) *The Protection of Children: State Intervention and Family Life.* Oxford: Basil Blackwell.

Ditton, J. (1990) *Scottish Cocaine Users: Yuppie Snorters or Ghetto Smokers?* Update 6. Glasgow: Scottish Cocaine Research Group, University of Glasgow.

Dore, M.M., Doris, J.M. and Wright, P. (1995) 'Identifying substance misuse in maltreating families: a child welfare challenge.' *Child Abuse and Neglect 19*, 5, 531–543.

Drugscope (2001) *Drug Abuse Briefing.* London: Drugscope.

Dubowitz, H., Black, M., Starr, R.H. and Zuravin, S.A. (1993) 'A conceptual definition of child neglect.' *Criminal Justice and Behaviour 20*, 1, 8–26.

Duncombe, J. and Marsden, D. (1995) "Workaholics" and "whingeing women": theorising intimacy and emotional work – the last frontier of gender equality?' *Sociological Review 43*, 1, 150–169.

Dunn, J. (1993) *Young Children's Close Relationships: Beyond Attachment.* London: Sage.

Dunn, J. and McGuire, S. (1992) 'Sibling and peer relationships in childhood.' *Journal of Child Psychology and Psychiatry 33*, 1, 67–105.

Dunst, C.J. and Trivette, C.M. (1990) 'Assessment of social support in early intervention programmes.' In S.J. Meisels and J.P. Shonkoff (eds) *Handbook of Early Childhood Intervention.* New York: Cambridge University Press.

Edwards, G. and Gross, M.M. (1976) 'Alcohol dependence: provisional description of a clinical syndrome.' *British Medical Journal 1*, 1058–1061.

Edwards, G., Gross, M.M., Keller, M., Moser, M. and Room, R. (1977) *Alcohol Related Disabilities.* WHO Offset Publication no.32. Geneva: World Health Organisation.

Edwards, G., Marshall, E. and Cook, C. (1997) *The Treatment of Drinking Problems.* Cambridge: Cambridge University Press.

Elliott, E. and Watson, A. (1998) *Fit to be a Parent: The Needs of Drug Using Parents in Salford and Trafford.* Manchester: Public Health Research and Resource Centre, University of Salford.

Elliott, E. and Watson, A. (2000) 'Responsible carers, problem drug takers or both?' In F. Harbin and M. Murphy (eds) *Substance Misuse and Child Care: How to Understand, Assist and Intervene when Drugs Affect Parenting.* Lyme Regis: Russell House.

Ely, M., Hardy, R., Longford, N. And Wadsworth, M. (2000) 'Improving methods of estimating alcohol consumption.' Alcohol Insight no.9. London: Alcohol Education and Research Council.

Erikson, E.H. (1995) *Childhood and Society,* 2nd edn. London: Vintage.

Etiore, E. (1992) *Women and Substance Use.* London: Macmillan.

Fagan, J. (1993) 'Interactions among drug, alcohol and violence.' *Health Affairs 12*, 4, 65–79.

Fahlberg, V. (1982) *Child Development.* London: British Agencies for Adoption and Fostering.

Fahlberg, V. (1991) *A Child's Journey through Placement.* London: British Agencies for Adoption and Fostering.

Falkov, A. (1996) *A Study of Working Together Part 8 Reports: Fatal Child Abuse and Parental Psychiatric Disorder.* London: The Stationery Office.

Falkov, A., Mayes, K., Diggin, M. and Cox, A. (1998) *Crossing Bridges – Training Resources for Working with Mentally Ill Parents and their Children.* Brighton: Pavillion Publishing.

Famularo, R.A., Stone, K., Barnum, R. and Wharton, R. (1986) 'Alcoholism and severe child maltreatment.' *American Journal of Orthopsychiatry 56*, 481–485.

Famularo, R., Kinscherff, R. and Fenton, T. (1992) 'Parental substance abuse and the nature of child maltreatment.' *Child Abuse and Neglect 16*, 475–483.

Fanti, G. (1990) 'Helping the family.' In S. Collins (ed) *Alcohol, Social Work and Helping.* London: Routledge.

Farmer, E. and Owen, M. (1995) *Child Protection Practice: Private Risks and Public Remedies.* London: HMSO.

Farmer, E. and Owen, M. (1998) 'Gender and the child protection process.' *British Journal of Social Work 28*, 545–564.

Fawcett, M. (1996) *Learning through Child Observation.* London: Jessica Kingsley Publishers.

Featherstone, B. (1997) 'What has gender got to do with it? Exploring physically abusive behaviour towards children.' *British Journal of Social Work 27*, 419–433.

Feig, L. (1998) 'Understanding the problem: the gap between substance abuse programmes and child welfare services.' In R.L. Hampton, V. Senatore and T.P. Gullotta (eds) *Substance Abuse, Family Violence and Child Welfare: Bridging Perspectives.* Thousand Oaks, CA: Sage.

Fitch, M.J., Cadol, R.V., Goldson, E.J., Jackson, E.K. and Swarth, D.P. (1975) 'Prospective study in child abuse.' Paper presented at the Convention of America Public Health Association, Chicago.

Fitzgerald, H.E., Lester, B.M. and Zuckerman, B.S. (2000) *Children of Addiction: Research, Health and Public Policy Issues.* New York and London: RoutledgeFalmer.

Flores, P.J. (2001) 'Addiction as an attachment disorder: implications for group therapy.' *International Journal of Group Psychotherapy 51*, 1, 63–81.

Fonagy, P., Steele, M., Steele, H., Higgit, A. and Target, M. (1994) 'The theory and practice of resilience.' *Journal of Child Psychology and Psychiatry 35*, 2, 231–257.

Ford, C. and Hepburn, M. (1997) 'Caring for the pregnant drug user.' In B. Beaumont (ed) *Care of Drug Users in General Practice.* Abingdon: Radcliffe Medical Press.

Forrester, D. (2000) 'Parental substance misuse and child protection in a British sample: a survey of children on the child protection register in an inner London district office.' *Child Abuse Review 9*, 235–246.

Forrester, D. (2001) 'Prevalence of parental substance misuse in Britain.' *Children Law UK Newsletter Summer*, 4–6.

Freeman, M.D.A. (1992) *Children, their Families and the Law: Working with the Children Act.* London: British Association of Social Workers and Macmillan.

Freud, S. (1901) *The Psychopathology of Everyday Life*, Standard Edition vol. 6. London: Hogarth Press.

Gabel, S. (1992) 'Behavioural problems in sons of incarcerated or otherwise absent fathers.' *Family Process 31*, 3, 303–314.

Galanter, M. (1993) 'Network Therapy for substance misuse: a clinical trial.' *Psychotherapy 30*, 2, 251–258.

Galanter, M. (1999) *Network Therapy for Alcohol and Drug Abuse.* New York: Guilford.

Garbarino, J. (1977) 'The human ecology of child maltreatment: a conceptual model for research.' *Journal of Marriage and the Family 39*, 721–736.

Garbarino, J. (1990) 'The human ecology of early risk.' In S. Meisels and J. Shonkoff (eds) *Handbook of Early Childhood Intervention.* Cambridge, MA: Cambridge University Press.

Gensheimer, L.K., Roosa, M.W. and Ayers, T.S. (1990) 'Children's self-selection into prevention programmes: evaluation of an innovative recruitment strategy for children of alcoholics.' *American Journal of Community Psychology 18*, 5.

Gerada, C. (1996) 'The drug-addicted mother: Pregnancy and lactation.' In M. Gopfert, J. Webster and M.J. Seeman (eds) *Parental Psychiatric Disorder: Distressed Parents and their Families.* Cambridge: Cambridge University Press.

Gibbons, J., Conroy, S. and Bell, C. (1995) *Operating the Child Protection System.* London: HMSO.

Gilligan, R. (2001) 'Promoting positive outcomes for children in need: the assessment of protective factors.' In J. Horwath (ed) *The Child's World: Assessing Children in Need.* London: Jessica Kingsley Publishers.

Gilman, M. (2000) 'Social exclusion and drug using parents.' In F. Harbin and M. Murphy (eds) *Substance Misuse and Child Care: How to Understand, Assist and Intervene when Drugs Affect Parenting.* Lyme Regis: Russell House.

Glaser, D. (1995) 'Emotionally abusive experiences.' In P. Reder and C. Lucey (eds) *Assessment of Parenting: Psychiatric and Psychological Contributions.* London: Routledge.

Goffman, E . (1963) *Stigma: Notes on the Management of Spoiled Identity.* Harmondsworth: Penguin.

Gopfert, M., Webster, J. and Seeman, M.V. (eds) (1996) *Parental Psychiatric Disorder: Distressed Parents and their Families.* Cambridge: Cambridge University Press.

Gorell Barnes, G. (1998) *Family Therapy in Changing Times.* London: Macmillan.

Gossop, M. (2000) *Living with Drugs.* Aldershot: Ashgate.

Gray, J. (1993) 'Coping with unhappy children who exhibit emotional and behavioural problems in the classroom.' In V. Varma (ed) *Coping with Unhappy Children.* London: Cassell.

Greenberg, J.R. and Mitchell, S.A. (1983) *Object Relations in Psychoanalytic Theory.* Cambridge, MA: Harvard University Press.

Greenland, C. (1987) *Preventing CAN Deaths: An International Study of Deaths due to Child Abuse and Neglect.* London: Tavistock.

Hampton, R.L., Senatore, V. and Gullotta, T.P. (eds) (1998) *Substance Abuse, Family Violence and Child Welfare: Bridging Perspectives.* Thousand Oaks, CA: Sage.

Harbin, F. (2000) 'Therapeutic work with children of substance misusing parents.' In F, Harbin and M. Murphy (eds) *Substance Misuse and Child Care: How to Understand, Assist and Intervene when Drugs Affect Parenting.* Lyme Regis: Russell House.

Harbin, F. and Murphy, M. (eds) (2000) *Substance Misuse and Child Care: How to Understand, Assist and Intervene when Drugs Affect Parenting.* Lyme Regis: Russell House.

Harwin, J. (1982) 'The excessive drinker and the family: approaches to treatment.' In J. Orford and J. Harwin (eds) *Alcohol and the Family.* London: Croom Helm.

Harwin, J., Owen, M. and Forrester, D. (forthcoming) *Making Care Orders Work.* London: The Stationery Office.

Hastings, J. and Typpo, M. (1984) *An Elephant in the Living Room.* Minneapolis, MN: Comp. Care.

Hawker, R. (1999) 'Lone parents and alcohol.' Unpublished paper presented at Addictions Forum Conference, Durham.

Hawker, R. (in preparation) 'Lone parents and alcohol misuse.' PhD thesis in preparation.

Heal, A. (2000) 'Providing therapeutic services for drug using parents and their children.' In F. Harbin and M. Murphy (eds) *Substance Misuse and Child Care: How to Understand, Assist and Intervene when Drugs Affect Parenting.* Lyme Regis: Russell House.

Heather, N. and Robertson, I. (1981) *Controlled Drinking.* London: Methuen.

Hendry, L.B. (1999) 'Adolescents in society.' In D. Messer and F. Jones (eds) *Psychology and Social Care*. London: Jessica Kingsley Publishers.

Hepburn, M. (2000) 'Gender issues: women's perspectives in substance misuse.' Keynote speech at the Substance Misuse and Child Protection Conference, London, June.

Herrenkohl, E.C. and Herrenkohl, R.C. (1979) 'A comparison of abused children with their non abused siblings.' *Journal of the American Academy of Child Psychiatry 18*, 260–269.

Hester, M., Pearson, C. and Harwin, N. (2000) *Making an Impact: Children and Domestic Violence – A Reader*. London: Jessica Kingsley Publishers.

Hien, D. and Honeyman, T. (2000) 'A closer look at the drug abuse–maternal aggression link.' *Journal of Interpersonal Violence 15*, 5, 503–522.

Hill, M., Laybourn, A. and Brown, J. (1996) 'Children whose parents misuse alcohol: a study of services and needs.' *Child and Family Social Work 1*, 3, 159–167.

Hogan, D.M. (1997) *The Social and Psychological Needs of Children of Drug Users: Report on Exploratory Study*. Dublin: Children's Research Centre, Trinity College, Dublin.

Hogan, D.M. (1998) 'Annotation: the psychological development and welfare of children of opiate and cocaine users – review and research needs.' *Journal of Child Psychology and Psychiatry 39*, 609–619.

Hogan, D. and Higgins, L. (2001) *When Parents Use Drugs: Key Findings from a Study of Children in the Care of Drug-Using Parents*. Dublin: Children's Research Centre, Trinity College, Dublin.

Holland, S. (2000) 'The assessment relationship: interactions between social workers and parents in child protection assessments.' *British Journal of Social Work 30*, 149–163.

Home Office (1989) *The Children Act 1989*. London: HSMO.

Horwath, J. (2001) 'Assessing the world of the child in need: background and context.' In J. Horwath (ed) *The Child's World: Assessing Children in Need*. London: Jessica Kingsley Publishers.

Howe, D. (1995) *Attachment Theory for Social Work Practice*. London: Macmillan.

Howe, D. (1996) 'Surface and depth in social work practice.' In N. Parton (ed) *Social Theory, Social Change and Social Work*. London: Routledge.

Howe, D. (2001) 'Attachment.' In J. Horwath (ed) *The Child's World: Assessing Children in Need*. London: Jessica Kingsley Publishers.

Howe, D., Brandon, M., Hinings, D. and Schofield, G. (1999) *Attachment Theory, Child Maltreatment and Family Support*. London: Macmillan.

Howland Thompson, S. (1998) 'Working with children of substance-abusing parents.' *Young Children 53*, 1, 34–37.

Hudson, B. (2000) 'Inter-agency collaboration: A sceptical view.' In A. Brechin, H. Brown and M.A. Eby (eds) *Critical Practice in Health and Social Care*. London: Open Unversity/Sage.

Jack, G. (1997) 'An ecological approach to social work with children and families.' *Child and Family Social Work 2*, 109–120.

Jack, G. (1998) 'The social ecology of parents and children: implications for the development of child welfare services in the U.K.' *International Journal of Child and Family Social Work 2*, 109–120.

Jack, G. (2000) 'Ecological influences on parenting and child development.' *British Journal of Social Work 30*, 703–720.

Jack, G. (2001) 'Ecological perspectives in assessing children and families.' In J. Horwath (ed) *The Child's World: Assessing Children in Need*. London: Jessica Kingsley Publishers.

Jack, J. and Jack, D. (2000) 'Ecological social work: the application of a systems model of development in context.' In P. Stepney and D. Ford (eds) Social Work Models, Methods and Theories. Lyme Regis: Russell House.

Jack, G. and Jordan, B. (1999) 'Social capital and child welfare.' Children and Society 13, 242–256.

Jaudes, P.K., Ekwo, E. and Van Voorhis, J. (1995) 'Association of drug abuse and child abuse.' Child Abuse and Neglect 19, 9, 1065–1075.

Jellinek, E.M. (1960) The Disease Concept of Alcoholism. New Brunswick, NJ: Hillhouse Press.

Jewett, C. (1984) Helping Children Cope with Separation and Loss. London: British Agencies for Adoption and Fostering.

Jones, B.W. (1994) 'The clients and their problems.' In D.J. Besharov (ed) When Drug Addicts have Children. Washington, DC: Child Welfare League of America/American Enterprise Institute.

Jones, D. (2001) 'The assessment of parenting capacity.' In J. Horwath (ed) The Child's World: Assessing Children in Need. London: Jessica Kingsley Publishers.

Juliana, P. and Goodman, C. (1997) 'Children of substance abusing parents.' In J.H. Lowinson (ed) Substance Abuse: A Comprehensive Textbook. Baltimore, MD: Williams and Wilkins.

Julien, R.M. (1995) A Primer of Drug Action, 7th edn. New York: W.H. Freeman.

Kandel, D.B. (1990) 'Parenting styles, drug use and children's adjustment in families of young adults.' Journal of Marriage and the Family 52, 183–196.

Katz, I. (1997) Current Issues in Comprehensive Assessment. London: NSPCC.

Keane, F. (1996) 'Letter to my father.' In F. Keane, Letter to Daniel: Dispatches from the Heart. Harmondsworth: Penguin.

Kearney, P. (1994) 'Drug using parents and their children.' Irish Social Worker Summer, 12, 2, 6–8.

Kearney, P. and Ibbetson, M. (1991) 'Opiate dependent women and their babies: a study of the multidisciplinary work of a hospital and a local authority.' British Journal of Social Work 21, 105–126.

Kearney, P., Levin, E. and Rosen, G. (2000) Working with Families: Alcohol, Drug and Mental Health Problems. London: National Institute of Social Work.

Kearney, R.J. (1996) Within the Wall of Denial: Conquering Addictive Behaviours. New York and London: W.W. Norton.

Keith, L. and Morris, J. (1995) 'Easy targets: a disability rights perspective on the "children as carers" debate.' Critical Social Policy 44, 5, 36–50.

Kelley, S.J. (1992) 'Parenting stress and child maltreatment in drug-exposed children.' Child Abuse and Neglect 16, 317–328.

Kemshall, H. and Pritchard, J. (eds) (1996) Good Practice in Risk Assessment and Risk Management, vol. 1. London: Jessica Kingsley Publishers.

Kemshall, H. and Pritchard, J. (eds) (1997) Good Practice in Risk Assessment and Risk Management, vol. 2. London: Jessica Kingsley Publishers.

Klee, H. (1998) 'Drug using parents: analysing the stereotypes.' International Journal of Drug Policy 9, 437–448.

Klee, H. and Jackson, M. (1998) Illicit Drug Use, Pregnancy and Early Motherhood: An Analysis of the Impediments to Effective Service Delivery, Report to the Department of Health. Task Force to Review Services for Drug Misusers. Manchester: Manchester Metropolitan University.

Klee, H., Jackson, M. and Lewis, S. (2001) Drug Misuse and Motherhood. London: Routledge.

Klee, H., Lewis, S. and Jackson, M. (1995) 'Illicit drug users' experience of pregnancy: an exploratory study.' *Journal of Reproductive and Infant Psychology 13*, 219–227.

Klee, H., Wright, S. and Rothwell, J. (1998) *Drug Using Parents and their Children: Risk and Protective Factors.* Report to the Department of Health. Manchester: Centre for Social Research on Health and Substance Use, Manchester Metropolitan University.

Klein, M. (1963) *Our Adult World and its Roots in Infancy and Other Essays.* London: Heimemann.

Knapp, C. (2001) 'Women who drink too much.' *Sunday Telegraph* Magazine 4 August.

Korbin, J. (1991) 'Crosscultural perspectives and research directions for the 21st century.' *Child Abuse and Neglect 15 (supplement)*, 67–77.

Korbin, J. (1997) 'Culture and child maltreatment.' In M. Helfer, R. Kempe and R. Krugman (eds) *The Battered Child.* London: University of Chicago Press.

Krauthamer, C. (1979) 'Maternal attitudes of alcoholic and non-alcoholic upper middle class women.' *International Journal of Addictions 14*, 639–644.

Kroll, B. (1994) *Chasing Rainbows: Children, Divorce and Loss.* Lyme Regis: Russell House.

Kroll, B. (1995) 'Working with children.' In F. Kaganas, M. King and C. Piper (eds) *Legislating for Harmony: Working in Partnership under the Children Act 1989.* London: Jessica Kingsley Publishers.

Kroll, B. (1997) 'The sins of the mothers,' *Guardian* Society 20 August.

Kroll, B. and Taylor, A. (2000) 'Invisible children? Parental substance abuse and child protection: dilemmas for practice.' *Probation Journal 47*, 2, 91–100.

Laybourn, A., Brown, J. and Hill, M. (1996) *Hurting on the Inside.* Aldershot: Avebury.

Leiffer, M., Shapiro, J.P. and Kassem, L. (1993) 'The impact of maternal history and behaviour upon foster placement and adjustment in sexually abused girls.' *Child Abuse and Neglect 17*, 715–726.

Le Riche, P. and Tanner, K. (eds) (1998) *Observation and its Application to Social Work: Rather like Breathing.* London: Jessica Kingsley Publishers.

Leventhal, H. and Cleary, P. (1980) 'The smoking problem: a review of the research and theory in behavioural risk modification.' *Psychological Bulletin 88*, 370–405.

Lewis, C.E. and Bucholz, K.K. (1991) 'Alcoholism, antisocial behaviour and family history.' *British Journal of Addiction 86*, 177–194.

Lewis, V. (1997) 'Drunk in charge.' *Community Care* 11–17 September

Lloyd, C. (1998) 'Risk factors for problem drug use: identifying vulnerable groups.' *Drugs: Education, Prevention and Policy 5*, 3, 217–232.

Lodge, D. (2001) *Thinks...* London: Secker and Warburg.

London Borough of Brent (1985) *A Child in Trust.* London: London Borough of Brent.

London Borough of Greenwich (1987) *A Child in Mind.* London: London Borough of Greenwich.

Luthar, S.S. and Zigler, E. (1991) 'Vulnerability and competence: a review of research and resilience in childhood.' *American Journal of Orthopsychiatry 61*, 1, 6–22.

McKeganey, N., Barnard, M. and McIntosh, J. (2001) *Paying the Price for their Parents' Addiction: Meeting the Needs of the Children of Drug Using Parents.* Glasgow: Centre for Drug Misuse Research, University of Glasgow.

McMurran, M. (1994) *The Psychology of Addiction.* London: Taylor and Francis.

Magura, S. and Laudet, A.B. (1996) 'Parental substance abuse and child maltreatment: review and implications for intervention.' *Children and Youth Services Review 1*, 3, 193–220.

Main, M. (1991) 'Metacognitive knowledge, metacognitive monitoring and singular (coherent) vs. multiple (incoherent) model of attachment.' In C.M. Parkes, J, Stevenson-Hinde and P. Marris (eds) *Attachment across the Life Cycle.* London: Tavistock.

Main, M. and Solomon, J. (1986) 'Discovery of an insecure-disorganised/disoriented attachment pattern.' In T. Brazelton and M. Yogman (eds) *Affective Development in Infancy.* Norwood, NJ: Ablex.

Marlatt, G.A. and Gordon, J.R. (1985) *Relapse Prevention.* New York: Guilford.

Marsden, J., Gossop, M., Stewart, D., Best, D., Farrell, M., Lehmann, P., Edward, C. and Strang, J. (1998) The Maudsley Addiction Profile (MAP): A brief instrument for assessing treatment outcome.' *Addiction 93*, 12, 1857–1868.

Masten, A.S. and Coatsworth, J.D. (1998) 'The development of competence in favourable and unfavourable environments: lessons from research on successful children.' *American Psychologist 53*, 205–220.

Mayer, J. and Black, R. (1977) 'Child abuse and neglect in families with an alcohol or opiate addicted parent.' *Child Abuse and Neglect 1*, 85–98.

Miles, A. (1991) *Women, Health and Medicine.* Buckingham: Open University Press.

Miller, W.R. and Kurtz, E. (1994) 'Models of alcoholism used in treatment: contrasting A.A. and other perspectives with which it is often confused.' *Journal of Studies on Alcohol 55*, 159–166.

Miller, W.R. and Rollnick, S. (eds) (1991) *Motivational Interviewing: Preparing People to Change Addictive Behaviour.* New York: Guilford.

Milner, J. and O'Byrne, P. (1998) *Assessment in Social Work.* London: Macmillan.

Minuchin, S. (1974) *Families and Family Therapy.* London: Tavistock.

Mitchell, J. (ed) (1986) *The Selected Melanie Klein.* Harmondsworth: Penguin.

Moffitt, T.E. (1993) 'Adolescent-limited and life-course-persistent anti-social behaviour: a developmental taxonomy.' *Psychological Review 4*, 674–701.

Molyneux, J. (2001) 'Interprofessional teamworking: what makes teams work well?' *Journal of Interprofessional Care 15*, 1, 29–35.

Mountenay, J. (1998) *Children of Drug Using Parents.* Highlight no. 163. London: National Children's Bureau.

Mullender, A. and Morley, R. (eds) (1994) *Children Living with Domestic Violence: Putting Men's Abuse of Women on the Child Care Agenda.* London: Whiting and Birch.

Mulvey, E.P. (1994) 'Assessing the evidence of a link between mental illness and violence.' *Hospital and Community Psychiatry 45*, 7, 663–668.

Murphy, M. and Harbin, F. (2000) 'Background and current context of substance misuse and child care.' In F. Harbin and M. Murphy (eds) *Substance Misuse and Child Care: How to Understand, Assist and Intervene When Drugs Affect Parenting.* Lynne Regis: Russell House.

Murphy, J.M., Jellinek, M., Quinn, D., Smith, G., Poitrast, F.G. and Gashko, M. (1991) 'Substance abuse and serious child mistreatment: prevalence, risk and outcome in a court sample.' *Child Abuse and Neglect 15*, 197–211.

Murphy, M. and Oulds, G. (2000) 'Establishing and developing co-operative links between substance misuse and child protection systems.' In F. Harbin and M. Murphy (eds) *Substance Misuse and Child Care: How to Understand, Assist and Intervene when Drugs Affect Parenting.* Lyme Regis: Russell House.

Newcomb, M.D. and Rickards, S. (1995) 'Parent drug-use problems and adult intimate relations: associations among community samples of young adult women and men.' *Journal of Counselling Psychology 42*, 2, 141–154.

Nicholson, J. (1984) *Men and Women*. Oxford: Oxford University Press.

Nottingham Area Child Protection Committee (1997) *Nottingham Area Child Protection Committee Procedures*. Nottingham: Nottingham Area Child Protection Committee.

Oates, M. (1997) 'Patients as parents: the risk to children.' *British Journal of Psychiatry 170* (Supplement 32) 22–27.

O'Hagan, K. (1993) *Emotional and Psychological Abuse of Children*. Buckingham: Open University Press.

O'Hagan, K. (1997) 'The problem of engaging men in child protection work.' *British Journal of Social Work 27*, 1, 25–42.

Olsen, L.J., Allen, D. and Azzi-Lessing, L. (1996) 'Assessing risk in families affected by substance misuse.' *Child Abuse and Neglect 20*, 9, 833–842.

OPCS (Office of Population, Censuses and Surveys) (1996) *The Prevalence of Psychiatric Morbidity among Adults Living in Private Households*. London: HMSO.

Orford, J. (1985) *Excessive Appetites: A Psychological View of Addictions*. Chichester: John Wiley.

Orford, J (1998) 'The coping perspective.' In R. Velleman, A. Copello and J. Maslin (eds) *Living with Drink: Women who Live with Problem Drinkers*. London: Longman.

Orford, J. (2001) *Excessive Appetites: A Psychological View of Addictions*, 2nd edn. Chichester: John Wiley.

Orford, J., Natera, G., Davies, J., Nava, A., Mora, J., Rigby, K., Bradbury, C., Copello, A. and Velleman, R. (1998a) 'Stresses and strains for family members living with drinking or drug problems in England and Mexico.' *Salud Mental V*, 21, 1.

Orford, J., Natera, G., Davies, J., Nava, A., Mora, J., Rigby, K., Bradbury, C., Copello, A. and Velleman, R. (1998b) 'Tolerate, engage or withdraw: a study of the structure of families coping with alcohol and drug problems in south west England and Mexico City.' *Addiction 93*, 1799–1813.

Orford, J., Natera, G., Davies, J., Nava, A., Mora, J., Rigby, K., Bradbury, C., Copello, A. and Velleman, R. (1998c) 'Social support in coping with alcohol and drug problems at home: findings from Mexican and English families.' *Addiction Research 6*, 359–420.

Parker, R., Ward, H., Jackson, S., Aldgate, J. and Wedge, P. (eds) (1991) *Looking after Children: Assessing Outcomes in Child Care*. London: HMSO.

Parkes, C.M. (1996) *Bereavement: Studies of Grief in Adult Life*, 3rd edn. London: Routledge.

Parsloe, P. (ed) (1999) *Risk Assessment in Social Care and Social Work*. London: Jessica Kingsley Publishers.

Parton, N. (1991) *Governing the Family: Child Care, Child Protection and the State*. London: Macmillan.

Parton, N. (ed) (1996) *Social Theory, Social Change and Social Work: The State of Welfare*. London: Routledge.

Parton, N. (ed) (1997) *Child Protection and Family Support: Tensions, Contradictions and Possibilities*. London: Routledge.

Parton, N., Thorpe, D. and Wattam, C. (1997) *Child Protection: Risk and the Moral Order*. London: Macmillan.

Patel, K. (2000) 'The missing drug users: minority ethnic drug users and their children.' In F. Harbin and M .Murphy (eds) *Substance Misuse and Child Care: How to Understand, Assist and Intervene when Drugs Affect Parenting.* Lyme Regis: Russell House.

Pearson, G (1987) *The New Heroin Users.* Oxford: Blackwell.

Peele, S. (1985) *The Meaning of Addiction.* Lexington, MA: Lexington Books.

Phares, V. (1992) 'Where's Poppa? The relative lack of attention to the role of fathers in child and adolescent psychopathology.' *American Psychologist 4,* 656–664.

Phares, V. (1997) 'Psychological adjustment, maladjustment and father–child relationships.' In M.E. Lamb (ed) *The Role of the Father in Child Development.* New York: John Wiley.

Phinney, J.S. and Devich-Navarro, M. (1997) 'Variations in bi-cultural identification amongst African American and Mexican American adolescents.' *Journal of Research on Adolescents 7,* 3–32.

Piaget, J. (1969) *The Psychology of the Child.* London: Routledge and Kegan Paul.

Plant, M. (1997) *Women and Alcohol: Contemporary and Historical Perspectives.* London: Free Association.

Preston-Shoot, M. and Agass, D. (1990) *Making Sense of Social Work: Psychodynamics, Systems and Practice.* London: Macmillan.

Prins, H. (1999) *Will they do it Again?* London: Routledge.

Prochaska, J.O. and DiClemente, C.C. (1982) 'Transtheoretical therapy: towards a more integrative model of change.' *Theory, Research and Practice 19,* 276–278.

Prochaska, J.O. and DiClemente, C.C. (1984) *The Transtheoretical Approach: Crossing the Traditional Boundaries of Therapy.* Homewood, IL: Dow Jones/Irwin.

Prochaska, J.O., DiClemente, C.C. and Norcross, J.C. (1992) 'In search of how people change: applications to addictive behaviours.' *American Psychologist 87,* 825–835.

Project MATCH Research Group (1997) 'Matching alcoholism treatment to client heterogeneity: Project MATCH post-treatment drinking outcomes.' *Journal of Studies on Alcohol 58,* 1671–1698.

Project MATCH Research Group (1998) 'Matching alcoholism treatment to client heterogeneity: Project MATCH three-year drinking outcomes.' *Alcoholism: Experimental and Clinical Research 22,* 1300–1311.

Quinton, D. and Rutter, M. (1985) 'Family pathology and child psychiatric disorder: a four year prospective study.' In A.R. Nichol (ed) *Longitudinal Studies in Child Psychology and Psychiatry.* London: John Wiley.

Reder, P. and Duncan, S. (1999) *Lost Innocents: A Follow-Up Study of Fatal Child Abuse.* London: Routledge.

Reder, P., Duncan, S. and Gray, M. (1993) *Beyond Blame.* London: Routledge.

Reder, P. and Lucey, C. (eds) (1995) *Assessment of Parenting: Psychiatric and Psychological Contributions.* London: Routledge.

Rickford, F. (1996) 'Bad habits.' *Community Care 8,* 4 February, 16–17.

Robinson, B.E. and Rhoden, J.L. (1998) *Working with Children of Alcoholics,* 2nd edn. London: Sage.

Robinson, W. and Dunne, M. (1999) *Alcohol, Child Care and Parenting.* London: NSPCC.

Robinson, W. and Hassle, J. (2001) *Alcohol Problems and the Family: From Stigma to Solution.* London: Alcohol Recovery Project and NSPCC.

Robson, P. (1999) *Forbidden Drugs,* 2nd edn. Oxford: Oxford University Press.

Roosa, M.W., Sandler, I.N., Beals, J. and Short, J. (1988) 'Risk status of adolescent children of problem drinking parents.' *American Journal of Community Psychology 16*, 225–229.

Rose, D. (2001) 'Battle begins in junkies' very personal war zone.' *Observer* 15 July.

Rose, W. (2001) 'Assessing children in need and their families: an overview of the framework.' In J. Horwath (ed) *The Child's World: Assessing Children in Need.* London: Jessica Kingsley Publishers.

Rose, W. and Aldgate, J. (2000) 'Knowledge underpinning the assessment framework.' In Department of Health, *Assessing Children in Need and their Families: Practice Guidance.* London: The Stationery Office.

Rounsaville, B.J., Anton, S.F., Carroll, K., Budde, D., Prusoff, B.A. and Gavin, F.H. (1991) 'Psychiatric diagnosis of treatment-seeking cocaine abusers.' *Archives of General Psychiatry 48*, 739–745.

Royal College of Physicians (1995) *Alcohol and the Young.* London: Royal Lavenham Press.

Rubin, L. (1996) *The Transcendent Child: Tales of Triumph over the Past.* New York: Basic Books.

Rutter, M. (1974) 'Dimensions of parenthood: some myths and some suggestions.' In Department of Health and Social Security, *The Family in Society: Dimensions of Parenthood.* London: HMSO.

Rutter, M. (1975) *Helping Troubled Children.* Harmondsworth: Penguin.

Rutter, M. (1986) 'Intergenerational continuities and discontinuities in serious parenting difficulties.' In D. Cicchetti and V. Carlson (eds) *Research on the Consequences of Child Maltreatment.* New York: Cambridge University Press.

Rutter, M. (1990) 'Psychosocial resilience and protective mechanisms.' In D. Cicchetti, A. Neuchterlain and S. Weintraub (eds) *Risk and Protective Factors in the Development of Psychopathology.* Cambridge: Cambridge University Press.

Rutter, M. (1993) 'Resilience: some conceptual considerations.' *Journal of Adolescent Health 14*, 626–631.

Rutter, M. (1995a) 'Clinical implications of attachment concepts, retrospect and prospect.' *Journal of Child Psychology and Psychiatry 36*, 4, 549–571.

Rutter, M. (1995b) 'Psychosocial adversity: risk, resilience and recovery.' *Southern African Journal of Child and Adolescent Psychiatry 7*, 75–88.

Rutter, M. (1999) 'Resilience concepts and findings: implications for family therapy.' *Journal of Family Therapy 21*, 119–141.

Rutter, M. and Quinton, D. (1984) 'Parental psychiatric disorder: effects on children.' *Psychological Medicine 14*, 853–880.

Rutter, M. and Rutter, M. (1993) *Developing Minds: Challenges and Continuity across the Lifespan.* Harmondsworth: Penguin.

Ryan, M. (2000) *Working with Fathers.* Abingdon: Radcliffe Medical Press.

Ryan, T., Smith, I., Hancock, G. and Smith, M. (1999) 'Applying aspects of the Community Reinforcement Approach to alcohol and drug services.' *Journal of Substance Use 4*, 70–75.

Sargent, K. (1999) 'Assessing risks for children.' In P. Parsloe (ed) *Risk Assessment in Social Work and Social Care.* London: Jessica Kingsley Publishers.

Schaffer, H.R. (1990) *Making Decisions about Children.* Oxford: Blackwell.

Schetky, D.H., Angell, R., Morrison, C.V. and Sack, W.H. (1979) 'Parents who fail: a study of 51 cases of termination of parental rights.' *Journal of the American Academy of Child Psychiatry 18*, 366–383.

SCODA (1997) *Drug Using Parents: Policy Guidelines for Inter-Agency Working.* London: Local Government Association Publications.

Scott, D. (1997) 'Inter-agency conflict: an ethnographic study.' *Child and Family Social Work 2,* 73–80.

Seilhammer, R.A., Jacob, T. and Dunn, N.J. (1992) 'The impact of alcohol consumption on parent–child relationships in families of alcoholics.' *Journal of Studies on Alcohol 54,* 189–198.

Sellar, A. (1990) 'Kicking the habit.' *Young People Now May,* 31–32.

Shaffer, H.J. and Jones, S.B. (1989) *Quitting Cocaine: The Struggle against Impulse.* New York: Lexington Books.

Sheehan, M., Oppenheimer, E. and Taylor, C. (1988) 'Who come for treatment? Drug misusers at three London agencies.' *British Journal of Addiction 83,* 311–320.

Shemmings, Y. and Shemmings, D. (2001) 'Empowering children and family members to participate in the assessment process.' In J. Horwath (ed) *The Child's World: Assessing Children in Need.* London: Jessica Kingsley Publishers.

Shephard, A. (1990) *Substance Dependency.* Birmingham: Venture Press.

Sheppard, J. (2000) 'Learning from personal experience: reflexions on social work practice with mothers in child and family care.' *Journal of Social Work Practice 14,* 1, 37–50.

Sheppard, M. (1998) 'Practice validity, reflexivity and knowledge for social work.' *British Journal of Social Work 28,* 763–781.

Sheppard, M. (2001) *Social Work Practice with Depressed Mothers in Child and Family Care.* London: The Stationery Office.

Sher, K.J. (1991) 'Psychological characteristics of children of alcoholics: overview of research methods and findings.' *Recent Developments in Alcohol 9,* 301–326.

Sheridan, M. (1986) *From Birth to Five Years: Children's Developmental Progress.* Windsor: NFER-Nelson.

Silverstein, L., Edelwich, J. and Flanagan, D., with commentary by Brodsky, A. (1981) *High on Life: A Story of Addiction and Recovery.* Pompano Beach, FL: Health Communications.

Sloan, M. (1998) *Substance Misuse and Child Maltreatment,* Social Work Monographs. Norwich: University of East Anglia.

Smith, J.A.S. and Adler, R.G. (1991) 'Children hospitalised with child abuse and neglect: a case controlled study.' *Child Abuse and Neglect 15,* 437–445.

Smith, J.E. and Meyers, R.J. (1995) 'The Community Reinforcement Approach.' In R. Hester and W. Miller (eds) *Handbook of Alcoholism Treatment Approaches.* Boston, MA: Allyn and Bacon.

Smith, P.K. and Cowie, H. (1991) *Understanding Children's Development.* Oxford: Blackwell.

Social Exclusion Unit (1998) *Bringing Britain Together: A National Strategy for Neighbourhood Renewal.* London: The Stationery Office.

Social Services Inspectorate (1997a) *Messages from Inspections: Child Protection Inspections 1992–6.* London: HMSO.

Social Services Inspectorate (1997b) *Assessment Planning and Decision Making: Family Support.* London: Department of Health.

Solomon, A. (2001) *The Noonday Demon.* London: Chatto and Windus.

South, N. (1999) 'Debating drugs and everyday life: normalisation, prohibition and "Otherness".' In N. South, *Drugs: Cultures, Controls and Everyday Life.* London: Sage.

Sowder, B. and Burt, M.R. (1980) 'Children of addicts and non addicts: a comparative investigation in five urban sites.' In National Institute on Drug Abuse Services Research Report, *Heroin Addicted Parents and their Children*. Rockville, MD: National Institute of Drug Abuse.

Spicer, P. and Fleming, C. (2000) 'American Indian children of alcoholics.' In H.E. Fitzgerald, B.M. Lester and B.S. Zuckerman (eds) *Children of Addiction: Research, Health and Public Policy Issues*. New York and London: RoutledgeFalmer.

Steinglass, P. (1987) *The Alcoholic Family*. New York: Basic Books.

Stern, D. (1977) *The First Relationship: Mother and Infant*. Cambridge, MA: Harvard University Press.

Stevenson, O. (1998) *Neglected Children: Issues and Dilemmas*. Oxford: Blackwell Science.

Stone, B. (1998) *Child Neglect: Practitioners' Perspectives*. London: NSPCC.

Stroud, J. (1997) 'Mental disorder and the homicide of children.' *Social Work and Social Sciences Review: An International Journal of Applied Research 6*, 3, 149–162.

Sutton, S. (1996) 'Can "Stages of Change" provide guidance in the treatment of addictions? A critical examination of Prochaska and DiClemente's model.' In G. Edwards and C. Dare (eds) *Psychotherapy, Psychological Treatments and the Addictions*. Cambridge: Cambridge University Press.

Svedin, C.G., Wadsby, M. and Sydsjo, G. (1996) 'Children of mothers who are at psycho-social risk: mental health, behaviour problems and incidence of child abuse at age eight years.' *European Child and Adolescent Psychiatry 5*, 162–171.

Swadi, H. (1994) 'Parenting capacity and substance misuse: an assessment scheme.' *Association of Child Psychology and Psychiatry Review and Newsletter 16*, 237–245.

Szasz, T. (1974) *Ceremonial Chemistry*. New York: Anchor Press/Doubleday.

Tanner, K. and Turney, D. (2000) 'The role of observation in the assessment of child neglect.' *Child Abuse Review 9*, 337–348.

Taylor, A. (1999) 'The elephant in the interview room: working with the process of denial in chronic drinkers.' *Probation Journal 46*, 1, 19–26.

Taylor, A. (in preparation) 'Children of substance misusing parents: do professionals meet their needs?' PhD Research Project in preparation, Department of Psychology, University of Bath.

Thoburn, J., Brandon, M. and Lewis, A. (1997) 'Need, risk and significant harm.' In N. Parton (ed) *Child Protection and Family Support: Tensions and Contradictions*. London: Routledge.

Tizard, B. and Phoenix, A. (1993) *Black, White or Mixed Race? Race and Racism in the Lives of Young People of Mixed Parentage*. London: Routledge.

Tsui, M. (2000) 'The harm reduction approach revisited: an international perspective.' *International Social Work 43*, 2, 243–251.

Tunnard, J. (2002) *Parental Problem Drinking and its Impact on Children*. Dartington: Research in Practice.

Turney, D. (2000) 'The feminising of neglect.' *Child and Family Social Work 5*, 47–56.

Tweed, S.H. and Ryff, C.D. (1991) 'Adult children of alcoholics: profiles of wellness amidst distress.' *Journal of Studies on Alcohol 52*, 2, 133–141.

Tyler, R., Howard, J., Espinosa, M. and Doakes, S.S. (1997) 'Placement with substance abusing mothers vs. placement with other relatives: infant outcomes.' *Child Abuse and Neglect 21*, 4, 337–349.

United Kingdom Alcohol Treatment Trial Research Team (2001) 'United Kingdom Alcohol Treatment Trial: hypotheses, design and methods.' *Alcohol and Alcoholism 36*, 1, 11–21.

Valliant, G.E. (1983) *The Natural History of Alcoholism.* Cambridge, MA: Harvard University Press.

Velleman, R. (1992) *Counselling for Alcohol Problems.* London: Sage.

Velleman, R. (1993) *Alcohol and the Family.* London: Institute of Alcohol Studies.

Velleman, R. (1996) 'Alcohol and drug problems in parents: an overview of the impact on children and the implications for practice.' In M. Gopfert, J. Webster and M.V. Seeman (eds) *Parental Psychiatric Disorder: Distressed Parents and their Families.* Cambridge: Cambridge University Press.

Velleman, R., Copello, A. and Maslin, J. (eds) (1998) *Living with Drink: Women who Live with Problem Drinkers.* London: Longman.

Velleman, R. and Orford, J. (1985) 'Methodological problems in social research: the reliability of the retrospective remembrances of 250 young adults aged 16–25.' Paper presented at annual Conference of the British Psychological Society, Social Psychology Section, Cambridge, UK.

Velleman, R. and Orford, J. (1990) 'Young adult offspring of parents with drinking problems: recollections of parents.' drinking and its immediate effects' *British Journal of Clinical Psychology 29*, 297–317.

Velleman, R. and Orford, J. (1993) 'The importance of family discord in explaining childhood problems in the children of problem drinkers.' *Addiction Research 1*, 39–57.

Velleman, R. and Orford, J. (1999) *Risk and Resilience: Adults who were the Children of Problem Drinkers.* Amsterdam: Harwood Academic.

Vetere, A.L. (1987) 'General system theory and the family: a critical evaluation.' In A.L. Vetere and A. Gale (eds) *Ecological Studies of Family Life.* Chichester: John Wiley.

Vetere, A.L. (1998) 'A family systems perspective.' In R. Velleman, A. Copello and J. Maslin (eds) *Living with Drink: Women who Live with Problem Drinkers.* London: Longman.

Wade, J. and Biehal, N. (1998) *Going Missing: Young People Absent from Care.* Report to the Department of Health. Chichester: John Wiley.

Warren, C. (1993) *Family Centres and the Children Act 1989.* Arundel: Tarrent Publishing Ltd.

Waterhouse, L. and Carnie, J. (1991) 'Social work and police response to child sexual abuse in Scotland.' *British Journal of Social Work 21*, 373–379.

Wegscheider-Cruse, S. (1981) *Another Chance: Hope and Healing for the Alcoholic Family.* Crystal, MN: Nurturing Networks.

Weir, A. and Douglas, A. (eds) (1999) *Child Protection and Adult Mental Health: Conflict of Interests?* Oxford: Butterworth Heinemann.

Weiss, R.D. (1992) 'The role of psychopathology in the transmission from drug use to abuse and dependence.' In M.D. Glantz and R.W. Pickens (eds) *Vulnerability to Drug Use.* Washington, DC: American Psychological Association.

Wellisch, D.K. and Steinberg, M.R. (1980) 'Parenting attitudes of addict mothers.' *International Journal of Addictions 15*, 809–819.

Werner, E. (1986) 'Resilient offspring of alcoholics: a longitudinal study from birth to age 18.' *Journal of Studies on Alcohol 47*, 34–40.

Werner, E. (1990) 'Protective factors and individual resilience.' In S. Meisels and J. Shonkoff (eds) *Handbook of Early Childhood Development.* Cambridge, MA: Cambridge University Press.

West, M.O. and Prinz, R.J. (1987) 'Parental alcoholism and childhood psychopathology.' *Psychological Bulletin 102*, 2, 204–218.

Wilczynski, A. (1997) *Child Homicide.* Glasgow: Bell and Bain.

William-Peterson, M.G., Myers, B.J., McFarland, D.H., Knisely, J.S., Elswick, R.K. and Schnoll, S.S. (1994) 'Drug using and non using women: potential for child abuse, child rearing attitudes, social support and affection for expected baby.' *The Journal for the Addictions 29*, 12, 1631–1643.

Williams, H.A. (1972) *True Resurrection.* London: Mitchell Beazley.

Williams, H., O'Connor, J.J. and Kinsella, A. (1990) 'Depressive symptoms in opiate addicts on methadone maintenance.' *Irish Journal of Psychology 7*, 45–46.

Wilson, J. (1999) 'Mo Mowlam tells of childhood with alcoholic father.' *Guardian* 30 January.

Winnicott, D. (1960) 'The theory of the parent–infant relationship.' In *The Maturational Process and the Facilitating Environment.* London: Hogarth Press.

Winnicott, D. (1964) *The Child, the Family and the Outside World.* Harmondsworth: Penguin.

Wisely, C., Gledhill, N., Cyster, R. and Shaw, H. (1997) 'The new young heroin users.' Unpublished report.

Woititz, J.G. (1990) *Adult Children of Alcoholics,* 2nd edn. Pompano Beach, FL: Health Communications.

Wolin, S. and Wolin, S. (1993) *The Resilient Self: How Survivors of Troubled Families Rise above Adversity.* New York: Random House.

Woodcock, J. (forthcoming) 'The social work assessment of parenting: an exploration.' *British Journal of Social Work.*

Woodcock, J. and Sheppard, M. (forthcoming) 'Double trouble: maternal depression and alcohol dependence as combined factors in child and family social work.' *Children and Society.*

Woollett, A. and Phoenix, A. (1991) 'Psychological views of mothering.' In A. Phoenix, A. Woollett and E. Lloyd (eds) *Motherhood, Meanings, Practice and Ideology.* London: Sage.

Yandoli, D., Mulleady, G. and Robbins, C. (1989) 'Family therapy and addiction.' In G. Bennett (ed) *Treating Drug Abusers.* London: Routledge.

Young, L. (1964) *Wednesday's Children: A Study of Child Neglect and Abuse.* New York: McGraw-Hill.

Zeitlin, H. (1994) 'Children with alcohol misusing parents.' *British Medical Bulletin 50*, 139–151.

Zinberg, N. (1975) 'Addiction and ego function.' *Psychoanalytic Study of the Child 30*, 567–588.

Zuckerman, B. (1994) 'Effects on parents and children.' In D.J. Besharov (ed) *When Drug Addicts have Children.* Washington, DC: Child Welfare League of America/American Enterprise Institute.

Subject Index

ability to use adults as resources 154
abuse, violence and living with fear 169–71
accommodation and home environment 261–2
  SCODA guidelines 317–18
active behaviours 141
adapting and surviving 172–8
addiction
  and dependence 60
  and volition 58–9
  see also attachment; dependence
adolescent crisis 209
adults
  ability to use as resources 154
  availability of supportive, as role models and caregivers 157
  needs of vs needs of children 223–9
Afro-Caribbean communities 105
agencies
  communicating across, and issue of confidentiality 232–3
  differences between 223–9
alcohol 311–12
  dependence
    and types of maltreatment 40–1
    prevalence of 30–2
    research on 32, 34
Al-Anon 69
Al-Ateen 69, 294
Alcohol Recovery Project 303
Alcoholics Anonymous 67, 274, 281, 294
amphetamines 309–10
analgesics/opiates 308–9
Asian communities 105
assessment
  approaches to 256–9
  evaluating 266–7
  of harm 63–4
  to intervention: a family perspective 269–95
    child-centred practice in family intervention 291–5

Community Reinforcement Approach 278–80
    coping perspectives 275–6
    ecological perspective and social support 272–5
    Network Therapy 280–1
    obstacles to working holistically 270–2
    Social Behaviour and Network Therapy (SBNT) 281–3
    Stress-Coping-Health Model 276–8
    towards a family-centred model for intervention 283–91
  issues in 244–6
  of parenting 242–4
  role of observation in 255–6
Assessment Framework 21–2
attachment 139–43
  developing 86–8
  and loss 92–3
  patterns and defensive strategies 143–5
  physical dependence or emotional attachment? 88–90
  problems, substance misuse and child maltreatment 49–51
  and reinforcement 85–97
  secure 153
  separation and loss 165–7
  to substances as management of pain 91–2
  vulnerability, risk and resilience 137–62
  see also addiction; dependence
Australia 47
aversive behaviour 141
awareness 154

barbiturates 314
basic care 22, 103
Baumrind's Parenting Attitudes Questionnaire 121
Beck Depression Inventory 46
behavioural development 22, 195, 203–6
benefits of parental substance misuse 187–9
benzodiazepines 314
binge drinking 72
Bolton survey 36
boundaries 22, 103
British research studies 34–6, 43, 257

bullying 187

Canada 179
cannabis 312–13
care, basic 22, 103
caretaker, availability of stable, nurturing 155
chaos
  and control: adapting and surviving 172–8
  theory, and lifestyle 118–19
childcare 157
  substance use and risk management 114
child as carer, role reversal, role confusion and 178–80
child-centred practice
  in family assessment 251–4
  in family intervention 291–5
child development
  and developmental domain 194–5
  education and cognitive ability 199–202
  emotional and behavioural development 203–6
  family and social relationships 212–14
  health 195–9
  identity and social presentation 207–11
  and parental substance misuse 193, 215
  self-care skills 214–15
Child and Family Court Advisory and Support Service (CAFCASS) 107
child homicide and parental substance misuse 47–9
child maltreatment
  alcohol, drugs and types of 40–1
  definition 29–30
  and parental substance misuse 27–53
child protection
  and parental substance misuse 18–20
  registers 41
child welfare 15–26
  role of parenting in 100
child, world of the 137–62
  attachment 139–43
  object relations, holding environment and containment 138–9

resilience and protective factors 151–8
risk assessment: perils and pitfalls 146–8
risk and vulnerability 149–50
vulnerability: who is most at risk of significant harm? 158–61
Child's World training pack (DoH) 253
Children Act 1; 1989 9, 10, 18, 19, 147, 232
children in need 18–20
children of alcoholics (COAs) 50–1
Children of Alcoholics Life Events Schedules (COALES) 168
children's developmental needs, meeting 262
children's roles 173–6
cocaine 34, 309–11
cognitive competence 153, 195
education and 195, 199–202
communicating across agencies and issue of confidentiality 232–3
communication between parents and children, good 155
community
characteristics 157
context: social life, social isolation and family support 126–9
resources 22, 103, 157
Community Reinforcement Approach 76, 278–80, 282
compulsion to drink, subjective awareness of 69, 72–3
confidant 176
confidentiality, issue of, and communicating across agencies 232–3
constant opportunistic drinking 74
containment, holding environment and object relations 138–9
coping
perspectives 275–6
strategies 176–8
Cornwall survey 36–7
crack 34, 309–10
criminal behaviour 124
cross-tolerance 71
cultural connection, value and identity 157
cultural relativism, optimism and 'natural love', influence of rule of 247–50

culture, gender and parenting 105–8

definitions vs labels 61–62
denial
distortion and secrecy 183–7
as natural response to pain and loss 93–6
dependence
and addiction 58
frequency of use and time spent with children 72–3
physical dependence or emotional attachment? 88–90
syndrome 68
progressive states of 72–3
see also addiction; attachment
depressants 311
depression 45–7, 87
detached/avoidant pattern 144
developmental dance 100
developmental needs 22
dilemmas for practice 219–39
child-centred practice in family assessment 251–4
communicating across agencies and issue of confidentiality 232–3
differences between agencies: adults' needs, children's needs 22, 39
different approaches to assessment 234–6
inter-agency dynamics: working together 250–1
joining 'snapshots' 236–7
practice with children: engagement, low visibility and parents' needs 229–32
problem of engagement: access denied 220–3
disclosure 254–5
disease
free will or responsibility? 66–7
model
growth of 65–6
implications of 66–7
stigmatising or liberating? 68–70
and moral lassitude 65
Disease Concept of Alcoholism, The (Jellinek) 66
disorganised/disoriented pattern 145
dissocialisation 81

distorted perceptions and emotional control 125
distortion, denial and secrecy 183–7
divorce, family dislocation, separation and 172
domestic violence and substance misuse 44–5
drinking, patterns of 73–4
drugs
and alcohol: classifications and effects 307–15
analgesics/opiates 308–9
depressants 311
hallucinogenic/psychedelic 312–14
impact of mixing 307–8
procurement of, SCODA guidelines 318
stimulants 309–12
tranquillisers and sleeping pills 314
and types of maltreatment 40–1
dynamics of substance misuse 57–84
addiction or volition? 58–9
assessing harm 63–4
conceptualising problem substance use 64–70
'disease', free will or responsibility? 67–8
from moral lassitude to 'disease' 65
growth of disease model 65–6
implications of disease model 66–7
interactive dimension 70–73
stigmatising or liberating? 68–70
dependence, frequency of use and time spent with children 73–5
impact of labelling 80–82
issue of terminology 60
and labelling, between professionals and substance-misusing parents 83
labels or definitions? 59–60
legality and illegality 60–1
social constructionist perspective 60–61
social pressures and substance misuse 77–9

substance misuse as learned
behaviour 74–7
learning theory and family
functioning 76–7

early loss and trauma, absence of
153
ecological perspective and social
support 272–5
ecomaps 286–90
example 288
structure and links 287
economic status, adequate 155
ecstasy (MDMA) 313–14
education 22, 157
and cognitive ability 195,
199–202
risks posed to by parental
substance misuse
201–2
embarrassment and exposure, fear
of affecting friendships
186–7
emotion focused coping strategies
176, 177
emotional attachment or physical
dependence? 88–90
emotional and behavioural
development 22, 195,
203–6
emotional control and distorted
perceptions 125
emotional homeostasis 92
emotional warmth 22, 103
empathy 154
employment 22, 103
enabler role 175
enmeshed relationships 74
engagement
engagement
low visibility and parents' needs
229–32
problem of 220–3
England 30, 31, 47, 220
enslavement 87
environment
factors 261–2
socially rich 157
evaluating the assessment 266–7
externalising behaviours 177, 204

false selves 174
Families Anonymous 69
familial characteristics 155
family
assessment, child-centred
practice in family 251–4

discord, minimal 155
dislocation, separation and
divorce 172
functioning
conflict and breakdown
167–72
and history 22, 103
and learning theory 76–7
and relationships 116–18
rhythms, effects of
substance abuse on
118
rituals 155
rules, consistently enforced 155
social integration of 22, 103
social network and support
systems: SCODA
guidelines 319
and social relationships 22,
195, 212–14
structured activities 155
support, social life and social
isolation 126–9
wider 103
family-centred model for
intervention 283–91
fathers 107–8
fear, violence, abuse and living
with 169–71
finances, work and living
conditions 126
*Framework for the Assessment of
Children in Need and Their
Families* (DoH) 21, 24, 29,
79, 137–8, 194, 226, 234,
243, 259, 272
free will, 'disease' or
responsibility? 67–8
frequency of use, dependence and
time spent with children
73–4
friendships affected by fear of
embarrassment and
exposure 186–7

gender, culture and parenting
105–8
genograms 286, 290
Glasgow drug action team 31
goal directedness 154
'good enough' parenting 100–1
growing up with parental
substance misuse 163–91
attachment, separation and loss
165–7
benefits of parental substance
misuse 187–9

chaos and control: adapting and
surviving 172–8
coping strategies 176–8
maintaining harmony:
children's roles
173–6
denial, distortion and secrecy
183–7
implications for
friendships:
embarrassment and
exposure 186–7
family functioning, conflict and
breakdown 167–72
family dislocation,
separation and
divorce 172
violence, abuse and living
with fear 169–71
model for problem-solving
180–2
role reversal, role confusion and
child as carer 178–80
what children said they needed
189–90
guidance and boundaries 22, 103
guilt, shame and remorse 115

hallucinogenic/psychedelic drugs
312–14
harm, assessing 63–4
harmony, maintaining: children's
roles 173–6
health 22, 195–9
care 157
risks posed to, by parental
substance misuse 196–9
SCODA guidelines
318–19
hero role 174
heroin 34, 308–9
holding environment, containment
and object relations 138–9
holistic approach to assessment,
towards 241–67
accommodation, home, social
support and environment
factors 261–3
assessing parenting 242–4
child-centred practice in family
assessment 251–4
child's perception of the
situation 260–1
disclosure 254–5
effects on parental mental state
265

evaluating the assessment 266–7
how substances are obtained 265
influence of rule of optimism, cultural relativism and 'natural love' 247–50
learning from experience: approaches to assessment 256–9
issues in assessment 244–6
meeting children's developmental needs and provision of basic necessities 262
parents' perceptions of the situation 265–6
patterns of parental substance misuse 262–4
power dynamics 250
role of observation in assessment 255–6
substance misuse: values, beliefs and feelings 246–7
home, accommodation, social support and environment factors 261–2
housing 22, 103
how substances are obtained 265
humour, good sense of 154

identity 22
and social presentation 195, 207–11
illegality and legality 60–1
improving practice 299–306
listening to children and their parents: service provision 302
practice and policy initiatives 303–5
research initiatives 305–6
tackling organisational barriers 301–2
training 300–1
income 22, 103
increased tolerance 68, 69
insignificant harm 18
interaction of physical and psychological effects of chronic substance misuse 70–73
inter-agency dynamics: working together 250–1
internal locus of control 154
internalisation 82
internalising behaviours 204

interpersonal conflict 95
intervention
from assessment to 269–95
family-centred model for 283–91
intrapsychic conflict 95

Jasmine Beckford tragedy 248

keeping watch as coping strategy 177

labelling
disjunction in 81
and dynamics between professionals and substance-misusing parents 83
impact of 78–80
labels vs definitions 59–60
learned behaviour, substance misuse as 74–7
learning from experience: approaches to assessment 256–9
learning theory and family functioning 76–7
legality and illegality 62–3
leisure facilities 157
lifestyle and 'chaos' theory 118–19
listening to children and their parents: service provision 302
living conditions, work and finances 126
Local Government Drugs Forum (LGDF) 257
lone parenting 39–40
loss
and attachment 92–3
and separation 165–7
and pain, denial as natural response to 93–6
lost child role 175
low visibility, engagement and parents' needs 229–32
LSD 313

maintaining habit 85–97
maintaining harmony: children's roles 173–6
maltreatment, neglect, risks and hazards 122–4
management of pain, attachment of substances as 91–2
Maria Colwell inquiry 146

mascot role 175
maternal substance misuse 38–9
MDMA (ecstasy) 313–14
mediator role 176
mental states, mental health problems and substance misuse 45–7
methadone 308–9
mixing drugs, impact of 307–8
moral lassitude and 'disease' 65
mothering 104
see also parenting
mothers, blaming 106–7
motivational interviewing 285

narrowing of repertoire 70, 71
National Society for the Prevention of Cruelty to Children (NSPCC) 37, 43, 303
Kilburn Project/Caversham Children's Centre group-work initiative 294
'natural love', cultural relativism and optimism, influence of rule of 247–50
negative chain events 149
neglect
maltreatment, risks and hazards 122–4
and parental substance misuse 41–4
Network Therapy 76, 274, 280–1, 282
neurobiological problems, absence of 153
nightly drinking 74
New York studies 48
non-attachment 144
Northern Ireland 30

object relations, holding environment and containment 138–9
observation, role of in assessment 255–6
obstacles to working holistically 270–2
opiates/analgesics 308–9
optimism, cultural relativism and 'natural love', influence of rule of 247–50
organisational barriers, tackling 301–2

pain
attachment of substances as management of 91–2

and loss, denial as natural
      response to 93–6
parental esteem, high 155
parental mental state, effects on
      265
'Parental Modelling Theory' 182
parental substance misuse
   benefits 187–9
   and child development
      193–215
   and child maltreatment 27–53
      alcohol, drugs and types of
         maltreatment 40–1
      attachment problems
         49–51
      child homicide 47–9
      domestic violence 44–5
      how many children are
         affected? 30–2
      lone parenting 39–40
      maternal substance misuse
         38–9
      mental states and mental
         health problems
         45–7
      neglect 41–4
      research in context 32–4
      what is meant by child
         maltreatment? 29–30
      what is meant by
         'substance misuse'?
         28–9
   and child welfare 15–26
      children in need,
         significant harm and
         child protection
         18–20
      Quality Protects initiative
         and Assessment
         Framework 21–2
      research on 20–1
   growing up with 163–91
   patterns of 262–4
   SCODA guidelines 317
parental tension, low 155
parenting
   assessing 242–4
   behaviour and substance misuse
      111–12
   domain and capacity 103–5
   gender and culture 105–8
      fathers 107–8
      mothers 106–7
   'good enough' 100–1
   impact of substance abuse on
      99–133

needs of substance-misusing
      parents 130–2
   practical, psychological and
      emotional consequences
      of substance misuse on
      112–25
      criminal behaviour 124
      distorted perceptions and
         emotional control
         125
      family functioning and
         relationships 116–18
      guilt, shame and remorse
         115
      lifestyle and 'chaos' theory
         118–19
      neglect, maltreatment, risks
         and hazards 122–4
      parenting skills and styles
         120–2
      rhythms of family life 118
      role reversal and role
         confusion 119–20
      substance use, childcare
         and risk management
         114
   social consequences of
      substance misuse on
      125–30
      community context: social
         life, social isolation
         and family support
         126–9
      living conditions, work
         and finances 126
      social exclusion 129–30
   role of in child welfare 100
      assumptions and
         stereotypes 101–3
   and substance misuse in context
      109
parents' perceptions of the
      situation 265–6
   SCODA guidelines 320
perceptions, distorted and
      emotional control 125
physical dependence or emotional
      attachment? 88–90
positively regarded temperament
      153
power dynamics 250
practical, psychological and
      emotional consequences of
      substance misuse on
      parenting 112–25
practice and policy initiatives
      303–5

problem focused coping strategies
      176
problem-solving
   model for 180–2
   skills, good 153
procurement of drugs, SCODA
      guidelines 318
progressive states of dependence
      syndrome 73–4
Project MATCH Research Group
      trials 274
Protecting Children: A Guide for Social
      Workers Undertaking a
      Comprehensive Assessment
      ('orange book') 234
protective mechanisms 153
protector role 175–6
provision of basic necessities 262
   SCODA guidelines 318
psychedelic/hallucinogenic drugs
      312–14

Quality Protects initiative 21

reflective function 155
reinforcement and attachment
      85–97
relationships and family
      functioning 116–18
relief of withdrawal symptoms by
      further drinking 71, 72
religious/spiritual faith 154
remorse, shame and guilt 115
research 20–1
   in context 32–4
   initiatives 305–6
resilience and protective factors
      151–8
resistant/ambivalent pattern 144
responsibility, free will or 'disease'?
      65–6
risk(s)
   assessment: perils and pitfalls
      146–8
   maltreatment, neglect, hazards
      and 122–4
   management, substance use,
      childcare and 114
   posed by parental substance
      misuse
      to education and cognitive
         ability 201–2
      to emotional and
         behavioural
         development 20, 56
      to family and social
         relationships 213–14

to health 196–9
to identity and social
    presentation 210–11
to self-care skills 215
variable 150
Risk Inventory for Substance
    Abuse-Affected Families
    256
role(s)
    children's 173–6
    engulfment 82
    reversal and role confusion
        119–20
    and child as carer 178–80
rural communities 105

safety, ensuring 22, 103
salience of drinking 70, 71
scapegoat role 174–5
school experiences, positive,
    nurturing 157
Scotland 30, 31
secrecy, distortion and denial
    183–7
secure attachment 153
self-care skills 22, 195, 214–15
self-esteem, strong 153
separation
    attachment and loss 165–7
    family dislocation and divorce
        172
service provision 302
sexual identity 209
shame, guilt and remorse 115
signalling behaviour 141
significant harm 18–20
sleeping pills 314
'snapshots', joining 236–7
Social Behaviour and Network
    Therapy (SNBT) 74, 281–3
social consequences of substance
    misuse on parenting
    125–30
social constructionist perspective
    58–9
social exclusion 129–30
social life, social isolation and
    family support 126–9
social presentation 22, 195
social pressures and substance
    misuse 77–80
social relationships 22
social support
    ecological perspective and
        272–5

home, accommodation and
    environment factors
    261–2
social understanding 154
spiritual/religious faith 154
stability 22, 103
Standing Conference on Drug
    Abuse (SCODA) 28, 46,
    119, 148, 234, 257, 258
    guidelines 317–20
        accommodation and home
            environment 317–18
        family social network and
            support systems 319
        health risks 318–19
        parental drug use 317
        parents' perception of the
            situation 320
        procurement of drugs 318
        provision of basic needs
            318
stigmatising or liberating, disease
    model as 68–70
stimulants 309–12
stimulation 22, 103
'strange situation' procedure
    143–4
Stress-Coping-Health Model 274,
    276–8, 282
subjective awareness of compulsion
    to drink 71, 72–73
substance misuse
    childcare and risk management
        114
    conceptualising 63–70
    definition of 28–9
    dynamics of 57–84
    and domestic violence 44–5
    impact on parenting 99–133
    as learned behaviour 74–7
    maternal 38–9
    mental states, mental health
        problems and 45–7
    parental and child welfare
        15–26
    and parenting 109–11
    and parenting behaviour
        111–12
    social pressures 77–80
    treatment for 155
    values, beliefs and feelings
        246–7
switching off as coping strategy
    177

temperament, positively regarded
    153

terminology 60
time spent with children,
    dependence frequency of
    use and 73–4
tolerance, increased 70, 71
Torbay survey 39–40
Trafford, Greater Manchester
    community alcohol and
    drug services 279
training 300–1
tranquillisers 312, 314
transcendence 151–2
transport 157
'Transtheoretical Model of
    Change' (Prochaska and
    DiClemente) 75–6
trauma and early loss, absence of
    153
traveller communities 105
treatment for substance misuse 155

unattached children 143
United Kingdom 31, 34, 278, 281
United Kingdom Alcohol
    Treatment Trial 282
United States 31, 278, 281
    research studies 33, 34, 48, 51,
        181

verbal skills, good 154
Victoria Climbié; inquiry 146, 248
violence, abuse and living with fear
    169–71
volition or addiction 56–7
vulnerability
    and risk 149–50
    who is most at risk of
        significant harm? 158–61

Wales 30, 31
weekly heavy drinking 74
withdrawal symptoms 70, 72
    relief of by further drinking 71,
        72
women
    and maternal substance misuse
        38–9
work, finances and living
    conditions 126
Working Together to Safeguard
    Children (DoH) 245
World Health Organisation 68

Author Index

Ackerman, R. 191, 321
Adams, P. 321
Adams, T. 66–7, 102, 244, 246, 321
Adler, R.G. 51, 340
Advisory Council on the Misuse of Drugs 77, 321
Agass, D. 138, 338
Ainsworth, M.D.S. 108, 143, 321, 327
Alcohol Concern 321
Aldgate J. 9–11, 16, 19, 242, 266, 321, 326, 337, 338
Aldridge, J. 178, 206, 321, 323
Aldridge, T. 53, 72, 115, 125, 148, 157, 181, 213, 241, 248, 255, 257–8, 321
Alfaro, J. 48, 321
Alison, L. 28, 41, 122, 198, 202, 321
Allen, D. 256, 336
Ammerman, R.T. 34, 42, 105
Angell, R. 339
Antaki, C. 326
Anthony, E.J. 151, 321
Anton, S.F. 338
Appleby, A. 64, 270, 322
Ashton, M. 237, 322
Aters, DE. 321
Audit Commission 39, 45, 159, 322
Avis, H. 196, 322
Awiah, J. 186, 322
Ayers, T.S. 292, 330
Azrin, N.H. 74, 322
Azzi-Lessing, L. 256, 336

Bachay, J. 160, 322
Bacon, S. 79, 269, 322
Baker, S. 30, 324
Baldwin, S. 74, 322
Banks, N. 105, 194, 248, 252, 322
Bannister, A. 252, 253, 322
Barber, J.G. 272, 276, 280, 307, 322
Barber, L. 99, 322
Barker, P. 285, 322

Barlow, J. 16, 35, 112, 117, 152, 163, 164, 165, 166, 169, 176, 183, 184, 186, 187, 189, 191, 202, 205, 214, 292, 305, 322
Barnard, M. 16, 27, 31, 35, 103, 112, 117, 118, 121, 122, 124, 152, 163, 164, 165, 166, 169, 176, 183, 184, 186, 187, 189, 191, 202, 205, 214, 241, 292, 301, 305, 322, 335
Barnett, B. 206, 322
Barnum, R. 329
Barr, A. 65, 322
Barrett, C. 326
Barth, R. P. 322
Bates, T. 35, 46, 80, 102, 113, 115, 117, 119, 123, 126, 127, 128, 130, 131, 221, 242, 244, 246, 323
Bauman, P. S. 121, 122, 323
Baumrind, D. 121, 181, 201, 323
Bays, J. 28, 42, 44, 122, 197, 201, 323
Beals, J. 338
Bebbington, A. 20, 32, 323
Becker, H. 82, 323
Becker, S. 178, 206, 321, 323, 327
Bee, H. 143, 144, 173, 194, 196, 200, 204, 205, 207, 208, 209, 210, 323
Behrman, R.E. 339
Bell, C. 36, 330
Bell, M. 141, 252, 301, 323
Belsky, J. 100, 109, 141, 243, 257, 323
Belz, A. 181, 325
Bennett, G. 75, 76, 323
Bennett, M. 61, 323
Bentovim, A. 178, 323
Berridge, V. 63, 323
Besharov, D.J. 48, 164, 321, 323, 333
Best, D. 335
Bettelheim, B. 100–1, 243, 323
Biederman, J. 181, 323
Biehal, N. 214, 342
Biernacki, P. 279, 323
Bifulco, A. 41, 122, 140, 324
Bion, W. 139, 324
Black, C. 173, 174, 324
Black, M. 328
Black, R. 34, 35, 36, 40, 42, 324, 335
Blake, W. 137, 138

Blehar, M. 321
Blos, P. 208, 213, 324
Bonner, A. 59, 324
Boushel, M. 160, 324
Bowlby, J. 49, 139, 140, 141, 142, 324
Bradbury, C. 336, 337
Brandon, M. 18, 49, 140, 166, 173, 204, 205, 208, 252, 253, 324, 332, 341
Brazelton, T. 335
Brechin, A. 332
Bridge, G. 255, 324
Bridge Child Care Development Service 324
Brisby, T. 30, 31, 41, 43, 117, 118, 119, 120, 122, 125, 140, 152, 153, 163, 166, 180, 183, 186, 190, 214, 297, 324
Brodsky, A. 340
Bronfenbrenner, U. 77, 324
Brookoff, D. 44, 324
Brooks, C.S. 49, 51, 68, 125, 127, 140, 151, 152, 153, 154, 163, 165, 167, 168, 176, 177, 178, 180, 183, 184, 185, 202, 206, 210, 265, 284, 324
Brow, J. 185
Brown, H. 332
Brown, J. 16, 275, 331, 334
Brown, S. 66, 67, 127, 183, 265, 325
Brownstein, H.H. 326
Buchanan, A. 20, 28, 29, 44, 159, 325
Buchanan, J. 323
Bucholz, K.K. 198, 334
Buckley, H. 105, 106, 107, 160, 222, 238, 243, 244, 246, 248, 250, 251, 325
Budde, D. 338
Burnham, J.B. 285, 286, 325
Burns, E.C. 52, 118, 201, 325
Burt, M.R. 36, 341
But, S. 322
Butler, I. 252, 325
Butler, K. 151, 325

Cadol, R.V. 329
Cadoret, R.J. 181, 325
Camden and Islington Area Child Protection Committees (ACPC) 253, 258, 260, 325
Cantwell, R. 66, 325

Caplan, P.J. 106, 325
Carlson, V. 323, 327, 339
Carnie, J. 226, 343
Carroll, K. 338
Cassell, D. 30, 35, 51, 52, 118, 119, 120, 125, 126, 128, 198, 311, 326
Cassidy, J. 141, 323
Cawson, R. 326
Chaffin, M. 34, 325
Chassin, L. 181, 325
Chess, S. 106, 325
Chick, J. 66, 325
Chiland, C. 321
ChildLine 35, 37, 39, 41, 43, 117, 122, 125, 163, 164, 166, 167, 168, 169, 170, 171, 172, 177, 179, 180, 182, 187, 211, 325
Christie, N. 60, 325
Cicchetti, D. 323, 327, 339
Cingel, P. 160, 322
Cleary, P. 92, 334
Cleaver, H. 16, 20, 27, 28, 31, 35, 39, 40, 44, 83, 99, 100, 111, 118, 121, 122, 128, 131, 146, 159, 166, 193, 195, 196, 197, 198, 203, 206, 210, 211, 215, 242, 245, 246, 250, 251, 274, 290, 299, 300, 301, 302, 307, 309, 325, 326
Coatsworth, J.D.194, 335
Cody, M. 83, 326
Cohen, B. 263, 326
Colby, S.M. 237, 238, 326
Coleman, J.C. 210, 326
Coleman, R. 30, 35, 51, 52, 118, 119, 120, 125, 126, 128, 198, 311, 326
Collins, S. 67, 76, 322, 326
Colten, M.E. 121, 326
Conroy, S. 36, 330
Cook, C. 66, 324, 326, 328
Copello, A. 76, 272, 276, 280, 282, 284, 326, 327, 336, 337, 342
Corby, B. 146, 323, 326
Cork, M. 163, 166, 167, 179, 186, 326
Cowie, H. 207, 212, 340
Cox, A. 329
Crawford, R.J. 173, 326
Crimmins, S. 47, 326
Crisp, B.R. 276, 322
Crittenden, P.M. 108, 327
Cutland, L. 67, 69, 327

Cutrona, C.E. 273, 327
Cyster, R. 343

Dale, P. 327
Daniel, B. 49, 101, 105, 107, 108, 141, 207, 208, 209, 213, 238, 242, 243, 246, 327
Dare, C. 327, 341
Davidson, R. 285, 327
Davies, J.B. 58, 59, 63, 70, 88, 263, 327, 336, 337
Davies, M. 327
Dawes, M.A. 321
Dearden, C. 178, 323, 327
Department of Health 11, 19, 20, 21, 22, 24, 29, 32, 79, 99, 100, 103, 109, 120, 121, 138, 146, 147, 193, 194, 220, 226, 234, 242, 245, 253, 255, 257, 259, 272, 300, 327, 338
Deren, S. 32, 33, 34, 36, 38, 48, 327
Devich-Navarro, M. 210, 337
DiClemente, C.C. 75, 284, 338, 339
Diggin, M. 329
Dingwall, R. 247, 328
Ditton, J. 263, 328
Doakes, S.S. 342
Dobson, F. 21
Dore, M.M. 34, 38, 45, 149, 193, 196, 197, 206, 256, 328
Doris, J.M. 34, 149, 328
Dorn, N. 322
Dougherty, F.E. 121, 323
Douglas, A. 16, 17, 45, 46, 298, 299, 343
Drugscope 58, 307–8, 309, 310, 311, 312, 314, 328
Dubowitz, H. 41, 328
Duncan, S. 20, 30, 45, 46, 48, 52, 104, 111, 119, 125, 146, 147, 159, 244, 338
Duncombe, J. 160, 328
Dunn, J. 144, 212, 261, 328
Dunn, N.J. 52, 340
Dunne, M. 293, 294, 338
Dunst, C.J. 77, 273, 274, 328

Eby, M.A. 332
Edelwich, J. 340
Edward, C. 335
Edwards, G. 66, 70, 72, 73, 84, 90, 327, 328, 341
Eekelaar 247, 328
Ekwo, E. 34, 332

Elliott, E. 78, 95, 99, 102, 112, 113, 114, 115, 130, 131, 132, 209, 221, 237, 298, 328
Elswick, R.K. 341
Ely, M. 263, 328
Erikson, E.H. 194, 200, 201, 208, 328
Espinosa, M. 342
Etiore, E. 106, 328

Fagan, J. 328
Fahlberg, V. 199, 203, 204, 207, 210, 328
Falkov, A. 20, 45, 47, 48, 329
Famularo, R.A. 28, 34, 35, 36, 39, 40, 42, 329
Fanti, G. 40, 168, 173, 329
Faraone, S.V. 323
Farmer, E. 105, 106, 107, 108, 116, 246, 329
Farrell, M. 335
Fawcett, M. 255, 329
Featherstone, B. 105, 329
Feig, L. 64, 237, 329
Feighner, J.A. 323
Fenton, T. 28, 329
Fergusson, D.M. 334
Fitch, M.J. 35, 329
Fitzgerald, H.E. 164, 197, 201, 325, 329, 341
Flanagan, D. 340
Fleming, C. 180, 188, 341
Flores, P.J. 50, 89, 91, 329
Fonagy, P. 151, 153, 155, 329
Ford, C. 38, 52, 106, 198, 329
Ford, D. 7
Forrester, D. 28, 30, 33, 34, 35, 37, 41, 43, 63, 102, 129, 247, 263, 299, 329, 331
Freeman, M.D.A. 18, 19, 329
Freeman, P. 20, 83, 99, 100, 131, 246, 250, 290, 325
Freud, S. 194, 329

Gabel, S. 205, 330
Galanter, G. 74, 280, 281, 330
Galanter, M. 280, 281, 330
Garbarino, J. 33, 79, 80, 153, 156, 157, 272, 330
Gashko, M. 336
Gavin, F.H. 338
Gensheimer, L.K. 292, 330
Gerada, C. 197, 330
Gibbons, J. 36, 330
Gilligan, R. 160, 207, 327, 330
Gilman, M. 33, 77, 91, 129, 330

Glantz, M.D. 325, 343
Glaser, D. 237, 330
Gledhill, N. 343
Goffman, E. 80, 330
Goldson, E.J. 329
Gomberg, E. 330
Goodman, C. 196, 201, 206, 333
Gopfert, M. 45, 330, 342
Gordon, J.R. 335
Gordon, R. 76, 326
Gorell Barnes, G. 285, 330
Gossop, M. 66, 67, 88, 91, 330, 335
Gray, J. 20, 211, 330
Gray, M. 338
Greenberg, J. 138, 330
Greenland, C. 46, 148, 330
Griffiths, H. 332
Gross, M.M. 68, 328
Gullotta, T.P. 16, 326, 329, 330

Hall-McCorquodale, I. 106, 325
Hampton, R.L. 16, 231, 256, 326, 329, 330
Hancock, G. 339
Harbin, F. 16, 27, 106, 115, 163, 165, 191, 201, 251, 256, 258, 259, 264, 266, 292, 294, 302, 321, 328, 330, 331, 336, 337
Hardy, R. 328
Harrison, L.D. 332
Harwin, J. 35, 37, 44, 67, 280, 305, 331
Hassle, J. 269, 270, 293, 303, 338
Hastings, J. 184, 331
Hawker, R. 35, 39, 47, 159, 331
Hay, D. 323
Heal, A. 331
Heather, N. 66, 75, 331, 333, 338
Hedderwick, T. 30, 324
Helfer, M. 334
Hellawell, K. 15
Hendry, L.B. 196, 209, 210, 213, 326, 331
Hepburn, M. 34, 38, 52, 103, 106, 107, 115, 197, 198, 329, 331
Herrenkohl, E.C. 198, 331
Herrenkohl, R.C. 198, 331
Hester, M. 44, 45, 116, 211, 254, 255, 331
Hien, D. 121, 331
Higgins, L. 35, 46, 112, 113, 114, 116, 120, 123, 124, 132, 166, 179, 183, 184, 187, 202, 302, 303, 331

Higgit, A. 329
Hill, M. 16, 275, 291, 292, 294, 295, 331, 334
Hinings, D. 332
Hodgson, R. 326
Hogan, D.M. 28, 33, 35, 46, 91, 95, 112, 113, 114, 116, 117, 118, 120, 122, 123, 124, 128, 129, 130, 132, 166, 179, 183, 184, 187, 191, 202, 205, 214, 302, 303, 331
Holland, S. 243, 332
Hollenberg, J. 34, 325
Home Office 18, 332
Honeyman, T. 121, 331
Horwath, J. 19, 138, 147, 255, 322, 327, 330, 332, 333, 338
Horwood, L.J. 334
Houston, S. 332
Howard, J. 342
Howe, D. 19, 49, 86, 92, 104, 109, 138, 139, 140, 141, 142, 143, 144, 145, 149, 150, 153, 155, 210, 242, 291, 332
Howland Thompson 163, 165, 166, 169, 189, 193, 332
Hudson, B. 297, 332

Ibbetson, M. 35, 333
Inciardi, J.A. 332

Jack, D. 273, 332
Jack, G. 7, 20, 33, 79, 157, 271, 272, 273, 274, 332
Jack, J. 273, 332
Jackson, E.K. 329
Jackson, M. 38, 52, 333, 334
Jackson, S. 337
Jacob, T. 52, 340
Jaudes, P.K. 34, 38, 42, 43, 47, 332
Jellinek, E.M. 66, 69, 332, 336
Jewett, C. 173, 206, 207, 211, 332
Jones, B.W. 107, 333
Jones, D. 100, 333
Jones, F. 331
Jones, S.B. 274, 279, 340
Jordan, B. 157, 332
Juliana, P. 196, 201, 206, 333
Julien, R.M. 197, 333

Kaganas, F. 334
Kandel, D.B. 121, 201, 333

Kanfer, F.H. 333
Kassem, L. 40, 334
Katz, I. 19, 333
Keane, F. 163, 167, 333
Kearney, P. 31, 32, 35, 104, 106, 244, 299, 300, 302, 303, 333
Kearney, R.J. 96, 333
Keene, J. 67, 76, 326
Keith, L. 178, 333
Kelleher, K. 34, 325
Keller, M. 328
Kelley, S.J. 38, 122, 333
Kempe, R. 334
Kemshall, H. 146, 147, 326, 333
Kerr, N. 65
King, M. 334
Kinscherff, R. 28, 329
Kinsella, A. 46, 343
Kirisci, L. 321
Kleber, H. 87
Klee, H. 27, 35, 38, 46, 49, 50, 52, 95, 102, 106, 108, 112, 113, 116, 119, 120, 122, 123, 124, 125, 126, 128, 150, 152, 157, 201, 244, 333, 334
Klein, M. 194, 334
Knapp, C. 57, 59, 61, 62, 85, 334
Knisely, J.S. 343
Kolko, D.J. 321
Korbin, J. 29, 100, 334
Koupernik, C. 321
Krauthamer, C. 122, 334
Krishnan, M. 326
Kroll, B. 16, 102, 106, 140, 181, 252, 253, 255, 334
Krugman, R. 334, 339
Kurtz, E. 68, 335

Lamb, M.E. 337
Laudet, A.B. 34, 335
Langley, S. 326
Laybourn, A. 16, 35, 41, 43, 49, 52, 72, 73, 74, 114, 115, 117, 122, 124, 125, 128, 130, 152, 153, 154, 156, 160, 163, 166, 167, 169, 170, 171, 172, 173, 176, 177, 179, 180, 182, 183, 186, 187, 188, 189, 193, 210, 211, 214, 263, 275, 291, 292, 295, 331, 334
Lehmann, P. 335
Leiffer, M. 40, 334
Le Riche, P. 255, 334
Lester, B.M. 164, 325, 329, 341

Levanthal, H. 92, 334
Levin, E. 31, 333
Lewis, A. 341
Lewis, C.E. 198, 334
Lewis, S. 18, 38, 333, 334
Lewis, V. 37, 40, 43 334
Lloyd, C. 33, 34, 46, 77, 130, 171, 181, 334
Lloyd, E. 344
Lodge, D. 93, 334
London Borough of Brent 248, 334
London Borough of Greenwich 145, 334
Longford, N. 328
Lowinson, J.H. 333
Lucey, C. 20, 100, 104, 109, 120, 238, 243, 247, 257, 338
Luthar, S.S. 153, 334
Lynskey, M.T. 334

McCormick, N. 335
MacCoun, J. 338
McFarland, D.H. 343
McGuire, S. 212, 328
McIntosh, J. 31, 335
McKeganey, N. 31, 95, 112, 113, 114, 115, 116, 117, 118, 120, 123, 124, 214, 302, 304, 335
McLaughlin, L. 81, 326
McMurran, M. 65, 66, 69, 83, 335
Magura, S. 34, 335
Main, M. 143, 155, 335
Marlatt, G.A. 76, 335
Marlow, A. 322
Marris, P. 335
Marsden, D. 160, 328
Marsden, J. 262, 335
Marshall, E. 64, 328
Maslin, J. 284, 327, 336, 342
Masten, A.S. 194, 335
Mayer, J. 34, 35, 36, 40, 42, 324, 335
Mayes, K. 329
Meisels, S.J. 328, 330, 343
Messer, D. 331
Meyers 74, 279, 340
Miles, A. 335
Miles, G. 255, 324
Miles, J. 20, 32, 108, 323, 324
Miller, W.R. 68, 285, 333, 335, 339
Milner, J. 242, 259, 335
Minuchin, S. 335
Mitchell, S.A. 138, 194, 330, 335
Moffitt, T.E. 206, 213, 335

Molyneux, J. 304, 335
Monuteaux, M.C. 323
Mora, J. 336, 337
Moran, P. 41, 122, 140, 324
Morley, R. 44, 336
Morris, J. 178, 333
Morrison, C.V. 339
Morrison, T. 327
Moser, M. 328
Mountenay, J. 27, 37, 335
Mowlam, M. 186
Mulleady, G. 74, 344
Mullender, A. 44, 336
Mulvey, E.P. 44, 336
Murphy, M. 16, 27, 35, 36, 42, 43, 52, 106, 115, 191, 201, 219, 237, 251, 256, 258, 259, 264, 266, 300, 302, 321, 328, 330, 331, 336, 337
Murray, T. 247, 328
Murrell, W. 237, 238, 326
Myers, B.J. 343

Natera, G. 336, 337
Nava, A. 336, 337
Newcomb, M.D. 163, 168, 171, 187, 336
Newman, T. 178
Nicholson, J. 160, 336
Norcross, J.C. 75, 338
Nottingham Area Child Protection Committee 42, 336

Oates, M. 62, 336
O'Brien, K.K. 324
O'Byrne, P. 242, 259, 335
O'Connor, J.J. 46, 343
O'Driscoll 52, 325
Office of Population, Censuses and Surveys (OPCS) 30, 39, 159, 336
O'Hagan, K. 41, 105, 108, 336
Olsen, L.J. 256, 336
Oppenheimer, E. 181, 340
Orford, J. 28, 31, 32, 35, 41, 44, 46, 59, 61, 66, 68, 69, 70, 76, 81, 85, 87, 92, 93, 94, 95, 116, 122, 128, 129, 149, 156, 163, 164, 166, 167, 171, 174, 176, 177, 178, 182, 186, 188, 189, 191, 193, 202, 205, 206, 214, 219, 269, 272, 274, 275, 276, 277, 278, 279, 281, 285, 291, 292, 326, 331, 336, 337, 342

Oulds 36, 219, 237, 251, 300, 336
Owen, M. 35, 37, 105, 106, 107, 108, 116, 246, 329, 331

Parker, G. 20, 206, 322, 337
Parkes, C.M. 140, 335, 337
Parsloe, P. 146, 337, 339
Parton, N. 29, 32, 101, 104, 146, 160, 222, 242, 247, 248, 249, 271, 337
Patel, K. 30, 105, 128, 164, 186, 303, 322, 337
Pearson, G. 44, 88–9, 322, 337
Peele, S. 77, 337
Phares, V. 106, 107, 108, 337
Phinney, J.S. 210, 338
Phoenix, A. 104, 208, 341, 344
Phyfer, A.Q. 173, 326
Piaget, J. 194, 199, 200, 207, 212, 337
Pickens, R.W. 325, 343
Pierce, G.R. 327
Pietrzak, J. 322
Piper, C. 334
Plant, M. 197, 338
Poitrast, F.G. 336
Preston-Shoot, M. 138, M.
Prins, H. 247, 338
Prinz, R.J. 206, 210, 343
Pritchard, J. 146, 147, 148, 326, 333
Prochaska, J.O. 75, 76, 284, 338, 339
Project MATCH Research Group 80, 338
Prusoff, B.A. 338

Quinn, D. 336
Quinton, D. 159, 211, 338, 339

Ramler, M. 322
Reder, P. 20, 28, 30, 45, 46, 48, 52, 100, 104, 109, 111, 119, 120, 125, 146, 147, 159, 238, 243, 244, 246, 247, 249, 257, 330, 338
Reuter, P. 338
Rhoden, J.L. 16, 49, 50, 51, 151, 152, 153, 154, 163, 165, 166, 168, 173, 174, 180, 182, 183, 184, 185, 186, 187, 190, 205, 215, 284, 338
Rice, K.F. 49, 51, 68, 125, 127, 140, 151, 152, 153, 154, 163, 165, 166, 167, 168,

176, 177, 178, 180, 183, 184, 185, 202, 206, 210, 265, 284, 324
Rickards, S. 163, 168, 171, 187, 336
Rickford, F. 31, 36, 338
Ridley, I. 69, 321
Rigby, K. 336, 337
Robbins, C. 76, 344
Robertson, I. 66, 75, 331
Robinson, B.E. 16, 49, 50, 51, 151, 152, 153, 154, 163, 165, 166, 168, 173, 174, 180, 182, 183, 184, 185, 186, 187, 190, 205, 215, 284, 338
Robinson, W. 269, 270, 293, 294, 303, 338
Robson, P. 28, 307, 308, 309, 310, 311, 312, 313, 338
Rollnick, S. 285, 335
Room, R. 328
Roosa, M.W. 168, 292, 330, 338
Rose, D. 76, 338
Rose, W. 19, 20, 32, 242, 266, 338
Rosen, G. 31, 333
Rothwell, J. 27, 334
Rounsaville, B.J. 46, 338
Royal College of Physicians 197, 339
Rubin, L., 339
Russell, D.W. 273, 327
Rutter, M. 100, 109, 140, 149, 150, 151, 153, 159, 161, 211, 291, 323, 338, 339
Rutter, M. and Rutter, M. 28, 204, 205, 209, 339
Ryan, M. 105, 107, 339
Ryan, T. 74, 274, 278, 279, 280, 339
Ryff, C.D. 160, 163, 174, 191, 342

Sack, W.H. 339
Sandler, I.N 338
Sarason, B.R. 327
Sarason, I.G. 327
Sargent, K. 147, 339
Schaffer, H.R. 160, 339
Schetky, D.H. 36, 339
Schmitt, B.D. 339
Schnoll, S.S. 343
Schofield, G. 49, 324, 332
SCODA (Standing Conference on Drug Abuse) 27, 28, 46,

119, 126, 127, 148, 227, 242, 251, 257, 320, 339
Scott, D. 226, 227, 251, 339
Seeman, M.J. 45, 330, 342
Seilhammer, R.A. 52, 340
Self, W. 99, 109, 130
Sellar, A. 185, 340
Senatore, V. 16, 326, 329, 330
Shaffer, H.J. 274, 279, 340
Shapiro, J.P. 40, 334
Shaw, H. 343
Sheehan, M. 181, 340
Shemmings, D. 251, 340, 341
Shemmings, Y. 251, 340
Shephard, A. 58, 72, 73, 340
Sheppard, J. 104, 340
Sheppard, M. 35, 39, 41, 45, 46, 106, 122, 140, 243, 340, 344
Sher, K.J. 28, 163, 164, 181, 340
Sheridan, M. 199, 203, 340
Shonkoff, J.P. 328, 330, 335, 343
Short, J. 338
Silverstein, L. 76, 82, 92, 93, 340
Sloan, M. 30, 35, 36, 52, 118, 315, 340
Smith, G. 336
Smith, I. 339
Smith, J.A.S. 51, 340
Smith, J.E. 74, 279, 340
Smith, M. 339
Smith, P.K. 207, 212, 340
Social Exclusion Unit 20–1, 340
Social Services Inspectorate (SSI) 20, 21, 340
Solomon, A. 87, 340
Solomon, J. 143, 335
South, N. 60, 341
Sowder, B. 36, 341
Spicer, P. 180, 188, 341
Spunt, B. 326
Starr, R.H. 328
Steele, H. 329
Steele, M. 329
Steinberg, M.R. 121, 343
Steinglass, P. 269, 341
Stern, D. 138, 341
Stevenson, O. 20, 29, 42, 100, 160, 250, 341
Stevenson-Hinde, J. 335
Stewart, D. 335
Stone, B. 41, 146, 341
Stone, K. 329
Strang, J. 335
Stroud, J. 47, 341
Sutton, S. 284, 341
Svedin, C.G. 205, 341

Swadi, H. 35, 45, 46, 111, 118, 198, 211, 253, 257, 259, 260, 264, 341
Swarth, D.P. 329
Sydsjo, G. 205, 341
Szasz, T. 58, 341

Tanner, K. 41, 43, 255, 334, 341
Target, M. 329
Taylor, A. 16, 61, 94, 102, 140, 181, 290, 334, 341
Taylor, C. 340
Taylor, J. 49, 105, 107, 108, 141, 327
Templeton, L. 326
Thoburn, J. 18, 146, 341
Thompson, T.D. 324
Thorpe, D. 32, 337
Tizard, B. 208, 341
Tober, G. 326
Trinder, L. 49, 324
Trivette, C.M. 79, 261, 273, 274, 328
Tsui, M. 61, 342
Tunnard, J. 116, 126, 128, 164, 231, 299, 301, 342
Tunstill, J. 19, 321
Turney, D. 41, 43, 243, 255, 341, 342
Tweed, S.H. 160, 163, 174, 191, 342
Tyler, R. 34, 47, 201, 342
Typpo 184, 331

Unell, I. 16, 326
United Kingdom Alcohol Treatment Trial Research Team 74–5, 274, 282, 342

Valliant, G.E. 279, 342
Van Hoorhis, J. 34, 332
Varma, V. 330
Velleman, R. 28, 31, 32, 35, 41, 44, 46, 62, 68, 116, 118, 122, 126, 128, 149, 156, 160, 163, 164, 166, 167, 171, 174, 176, 177, 178, 182, 186, 188, 189, 191, 193, 202, 205, 206, 214, 219, 272, 278, 284, 291, 292, 326, 327, 336, 337, 342
Vetere, A.L. 284, 342
Vondra, J. 109, 243, 257, 323

Wade, J. 214, 342
Wadsby, M. 341

Wadsworth, M. 328
Wall, S. 321
Wared, H. 337
Warren, C. 275, 286, 288, 289,
    343
Wason, G. 52, 325
Wassell, S. 207, 327
Waterhouse, J. 324
Waterhouse, L. 59, 226, 343
Waters, J. 327
Watson, E. 78, 95, 99, 102, 112,
    113, 114, 115, 130, 131,
    132, 221, 237, 298, 328
Watson, J. 341
Wattam, C. 32, 326, 337
Webster, J. 45, 330, 342
Wedge, P. 337
Wegscheider-Cruse, S. 173, 343
Weir, A. 16, 17, 45, 46, 298, 299,
    343
Weiss, R.D. 46, 343
Wellisch, D.K. 121, 343
Werner, E. 151, 154, 191, 343
West, M.O. 206, 210, 343
Wharton, R. 329
Wilczynski, A. 45, 47, 343
Wilding, J. 341
William-Peterson, M.G. 122, 343
Williams, B. 46, 91, 178, 323
Williams, C. 324
Williams, H.A. 343
Williamson, H. 252, 325
Wilson, J. 186, 343
Winnicott, D. 100, 137, 138, 343
Wisely, C. 181, 343
Wodsby 205
Woititz, J.G. 163, 165, 168, 183,
    187, 190, 343
Wolin, S. and Wolin, S. 151, 343
Woodcock, J. 7, 35, 39, 45, 46,
    104, 243, 343, 344
Woollett, A. 104, 344
Wright, P. 27, 34, 149, 328
Wright, S. 334

Yandoli, D. 76, 284, 344
Yogman, M. 335
Young, L. 35, 323, 344

Zeitlin, H. 28, 181, 193, 196,
    197, 344
Zigler, E. 153, 334
Zinberg, N. 81, 344
Zuckerman, B.S. 164, 197, 325,
    329, 341
Zuravin, S.A. 328